D0170334

DEMOCRACIES AT WAR

DEMOCRACIES AT WAR

Dan Reiter and Allan C. Stam

PRINCETON UNIVERSITY PRESS

PRINCETON AND OXFORD

LIBRARY OF CONGRESS CATALOGING-IN-PUBLICATION DATA

REITER, DAN, 1967–

DEMOCRACIES AT WAR / DAN REITER AND ALLAN C. STAM.

P. CM.

INCLUDES BIBLIOGRAPHICAL REFERENCES AND INDEX.

ISBN 0-691-08948-5 (ALK. PAPER) — ISBN 0-691-08949-3 (PBK. : ALK. PAPER)

1. DEMOCRACY.   2. WAR.   I. STAM, ALLAN C.   II. TITLE.

JC421.R4185 2002

355.02—DC21

2001019859

THIS BOOK HAS BEEN COMPOSED IN GALLIARD

PRINTED ON ACID-FREE PAPER. ∞

WWW.PUP.PRINCETON.EDU

PRINTED IN THE UNITED STATES OF AMERICA

1   3   5   7   9   10   8   6   4   2

3   5   7   9   10   8   6   4   2

(PBK.)

We dedicate this book with love to our wives,
Carolann Reiter and Cyndi Stam

CONTENTS

TABLES AND FIGURES

Tables

Figures

ACKNOWLEDGMENTS

D
URING THIS BOOK'S gestation, we received tremendously
helpful comments from a number of different sources. At various stages of the manuscript's development, we received much
advice and many useful suggestions. Early on, Scott Bennett, Bruce
Bueno de Mesquita, Scott Gartner, Ali Ghobadi, Joshua Goldstein,
Shoon Murray, Eric Reinhardt, and Chris Zorn provided important in-
sights and criticisms. As we completed our initial draft, a number of individuals were kind enough to read the entire manuscript and provide extensive comments. They include Robert Bartlett, Erik Gartzke, Hein
Goemans, Paul Huth, Peter Katzenstein, John McCormick, Steve Rosen,
Bruce Russett, Ian Shapiro, and Alastair Smith. The resulting book is far
better than it would have been absent their help, though we remain exclusively responsible for all opinions and any remaining errors.

We thank Scott Bennett for permitting us to use in chapter 7 portions
of an article he coauthored with Stam (D. Scott Bennett and Allan C.
Stam, "The Declining Advantages of Democracy: A Combined Model of
War Outcomes and Duration," *Journal of Conflict Resolution* 42 (June
1998): 344–366). Earlier versions of chapters 2 and 3 appeared as Dan
Reiter and Allan C. Stam III, "Democracy, War Initiation, and Victory,"
American Political Science Review 92 (June 1998): 377–389, and Dan
Reiter and Allan C. Stam III, "Democracy and Battlefield Military Effectiveness," *Journal of Conflict Resolution* 42 (June 1998): 259–277, respectively. Jay Kim and Asit Gosar provided much needed research assistance. Chuck Myers at Princeton University Press provided unflagging
support for the project for which we are very grateful. For financial support, we thank at Emory University the Institute for Comparative and
International Studies and the University Research Committee. Yale University provided substantial resources in both time and research support.

We presented early versions of various portions of this project at different institutions, including the John M. Olin Institute at Harvard University, the Program on International Security Policy at the University of
Chicago, the Center for International Security and Cooperation at Stanford University, the Center for Political Studies at the University of
Michigan, the Rockefeller Center at Dartmouth College, the Research
Program in International Security at Princeton University, and the departments of political science and government at the University of Cali-
fornia-Riverside, the University of California-San Diego, Duke Univer-
sity, Rutgers University, the University of Washington, the University
of Colorado, Arizona State University, and Yale University. We received

useful feedback from those attending our talks. We thank the assembled attendees for their indulgence and considered criticism.

Gazing on back lets us extol; book-writing exhausts, and thankfully others supported us. With loving gratitude, we thank our wives for their endless patience and support of the more personal kind. Our book is dedicated to them, Carolann Reiter and Cyndi Stam.

DEMOCRACIES AT WAR

ONE

DEMOCRACY'S FOURTH VIRTUE

The world crisis has given new urgency to the question of
the "meaning" of democracy. If democracy is indeed to be
the hope of the future, we know now that we must have its
lineaments clearly in mind, so that we the more surely
recognize it and the more responsibly act upon it.
—*Arthur Schlesinger*

THE TWENTIETH CENTURY ended with near consensus among
leaders, populations, and academics alike on the virtues of democracy. Successive waves of democratization crashed upon the
world with unexpected rapidity and completeness: in all regions of the
world, autocratic regimes have been swept from power to be replaced by
new, more democratic forms of government. Even states such as the Soviet Union, Nicaragua, South Korea, and Chile that had seemed in the
middle 1980s to be paragons of authoritarian stability were by the early
1990s fledgling democracies. This most recent wave of democratization
has renewed democrats' faith in their political system: as the American
President William Jefferson Clinton proclaimed in his 1994 State of the
Union address, "Ultimately, the best strategy to ensure our security and
to build a durable peace is to support the advance of democracy elsewhere. Democracies don't attack each other, they make better trading
partners and partners in diplomacy."[1] Many politicians and most political
scientists base their devotion to democracy on the belief that liberal democracy brings with it at least three important virtues: freedom, prosperity, and peace.

While some may contest these beliefs, of late, dissenting voices sound
out less frequently and with diminished fervor. For instance, regarding
democracy's first virtue, freedom, most critics have abandoned the old
Marxist canards about the sham of voting and supposed fascist norms
that identified the individual with the state. Instead, demands for free
and fair elections and the protection of individual liberties in the formerly
Communist states of Eastern Europe and the Soviet Union led to what
some refer to today as the Velvet Revolution.[2]

Belief in the second virtue, prosperity, has been a central driving force
behind the new wave of democratization. Citizens in Communist bloc
nations found it increasingly difficult to ignore their societies' economic

stagnation, particularly when compared to the material prosperity of the democratic, capitalist West. As technological advances in communication made it increasingly difficult for Communist leaders to maintain the veil of ignorance pulled over their societies, citizens in those countries demanded a rapid combination of democratic and market reforms that they believed would allow them the ability to emulate the heavenly cities of the West, known as the European Union and American consumer markets.

Third, successful democratization appears to bring peace to otherwise potentially warring nations. Resurrecting an empirical observation first speculated on by the political philosopher Immanuel Kant, a consensus formed in the academic community during the early 1990s that democracies almost never fight each other.[3] This belief spread to the American presidency, leading the Clinton administration to emphasize democratization in its foreign policy as it concluded that the best way to stabilize traditionally dangerous regions like Eastern Europe was to foster the spread of liberal democratic institutions.

Together, these three virtues seem to offer elegant and just solutions to the human condition, the perfect recipe for the organization of society, and even, in the words of one observer, "the end of history."[4] But what if, in their dealings with other nations, democracies prove vulnerable to predation? Is democracy a luxury that states can afford only during times of peace? Or are the attributes associated with democratic institutions, those that provide for the personal liberty, freedom of expression, and collective material growth of common citizens, also the same attributes that, in the worst of times, allow states to provide for their national security as well? Largely underappreciated by scholars and political observers has been a fourth virtue of democracy: democracies win wars. Since 1815, democracies have won more than three quarters of the wars in which they have participated. This is cause for cheer among democrats. It would appear that democratic nations not only might enjoy the good life of peace, prosperity, and freedom; they can also defend themselves against outside threats from tyrants and despots.

The martial effectiveness of democracies comes as a surprise to some. Critics of the democratic experiment pessimistically believed that the obverse side to a liberal political culture's fostering of prosperity and commerce would be a corresponding inability to muster the military discipline and spirit necessary to conduct an effective foreign policy, particularly in times of war. The American Founding Fathers saw that threats to national security might require the sacrifice of liberty, as freedom hampers the ability of the state to conduct war. That great and perceptive observer of America, Alexis de Tocqueville, agreed, stating his qualms frankly: "I have no hesitation in saying that in the control of society's foreign affairs democratic governments do appear decidedly inferior to others." Decades later, disheartened after the Union Army's debacle at Bull Run, General William Tecumseh Sherman put the point somewhat differently: "I doubt if our democratic form of government admits of that organization and discipline without which an army is but a mob." Indeed, doubts about the ability of democratic government to defend itself have plagued American presidents as diverse as Abraham Lincoln and John F. Kennedy. Some pessimists recommended that elected governments would have to subvert democracy in order to make effective foreign policy; others doubted that the democratic experiment would even survive.[5]

In this book, we explore why democracies win wars. In doing so, we will try to show why events repeatedly prove the pessimists wrong, ironically among whom rank some of democracy's greatest leaders. We also discuss how it is that the nation-states most capable of safeguarding freedom also exhibit prowess on the battlefield, paradoxically to some, by putting governance in the hands of the people. By addressing these puzzles, we hope to say something about both democracies and wars.

About democracies, we want to find out what characteristics enable them to prevail on the battlefield more often than not. Democracies are complicated creatures, exhibiting many anatomical and behavioral qualities that distinguish them from other political systems such as dictatorships or monarchies. We explore which of these differences explain why they win wars, and in turn, we aim to say something about which of these differences are more important than others to students of pluralism, democratic institutions, and international relations.

About wars, we aim to improve our understanding of the tragedy of war by exploring why states win them. Some readers may find our detailed study of the process by which states prosecute war as somewhat repellant, given war's obvious horrors. Indeed, the modern academic study of conflict by political scientists has focused almost myopically on the causes of war. Perhaps this is because the study of war outcomes seemed either pointless in the shadow of nuclear weapons or politically incorrect in the wake of the Vietnam War.[6] However, like it or not, the history most commonly taught is that which is written by the victors in war; understanding the course of history and the lessons we might divine from it requires, in part, tracing the steps to victory on the battlefield. Perhaps most importantly, thinking about how countries win wars is a necessary step to understanding how wars begin, since leaders think about whether or not they will win wars before they start them. Fleshing out our understanding of how states win wars will help us, in turn, to understand how wars begin.

Our central argument is that democracies win wars because of the off-shoots of public consent and leaders' accountability to the voters.

Regardless of the particular permutation, at the core of democracy is the notion that those who govern are accountable in some way to the consent of the people. In democracies, leaders who act without the consent of the voters do so at considerable political risk of removal from office. This commitment to consent, contrary to the negative declarations of observers such as Tocqueville, George Kennan, and Walter Lippmann, offers democracies a set of peculiar advantages that enable them to prevail in war.

We outline two specific advantages that flow from the democratic commitment to consent of the governed. First, being vulnerable to the will of the people restrains democratic leaders and helps prevent them from initiating foolhardy or risky wars. Democratic leaders know that there are few greater political disasters than wasting the lives of their citizens in a losing cause. The explicit threat of electoral punishment and the need to generate consent of the governed at the time of action pushes democratic leaders to be particularly cautious when starting wars and, typically, to start only those wars that they will go on to win. Though Tocqueville and others feared this caution would paralyze democratic leaders, we demonstrate the opposite, that democrats are prepared to use military force but are unwilling to risk decisive defeat when compared to their autocratic counterparts. We present and test this argument in chapter 2. In the same vein, democratic leaders are also quite fearful of fighting wars that may drag on for too long, as public support for war steadily and inevitably erodes as casualties mount. As a result, democracies also tend to fight wars that are both short and victorious, or they willingly compromise and accept bargain outcomes short of outright victory; we develop this point in chapter 7.

A second advantage that emerges from consent occurs on the battlefield itself. What kinds of soldiers might we expect a society based on popular consent to produce? Sherman worried that the soldiers of liberal societies stand to be beaten, as most individuals, if given the choice, will resist the rigors of military discipline necessary for victory on the battlefield. We turn Sherman's worry inside out: the soldiers produced by consent-based societies will in fact enjoy certain advantages. Specifically, the emphasis on individuals and their concomitant rights and privileges in democratic societies produces better leaders and soldiers more willing to take the initiative on the battlefield. Rather than empowering the individual at the expense of the collective, democratic institutions are associated with states filled with individuals more capable of serving the state's needs in times of duress. We develop this argument and test it in chapter 3.

To approach the multifaceted question of why and how democracies prevail in war, we present four different theoretical perspectives on the nature and behavior of democracies. Each perspective offers a slightly different answer to the questions, what is a democracy, and what are the links between these political institutions and war? Though we might agree on the general conception that democracies offer the people greater control over their leaders, beyond this, disagreements emerge over what it means to be a democracy.[7] Our goal here is to ask which theoretical perspectives explain best the specific phenomenon of why democracies win. Each of these perspectives offers an alternative vision of why democracies might appear powerful and contains different implications for the relations between the governed and those that represent them.

Each perspective generates a set of hypotheses as to why democracies win wars. We develop and test these hypotheses in a series of chapters that compose the bulk of this book. To this end, we show that the historical record supports some hypotheses but not others. We also use these findings to gain purchase on two different questions: how do democracies generate the consent needed to initiate a war, and when do democracies seek to end wars? These we explore in chapters 6 and 7. In the concluding chapter, we discuss the implications of our findings for democracy, war, and the future of the international order.

Perspective 1: The Skeleton of Democracy—Political Structures

There is universal agreement that political institutions create the essence of democracy: some set of rules or law that provides for the direct or indirect control of a state's leaders by the citizens of that state. In order for us to consider a state a democracy, its leaders must be, at some level, answerable to the people. Typically, in democratic states, voting in regular, fair, and competitive elections is one means by which citizens hold leaders accountable for potentially reckless behavior. More specifically, this accountability can be of three basic forms, either in combination or singularly. In one form, known as retrospective voting, voters may use their franchise to punish or reward leaders' past behavior. In another conception of accountability, known as prospective voting, voters will select leaders believed to be the ones most competent to deal with the challenges ahead in the foreseeable future—those leaders offering the best "prospects," expectations of this competence perhaps being formed on the basis of past behavior. Last, political institutions may explicitly or implicitly require leaders to generate popular consent for a policy at the time of its enactment, what we will refer to as a contemporaneous consent model.

The distinguishing characteristics of prospective versus retrospective voting models hinge on assumptions about where the voters' and their leaders' uncertainty lies. Voters may focus on the future and may expect the future to be quite different from the past. If this were the case, citizens might well vote out of office officials who performed well in the past because they nevertheless believed other potential leaders might have some special competence to deal with new challenges in the future, regardless of the current leader's prior performance. Voters would not necessarily punish failure in the past either—rather, in the prospective view, voters would search for other possible leaders, sometimes changing course, sometimes staying the course, relying on the financial investment maxim that past performance is no guarantee of future returns. Retrospective voting is a somewhat less sophisticated notion of voting, that voters simply reward success and punish failure, focusing myopically, and perhaps a bit irrationally, on the past. Rather than developing a sophisticated gauge of leader competence in the face of an uncertain future, retrospective voters implicitly assume the future will be like the past and the past performance is a fair indicator of future performance. Our view is that voters and leaders alike tend to focus on the matter at hand. Leaders in liberal democracies seek out contemporaneous approval for political choices. Voters then punish leaders not so much for particular failure or success, but instead for failing to heed the more popular sentiments at the time the leaders settle on a particular policy. We discuss these distinctions in more detail in chapters 6 and 8.

Beyond the basic vote, there are of course a myriad of democratic forms of checks and balances: presidential versus parliamentary systems, representative versus participatory systems, variations in the separation of powers and protection of individual rights, and so forth. How does the existence of the vote and other systems of checks and balances affect foreign policy in general, and democracies' proclivity for victory in particular? A number of observers going back to Kant and forward to modern scholars of international relations have argued that the vote acts to constrain democratic leaders from engaging in any and all military action. According to this logic, the people who ultimately pay the price of war in higher taxes and bloodshed would oust any leader who recklessly threw their nation into war.

The insight that democratic political structures provide foreign policy constraints makes an interesting prediction for democracies' tendencies to victory. The people certainly do not want to suffer costly or meaningless wars; correspondingly, they also do not want to fight losing wars. We argue that this means that democratic leaders pick only winnable wars; that is, when they do start wars, they will be especially likely to win. Conversely, autocratic leaders know that in all but the worst of conditions, their power is secure, even following defeat in war. This political insulation leads them to start wars they know they may have little chance to win but where the prize at hand might be particularly enticing.

We also consider an important corollary to this insight: what happens when democrats are unable to gather popular consent and instead carry out policies beyond the shadow of public consent, bypassing constraining checks and balances? Specifically, what happens when the government carries out foreign policy in secret, out of the popular view? We argue that when carrying out such covert actions, democracies begin to act more like other kinds of states; they take violent actions against other democracies, engage in doomed foreign policy ventures, and violate the human rights of their opponents in ways that democratic citizens would likely find repugnant. In chapter 6, we explore patterns of democratic behavior regarding covert action.

Perspective 2: The Spirit of Democracy—Political Culture

Political culture has been at the center of the modern study of politics. Do the societies of different political regimes exhibit different values and norms that would either emerge on the battlefield or indirectly lead to democratic elites selecting out of certain types of wars for normative reasons? Is a state's proclivity to develop or depend on a violent political culture (both at home and abroad) a cause or effect of its regime type? What exactly are the foreign policies associated with different forms of political culture?

Democracy has been at the center of the debate over political culture, presenting a number of central questions. Does democracy require a certain political culture to thrive? Does democracy promote changes in political culture? Do citizens in democracies exhibit different norms and values from citizens of other societies? We argue that differences in political culture help democracies to win wars, but not in the ways most political scientists and military historians might suspect. Rather than weakening the whole to empower the individual, we argue the opposite, that democratic institutions that empower the individual in the end empower the whole as well. Specifically, in chapter 3 we argue that democracies' emphasis on the prerogative of the individual translates into soldiers and leaders that perform better and exhibit stronger initiative on the battlefield.

Perspective 3: The Family of Democracy—International Community

When Kant thought about the connections between domestic politics and international relations, he saw an opportunity for democracies to form an international community and transform the nature of global politics. The idea that democracies see themselves as a group advocating common interests was revived by Woodrow Wilson at the close of World War I, as he sketched out a new world order based on peaceful relations among democratic states with his famous Fourteen Point manifesto. Though that effort failed, some observers interpreted the post–World War II era as one characterized by the emergence of a democratic community of states, a community that has persevered and prospered even past the end of the Cold War.[8]

What are the observable manifestations of this sense of democratic community, aside from lofty sounding speeches from presidents and prime ministers? Some attribute the near absence of war between democracies to a powerful sense of democratic community. Under the logic of this argument, when one democracy comes under attack, others will come to its rescue, that is, democracies heretofore on the sidelines will join the cause and help one of their own. We explore and test this proposition in chapter 4.

Perspective 4: The Power of Democracy—Economic Might

A central part of war is the clash of military and industrial power. Interstate war is the ultimate test in world politics by which one state uses its human and industrial capital to impose its will on another. An important, though not complete, determinant of war outcomes is the relative balance of military-industrial power—victory often going to the stronger. What, therefore, are the relationships among democracy, industrial power, and war?

A common explanation of democratic victory is that democracies win wars by amassing more material and industrial power.[9] We consider two different ways that democracies might be able to muster more power in time of war. First, democracies in general might be more prosperous than other kinds of states and therefore able to assemble more massive and better-equipped armies than their opponents. This was the faith leaders on both sides of the Atlantic put in the United States in both world wars, that its industrial might would tip the balances in favor of victory, moving Franklin Roosevelt to call on his country to be the "arsenal of democracy." Second, democracies might be able to muster greater collective material sacrifices from society than other kinds of states.[10] The greater popularity of democratic systems might inspire their people to be more willing to make the sacrifices to assure victory, perhaps by allowing deeper cuts in civilian consumption and thereby providing relatively greater resources for the state's military forces. Alternatively, democracies might emerge more powerful by sending more brothers and sons to join the armed forces. Therefore, whereas the first general point proposes that the democratic pie of power might be larger, this second point posits that from that pie, democracies are willing to cut a larger slice—in terms of either material resources or manpower—to commit to the demands of war.

Our Perspectives Reduced: Why Do Democracies Win Wars?

In the chapters that follow, we show that, in fact, democracies do not win wars because of some sense of international democratic community. Nor do they win because they are generally richer or typically better able to extract resources from their economies. Instead, as we shall see, the power of democracies lies not in the leaders or political elite, but instead in the people themselves—ultimately, power lies in the governed, not in the governors. Democratic war initiators are especially likely to win. In fact, just as some have claimed that democracies have almost never fought each other, we show in chapter 2 that a democracy has almost never started a war it went on to lose. We will show that this is a direct result of the constraining power of political consent granted to the leaders and the people's ability to withdraw it. We also find support for the hypothesis that soldiers fight better for democracies than for other kinds of states, as they exhibit qualities of better initiative and leadership. In short, we find the skeleton and spirit of democracy to explain best why democracies win wars, and the power and family of democracy to be less useful.

Primarily, we use statistical methods of analysis to test our hypotheses. We do this for two main reasons. First, it permits the simultaneous and rigorous testing of a large array of cases. By looking at the entirety of war in the last two centuries, we can be more confident in generalizing our results to war in general, as opposed to, for example, restricting our analysis to one or two wars. Happily, there is plentiful data in quantified form that permits this analysis. Second, statistical analysis permits the comparative testing of competing hypotheses. This allows us to assess alternative explanations for our hypotheses of interest, improving our ability accurately to assign causality.

We recognize, however, that the interest in the statistical details will vary from reader to reader. To make the book accessible to a wide variety of readers, we have minimized the statistical context of the texts of each chapter, with references only to percentages and line graphs. However, each empirical chapter (chapters 2–5 and 7) contains an extensive appendix that describes in detail the research design and methodology used to produce the findings summarized in the chapter itself. In the next chapter, we take up the issues of democracy, war initiation, and victory.

TWO

DEMOCRACY, WAR INITIATION, AND VICTORY

*I am thinking of how best to win this war with a least
possible amount of casualties and in the quickest time.*
—*United States Secretary of War Harold L. Ickes,
February 1943*

WARS DO NOT occur by chance. They are not the result of some fanciful alignment of the planets and moons; rather, states choose to start them. States deliberately select themselves into the population of war participants by attacking other states. Armies clash on battlefields not because of mechanical accidents, flights from reason, or the whimsy of the gods, but because at least one national government or leader prefers war to peace. Belligerents in war are closer to Oedipus, meeting his peculiar fate because of his personal tragic flaws and fatal choices, than to Job, a pure innocent, made to suffer by divine action rather than his own failings.[1]

We assume that states pick their fights: they start wars when the stakes are high enough, and when they are confident they will win. Note that this latter point directly connects the causes of wars to their outcomes. If states think about whether or not they will win a war when they make the decision to initiate the use of force, then understanding who wins wars sheds light on the decision to attack. To push this point a bit further, we might expect that the more conservative, risk-avoidant states will win more of the wars they start, as they will attack only when they are very confident they will win. One could think of such states as one might a boxing champion who fights only weak opponents to safeguard his grip on his title.

In this chapter, we construct an argument explaining war outcomes that integrates the initiation and the fighting of wars. Our aim is to explain how both the initial decision to take up arms and the eventual conduct of military operations on the battlefield can affect who wins and loses wars. This will then help us tackle our specific puzzle, understanding why democracies win wars. The story that follows produces two general answers to this puzzle. First, democracies win wars because they start wars only when they are very confident they will go on to win. Democratic leaders, compared to tyrants, are more likely to lose political office if they fight a losing war. This possibility makes liberal democrats especially cautious when starting wars, fighting only when they are very confident they will win.

We call this proposition the "selection effects" explanation. The process leaders use to "select" which wars to start and which wars to avoid leads directly to the "effect" we observe, democratic victory. While the term "selection effects" smacks of social science jargon, it gets precisely to the point. Who wins and who loses wars is, in part, a direct consequence of the choices state leaders make before the wars ever begin. Typically, when we think of the kinds of prewar choices that might affect war outcomes, we think of strategy choice, decisions about mobilization or perhaps choices of which weapons to acquire. Here we extend the intuition to its logical extreme. If we assume that leaders can choose to start a fight, selecting their country into a war, then they can also choose not to fight, selecting out of war. We are interested in the systematic effects on winning and losing when leaders choose not to fight, or select their states out of wars based on how they expect the wars to turn out in the end, if they were actually to happen. We develop this argument in detail below and then present tests using historical data that provide strong support for it.

The second general answer to the puzzle is that democracies win wars because they are more effective at fighting wars once hostilities begin. This is true whether the democracy itself chose to start the war or if it was the target of attack. We call this second proposition the "warfighting explanation" and find much support in the historical record for it as well. In later chapters, we delve into both explanations more deeply, considering in chapters 3–5 specific arguments as to why liberal democracies fight more effectively. We investigate arguments that democracies' soldiers fight harder, that democracies ally together during wartime, and that they can muster more economic resources. In chapters 6 and 7, we explore more deeply the political assumptions underlying the selection effects explanation, that democratic foreign policy is driven by the motivation of elected leaders to maintain public consent. In these chapters, we explore how the factor of consent affects the democratic decisions to initiate and terminate war.

A Theory of War Initiation and Outcomes

If wars result from choices rather than chance, how do leaders make these crucially important decisions, selecting paths that may bring their nations to the heights of greatness or the depths of annihilation? We propose that leaders think about war the way they do about any other policy issue, seeking to capture benefits while minimizing costs. This is not to say that leaders do not make mistakes and sometimes launch wars that they go on to lose, but merely that they act on the basis of reason rather than fancy. In particular, leaders prefer winning to losing, and to retain the offices of leadership.

We first note that war begins when at least one state chooses to attack another. In social science terms, we mean that war initiators select themselves into the population of war participants.[2] We also assume that before attacking they make some guess as to whether or not they will win. The estimate is subjective and particular to them, although it likely correlates with the other side's estimate, although certainly not perfectly so. This estimate of the chances of winning can approach 0 percent if the leader thinks his or her side has essentially no chance to win, or 100 percent if the leader is almost certain of victory.

When a state considers launching a war, we further assume it will do so if its estimate of its chances of winning is high enough.[3] We might think about leaders having in their mind a minimum acceptable chance of victory; if this estimated chance of victory is above their threshold, leaders will order an attack, and if it is below, they will not. Of course, the level of acceptable risk will vary from state to state and leader to leader. Real gamblers might be willing to attack if they think there is only a 55 percent chance of victory, whereas conservative leaders averse to risk might attack only if they think there is at least a 90 percent chance of victory. All other things being equal, we expect that as the estimate of a state's chances of winning goes up, leaders will become more likely to approve an attack.

Lastly, we assume that there is some actual objective probability, distinct from the state's subjective beliefs, that the attacker will claim victory, a number that again ranges from 0 percent if the state will almost certainly lose to 100 percent if the state will almost certainly emerge the victor. A state's subjective estimate of winning approximates its objective chances of victory. The more accurate a state's estimation of its chances, the closer its guess is to reality. Though we do not assume that leaders are completely clairvoyant in being able to forecast beforehand who will win, their guesses are usually reasonable estimates and almost always bear some relation to their actual chances of winning once the "iron dice" of war are rolled.

How realistic are these assumptions? Leaders do of course forecast their country's probability of victory before war begins. They also frame the decision to attack in the context of some sense of what is an acceptable probability of victory (and, conversely, an acceptably low probability of defeat). Sometimes leaders are quite precise in these calculations. During the 1911 Morocco Crisis between France and Germany, the high-ranking French civilian leader Joseph Caillaux asked French Marshall

Joseph Joffre point blank: "General, it is said that Napoleon did not give battle except when he thought his chances of success were 70 out of 100. Do we have a 70 in 100 chance of victory if the situation forces us into war?" When Marshall Joffre replied in the negative, Caillaux stated, "In that case we will negotiate." The American government during the Vietnam War brought quantification of wartime prospects to new heights, making very precise calculations of the chances of different outcomes given different policy inputs (although in hindsight these calculations, while precise, were also quite inaccurate). A famous 1965 policy memo by Undersecretary of State John McNaughton laid out subjective estimates of U.S. chances of success and collapse in Vietnam over the next three years for a variety of policy options. McNaughton estimated, for example, that the United States had a 70 percent chance of victory by 1968 if it escalated its ground commitment to several hundred thousand troops. More chillingly, President John F. Kennedy related that during the Cuban Missile Crisis he thought the odds of nuclear war to be between one in three and even.[4]

There is a more basic, urgent question implied here: Can we accurately predict the outcomes of war? Even more bluntly, what can we objectively understand about war? Some are extremely doubtful of our ability to forecast war outcomes, drawing on Carl von Clausewitz's concerns about factors such as friction, or the inherently unpredictable aspects of battlefield events. Pessimism in the extreme is probably unwarranted, however. The outcomes of war can be well understood in at least a post hoc manner; one model successfully predicted the outcomes of 90 percent of all wars between 1816 and 1990.[5] But what about before the fact? Can we determine historically whether leaders' estimates about their chances of winning reflect their real chances of winning?

One way to get at this question is to look at whether or not states that launch wars win more often than they lose. States that think they will win are more likely to attack, whereas states that think they will probably lose are less likely to attack. Hence, if states' guesses about their odds are on average close to the mark, then states that attack will generally be more likely to win wars and states that are targeted will be more likely to lose wars. Conversely, if states' estimates are unrelated to their actual chances of winning, either because of flaws in their decision making or perhaps because traditional factors thought to determine victory, such as troop morale and strategy, are overwhelmed by the unforeseen, then attacking states should be about as likely to win as targets. The historical record reveals that states that start wars are far more likely to win them.[6] Again, we do not assume that states know with certainty whether they will win or lose before war begins, rather that they make guesses about their chances of winning before war breaks out, and these guesses approximate their actual chances. Some states prove to be better than others at estimating their chances, and these states are the most likely to win.

One important and explicit assumption we make here is that targets must fight when attacked. Some might challenge this assumption, arguing that most overmatched targets of international aggression will recognize the hopelessness of their situation and surrender without fighting, as Denmark did in 1940 when Nazi troops crossed its border. This point is worth closer examination. Consider that if we instead assumed that states could avoid losing wars simply by giving in to the aggressors' demands just before war begins, then a couple of puzzles even more confounding than why democracies win wars confront us. The first puzzle is: Why do wars ever occur? One could argue that if both aggressor and target knew who would win a hypothetical war, the two sides could almost always avoid war. Each would recognize which side would win and by how much, and so both would know who would get what in the postwar political settlement. Both sides would be better off, the argument goes, if they could agree before the war to accept the political settlement that fighting the war would have brought anyway (such as an exchange of territory). In this way, both sides would get the same political outcome as they would have received if they had fought the war, and both would also avoid suffering the costs of war. So, it would be in the interests of both sides to cut this prewar political deal rather than fight the war. When the aggressor is more powerful than the target, the target would recognize its weakness and make the concessions the aggressor demands, which would be preferable to losing a war, which would mean making those concessions anyway as well as expending blood and treasure on a losing military effort. If the target is more powerful than the aggressor, then the target would refuse the aggressor's demand, knowing it can avoid making the demanded concession by fighting and winning. The aggressor recognizes this and decides not to attack when its demand is rebuffed, as accepting the status quo is preferable to fighting a losing war.[7]

This speculation notwithstanding, wars are regular events in the landscape of international politics. The question is, why? One traditional answer focuses on misperception of states' military capabilities.[8] It claims that wars occur when at least one side makes an inaccurate estimate of its chances of winning, leading one or both sides to overestimate its chances of winning. So, an aggressor demands concessions of a target, the target thinks it can win, and if the aggressor also thinks it can win, it attacks. The assumption that underlies this answer is that states have good knowledge about their own capabilities but typically underestimate the strength of their opponent. Wars in this misperception perspective occur in two situations. In the first, the potential initiator underestimates the target's capabilities: it demands concessions, the target refuses, and the overconfident aggressor starts and loses a war. In the second scenario, the target underestimates the threat it faces: the aggressor demands concessions, the target boldly refuses the concessions, and the aggressor recognizes the target's mistake, attacks, and wins.

Importantly, according to this misperception perspective, we have no reason to believe that potential aggressors are any more or less likely to overestimate their capabilities. Both aggressors and targets are equally at risk of exaggerating their military power in relation to their opponent and stumbling into a war they will go on to lose. Therefore, if most wars are driven by this kind of misperception, then in about half of the wars it will be the target's misperception, and half the time it will be the aggressor's misperception. In short, this means that the misperception perspective would predict that about half the time initiators of wars should win (instances when targets overestimated their capabilities), and about half the time targets in wars should win (instances when aggressors overestimated their capabilities). Having no reason to believe that initiators should have better information about their opponents than targets do, if this misperception argument accounted for most of the wars that occurred, we should not observe initiators winning more than 50 percent of the wars they begin. In about half of the wars that do occur, initiators ought to have overestimated their chances of winning, attacked, and lost. In the other half, targets ought to have overestimated their chances of winning, refused to make the demanded concessions, been attacked, and lost. If this perspective is correct, it leads to the second puzzle: Why do war initiators win more often than the states they target? The historical record indicates, as noted above, that not only do wars occur but initiators are significantly more likely to win them. Our assumption that targets often fail to avoid war even when they believe that they are likely to lose allows us to provide answers to both puzzles, explaining why wars ever occur and why initiators tend to win more than they lose.

Our assumption, even if true, presents its own question: If targets know they are likely to lose, why don't they avoid war by making concessions? There are several reasons. Sometimes an overmatched target underestimates the attacker's willingness to go to war.[9] To use a card game metaphor, these targets end up calling a strong hand rather than the bluff they had expected. Saddam Hussein probably became convinced in the summer of 1990 that the United States would not go to war to liberate Kuwait because of perceived American sensitivity to casualties, directly telling an American ambassador that America could not stomach high military casualties.[10] Other obstacles may prevent a state from choosing diplomatic concessions to military defeat. The aggressor may find it difficult to prove to the target that it will go to war over the issue absent using force, as Argentina could not convey to Britain its seriousness over the Falkland Islands in the negotiations preceding the 1982 Argentine invasion of the islands.[11] Leaders on the target side may take verbal statements about the imminence of war with a grain of salt, believing them to be cheap talk. This is because a state that really did not prefer war might still make belligerent statements in an attempt to get the other side to back down, just as China has repeatedly used bellicose language in conflicts ending short of war in the Taiwan Straits.

Alternatively, an aggressor state may decide at some point during negotiations that war is inevitable. It might then stop making belligerent statements and instead make apparently peaceful gestures. The aggressor's new strategy of deceitful conciliation would, if accepted, lull the target into a false sense of security. As the target lowers its alert posture, it will unwittingly add to the aggressor's surprise attack advantage. Importantly, this tactic also removes an opportunity to avoid war, as the states end negotiations prematurely, before the aggressor makes a "final offer" in the bargaining, an offer that the target might have been willing to accept to avoid war. A good example is diplomacy between the United States and China in the fall of 1950 in the first months of the Korean War. As American forces began to push into North Korea and toward the Chinese border, the Chinese at first issued a series of deterrent warnings. Around late October the warnings stopped, and China began to talk of settlement. This strategy recognized growing American military vulnerabilities to a Chinese surprise attack. At the diplomatic level, the Chinese had switched to a more conciliatory tone. By making it appear that they were not preparing to intervene, the Chinese hoped to forestall any increase in the Americans' military capabilities as U.S. forces moved north. The United States had been correct to fear a possible Chinese attack; the November 1950 intervention changed the course of the war, pushing the military front back to the prewar border and setting the stage for three years of bloody and inconclusive conflict. If China had kept up its deterrent strategy, it might have persuaded the United States to halt its military advance, but the military advantages of a surprise attack proved too enticing and the deterrent option came off the table. In this type of situation, targets may be able to select themselves out of losing disputes before the escalation to war, but when disputes do escalate to war, the initiator is significantly more likely to win. Recent systematic empirical research bears out this expectation.[12]

These diplomatic failures aside, even when a target knows that war is coming and that defeat is probable, it may choose to fight and lose rather than surrender and accept the imposed concessions for at least three reasons. First, abject surrender in all likelihood would end the personal political careers of the target's leadership, while choosing to fight vainly would permit the possibility of postwar leadership. During the October 1939 crisis that preceded the Winter War between Finland and the Soviet Union, the Finnish public strongly supported standing firm, thereby hampering the ability of the Finnish leadership to make major concessions to the Soviets. All Finnish political parties opposed major concessions; each time the Finnish diplomatic delegation left for Moscow for a new round of negotiations, Finnish citizens gathered around the railway stations, singing patriotic songs in support of their leaders. The leadership knew that the gatherings were encouragements for them to hang tough in the negotiations. More importantly, the negotiators also knew they would be held responsible for making significant concessions, such as handing over the Hanko Peninsula to Soviet control. The top Finnish negotiator remarked, "They won't sing for us if we tell them we have given away Hanko." Eventually the Soviets grew impatient with Finnish stalling and attacked on November 30.[13]

Second, it is a commonly held belief that honor supports power. A country that allows itself peacefully to be conquered brands itself for decades to come as a feckless weakling ripe for bullying.[14] Sometimes war is preferred to even moderate concessions. The Finns in 1939 perceived that a decision to concede the Soviet demand for the Hanko peninsula would only encourage further Soviet demands. Western leaders would fret about these kinds of salami tactics during the Cold War, as "domino theory" logic shaped American policies regarding, for example, Berlin and Vietnam.[15]

Third, leaders treat the choice to defend one's own land as an insubvertible good and assume that honor in defeat is intrinsically preferable to ignominious surrender. Consider Belgium's choice at the outbreak of World War I. In the first days of the war, Germany presented Belgium with an ultimatum: allow German troops to move peacefully through Belgian territory to get to France, and Germany would honor Belgian sovereignty after the war and recompense any damages; oppose such movement, and face destruction. Even with this relatively attractive offer in hand and facing the prospect of annihilation on the battlefield, the Belgians still fought. As the Belgian Undersecretary for the Foreign Office Baron de Bassompierre put it at the time, "If we are to be crushed, let us be crushed gloriously."[16]

A last point about our assumption that targets must fight: like all models (including Newtonian physics, Keynesian economics, and Darwinian evolution), ours is only a sketch of reality, intended to help improve our understanding of the world rather than provide a complete description. Our assumption that targets must fight is just that, an assumption, which may be right or wrong. In the end, the proof will lie not in a theoretical debate but in what the historical record reveals. Historically, of course, we do observe wars happening and targets fighting even when obviously overmatched. There are almost no cases of peaceful surrender aside from the Denmark 1940 example. To the contrary, there are several cases of small targets electing to fight even when facing overwhelming odds, including all the other small European neutrals in World War II. If our theory contains fundamental flaws, then we would expect that the historical evidence would not support our arguments. Specifically, if we are wrong, initiators would not be significantly more likely to win wars, as targets would avoid losing wars, fighting only when their chances were good, thereby reducing the potential initiator's chances of victory in the wars we actually observe.

Given our theory, which states are especially likely to win wars? Here we posit two distinct explanations of victory: the selection effects explanation, based on the choices that lead to the outbreak of war, and the warfighting explanation, based on what happens once a war begins.[17] The selection effects explanation proposes that states that start wars should be more likely to win overall. Within our framework, states might more frequently start winnable wars in two ways. First, more conservatively minded or risk-averse states enter wars when they believe they have high chances of winning. States that are very averse to risk because they greatly fear fighting a losing war are likely to start wars only when they think their chances of winning are very high. This means that such conservative states will win more of the wars they start, because the wars they start are all virtual "sure bets" and they avoid launching risky military ventures that might end disastrously. These states will likely start fewer wars than states willing to take bigger risks, but overall they will win in a higher proportion of wars they do start.

The second selection effects mechanism pertains to the accuracy of states' estimates of their chances of victory. States that can make systematically more accurate estimates of how potential wars will turn out will win more wars that they start. Such states will more effectively distinguish promising opportunities for victory from possible military quagmires and catastrophes, allowing them to attack and defeat vulnerable targets and avoid wars that may turn disastrous. Conversely, a state that mistakes a low chance of victory for a high chance of victory will more often start doomed military ventures, and if it mistakes a high chance of victory for a low chance of victory it will pass up opportunities for easy victories. In short, accurately assessing one's chances raises the number of victories and lowers the number of defeats.

Separate from the selection effects explanation is the warfighting explanation. This latter proposition argues simply that states that are relatively more effective at prosecuting war are likely to win more frequently than states that are less effective at waging war. Within our framework, such states will have a higher objective probability of victory once war starts.

Democracy's Propensity for Victory

In this book, we consider an array of reasons why democracies might win the wars they participate in, some of which fall into the selection effects category, others of which fall into the warfighting category. The focus in this chapter, however, is on our selection effects explanation—that democracies only start wars they will go on to win; most of the theoretical discussion here is an extensive presentation of selection effects arguments. We then briefly present the logic of the warfighting propositions before examining how well these two explanations account for the historical record. In later chapters, we offer more extensive theoretical treatments and tests of specific warfighting propositions.

Our first proposition is:

Proposition 2.1: *Among war initiators, the more democratic a state is, the more likely it is to win.*

Democracy and the Selection of War as a Policy Option

The essence of democracy is popular control of the government. One way or another, the leadership of a democracy must answer to its people, usually through elections. Undemocratic governments, on the other hand, need not hold regular, competitive elections and are not ultimately answerable to the will of the people. Displeased publics are far more likely to oust democratically elected governments than nonelected governments. We may become cynical of contemporary leaders obsessed with public opinion polls, but the undistracted focus of a democratic leader on what the public thinks of his or her performance is the central spirit of democracy: government as an expression of the will of the people.[18]

One of the gravest policy failures a nation can confront is defeat in war. Defeat damages the pride of the nation, needlessly expends blood and treasure, and may endanger the very existence of the nation. As one historian put it, societies demand cheap victory: "The American public has wanted only one thing from its commanders in chief: quick wars for substantial victories with minimal costs."[19] Governments that lead their nations into unsuccessful wars are especially likely to confront an angered citizenry. Democratic governments have much to fear from an angered public, as their hold on power is particularly dependent on the continuing pleasure of the people. President George Bush recognized this on the eve of the Gulf War in 1990, stating the possibility in the bluntest terms: "I'll prevail or I'll be impeached."[20] Repressive governments, less vulnerable to the displeasure of their peoples, are less likely to be myopically concerned with defeat; they need not face the public in elections, and they can violently repress opposition if the need arises. The historical evidence bears out this expectation, as following military defeats, democratic governments fall from power faster and more frequently than autocratic governments.[21]

An important implication follows from this notion of postwar political punishment. Because democratic executives know they risk ouster if they lead their state to defeat, they will be especially unwilling to launch risky military ventures. In contrast, autocratic leaders know that defeat in war is unlikely to threaten their hold on power. As a result, they will be more willing to initiate risky wars that democracies avoid. The proposition that democracies are unwilling to risk long-shot gambles in war means that they have systematically higher war initiation thresholds. Simply put, compared to other kinds of states, democracies require a higher confidence of victory before they are willing to launch a war. As mentioned earlier, democratic France was unwilling to risk war with Germany in 1911 with a less than 70 percent chance of victory. This was not an isolated incident, either. France's leaders had similarly backed down in the 1898 Fashoda Crisis with Britain when they realized the considerable military inferiority France faced on the ground in Egypt and at sea against the British navy.[22] The prediction that then follows is that democracies are especially likely to win wars that they initiate. This does not imply that they win because they are necessarily more powerful, rather that they are better at avoiding wars they would have gone on to lose had they actually fought them. This may explain, for example, why democratic Israel has won all of the wars it has initiated.

Conversely, autocratic leaders are willing to risk chancy wars, as they are likely to retain political power even if the war turns out badly. Saddam Hussein initiated a disastrous and bloody stalemate against Iran in the 1980s, blundered into one of the greatest military defeats in modern history against the United States in the 1990s, and yet remained the leader of Iraq. Had he been a democratically elected leader, he most certainly would have thought more carefully about accepting such grave gambles. This is not to say that autocratic leaders are completely blind to the consequences of war; even Joseph Stalin declined to support a Communist Chinese invasion of Taiwan in 1949 because he feared that such a move would lead to a war with the United States, which would threaten the Soviet Communist Party's hold on power.[23] The broader point, however, is that authoritarian leaders are more willing to accept higher risks of defeat than democratic leaders because of their more secure hold on power.

Other empirical evidence points to the greater caution of democracies when initiating wars. If democratic leaders were insensitive to public support and opposition, we might expect that in some wars we would see significant opposition to the effort, and in some not. In reality, however, democratic governments have enjoyed a lack of political opposition at the outset of the wars they have initiated. They do this by avoiding the risky ventures that would lead to significant open protest against the war effort. Since World War I, the only instance in which a democracy participated in war and its government faced substantial overt political opposition at the outset that threatened the stability of the government was Britain in the 1956 Suez War.[24]

Connected to the concern with victory and sensitivity to public opposition, democracies are also quite concerned about casualties, which, in the end, are related to both defeat and popular support for a war. One study found that democracies avoid bloody wars, as democratic initiators of war suffer significantly fewer casualties than do other types of belligerents. Other research has shown that as casualties mount, so does opposition to war.[25] Scholarship on American public opinion is consonant with this view, portraying the public as essentially stable, rational, and prudent, appropriately recognizing risks and interests in world affairs.[26] As we will discuss in chapter 7, democracies also prefer to avoid long wars, as they need to bring wars to successful conclusions before casualties mount and public support wanes.

Autocratic leaders appear to recognize democratic sensitivity to casualties and in turn have sought to exploit it by threatening to draw democracies into long and bloody conflicts. When planning for war in 1973, the Egyptians expected that the Israelis would wince from high casualties and accept defeat. Similarly, the Syrians inferred from the 1967 and 1973 wars that democratic Israel "cannot stand pain" and claimed in the 1975 peace negotiations that it would aim to inflict a high number of casualties in some future war with Israel. Authoritarian leaders also sometimes believe that once war starts democracies are likely to "cry uncle" and sue for peace as casualties begin to mount. When planning for the invasion of France, Hitler waived off concerns that the offensive could cost the Germans a million casualties, noting that it would not be just Germany that might suffer terribly, "but also the enemy, who cannot bear it."[27]

Perceived sensitivity to casualties has been an especially acute problem for American foreign policy in the years after the Vietnam War, from which many world leaders drew the conclusion that the United States would ultimately not back up its threats to use force. In July 1990 Saddam Hussein brusquely told U.S. Ambassador April Glaspie, "Yours is a society which cannot accept ten thousand dead in one battle." Months later, Iraqi Foreign Minister Tariq Aziz continued this theme, telling Secretary of State James Baker, "It will not be a short war. Americans do not know how to fight in the desert." Years later, Somali political leader Mohamed Farah-Aideed followed this theme and bluntly told Ambassador Robert Oakley, U.S. special envoy to Somalia: "We have studied Vietnam and Lebanon and know how to get rid of Americans, by killing them so that public opinion will put an end to things." Recognition of the American sensitivity to casualties spurred on the Somali fighters in the Mogadishu battles of October 1993. Even though the American Rangers overmatched the Somali fighters with superior technology and firepower, the Americans' unwillingness to accept casualties was a critical Achilles heel that the Somalis believed they could exploit.[28]

One theoretical issue, which we do not take up here, is the particular way that leaders fall from power, which may vary from state to state. Specifically, losing power in a democracy means losing political office, with the opportunity of entering economic life or reentering politics in the future. Losing office in an autocracy can have much more negative consequences, as it can mean imprisonment or even death for the ousted leader. Hein Goemans has built on this observation to argue that leaders of mixed oligarchic regimes, such as Germany in World War I, fear moderate military defeat much more so than leaders in democratic or totalitarian regimes. This is because moderate defeat for the leader of a mixed regime means imprisonment or death, whereas a dictatorial leader will not lose power because of his ability to use repression to stay in power, and for a democratic leader a military defeat only translates into the loss of political power. Hence, Goemans predicts that when facing moderate military defeat in war, rather than accepting the moderate loss, leaders of mixed regimes are more likely to engage in dramatic escalation and adopt highly risky military strategies that may provide some previously elusive small chance of victory, while at the same time dramatically increasing the risk of decisive, crushing defeat. Democratic and dictatorial leaders, facing far less draconian punishments for their failed policies, are more likely to accept moderate defeat. Though Goemans does not take up the decision to initiate war or the factors that determine war outcomes, his argument could be used to support the conclusion that mixed regimes are even more risk averse than democracies. Like democracies, mixed regime leaders cannot easily use the tools of repression to stay in power in the face of a dissatisfied public, and they are strongly motivated to avoid political ouster because the personal costs would be greater. Contrary to this speculation, however, we find below that among initiators, mixed regimes are less likely to win than either democracies or highly repressive states.[29]

So far, we have argued that the vulnerability of democratic governments to public discontent forces them to start only wars they believe they can win. There is also a second factor that interacts with the selection effects mechanism: democracies produce better estimates of the probability of victory than their autocratic counterparts do. That is, their estimates of winning are more accurate representations of their actual probabilities of victory. Not only do democracies start wars they believe they will win, but also their beliefs about outcomes are less biased than are the outcome estimates produced by autocratic leaderships.

How is it that democracies are better at forecasting war outcomes and associated costs? Democratic governments benefit from more and higher quality information, meaning that they are more likely to make better policy choices and therefore initiate only winnable wars. The proposition that the vigorous discussion of alternatives and open dissemination of information in democratic systems produce better decisions is an idea at the core of political liberalism, traceable to thinkers such as John Milton, Thomas Jefferson, and John Stuart Mill. Two principle factors facilitate the open discussion of ideas. First, unfettered opposition parties, acting in their own self-interest, work to expose the flaws in policies the party in power advocates. Whether the system is a two-party one, as in the United States, or a multiparty one, as found more commonly in parliamentary systems, the party or parties out of power face strong electoral incentives to expose incompetent leaders in their attempt to gain power in the next election. A signature characteristic of oligarchies and dictatorships is the lack of a true opposition. While eliminating the opposition helps dictators stay in power, it also shields them from criticism that frequently exposes flawed policies in democracies. Opposition parties lead to more rapid leadership turnover in democracies, but they also lead to better policy outcomes over the long haul.

The second powerful institution that works to expose flawed policy options is the free press found in liberal democracies. A free press with limited government control or censorship is more likely to expose the flaws in policy and improve government stewardship. In modern international relations literature, scholars have posited that the relatively open marketplace of ideas engendered by a free press decreases the chances that democratic leaders will engage in foolhardy wars. Additionally, the less politicized bureaucracies of democratic governments are more likely to generate higher quality, less biased information. The political consequences of defeat on the battlefield motivate democratic leaders to be certain that they promote the best officers available to high positions of leadership. During the crisis preceding the Gulf War, American Secretary of State Dick Cheney fretted to Joint Chiefs of Staff Chairman General Colin Powell about whether General Norman Schwartzkopf was the best choice to command the coalition forces in Saudi Arabia: "This is for all the marbles, you know. The presidency is riding on this one. Are you absolutely confident about Schwartzkopf?"[30]

Regarding this last point, it is worth noting that authoritarian militaries in particular provide lower quality information to their leaderships than do their democratic counterparts. Authoritarian governments are more likely to promote military officers based on political loyalty, as disloyal officers (rather than failed public policies) pose greater potential threats to their hold on power. This toadyist phenomenon has been called "commissarism," a side effect of which is that the collection of military intelligence is likely to be severely biased, as military officers are more interested in maintaining the approval of the civilian leadership than in presenting sound military or strategic analysis. Fearful military subordinates probably prevented Saddam Hussein from getting an accurate picture of American military power, which in turn led Iraq into an utterly disastrous military confrontation.[31] The bottom line is that since democratic leaders get better information from both society and their own bureaucracy, they are more likely to make better policy and therefore avoid starting wars they are likely to lose.

So far, we have discussed democracy in a simple, rather one-dimensional fashion: states are either more or less democratic. An alternative approach is to relax this assumption and enrich our typology of states. Consider instead three different kinds of states: democracies (such as the United States), oligarchic or cartelized regimes that share democratic and autocratic characteristics (such as Wilhelmine Germany), and unitary dictatorships that are highly repressive and undemocratic systems (such as Stalinist Russia or Hussein's Iraq). Though these three kinds of states can be placed on a spectrum, with democratic states being the freest, mixed regimes being less free, and dictatorships being the least free, the expected foreign policy behavior of these three states is not comparable. One scholar predicted that democracies are least likely to experience imperial overexpansion, dictatorships are somewhat more likely to overexpand, and mixed regimes are the most likely to expand beyond the size that provides net gains to the state. The reason that mixed regimes are most vulnerable is that their oligarchic system of governance makes them especially susceptible to logrolling coalitions, where rather than trying to settle on the single best policy, political opponents join together to produce a single overambitious policy that, to the detriment of the national interest, offers something for everyone. Because of this tendency toward logrolling, oligarchic governments tend to stagger into foolish military and colonial ventures. Such systems are also more likely to fall prey to imperial mythmaking that makes expansion seem falsely appealing. The unitary nature of dictatorships makes them less likely to fall prey to logrolling or mythmaking but forgoes democratic advantages of the marketplace of ideas that provide broad checks on a single leader.[32]

These arguments have direct application here and lead to our second proposition. They indicate that among initiators, mixed regimes are least likely to win, followed by dictatorships, followed by the relatively victory-prone democracies. The reason is that although both mixed regimes and dictatorships feel less of a domestic political threat from defeat in war than do democracies, mixed regimes are more likely to suffer from imperial mythmaking and overestimate their chances of victory. In the framework of our model, mixed regimes and totalitarian states are more risk acceptant than liberal democracies, hence both are willing to start wars with lower estimates of their chances for victory, but mixed regimes make less accurate estimates of their chances of victory than do totalitarian states.[33]

Proposition 2.2: *Among war initiators, democracies are most likely to win, dictatorships are next most likely to win, and mixed regimes are least likely to win.*

Having laid out our two selection effects arguments, what of the war-fighting argument? To this point, we have focused on the decisions leading to war and have argued that democracies win because they are careful to start only wars that they are sure they can win. This leads us to the next potential source of state power, strength on the battlefield.

Democracy and Warfighting

Do democracies win simply because they cleverly attack only easy targets, or because they are actually more effective on the battlefield? This question is important in understanding the evolution of world order. If democracies are more clever at starting wars but no more effective or perhaps less effective—as some pessimists have feared—at fighting them, then it is possible that democracy might eventually be eliminated from the international system by aggressive dictatorships, such as Hitler's Germany. Alternatively, if democracies are more effective at the actual process of fighting wars, over time we might expect to see democracy become more common through a Darwinian selection process where democracies win even when targeted by dictatorships.

In war, the belligerents' primary goals are to inflict costs on each other.[34] A belligerent will increase its chances of winning if it increases its ability to inflict or absorb costs. We will consider three arguments as to why democracies might be more effective at imposing costs and hence fighting and winning wars.[35] In this chapter, we present them only briefly, as they are described and tested in detail in chapters 3–5. We postpone in-depth discussion of these arguments, as the empirical tests we present in this chapter are helpful for a general test of the selection effects explanation against the warfighting explanation, but not for testing specific warfighting explanations against one another. The three arguments as to why democracies might fight more effectively are as follows:[36]

- *Soldiering:* On the battlefield, soldiers fight harder for democracies. Soldiers may be more motivated to fight and die on the battlefield if they are fighting for a popular government. Further, a political culture focused on the rights and privileges of the individual may produce soldiers who fight with higher levels of initiative on the battlefield serving under more inspired leadership. Lastly, enemy soldiers are more likely to surrender to democratic foes because they are more confident they will be treated fairly as prisoners of war by democratic captors. We test these arguments in chapter 3.
- *Community:* Democracies balance together in time of war, building overwhelming countercoalitions against autocratic aggressors. Some have argued that democracies together form an international liberal community, and that when one comes under fire, others come to its rescue. Conversely, authoritarian states feel no such impulse to collective defense, and the result of single authoritarian states fighting against groups of democracies affords democracies an important advantage. In chapter 4, we develop and test this line of reasoning.
- *Economic Power:* Democracies may win wars because their economies are stronger and relatively more efficient at delivering war materiel to the front lines. Some have argued that democracies have more prosperous economies than other kinds of states and/or that in wartime they can extract relatively more resources from their societies for the war effort. This affords democracies important military advantages, as they can produce more war materials that will actually end up on the battlefield. We explore these areas in chapter 5.

These three arguments together suggest that during wartime, democracies are likely to be more effective at achieving victory given the fact that a war has begun. According to the warfighting explanation, democracies enjoy these advantages whether they have started the war or they are targets. An important difference between the warfighting and selection effects explanations is that while the latter proposes that only democratic initiators are more likely to win, the former proposes that both democratic initiators and targets are more likely to win. This leads us to our third proposition.

Proposition 2.3: *Democratic targets are more likely to win wars than other kinds of targets.*

Democracy and Victory: No Effect?

Before jumping into our discussion of the historical record, we should note that not everyone agrees that democracies win wars more frequently. Realism, one of the dominant theories of international relations, focuses on material power, identifies states as primary actors, and downplays the significance of domestic politics in international relations. This emphasis has led realists famously to play down the connection between domestic politics and the outbreak of war.[37] Some realists have argued that democracies experience no advantage in fighting war. Hans Morgenthau, perhaps the most influential realist of the twentieth century, did argue that the quality of a state's government and national character or morale were important factors that contributed to state power, but he did not believe that these characteristics were systematically related to whether the state was democratic or not.[38] Realists propose that democracies are no more likely to win wars than other kinds of states, as either targets or initiators.

Other critics might point to our focus on initiation as a potential flaw, that most of the wars we actually observe are not wars of aggression dictated by the interests of the initiators, but rather defensive wars started by states with preemptive motives. That is, states frequently initiate wars not because they wish to, believing that they will win, but rather because they fear imminent attack and see some tactical advantage in preempting the putative aggressor. If this were true, we might see many likely losers initiate wars out of preemptive motives. The historical record, however, reveals almost no instances of preemptive war in the modern era, and of the three preemptive wars since 1815, the preemptor has won twice (Germany's victory over Russia in World War I and Israel's victory over its Arab neighbors in 1967) and drawn once (China's draw with the United States in the Korean War). There are, in fact, important reasons not to preempt. By preempting, a likely loser forgoes any further diplomatic attempts to reduce the concessions needed to reach a peaceful settlement. The likely loser also increases the costs it will have to pay compared to the costs it might have settled on otherwise since it will have to give up the policy at stake as well as compensate the winner for the costs it incurred during the fighting. Further, preemption itself can impose domestic political and international costs on the preemptor. Finally, the military advantages of achieving surprise are overrated.[39] Now, let us move on to the historical tests of our propositions.

The Historical Record

Our empirical strategy in this book is to present an array of empirical tests drawn from a variety of different levels of analysis. In the chapters to follow, we explore questions such as: Do democratic armies fight better on the battlefield? Do democracies join each other when autocracies attack? Do democracies extract more resources from society during wartime? Before going into such detail, we look first at a more basic question. Do democracies win wars?

To evaluate this question, we look at all wars from 1816 to 1990, a war being defined as a military clash between two countries in which there are at least a thousand battle casualties.[40] Table 2.1 sorts each war participant according to whether it was a democracy, an oligarchy, or a dictatorship, and whether it won or lost.[41] The table also separates initiators from targets. Again, the warfighting explanation predicts that democracies will in general be more likely to win wars, and the selection effects explanation predicts that democratic initiators will be particularly likely to win wars.

Table 2.1 presents some interesting results. Consistent with the notion that states consider carefully their chances of victory before starting a war, initiators do better than targets, winning 65 percent of the time compared to 41 percent for targets. Of the three types of states in our typology, democratic initiators do best, winning 93 percent of the time compared with dictators who win 60 percent of the time, and oligarchs who win 58 percent of the time. Just as some have said that democracies almost never fight each other, it seems clear that democracies almost never start wars they go on to lose. When we look at the results for targets, we find something quite startling—dictators and oligarchs lose more than they win, as we would expect, winning only 34 percent and 40 percent of the time, respectively. Democratic targets, however, win as often as the dictators and oligarchs who initiate wars. This suggests that democracies, setting aside their risk aversion and the care they appear to use when choosing to initiate a war, are significantly more powerful than other kinds of states.

Before we can accept the notion that democracies truly are more powerful than other states, we need to think carefully about the implications of our selection effects argument. It is possible that democratic targets are more likely to win solely because of an illusory artifact of selection effects. Because democracies almost never fight each other, democracies

TABLE 2.1
Winning Percentage for War Initiators and Targets by State Type

	Dictatorships	Oligarchs	Democracies	Total
War Initiators				
Wins	21	21	14	56
Losses	14	15	1	30
Winning Percentage	60%	58%	93%	65%
Targets				
Wins	16	18	12	46
Losses	31	27	7	65
Winning Percentage	34%	40%	63%	41%

are never the target of the more powerful and choosiest states in the system, other democracies. Instead, democracies are the target of apparently weaker and less careful states, autocracies. Perhaps democratic targets win more often than they lose simply because they have been attacked by relatively weak, but risk acceptant, dictators and oligarchs. In other words, the set of democratic targets might be more likely to win not because they fight any better, but rather because the only states that attack them are willing to start very risky wars. Conversely, autocratic targets become targets when attacked by democratic initiators who choose to go to war only when they believe they are certain to win. A subset of autocratic targets are doomed to lose because they fall victim to democratic aggression, which in turn would make the entire group of autocratic targets appear to be more likely to lose. However, if we examine only those states that are targets, democratic targets are more likely to win even when we control statistically for the regime type of the initiator—factoring the risk acceptant nature of autocrats into the likelihood of a democratic target winning (see appendix). Autocratic targets are then doubly doomed. They are more likely to have the cards stacked against them as democracies attack them disproportionately (because democracies never target each other), and once war starts, autocrats in general execute the tasks of war fighting less effectively than democracies.

Our quick look at the historical record supports both the warfighting and selection effects explanations, but the statistics in table 2.1 do not take into account many of the other factors that directly determine war outcomes. Perhaps our confidence in democratic initiators and targets winning wars is unwarranted.[42] To be sure that the results in table 2.1 are the results of factors truly particular to democracies and are not simply spurious correlations of democracy and some other factor that actually determines the outcomes of war, we also conducted a battery of statistical tests found in appendix 2.1. In the appendix, we use statistical techniques to control for other possible explanations of why states win wars.[43] Remember, our claim is that democracies will be more powerful holding other determinants of war outcomes constant. If there is no real connection between democracy and victory, then the inclusion of these other factors should reveal there to be no real democracy-victory connection. The statistical models in the appendix include, in addition to variables that measure democracy levels, an array of other possible explanations of why states win wars:

- *Military-Industrial Capabilities:* An important component of warfare is the ability to produce war materials such as tanks, guns, and planes, and sometimes victory goes to the side that wins the battle of the factories.
- *Troop Quality:* The essence of war is fighting, ultimately done by troops. Highly trained and well-equipped troops are of course crucial to making any plan for victory work.
- *Military Strategy:* Generals must make grand plans for the employment of their forces, and the appropriate strategy can assure victory by emphasizing one's own strengths and exploiting the enemy's weaknesses.
- *Terrain:* The geography of the land makes a difference, both by making some strategies more effective and by constraining the ability to carry out planned operations.
- *Distance:* Sending military forces over great distances can make victory difficult, both because it is costly to project power across the globe and because troops become dispirited when fighting far away from home.
- *Alliances:* Greater foes can be met and defeated with the assistance of a powerful ally, as additional armies can be deployed on the battlefield.

The statistical tests in the appendix account for these factors; there, we explore whether inclusion of them alters the results in table 2.1. For interested readers, the appendix goes into the specifics of the variables, data, and the statistical results. These more sophisticated statistical tests bolster our confidence in our findings. Even when controlling for an array of important control variables, we still find that democracies are especially likely to win wars, whether they are initiators or targets.

Other empirical tests confirm our speculation that democracies win wars because they initiate war only when they are very confident they will win. Recall that our theory proposed that democracies have a higher threshold of acceptable risk than other kinds of states, meaning they will initiate war only when they are quite confident they will win. So far, our empirical analysis has tested this conceptualization indirectly, finding that democratic initiators are especially likely to win wars that they have initiated.

A more direct test would look at the actual decision to initiate wars. Our theory predicts that for all states, both democratic and nondemocratic, the chances that a state will initiate war go up as its estimated chance of victory rises. However, we would also predict that as a state's estimate of its chances for victory rises, the chances of initiation increase greatly for democracies, whereas the chances of initiation increase only moderately for nondemocracies. That is, when the odds of victory are low to medium, democracies are significantly less likely to initiate war than are nondemocracies, but as the chances of victory become high, the likelihood that a democracy will initiate war increases faster than the likelihood that a nondemocracy will initiate war. As a democracy becomes more confident it will win, the constraints on its decisions fall away and its foreign policy behavior resembles that of a nondemocracy.

To test this line of argument, we examined a sample of several thousand pairs of states (or dyads) that were not at war, studying the factors that make it more likely that one of the states within each pair will make a demand on the other state that escalates to the point at which military forces become involved (see appendix). For each dyad, we generated predictions of war outcomes—probabilistic estimates of who would win in the case that war broke out between the two states—using national characteristics such as military-industrial capability and strategy. We found that democracies become increasingly willing to initiate a dispute as their estimated chances of victory increase. We also found the same result when we examined the decisions of states to escalate smaller scale disputes to war. These results are consistent with our selection effects theory and with the results in table 2.1. Though democracies are less willing to initiate the use of force when they are unsure they will win, as they become more confident they will win they shrug off these constraints and become willing to use force. This in turn means that when democracies initiate war, they are especially likely to win.

Our results indicate that democracies are significantly more likely to win wars. Remaining is the question of actual impact: how big of an advantage do democratic initiators and targets actually have in defeating their foes?

In figures 2.1 and 2.2, we demonstrate the extent of the advantage that democratic targets enjoy in comparison to authoritarian states. In these figures, we use the statistical model of war outcomes presented in the appendix, then simulate how predicted war outcomes change when we vary the democracy level of the target in figure 2.1 and the initiator in figure 2.2. The statistical models we use to generate the predicted outcome values plotted in the figures control for the factors listed earlier. In the simulations, we set the other factors to the values we observe historically. We then simulate how the outcomes would have changed, if democracy had the same effect in the simulated war outcomes that it did historically, on average, in the population of wars we did observe.

First, in considering the effect of increasing democracy in target states

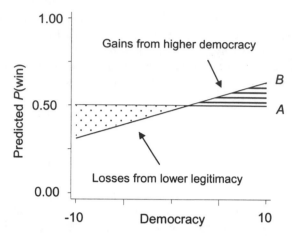

Figure 2.1. Probability of Victory by Level of "Democracy" among Target
States. A higher "Democracy" score indicates a more democratic state. Null (*A*)
is set at 0.50, 41% of all targets actually won. Line B represents *P*(Win).

in figure 2.1, note that the darkly striped area, which represents the potential gains from democracy compared with what the outcome would be
if democracy had no effect (the horizontal line), while positive, is rather
small. When we make the comparison of highly democratic states to dictatorships, however, the apparent effect is quite large. Recall that there
are several explanations as to why democratic targets should be more
likely to win—that soldiers fight harder for democracies, that democracies join together when attacked, and so forth. It is interesting to note
that we still observe effects for democratic targets even when we control
for two of these factors, industrial capabilities and alliance contributions
(see chapters 4 and 5). Indirectly, then, these findings point toward the
conclusion that democracies fight better because their soldiers fight
harder, and because soldiers are more likely to surrender to democratic
foes (see chapter 3). However, what of the selection effects argument?
   Figure 2.2 represents the changes in the expected chance of victory for
an initiating state as it becomes more democratic. The effect is considerable: democracy has a large impact on an initiator's chances of winning.
Note also, at the far left of the graph, that the most autocratic states,
while not doing as well as democracies, do substantially better than their
slightly more moderate oligarchic associates. This appears to lend support
to the argument that some totalitarian states may be able to gauge more
accurately their chances for success than mixed or cartelized regimes.
   In short, the statistical evidence provides strong support for both the
warfighting and selection effects hypotheses: democracies fight well when
attacked, democracies are more likely to start only those wars that they

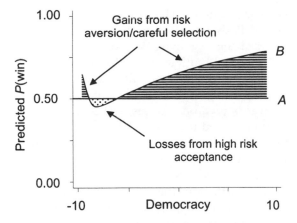

Figure 2.2. Probability of Victory by Level of "Democracy" among Initiator States. A higher "Politics" score indicates a more democratic state. Null (*A*) is set at 0.50, 64% of all initiators actually won. Line B represents *P*(Win).

can win, and, among authoritarian initiators of war, totalitarian regimes will do slightly better than mixed regimes. Next, we demonstrate and illustrate these points by briefly examining two wars, the India-Pakistan War of 1971 and the Pacific War between Japan and the United States during World War II. In each case, as our theory would lead us to expect, understanding the origins of the war is centrally important to explaining its outcome.

India-Pakistan War, 1971

India exploited the advantages of democracy in its 1971 war with Pakistan. Since decolonization in 1947, the two wings of Pakistan, West and East Pakistan, had united under the common bond of Islam to comprise one nation. However, political power had always fallen into the hands of the West Pakistanis, and the relationship between West Pakistan and East Pakistan was paternalistic at best. These facts, coupled with the gross economic disparities that existed between the two wings, prompted an East Pakistani movement for regional autonomy beginning in 1965. In 1971 the political conflict reached a head. A national election held in December 1970 gave the majority of seats in the Pakistani National Assembly to a single East Pakistani party, stunning the West Pakistanis. As a result, the West Pakistani president indefinitely postponed the convening of the Assembly.[44] This enraged the East Pakistanis, who responded with a general strike and systematic noncooperation, causing severe disruptions in the Pakistani economy. This in turn prompted the West Pakistani crackdown on East Pakistan on March 25, 1971.

March 25 marked the beginning of India's involvement in the Pakistani conflict. A principal motivation for Indian engagement in the dispute was the influx of East Pakistani refugees. Following the crackdown, close to ten million refugees crossed into India, creating an estimated $700 million a year burden on India as well as numerous political problems.[45] India was motivated to resolve the conflict in favor of East Pakistani autonomy, both to provide a permanent solution to the problem of East Pakistani refugees and to advance its interests in the ideological and regional competition with the Islamabad government.

India took several actions in the months following the March crackdown to build international support and bolster its chances for winning a war if one should come. The Indian government succeeded in persuading the World Bank to cut off economic assistance (minus humanitarian aid) to West Pakistan. It also convinced the United States to cut off military aid to West Pakistan. India signed a bilateral treaty with the Soviet Union that gave it protection from Security Council censure if it decided to enter the conflict, and it secured a steady supply of Soviet military supplies as well.[46]

While the Indian political leadership pursued diplomatic goals, it simultaneously trained and armed East Pakistani guerrilla forces, which were successful in harrying the West Pakistani authorities. Once the Indian leadership had achieved its diplomatic goals, however, it simply waited for the proper military circumstances to enter the conflict. On December 3, 1971, the Pakistanis attacked Indian Air Force bases near the West Pakistani-Indian border, providing the excuse the Indians needed to enter the conflict.[47] In just a few weeks, the Indians decisively defeated the West Pakistanis using a combined-arms, maneuver-based military strategy, reaching the capital of East Pakistan on the eastern front, and thwarting Pakistani attacks on the western front.[48] India was victorious over Pakistan, and East Pakistan achieved independence as Bangladesh.

The accoutrements of democracy helped India win its war with Pakistan. Prime Minister Indira Gandhi wanted victory, not just war for its own sake. In April 1971 her chief of staff dismissed calls for immediate war (something that we would not expect had India been an autocracy). He did this recognizing that the Indian Army was not yet ready for a two-front war (that is, simultaneously intervening in East Pakistan and parrying a likely counterattack launched from West Pakistan), and that India needed an additional six months to prepare for such a conflict.[49] Pausing several months before striking substantially increased India's chances for victory, as it allowed for the fighting to begin after the monsoon season ended in September. The delay also afforded the opportunity to train the Bangladeshi force Mukhti Bahini in guerrilla and conventional tactics, enabling them to aid regular Indian forces, and the signing of a Treaty of Peace, Friendship, and Cooperation with the Soviet Union in July 1971, which solidified Indo-Soviet ties. This reduced the possibility that the UN Security Council would make trouble once war started, given the Soviet veto in the Security Council.[50]

Offshoots of democratic institutions also helped India fight the war more effectively. Their desire for a short and successful war pushed them to adopt a maneuver-oriented military strategy, which helped them win.[51] India also benefited from superior civil-military relations. During the war, Indian officers were more professional and more closely identified with the rank-and-file of the army than their Pakistani counterparts were. The Pakistani president had been the army commander-in-chief before becoming president. This dual role contributed to the politicization of the military itself. He owed most of his loyalties to the army leadership and, as a result, nearly all his close advisors were members of the army leadership. This came at the expense, in part, of the other service branches. In addition, the headquarters of the army, navy, and air force were far apart, and these two factors together resulted in an extremely centralized command structure that bred interservice rivalries and misunderstandings. The Pakistani military frequently sacrificed efficiency and effectiveness for political expediency.[52]

In contrast, India's military had no political role because there was a clear separation between the civilian political and military leaderships. Civilian ministers collectively responsible to the Indian Parliament directed the military leadership. Within the military leadership, each of the three services was equal; the heads of the services met in the Chiefs of Staff Committee, and the most senior member of the committee was the chairman. The headquarters of all three services were located near the Ministry of Defense in Delhi. In addition to a nonpoliticized structure, the Indian military benefited from good personnel relations that crossed service boundaries at the highest level. As a result, the Indian military command, combined with good civilian leadership, was better able to manage the Indian war effort.[53]

The Japanese Attack on Pearl Harbor, 1941

Japan's attack on Pearl Harbor on December 7, 1941, contrasts starkly with India's careful consideration of war with Pakistan thirty years later. The Japanese leadership perceived itself to be in a dangerous bind in 1941, as its land war against China was bogging down and American opposition to the war in China had led to a trade embargo. The American economic sanctions limited Japanese access to crucial raw materials, particularly oil, which was essential to Japan's continued campaign for empire. Japan saw an adventurous bid to capture the raw materials of Southeast Asia as one way to make its empire economically sustainable. It also recognized, however, that widening the war in Asia would bring Japan into conflict with the United States. Since the Japanese believed capturing Southeast Asia was essential to their nation's continued existence as an Asian great power, war with the United States was inevitable. Japan chose to launch a surprise attack against Hawaii, the Philippines, and elsewhere to maximize its chances for victory, recognizing beforehand that in the end its overall chances for victory were likely quite low.[54]

What were Japan's estimates of its chances for victory in a war against the United States? Despite tendencies toward optimism that underestimated American military power, Japanese leaders recognized that the attack on the United States was a long shot at best. Their strategy for victory against the United States was to run up a string of victories in the first year and establish a defensive perimeter, hoping that American public opinion would become discouraged and press Roosevelt to sue for peace. Six days before Pearl Harbor, Admiral Yamamoto colorfully described this strategy: "One thing we could do now is disperse as many submarines as possible around the South Pacific so as to make the other side feel they've been set on by a swarm of hornets. If the hornets around it buzz loudly enough, even a hefty animal like a horse or a cow will get worried, at least. American public opinion has always been very changeable, so the only hope is to make them feel as soon as possible that it's no use tackling a swarm of lethal stingers."[55] The Japanese leadership recognized that they could not win a longer war because of American industrial might, and even that the short-war strategy had only a slim chance of victory.

Japan's war with the United States was an utter disaster for the Japanese. Millions of Japanese soldiers and civilians lost their lives, and the Japanese empire collapsed under its own weight and American guns. Using conventional or nuclear weapons, the United States flattened nearly every Japanese city. A democratic Japan might have been able to swallow its pride and avoid war with the United States by withdrawing from China, for two reasons. First, a democratic government might have made a less biased estimate of its chances of victory against the United States that was close to zero rather than just low. As it was, the hypernationalist military government in Japan drastically underestimated the American willingness to fight when attacked. It assumed that such a bourgeois and materialist society lacked the martial spirit for warfare. In addition, the leadership ignored the overwhelming power of the American economy. A Japanese colonel sent to the United States in the years before the war to study American industrial capacity reported that the United States could produce ten times the strategic goods and materials that Japan was capable of generating, making Japan's victory in a possible war an illusion, not a realistic possibility. The report disappeared into the toadyist bureaucracy; the army reassigned the colonel to an infantry regiment.[56] A democracy may have been more open to this sort of evaluation both within the state bureaucracy and from independent media sources within society.

In addition to a biased evaluation of its prospects against the United States, a democratic Japan would likely not have been willing to accept such low odds of victory simply to maintain the war effort in China. The militarization of Japanese society in the 1930s led to a crackdown on the expression of anti-imperial and anti-militarist sentiment from intellectuals, radicals, and artists. A citizenry better informed about the low chances of victory against the United States and unafraid of government oppression might have spoken out against such a war, and an elected Japanese government fearful of electoral backlash would have made the necessary concessions to avoid a catastrophic war. In the words of the Japanese historian Saburo Ienaga: "If the popular will had influenced national policies, the conflict might have been avoided or at least shortened. It was a vicious cycle: the weakness of democracy was one cause of the war, and the war further eroded freedom."[57]

How Democracies Choose Winnable Wars

We close this chapter with a final question focusing on selection effects. How exactly do democracies choose winnable wars? What criteria do they use to select winnable wars? Unfortunately, our quantitative data do not provide any easy answers to these questions. We looked for such evidence by examining the conditions under which democracies initiate wars. Confining ourselves to the data set offered few clues; statistical tests reveal that democratic initiators did not win because they were bigger or had more allies, better troops, or better strategy choices.

Broadening our empirical survey beyond just states that fought in wars offers some clues, however. Within our comprehensive survey of interstate wars, democracies do not seem especially likely to choose better military strategies. However, one study of states both at war and at peace shows that democracies are significantly more likely to choose maneuver strategies, which in turn are successful against the more frequently observed attrition strategy. This study offers a more complete picture of the strategy choices of states, as its inclusion of both peaceful and warring states avoids selection biases inherent to examining only belligerents. This finding is generally consistent with our selection effects explanation: democracies seek wars that are short, successful, and with low casualties, all of which are virtues promised by maneuver strategies.[58]

The relative infrequency of democratic initiators who use maneuver strategies encourages us to push a bit farther, however. It may be that democratic leaders do initiate wars when they are confident that they enjoy military advantages, but as shown in the case of India, the advantages vary depending on the circumstances. The United States was encouraged to attack Spain in 1898 because of its overwhelming material advantages; Israel felt confident to attack its Arab neighbors in 1967 because it had confidence in its maneuver-based military strategy; and the United States pushed for the liberation of Kuwait in 1990 because Iraq had inferior troop quality and stood without allies.[59]

Beyond selection effects, we do find some evidence of warfighting effects as well. In addition to making smarter choices when they select which wars to fight, democracies also seem to fight better once war starts. The fact that democratic targets fare systematically better than other types of targets provides cursory evidence in support of our claim. Of course, aggregate data in a simple table or figure cannot answer the following important question: what characteristics account for this warfighting power? At the outset of this chapter, we outlined three different arguments as to why democracies might fight better: they have more allies, their economies are stronger, and their soldiers fight better on the battlefield. In the broad-brush statistical tests of this chapter, we were able to include alliance contributions and capabilities as control variables alongside democracy. The fact that democratic targets are still more likely to win the wars they fight, even with the inclusion of these two controls, offers preliminary evidence that democracies fight better during wartime because of superior soldiering rather than stronger economies or more allies. In the next three chapters, we explore more closely which of these factors aid democracies' frequent march to victory.

Appendix 2.1: Research Design, Data, and Variables

This appendix describes the particulars of our data set, research design, and empirical results. Our unit of analysis is a belligerent nation in war, and we measure whether or not it experienced victory or defeat. Our population of cases for analysis includes all participants in interstate wars between 1816 and 1990.[60] To identify these wars we use the Correlates of War (COW) set of interstate wars and the *Encyclopedia of Military*

History.[61] The hypotheses we test in this chapter concerning polity type relate only to the likelihood of victory. Accordingly, we simplified the analysis by dropping draws from the data set, leaving 197 cases.[62] In chapter 7 we investigate draws.

We elected to disaggregate three long, multiple-actor wars—World War I, World War II, and the Vietnam War. Our goal is to be able to distinguish between separate military campaigns (for example, to separate the German campaign against France in 1940 and the German campaign against the Soviet Union). We acted conservatively, separating only the best candidates into multiple wars. World War I we divide into three wars: Germany versus Belgium, Germany/Austria/Turkey versus Russia, and Allied Powers (minus Russia and Belgium) versus Central Powers.[63]

World War II we divide into several wars, including Germany versus individual European countries (such as Norway and the Netherlands) as separate wars, Germany versus the Soviet Union, the Pacific War, war between the United States/Britain and Germany/Italy. The Vietnam War we divide into a United States/South Vietnam versus North Vietnam phase lasting until 1972, and a second phase of North versus South Vietnam.

This separation makes our data set more historically accurate; these long coalition wars are best thought of as aggregations of distinct conflicts. Decision makers rarely anticipate or think in terms of large systems of wars but instead usually think in terms of sequences of opponents. In the case of World War II, most historians have identified separate and distinct negotiated settlements or fundamentally independent war-fighting efforts between the participants.[64] Such disaggregation also affords two important advantages for testing the hypotheses. First, it permits us to distinguish more accurately between winners and losers. In long coalition wars there are distinct campaigns in which individual members of the losing coalition defeat members of the coalition that are ultimately victorious. For example, our method permits us to classify Russia and Belgium as losers in World War I and Poland and Norway as losers in World War II, whereas the COW data set, for example, views these four countries as winners. Conversely, our method recognizes the execution of successful military campaigns by countries that went on to lose, such as Germany's campaign against the Netherlands in World War II. Second, the disaggregation of cases allows us to code the independent variables more accurately. Dividing long wars of global reach into distinct campaigns greatly improves the accuracy of codings for variables like strategy and terrain.[65] Such advantages may not be trivial: one scholar found that how one treats cases from the world wars determines whether or not one finds significant correlations between military buildups and the outbreak of war.[66]

We code our variables as follows:

Initiation. Initiation is a dichotomous variable, 1 for initiators, and 0 for noninitiators. Our initiation codings differed slightly from those of the Correlates of War project. Aside from the three cases we divide—World War I, World War II, and the Vietnam War—we follow the descriptions provided by the *Encyclopedia of Military History* and Michael Clodfelter.[67] We made two changes from the COW initiation codings. In the Crimean War, we code Russia as the initiator, not Turkey, because of the Russian moves to occupy the Danubian principalities in May and June 1853. In the First Balkan War, we code the three members of the Balkan League as co-initiators as they declared war on Turkey first in October 1912. One might also argue that states that join wars are conceptually similar to those that initiate wars.[68] We tested for this possibility. When we recode the initiation variable to include states that join wars because they have a defense pact with a belligerent or because an ongoing war threatens their national interests, the results are largely the same, though the change weakens the substantive and statistical significance of the result. Note that including initiation as an interaction term essentially removes any selection bias problems that might occur with the analysis of wars only (that is, as opposed to analyzing both wars and crises that did not culminate in war) to test a selection effects hypothesis.[69]

Democracy. To test our propositions, we coded the political system of each nation using the democracy and autocracy scores from the Polity III data set. The democracy and autocracy scores are aggregations of the degree of openness of the system, the degree of participation, and the degree of competitiveness of candidate selection. The democracy scale ranges from 0 to 10, where 0 indicates the absence of democratic institutions and 10 the presence of very strong democratic institutions. The autocracy scale also ranges from 0 to 10, with 10 representing the most autocratic states. We combine the two scales into a single "Politics" index by subtracting the autocracy scale from the democracy scale, which results in a −10 to 10 scale, with 10 representing the most democratic states and −10 the least.[70]

To test our various hypotheses linking regime type and war outcomes, we used two functional forms, each with a different set of interaction terms. In one functional form, we added two interaction terms. One consists of a state's Politics score times the dichotomous initiation variable, and the second consists of a state's Politics score times a dichotomous target variable, which is coded 1 if the state is a target (not an initiator) and 0 if it is not a target (an initiator). Proposition 2.1 predicts that the Politics*Initiator term should be positive, and Proposition 2.3 predicts that the Politics*Target terms should be positive. The war-fighting explanation predicts that both terms ought to be significant, while the simpler, monotonic selection effects explanation predicts that only the Politics*Initiator term ought to be significant.

Testing Proposition 2.2, which envisions a nonmonotonic selection effects relationship, requires a different functional form for the independent variables. To test for the expected curvilinear relationship between the interaction of politics and initiation, we use a pair of fractional polynomials.[71] To compare the curvilinear selection effects explanation to the war-fighting explanation, we then need three terms. The first of the three is a state's Politics score multiplied by a dichotomous Target variable that is coded as 1 if a state is a target (meaning it is *not* an initiator) and 0 if a state is not a target (meaning it *is* an initiator). There are also two terms of a transformed independent variable: the transformation for the first term is $x^{-1/2}$ and for the second term is $x^{-1/2}(\ln(x))$, where $x = $ (Politics* Initiation + 11)/10. The polynomial specification allows for a curve that starts at a medium level for Politics scores of -10, dips down to a lower level as Politics scores increase, but then rises to a higher level as Politics scores approach 10. With this alternate functional form, the democratic selection effects are supported in the curvilinear manner predicted by Proposition 2.2 if the transformed independent variables are statistically significant. Among targets, democracies have an advantage (an effect predicted by Proposition 2.3) if the Politics*Target interaction term is positive and significant.

Material capabilities. We operationalize each actor's military and industrial capabilities as its proportion of all the capabilities available to all the war's participants. We use the Correlates of War composite capabilities index as our indicator of national capabilities. The index is composed of industrial production, military troops, military spending, energy consumption, and proportions of urban and total populations.[72]

Troop quality. We used an indicator for technology and training using *ex ante* information. We assume that states with higher spending rates per soldier, relative to their opponents, will have correspondingly higher levels of technological endowment, equipment, and training.[73] The military spending and troop numbers come from the COW data set.

Military strategy. We categorize military strategies as follows. States choose among three strategies, maneuver, attrition, and punishment. We then match each of these strategies with either offensive or defensive political goals (doctrine). Significantly, the effectiveness of a particular strategy depends on the adversary's choice of strategy. We predict the effectiveness of various strategy combinations based on the assumptions that minimizing one's own military losses are better, and the side trying to change the status quo prefers quicker outcomes.[74]

We coded military strategy as a set of dummy variables following the procedures in Stam's previous book, *Win, Lose, or Draw*. The first step is to code whether a state has offensive (O) or defensive (D) political goals, based on the *Encyclopedia of Military History* and Kalevi Holsti's book *Peace and War*. Next, we coded the choice between maneuver (M), attrition (A), and punishment (P) strategies, following the analysis in the *Encyclopedia of Military History*, Michael Clodfelter's *Warfare and Armed Conflicts*, and Trevor Dupuy's 1983 study under the Historical Evaluation and Research Organization. Cases in which the state used a strategy emphasizing high mobility were coded as being maneuver. Maneuver strategies are frequently characterized by attempts to avoid the enemy's strength, achieve breakthroughs at weak points, and disrupt the enemy's command, control, and communication. Maneuver strategies also seek to encircle and divide the enemy's forces. Examples of maneuver strategies include the blitzkriegs of the German Wehrmacht in World War II. Israel also used maneuver strategies frequently in its wars with its Arab neighbors. Cases in which the state's strategy focused on annihilation of the enemy and/or seeking decisive battles we coded attrition. In contrast to avoiding the enemy's strength, attrition strategies seek out the enemy's strength, aiming to pit strength against strength in order to erode directly the enemy's forces. Attrition emphasizes firepower over mobility. Both the Allied and Central Powers on the Western Front in World War I used attrition strategies. Punishment includes two classes of cases. The first is the guerrilla strategy, in which guerrilla forces seek to establish political support in the countryside and then conduct unconventional warfare against occupying troops, before finally moving to conventional military operations. Mao Zedong honed guerrilla warfare during the 1940s against both the Imperial Japanese Army and the Chinese Nationalists; in later years, the Viet Cong used it effectively against American and South Vietnamese forces during the Vietnam War. A second category of punishment is aerial bombing of civilians, in which the aim is to inflict damage against nonmilitary targets in order to coerce the other side to concede. In cases where states used multiple strategies, we coded the strategy that absorbed the majority of the state's military assets. If there was more than one country on one side, we coded the strategy of the largest state (in terms of capabilities).[75]

We code the goals and strategy of each belligerent and each belligerent's opponent. Therefore, a coding of OADP indicates that the belligerent has offensive goals and an attrition strategy, and its opponent has a defensive doctrine and punishment strategy. We group all possible strategy codings into pairs and rank the effectiveness of each pair. We do not observe all possible strategies, however. Among those that are observed, we rank the strategy pairs as follows starting with the most effective: OMDA/ DPOA; OPDA/DMOA; OADA/DAOA; OADM/DAOP; OADP/DAOM. We use five dummy variables to account for the observed strategy combinations. To avoid perfect multicollinearity among the strategy categories, we omit from the regression models the dummy category representing OADP/DAOM.[76]

Our strategy variables are certainly simplifications of reality. However, our effort to propose concepts about the execution of combat that transcend a particular military environment has also been the general aim of most military theorists. The essential question, though, is whether our conceptualizations explain more than they obscure. We believe the answer to be yes, if for no other reason than that this set of strategy variables has been found to be significantly correlated elsewhere with war outcomes, war duration, and war initiation.[77]

Terrain. Terrain interacts significantly with strategy choice by enhancing or detracting from the advantages offered by wise strategy choice. For example, a maneuver strategy can better exploit an attrition strategy in flat plains than it can in mountainous jungle. Terrain codings come from the *New York Times Atlas of the World* and correspond to the location of the majority of the battles fought during the war. We then scaled the terrain types to match the predicted movement times, using data from Trevor Dupuy's works that estimate movement speeds on various types of terrain. In cases where there were more than two actors on one side, we used the average of terrain scores weighted by the size of the forces fighting in particular terrain. The final terrain index ranges from 0.3 to 1.2, where 1.0 corresponds to the speed at which vehicles and troops can move on open rolling terrain, similar to the plains found in Eastern Europe. Scores above 1.0 correspond to desert areas with flat, hard-packed surfaces. Codings close to 0.3 match places where movement of vehicles is close to impossible, such as very rugged mountains and dense jungles. The results do not change if we scale the 0.3 to 1.2 scale to a 0 to 1 scale.[78]

Our model includes two terrain variables, a strategy-terrain interaction variable and, as a control, the terrain variable by itself. To measure the interaction of terrain and strategy, we would normally multiply the strategy and terrain variables. Unfortunately, with dummy variables to control for strategy choice, the inclusion of each terrain interaction dummy creates multicollinearity problems. We instead use a scaled strategy index with terrain, which reduces multicollinearity (as revealed by partial correlations) by creating a single variable with a larger range of values rather than several variables with more limited ranges of values. This scaled strategy variable is coded 1 through 5, a ranking of the observed strategies listed above.[79]

Distance. We measure distances from capital to capital in miles.[80]

Allies. The contributions to a state's power from its allies must be discounted compared to the state's own military and industrial capabilities. At the operational level, it is likely that differences in factors such as command structure, technology, training, and communication equipment may hinder allies from working together effectively. Allies are also less reliable because they have to defend themselves, so they may not be willing to commit completely their forces to the war at hand. We thus separate out alliance contributions from the resources of the belligerents. We measure alliance contributions in the same fashion as the state's military-industrial capability, using the COW data, where the alliance partner's contribution is the fraction of the total capabilities of all states involved in the war. Because we have no prior beliefs as to the absolute size of the anticipated discount factor for alliance power, we include alliance contributions as a separate term to permit measurement of its independent effect.

Empirical Results

In this section, we present more extensive analysis.[81] We use a probit model because of the dichotomous nature of the dependent variable. Applying a linear model would risk introducing specification error and biased coefficients. Table 2.2 presents the probit regression results of several models.[82]

In Model 1, our baseline, we include terms for the interaction between the politics variable and both initiators and targets. We also include a variable marking whether the state was an initiator or not. Note that in this model we cannot test the nonmonotonic Proposition 2.2; we address this hypothesis below. Regardless, concerning the effects of democracy, the Politics*Initiator term is in the hypothesized direction and statistically significant.[83] We also see that democratic targets appear to perform somewhat better during war and we find support for the selection effects argument. With this simple model we cannot, however, ascertain the individual validities of the rent-seeking, democratic countercoalitions, or state legitimacy arguments.

To test Proposition 2.2 (nonmonotonic relationship between Politics, Initiation, and Victory), we also fit a fractional polynomial model. In Model 2 we find similar results for the initiation term. The parameter estimate for the Politics*Target term is relatively stable, although it is no longer statistically significant. In this simple model, there is no support for the fractional polynomial terms (interacted with initiation) preliminarily leading us to reject Proposition 2.2. Before doing so, including additional data may allow us to make less biased estimates of the polynomial terms. Recall that one twist of the warfighting explanation posits that democracies should be more likely to win because they devote more resources to the military, that they will assemble overwhelming countercoalitions. These variables would be the ones actually determining the

TABLE 2.2
Probit Models of War Outcomes: Dependent Variable Is Win/Lose

Independent Variable	Model 1		Model 2		Model 3		Model 4		Model 5		Model 6	
	Coefficient	SE	Coefficient	SE	Coefficient	SE	Coefficient	SE	Coefficient	SE	Coefficient	SE
Poly-Pol 1* Initiation	—	—	−0.16	0.13					−3.67*	1.88	−3.90*	1.98
Poly-Pol 2* Initiation	—	—	0.013	0.075			—	—	−1.07#	0.57	−1.14#	0.60
Politics*Initiation	0.045*	0.021	—	—	—	—	0.069*	0.030	—	—	—	—
Politics*Target	0.036*	0.017	0.029	0.019	—	—	0.064**	0.027	0.064*	0.03	0.059	0.04
Initiation	0.51**	0.15	0.64***	0.21	—	—	0.91***	0.34	0.96**	0.35	1.24**	0.41
Capabilities	—	—	—	—	3.33***	0.70	3.73***	0.52	3.76***	0.53	3.85***	0.60
Alliance Contribution	—	—	—	—	3.85***	0.95	4.72***	0.68	4.71***	0.68	4.48***	0.78
Quality Ratio	—	—	—	—	0.082*	0.05	0.052	0.03	0.051	0.03	0.055	0.03
Terrain	—	—	—	—	−9.00***	3.36	−10.93***	2.94	−11.31***	3.02	−14.1***	3.31
Strategy*Terrain	—	—	—	—	2.86***	1.09	3.56***	0.97	3.68***	0.99	4.73***	1.10
Strategy 1	—	—	—	—	5.14	3.40	7.24**	2.89	7.62**	2.93	10.5***	3.13
Strategy 2	—	—	—	—	2.72	2.39	3.47*	1.99	3.76*	2.02	6.06**	2.15
Strategy 3	—	—	—	—	2.47	1.70	3.35*	1.43	3.57*	1.45	4.91**	1.55
Strategy 4	—	—	—	—	2.09*	1.27	3.07**	1.25	3.21*	1.26	5.23**	1.59
Constant	—	—	—	—	−4.11***	1.86	−5.51***	1.70	−2.14	2.49	−3.76	2.77
	LL = −128.3		LL = −128.2		LL = −69.3		LL = −64.9		LL = −64.9		LL = −50.2	
	Pseudo r^2 = 0.07		Pseudo r^2 = 0.07		Pseudo r^2 = 0.49		Pseudo r^2 = 0.52		Pseudo r^2 = 0.52		Pseudo r^2 = 0.57	
	n = 197		n = 197		n = 197		n = 197		n = 197		n = 168	

Note: Model 6 includes only core dyads. Reported standard errors are robust standard errors. Data are currently available from the authors at www.eugenesoftware.org. Strategy 1 is OMDA and DPOA; Strategy 2 is OPDA and DMOA; Strategy 3 is OADA and DAOA; Strategy 4 is OADM and DAOP.

* p < 0.05 all tests two-tailed.

** p < 0.01

*** p < 0.001

\# p < 0.06

wars' outcomes. This implies that if we control for these factors the effects of democracy may drop out of the equation. First, we test our model of military factors. Model 3 might best be termed a realist model of war outcomes. It is devoid of state characteristics and includes variables marking military-industrial capabilities, alliance contributions, military quality, and several markers for strategy and strategy and terrain interactions. In general, we find strong support for this realist approach.

Next, in Model 4, we include the regime type variables from Model 1, and all the Politics terms from our base model are still significant. This increases our confidence in the validity of the selection effects explanation. It also implies that democratic targets are more powerful, which is consistent with all three of the arguments underlying the warfighting explanation. However, in Model 4 we have controlled for alliances and industrial capabilities, two of the factors delineated in the warfighting explanation, and we still observe a relationship between democracy and war outcomes; indeed, this relationship appears stronger, not weaker, when we add the realist controls. This would seem to support the argument that the empirical generalization that democracies are more effective at fighting wars is correct, but not for all of the reasons we outlined. Though there is no direct evidence here, the results indirectly support the validity of the proposition that democracies fight wars well because their troops fight with higher battlefield military effectiveness. Additionally, we ran tests to see if the addition of political variables in Model 4 makes a statistically significant improvement to our explanation of the dependent variable. A likelihood ratio test demonstrates that the gains in Model 4 over Model 3 are statistically significant at the $p < 0.01$ level.

In Model 5 we substitute two fractional polynomial terms for the Politics*Initiation interaction. Differing from Model 2, the inclusion of a more fully specified model of outcomes indicates support for the non-monotonic Proposition 2.2. Note that although the Politics interaction terms in both Models 4 and 5 are statistically significant, Model 5 is preferable to Model 4. The improvement in the fit of the overall model from the inclusion of two fractional polynomial terms, compared to the linear term, is significant using a conservative test at the $p < 0.02$ level.[84] This encourages preference for the curvilinear selection effect described in Proposition 2.2 over the monotonic selection effect described in Proposition 2.1. We limit the remainder of our discussion to the estimates for Model 5, which tests all hypotheses other than the hypothesis which we discuss below.

As shown in Model 5, the coefficient estimate for initiation is statistically significant, indicating that initiators win more often. The coefficient estimates for the two Politics*Initiator interaction terms are also statistically significant. This indicates support for Proposition 2.2 (that democratic initiators win more often and dictatorships are more likely to win than anocracies). We discuss the meaning and the interpretation of the signs and magnitudes of the interaction terms below. This is an interesting result; the conventional belief from the rational choice literature on wars that initiators are more likely to win receives confirmation. Nevertheless, even when we control for the general increase in the likelihood of victory that all initiators benefit from, some initiators do better than others. Among initiators, democracies have a significantly higher likelihood of winning than other kinds of regimes.

Among the control variables, we have mixed findings. The probit models in table 2.2 are restricted models. They reflect our decision to drop two independent variables from models not presented in table 2.2: military personnel and distance. The p-values for these variables fall far outside the standard levels of statistical significance. Additionally, a likelihood ratio test indicates that we can safely exclude distance and military personnel from the model. When including distance and military personnel, the results are consistent with Models 4 and 5.

We find statistically significant relationships between a better ratio of military-industrial capabilities, greater allied contributions, superior troops and training, and victory. Distance was not significantly related to outcomes.[85] The strategy dummy variables are statistically significant, indicating that strategy choices do have a substantial effect on outcomes. Additionally, both the terrain and strategy-terrain interaction are statistically significant ($p < 0.001$). The strategy dummy variables Strategy 2 and Strategy 3, while having essentially the same coefficients, still predict to different outcomes because of the effects of the strategy-terrain interaction.

It is possible that the inclusion of war participants other than the core dyad belligerents biases our results. That is, for wars with more than two participants we should include for analysis only the two principle belligerents and exclude nations that have only secondary interests in the conflict. To be sure that our results are robust, we also estimated Model 6, which includes all the variables from Model 5 but on a smaller sample that is made up of the core dyad in each war ($n = 168$ versus $n = 197$).[86] In this model, the results do not change substantially.

Lastly, it is possible that democratic targets win wars not because they fight more effectively but rather because autocratic initiators, which are more risk-averse and more likely to lose, only attack democratic targets. Some autocratic targets are attacked by democratic initiators and are in turn especially likely to lose. Together, this means that the average autocratic target may be more likely to lose than the average democratic target not because democracies execute the tasks of war more effectively, but rather because some autocratic targets are doomed to lose as the targets of destined-to-win democratic initiators.

We can test this speculation. We reduce the data set to only targets. We include variables for the regime type of the target, and the regime type for the initiator that attacked that target. If democratic targets were more likely to win only because of this selection effect, then we would see that the regime type of the initiator is statistically significant, while the regime type of the target itself would no longer be significant, because we are controlling for the regime type of the initiator. However, as indicated in table 2.3, in such a model the regime type of both the target and the initiator are statistically significant. Hence, autocratic targets are doubly cursed: they are more likely to lose both because democratic initiators prey on them and because they do not execute the tasks of war as effectively.[87]

War Initiation

We also tested the proposition that democracies initiate conflicts only when they are very confident they will win. We assembled a data set on dispute and war initiation so that we could test more directly the proposition that democracies are relatively risk-averse. We estimated several probit models, where the variable of interest is the interaction of the predicted likelihood of defeat in a bilateral war (P(lose)) and the state's level of democracy. If our selection effects argument is valid, we would expect to find that the greater the chance of losing, and the more democratic a state is, the less likely it should be to initiate a militarized dispute or escalate an existing dispute to war.

We built the data set on a foundation of two data sets produced by Reiter and one produced by Bennett and Stam. The first of Reiter's data sets contains strategy and terrain codings for all states involved in wars and a random sample of states involved in crises during the years 1903–1992. The second set contains a random sample of states at peace for the same variables and temporal domain. We began by creating unique directed dyads for each year by including states at peace, states in dispute, and the opponents of states in dispute. We then used the EUGene program to create directed dyads for these states, thereby providing the base observations for the data set. We drop dyads with an ongoing MID and dyads of Target vs. Initiator.[88]

We then generated predicted durations for hypothetical bilateral wars using the parameter estimates found in Bennett and Stam's article, "The Duration of Interstate Wars." We used these estimates in the generation of predicted war outcomes for all dyads using the parameter estimates

TABLE 2.3
Probit Analysis of Determinants of Victory for Targets, 1816–1990

Variable	Coefficient Estimate
Politics Score of Initiator	−0.070*
	(.0303)
Politics Score of Target	0.060**
	(.0237)
Capabilities	4.34***
	(.826)
Quality Ratio	−0.0076
	(.0235)
Terrain	−4.23
	(3.84)
Strategy*Terrain	1.69
	(1.25)
Strategy 1	−3.86***
	(1.08)
Strategy 2	−4.58
	(no standard error estimates produced)
Strategy 3	−5.49***
	(1.10)
Strategy 4	−4.51**
	(1.92)
Constant	2.02*
	(1.17)

Note: $n = 110$; log likelihood $= −36.6$; pseudo r-squared $= 0.51$. Robust standard errors reported. Data set includes all participants in wars from 1816–1990 that were targets.
*Significant at 0.05 level.
**Significant at 0.01 level.
***Significant at 0.001 level. All significance tests are one-tailed.

found in Stam's *Win, Lose or Draw*. The duration and outcomes instruments were then combined with data measuring various indicators hypothesized to be associated with the onset of war. They range from bilateral balance of power, to systemic power concentration, to Bueno de Mesquita and Lalman's estimates of the expected utility for war.[89]

The variables are as follows:

Dependent Variables: We use two dependent variables: the decision to initiate a militarized interstate dispute (MID) and the decision to initiate a war.[90]

Independent Variables: The Democracy, Distance, and Dyadic Balance of Forces variables are coded the same as discussed above. The P(lose) and P(draw) variables are built using estimates from *Win, Lose, or Draw*, setting the ally capabilities, surprise, and ally quality variables to their means, allowing the issue salience variable to take values of 0 and 1 for different models, and taking the strategy and terrain data from the Reiter articles. The Nuclear Weapons variable is a count of the number of the states in the dyad that have nuclear weapons. Contiguity refers to geographical contiguity. The Politically Relevant variable is coded 1 if at least one state in the dyad is a major power, or the states are contiguous. The Arms Race variable is coded 1 if the three-year moving average of constant military expenditure growth is greater than 8 percent for both states, using COW data. EUGene generates the Expected Utility (EU) and uncertainty scores, which in turn uses *War and Reason*. The System Power Concentration variable is generated using the "concentration" and "movement" measures for the interstate system measuring each variable annually; our measures of change and movement are based on one-year differences.[91] We recomputed the values using the most recent COW capabilities data set and use all states in our computation. The value of the "concentration" index is 0 at an equal distribution of capabilities in the system and 1 when one state holds all capabilities; the "change in concentration" variable is high when concentration increases. The value of the "movement" index takes higher values when there have been more capability share shifts.

The results are in table 2.4. In Models 1 through 4, the dependent variable was the initiation of a MID, and in Model 5, the dependent variable is the initiation of a MID that escalates to the use of force. Throughout all four models, the interaction term of P(lose)*democracy is statistically significant and in the predicted direction (as a state's estimated probability of losing and democracy increase, it becomes increasingly likely to initiate a MID). Hence, we have robust results supporting our selection effects model: as democracies become more confident they will win, they become increasingly likely to initiate a dispute or the use of violence.

TABLE 2.4

Models of Dispute and War Initiation, 1904–1986

Variable	(1) Initiate MID	(2) Initiate MID	(3) Initiate MID	(4) MID with Force
P(Draw)	−0.222	−0.062	−0.075	0.021
	(2.42)*	(0.30)	(0.36)	(0.07)
P(Lose)	−0.102	−0.101	−0.157	0.466
	(0.85)	(0.37)	(0.58)	(1.15)
Democracy*P(Draw)	0.020	0.002	0.005	−0.020
	(1.63)	(0.06)	(0.19)	(0.44)
Democracy*P(Lose)	−0.049	−0.120	−0.115	−0.425
	(2.41)*	(2.30)*	(2.19)*	(2.13)*
Contiguous on Land	0.999	1.226	1.265	−0.037
	(11.07)**	(6.07)**	(6.09)**	(0.10)
Politically Relevant	0.922	2.490	2.518	2.792
	(11.09)**	(9.94)**	(9.70)**	(7.12)**
Arms Race	—	0.491	0.507	0.599
		(3.10)**	(3.20)**	(2.42)*
Balance of Power	—	−3.578	−3.599	−3.474
		(6.51)**	(6.19)**	(4.17)**
Change in System Concentration	—	−12.253	−11.383	−26.457
		(0.76)	(0.69)	(1.11)
System Power Concentration	—	6.839	7.105	7.993
		(2.19)*	(2.24)*	(1.58)
Dyadic Democracy	—	0.043	0.012	0.027
		(3.61)**	(3.54)**	(1.43)
EU War Equilibria	—	—	0.067	—
			(0.25)	
War Equilibria* Uncertainty	—	—	0.873	—
			(0.87)	
Uncertainty	—	—	−0.068	—
			(0.10)	
Constant	−2.062	−3.990	−4.155	−5.488
	(25.20)**	(3.72)**	(3.79)**	(3.17)**
Observations	4011	3452	3452	3452

Note: Robust z-statistics in parentheses.
*Significant at 0.05 level.
**Significant at 0.01 level.

Appendix 2.2: War Participants and Outcomes, 1816–1990

War	Participant	Initiator/ Target	Outcome
Franco-Spanish, 1823	France	Initiator	Win
Franco-Spanish, 1823	Spain	Target	Lose
Russo-Turkish, 1828–1829	Russia	Initiator	Win
Russo-Turkish, 1828–1829	Ottoman Empire	Target	Lose
Mexican-American, 1846–1848	USA	Initiator	Win
Mexican-American, 1846–1848	Mexico	Target	Lose
Austro-Sardinian, 1848–1849	Austria-Hungary	Target	Win
Austro-Sardinian, 1848–1849	Sardinia	Initiator	Lose
Austro-Sardinian, 1848–1849	Modena	Target	Lose
Austro-Sardinian, 1848–1849	Tuscany	Target	Lose
First Schleswig Holstein, 1849	Prussia	Initiator	Draw
First Schleswig Holstein, 1849	Denmark	Target	Draw
Roman Republic, 1849	France	Initiator	Win
Roman Republic, 1849	Austria-Hungary	Target	Win
Roman Republic, 1849	Papal States	Target	Lose
Roman Republic, 1849	Two Sicilies	Target	Lose
La Plata, 1851–1852	Brazil	Initiator	Win
La Plata, 1851–1852	Argentina	Target	Lose
Crimean, 1853–1856	United Kingdom	Target	Win
Crimean, 1853–1856	France	Target	Win
Crimean, 1853–1856	Italy/Sardinia	Target	Win
Crimean, 1853–1856	USSR (Russia)	Initiator	Lose
Crimean, 1853–1856	Ottoman Empire	Target	Win
Anglo-Persian, 1856–1857	United Kingdom	Initiator	Win
Anglo-Persian, 1856–1857	Persia	Target	Lose
Italian Unification, 1859	France	Target	Win
Italian Unification, 1859	Austria-Hungary	Initiator	Lose
Italian Unification, 1859	Italy/Sardinia	Target	Win
Spanish-Moroccan, 1859–1860	Spain	Initiator	Win
Spanish-Moroccan, 1859–1860	Morocco	Target	Lose
Italo-Roman, 1860	Italy	Initiator	Win
Italo-Roman, 1860	Papal States	Target	Lose
Italo-Sicilian, 1860–1861	Italy	Initiator	Win
Italo-Sicilian, 1860–1861	Two Sicilies	Target	Lose
Franco-Mexican, 1862–1867	Mexico	Target	Win
Franco-Mexican, 1862–1867	France	Initiator	Lose
Ecuadorian-Columbian, 1863	Colombia	Initiator	Win
Ecuadorian-Columbian, 1863	Ecuador	Target	Lose
Second Schleswig-Holstein, 1864	Prussia	Initiator	Win
Second Schleswig-Holstein, 1864	Austria-Hungary	Target	Win
Second Schleswig-Holstein, 1864	Denmark	Target	Lose
Lopez, 1864–1870	Brazil	Target	Win

War	Participant	Initiator/ Target	Outcome
Lopez, 1864–1870	Paraguay	Initiator	Lose
Lopez, 1864–1870	Argentina	Target	Win
Spanish-Chilean, 1865–1866	Peru	Target	Draw
Spanish-Chilean, 1865–1866	Chile	Target	Draw
Spanish-Chilean, 1865–1866	Spain	Initiator	Draw
Seven Weeks, 1866	Hanover	Target	Lose
Seven Weeks, 1866	Bavaria	Target	Lose
Seven Weeks, 1866	Prussia	Initiator	Win
Seven Weeks, 1866	Baden	Target	Lose
Seven Weeks, 1866	Saxony	Target	Lose
Seven Weeks, 1866	Wurtemburg	Target	Lose
Seven Weeks, 1866	Austria-Hungary	Target	Lose
Seven Weeks, 1866	Italy	Target	Lose
Franco-Prussian, 1870–1871	France	Initiator	Lose
Franco-Prussian, 1870–1871	Bavaria	Target	Win
Franco-Prussian, 1870–1871	Prussia	Target	Win
Franco-Prussian, 1870–1871	Baden	Target	Win
Franco-Prussian, 1870–1871	Wurtemburg	Target	Win
Russo-Turkish, 1877–1878	Russia	Initiator	Win
Russo-Turkish, 1877–1878	Ottoman Empire	Target	Lose
Pacific, 1879–1883	Peru	Target	Lose
Pacific, 1879–1883	Bolivia	Target	Lose
Pacific, 1879–1883	Chile	Initiator	Win
Sino-French, 1884–1885	France	Initiator	Draw
Sino-French, 1884–1885	China	Target	Draw
Central American, 1885	Guatemala	Initiator	Lose
Central American, 1885	El Salvador	Target	Win
Serbo-Bulgarian, 1885–1886	Serbia	Initiator	Lose
Serbo-Bulgarian, 1885–1886	Bulgaria	Target	Win
Sino-Japanese, 1894–1895	China	Target	Lose
Sino-Japanese, 1894–1895	Japan	Initiator	Win
Greco-Turkish, 1897	Greece	Initiator	Lose
Greco-Turkish, 1897	Ottoman Empire	Target	Win
Spanish-American, 1898	USA	Initiator	Win
Spanish-American, 1898	Spain	Target	Lose
Boxer Rebellion, 1900	USA	Initiator	Win
Boxer Rebellion, 1900	United Kingdom	Initiator	Win
Boxer Rebellion, 1900	France	Initiator	Win
Boxer Rebellion, 1900	Russia	Initiator	Win
Boxer Rebellion, 1900	China	Target	Lose
Boxer Rebellion, 1900	Japan	Initiator	Win
Russo-Japanese, 1904–1905	Russia	Target	Lose
Russo-Japanese, 1904–1905	Japan	Initiator	Win

War	Participant	Initiator/Target	Outcome
Central American, 1906	Guatemala	Initiator	Draw
Central American, 1906	Honduras	Target	Draw
Central American, 1906	El Salvador	Target	Draw
Central American, 1907	Honduras	Target	Lose
Central American, 1907	El Salvador	Target	Win
Central American, 1907	Nicaragua	Initiator	Win
Spanish-Moroccan, 1909–191	Spain	Initiator	Win
Spanish-Moroccan, 1909–191	Morocco	Target	Lose
Italo-Turkish, 1911–1912	Italy	Initiator	Win
Italo-Turkish, 1911–1912	Ottoman Empire	Target	Lose
First Balkan, 1912–1913	Yugoslavia/Serbia	Initiator	Win
First Balkan, 1912–1913	Greece	Initiator	Win
First Balkan, 1912–1913	Bulgaria	Initiator	Win
First Balkan, 1912–1913	Ottoman Empire	Target	Lose
Second Balkan, 1913	Serbia	Target	Win
Second Balkan, 1913	Greece	Target	Win
Second Balkan, 1913	Bulgaria	Initiator	Lose
Second Balkan, 1913	Rumania	Target	Win
Second Balkan, 1913	Ottoman Empire	Target	Win
WWI, Belgium Campaign, 1914	Belgium	Target	Lose
WWI, Belgium Campaign, 1914	Germany	Initiator	Win
WWI, Eastern Theater, 1914–1918	Germany	Initiator	Win
WWI, Eastern Theater, 1914–1918	Austria	Initiator	Win
WWI, Eastern Theater, 1914–1918	Russia	Target	Lose
WWI, Eastern Theater, 1914–1918	Turkey	Target	Lose
WWI, Western Theater, 1914–1918	USA	Target	Win
WWI, Western Theater, 1914–1918	Britain	Target	Win
WWI, Western Theater, 1914–1918	France	Target	Win
WWI, Western Theater, 1914–1918	Germany	Initiator	Lose
WWI, Western Theater, 1914–1918	Austria	Initiator	Lose
WWI, Western Theater, 1914–1918	Italy	Target	Win
WWI, Western Theater, 1914–1918	Greece	Target	Win
WWI, Western Theater, 1914–1918	Bulgaria	Target	Win
WWI, Western Theater, 1914–1918	Rumania	Target	Lose

War	Participant	Initiator/ Target	Outcome
WWI, Western Theater, 1914–1918	Turkey	Target	Lose
Russo-Polish, 1919–1920	Poland	Initiator	Win
Russo-Polish, 1919–1920	USSR	Target	Lose
Hungarian-Allies, 1919	Hungary	Target	Lose
Hungarian-Allies, 1919	Czechoslovakia	Initiator	Win
Hungarian-Allies, 1919	Rumania	Initiator	Win
Greco-Turkish, 1919–1922	Greece	Initiator	Lose
Greco-Turkish, 1919–1922	Turkey	Target	Win
Sino-Soviet, 1929	USSR	Initiator	Win
Sino-Soviet, 1929	China	Target	Lose
Manchurian, 1931–1933	China	Target	Lose
Manchurian, 1931–1933	Japan	Initiator	Win
Chaco, 1932–1935	Bolivia	Target	Lose
Chaco, 1932–1935	Paraguay	Initiator	Win
Italo-Ethiopian, 1935–1936	Italy	Initiator	Win
Italo-Ethiopian, 1935–1936	Ethiopia	Target	Lose
Sino-Japanese, 1937–1941	China	Target	Draw
Sino-Japanese, 1937–1941	Japan	Initiator	Draw
Changkufeng, 1938	USSR	Target	Draw
Changkufeng, 1938	Japan	Initiator	Draw
Germany-Poland, 1939	Germany	Initiator	Win
Germany-Poland, 1939	Poland	Target	Lose
Nomohan, 1939	USSR	Target	Win
Nomohan, 1939	Mongolia	Target	Win
Nomohan, 1939	Japan	Initiator	Lose
Russo-Finnish, 1939–1940	USSR	Initiator	Win
Russo-Finnish, 1939–1940	Finland	Target	Lose
Germany-Belgium, 1940	Belgium	Target	Lose
Germany-Belgium, 1940	Germany	Initiator	Win
Germany-Holland, 1940	Holland	Target	Lose
Germany-Holland, 1940	Germany	Initiator	Win
Germany-Denmark, 1940	Germany	Initiator	Win
Germany-Denmark, 1940	Denmark	Target	Lose
Germany-Norway, 1940	Germany	Initiator	Win
Germany-Norway, 1940	Norway	Target	Lose
Germany-France, 1939	France	Target	Lose
Germany-France, 1939	Germany	Initiator	Win
Italy-Greece, 1940	Italy	Initiator	Lose
Italy-Greece, 1940	Greece	Target	Win
Japan-United States, 1941–1945	United States	Target	Win
Japan-United States, 1941–1945	Japan	Initiator	Lose
United Kingdom/United States	United States	Initiator	Win

War	Participant	Initiator/ Target	Outcome
United Kingdom/United States	United Kingdom	Initiator	Win
United Kingdom/United States	Germany	Target	Lose
United Kingdom/United States	Italy	Target	Lose
Germany-Soviet Union, 1941–1945	Germany	Initiator	Lose
Germany-Soviet Union, 1941–1945	Soviet Union	Target	Win
Germany-Yugoslavia, 1941	Germany	Initiator	Win
Germany-Yugoslavia, 1941	Yugoslavia	Target	Lose
Germany-Greece, 1941	Germany	Initiator	Win
Germany-Greece, 1941	Greece	Target	Lose
First Kashmir, 1947–1948	India	Initiator	Draw
First Kashmir, 1947–1948	Pakistan	Target	Draw
Palestine, 1948–1949	Iraq	Initiator	Lose
Palestine, 1948–1949	Egypt/UAR	Initiator	Lose
Palestine, 1948–1949	Syria	Initiator	Lose
Palestine, 1948–1949	Lebanon	Initiator	Lose
Palestine, 1948–1949	Jordan	Initiator	Lose
Palestine, 1948–1949	Israel	Target	Win
Korean, 1950–1953	USA	Target	Draw
Korean, 1950–1953	China	Target	Draw
Korean, 1950–1953	Korea, N.	Initiator	Draw
Korean, 1950–1953	Korea, S.	Target	Draw
Russo-Hungarian, 1956	Hungary	Target	Lose
Russo-Hungarian, 1956	USSR	Initiator	Win
Sinai, 1956	United Kingdom	Target	Draw
Sinai, 1956	France	Target	Draw
Sinai, 1956	Egypt/UAR	Target	Lose
Sinai, 1956	Israel	Initiator	Win
Sino-Indian, 1962	China	Initiator	Win
Sino-Indian, 1962	India	Target	Lose
Vietnamese, 1965–1975	USA	Target	Draw
Vietnamese, 1965–1975	Vietnam, DRV (North)	Initiator	Draw
Vietnamese, 1965–1975	Vietnam, RVN (South)	Target	Draw
Second Kashmir, 1965	India	Initiator	Draw
Second Kashmir, 1965	Pakistan	Target	Draw
Six Day, 1967	Egypt/UAR	Target	Lose
Six Day, 1967	Syria	Target	Lose
Six Day, 1967	Jordan	Target	Lose
Six Day, 1967	Israel	Initiator	Win
Israeli-Egyptian, 1969–1970	Egypt/UAR	Initiator	Lose
Israeli-Egyptian, 1969–1970	Israel	Target	Win
Football, 1969	Honduras	Target	Draw

War	Participant	Initiator/ Target	Outcome
Football, 1969	El Salvador	Initiator	Draw
Bangledesh, 1971	India	Initiator	Win
Bangledesh, 1971	Pakistan	Target	Lose
Yom Kippur I, 1973	Egypt/UAR	Initiator	Lose
Yom Kippur I, 1973	Israel	Target	Win
Yom Kippur II, 1973	Iraq	Initiator	Lose
Yom Kippur II, 1973	Syria	Initiator	Lose
Yom Kippur II, 1973	Jordan	Target	Lose
Yom Kippur II, 1973	Israel	Target	Win
Yom Kippur II, 1973	Saudi Arabia	Initiator	Lose
Turco-Cypriot, 1974	Cyprus	Target	Lose
Turco-Cypriot, 1974	Turkey	Initiator	Win
Vietnamese, 1975	Vietnam, N	Initiator	Win
Vietnamese, 1975	Vietnam, S	Target	Lose
Vietnamese-Cambodian, 1975	Cambodia	Target	Draw
Vietnamese-Cambodian, 1975	Vietnam, DRV (North)	Target	Draw
Ethiopian-Somalian, 1977–1978	Cuba	Target	Win
Ethiopian-Somalian, 1977–1978	Somalia	Initiator	Lose
Ethiopian-Somalian, 1977–1978	Ethiopia	Target	Win
Ugandan-Tanzanian, 1978–1979	Uganda	Initiator	Lose
Ugandan-Tanzanian, 1978–1979	Tanzania	Target	Win
Ugandan-Tanzanian, 1978–1979	Libya	Target	Lose
Sino-Vietnamese, 1979	China	Initiator	Draw
Sino-Vietnamese, 1979	Vietnam, DRV (North)	Target	Draw
Iran-Iraq, 1980–1988	Iran	Target	Draw
Iran-Iraq, 1980–1988	Iraq	Initiator	Draw
Falklands, 1982	Argentina	Initiator	Lose
Falklands, 1982	United Kingdom	Target	Win
Israel-Syria (Lebanon), 1982	Syria	Target	Lose
Israel-Syria (Lebanon), 1982	Israel	Initiator	Win
Sino-Vietnamese, 1985–1987	China	Initiator	Draw
Sino-Vietnamese, 1985–1987	Vietnam, DRV (North)	Target	Draw

THREE

DEMOCRACY AND BATTLEFIELD SUCCESS

One might say that the physical seems little more than the
wooden hilt, while the moral factors are the precious metal,
the real weapon, the finely honed blade.
—*Carl von Clausewitz*

An officer's principal weapon is his mind.
—*Official doctrine of the United States Marine Corps*

WHAT IS IT that makes democracies more powerful? Exactly
how do democracies fight wars more effectively? In chapter 2,
we demonstrated that there are two aspects to democracies'
military prowess. The first is a selection effect that results from the
choices of which wars they start and which wars they avoid: democracies
almost always start only those wars they go on to win, successfully avoiding risky situations where they would otherwise find themselves overmatched. The second explanation is more of a story about tangible
power: democracies are actually better at waging war than other kinds of
states. To support this second and controversial claim, we demonstrated
that democracies are more likely to win whether they are initiators or
targets. We left as an open question, however, exactly what accounts for
democracies' apparent advantage during war. In this and the following
two chapters, we explore three different explanations of why democracies
are successful at fighting wars. First, democratic armies perform better on
the battlefield, making more efficient use of their military assets. This
implies that when two equally matched armies meet in battle, the one
drawn from a democratic society will outperform the one drawn from a
closed society. The two other explanations of democratic power argue
that democracies win more often than not simply because they bring
more resources to bear when they fight. One claim is that democracies
band together when attacked, forming overwhelming countercoalitions
of like-minded states. The other is that democracies can extract more
resources for war from their societies, enabling them to overwhelm their
opponents with larger numbers of soldiers and weapons.[1] Both of the
latter arguments maintain that democracies win because they bring more
of some resource to the battlefield, be it allies or war materiel. The for-

mer argument holds that democracies win not because they bring greater resources to bear, but because they use what they have more efficiently and effectively.

This chapter explores the first of these three different explanations: simply put, the soldiers of liberal democracies outfight the soldiers of closed, autocratic societies. This gets at a fundamental disagreement over the merits of free and oppressed societies. A conventional view is that free societies excel at the arts and commerce but lack the martial spirit that combat requires and authoritarian systems supposedly imbue. We might think of Athens, Britain, and the United States as three countries in their day classified as prosperous and culturally blessed free republics. In contrast, Sparta, Germany, and the Soviet Union were bland, brutal, and powerful.

An alternative to the view that oppression builds stoic societies stocked with warriors is that freedom produces better fighters. In this chapter, we make four propositions as to why democracies might produce armies that are more effective. First, soldiers serving popularly elected governments should fight with higher morale, enabling them to overcome obstacles and setbacks that would otherwise lead them to quit the field. Second, the emphasis on the rights and prerogatives of the individual in democratic political culture carries over to the battlefield, increasing individual initiative for both common infantry soldiers and their officers, and pushing them to innovate and succeed in combat. Third, soldiers fighting for authoritarian leaders are more likely to surrender to democratic enemies than vice versa. Soldiers believe that potential democratic captors will treat them better than will authoritarian captors. Finally, democratic armies enjoy better leadership, because of the emphasis on personal initiative within democratic culture and because officer advancement in democratic states is more likely to be merit-based, whereas in authoritarian states it tends to be politicized.

As is our strategy throughout this book, we give the empirical record the final word on which of these perspectives lies closest to the truth. We flesh out our analysis by using an underutilized data set of individual battles produced by the Historical Evaluation and Research Organization under contract to the U.S. Army Concepts Analysis Agency (CAA). The advantage of using the military battle as the unit of analysis (as opposed to the war itself) is that it helps eliminate other explanations as to why democracies win wars and isolate the precise effects of regime type on the battlefield—where most wars are won or lost. In other words, rather than observing that democratic states win wars and inferring that democratic soldiers therefore must fight better, the HERO/CAA data enable us to observe whether democratic armies are actually more effective on the battlefield and why. We take up a similar strategy in chapters 4 and 5, in which we test directly the propositions that democracies win wars because they ally together during wartime and that democracies extract more from their economies for the war effort.

Our findings in this chapter offer support to the proposition that democratic soldiers fight more effectively on the battlefield. Specifically, we find that soldiers of democracies fight with better initiative and leadership, though not necessarily with better morale. This offers a more nuanced view of the connection between democratic political culture and the battlefield. We find that democratic soldiers are not more inspired to lay down their lives for the cause of freedom or at the beck and call of popular governments, but that the emphasis on individual prerogative in democratic culture and the institutional incentives emphasizing merit over political correctness help make democratic armies fight better.

Fighting Battles to Win Wars

In large part, winning wars is about winning battles. Wars are defined by those battles that serve as turning points: Yorktown in the Revolutionary War; Gettysburg in the Civil War; Verdun and the failed spring 1918 offensives in World War I; Stalingrad and D-Day in World War II; Inchon in Korea; Dienbienphu and Tet in Vietnam. Frederick the Great minced no words: "War is decided only by battles and it is not decided except by them." We do not claim that competence at winning individual battles is sufficient to guarantee victory, but it is a crucial component of a successful military effort.[2] In the remainder of this section, we lay out four central propositions linking democracy to battlefield effectiveness.

Troop Morale

We first develop the argument that individual soldiers in democratic armies fight with higher morale. Across time, military thinkers have emphasized the importance of troop morale. Napoleon Bonaparte's famous remark that "The moral is to the physical as three to one" was echoed in the age of modern warfare by the World War II British Field Marshal Bernard Montgomery, who stated, "The morale of the soldier is the greatest single factor in war."[3]

How might the nature of the political system affect troop morale? Some have expressed the concern that liberalism imposes fundamental encumbrances on martial effectiveness. This is a fundamental controversy in political thought, whether or not the individualism unleashed within liberalism undermines collective action and respect for achieving communitarian goals. The twentieth-century German thinker Carl Schmitt considered this idea and proposed that liberalism's emphasis on the individual precluded the state from calling on individuals to self-sacrifice on the battlefield. In the 1930s Nazi sympathizers such as the American aviator Charles Lindbergh were pessimistic about the Western democracies' chances of prevailing over the new fascist dictatorships in the event of war. During the Cold War, observers of the Communist threat such as Aleksandr Solzhenitsyn worried that the devotion to individual, material pursuits in Western liberalism impeded the self-sacrifice demanded by national defense, so that the American Athens was systematically handicapped in its race for survival with the Soviet Sparta.[4]

The contrary view is that the popularity of democratic governments means that citizens are more willing to fight in service of the state. States must ask citizens to make individual sacrifices, whether to pay taxes, to sacrifice their liberty by serving in the military, or to risk their very lives on the battlefield. Soldiers are more likely to accept the dangers of the battlefield and place their lives at risk if they are serving in a military overseen by a government grounded in democratic political institutions. They are more likely to perceive the war effort and the leadership itself as reflecting their own interests if the need for popular consent constrains the government and can be removed from office if it fails to hold up its end of the social contract. Further, in this line of reasoning, soldiers are more confident that a democratically elected government will obey the laws and abide by its promises, because failure to do so may result in its removal from power. In essence, the source of political legitimacy lies in the rule of law rather than the cult of personality, as is the case in many autocracies.

The general proposition that popular governments engender loyalty in soldiers and thereby greater battlefield success is not a new one. Sun Tzu, a Chinese military thinker of sixth-century BCE China, emphasized moral influence as one of the five fundamental factors of war, defining it as "that which causes the people to be in harmony with their leaders, so that they will accompany them in life and unto death without fear of mortal peril."[5] The ancient Greeks also recognized the importance of popular government. Herodotus phrased it strongly in his analysis of the Athenian military:

> So Athens had increased in greatness. It is not only in respect of one thing but of everything that equality and free speech are clearly a good; take the case of Athens, which under the rule of princes proved no better in war than any of her neighbors but, once rid of those princes, was far the first of all. What this makes clear is that when held in subjection they would not do their best, for they were working for a taskmaster, but, when freed, they sought to win, because each was trying to achieve for his very self.[6]

Pericles made a similar point in praise of Athenian democracy at his funeral oration during the Peloponnesian War.[7]

The ancient Chinese and Greek proposition that troops fight harder for popular regimes has filtered into modern political thought. Liberals such as John Locke viewed checks on state power as enhancing military power and state capacity in general, as individuals in a liberal system would be more willing to make personal sacrifices to serve the common good. Some observers of the French Revolution thought that throwing off the shackles of monarchy would unleash human potential in all spheres of human behavior. The American Thomas Paine commented that a soldier of a republic would be worth "twice the value" of a soldier of a monarchy.[8]

Note, however, that the writings of proto-democrat Jean-Jacques Rousseau do not imply that citizens in republics have an obligation to fight and die for the state—rather, they may make that choice of their own free will. There have always been questions regarding liberal democracy's ability to oblige citizens to risk their lives in defense of the state. In the writings of Thomas Hobbes, his incipient liberal-democratic theory exhibits a tension between contractarianism and individualism. Hobbes states that citizens are obligated to defend their country because they have entered into a social contract with the sovereign state. Nevertheless, this obligation is tenuous at best since it is based on the state's guarantee of the individual's life, which obviously the state endangers by putting the soldier at the front in war. Thus, Hobbes indulges the "cowardice" of the soldier who flees battle.[9]

The idea that free men make better soldiers has been a popular one among American presidents, as well. John Quincy Adams wrote in a letter to his brother that "Individual liberty is individual power, and as the power of a community is a mass compounded of individual powers, the nation which enjoys the most freedom must necessarily be in proportion to its numbers the most powerful nation." Both Thomas Jefferson and Ronald Reagan proclaimed it in their first inaugural addresses: Reagan declared that "no arsenal, or no weapon in the arsenals of the world, is so formidable as the will and moral courage of free men and women."[10]

Modern political scientists have built more formal and extensively specified theories expanding on these ideas of the ancients. One focused on "contingent consent," examining the factors that are likely to determine the degree to which members of society comply with government military conscription policies. A key component of this model is the trustworthiness of government, a characteristic democratic governments are more likely than autocracies to exhibit. Importantly, it predicts that democratic governments are more likely to enjoy higher levels of social consent in reaction to military conscription policies. Along similar lines, we propose that governments installed by popular election operating under the constraints of democratic political institutions are more likely to earn the trust and loyalty of their citizens, which will translate into greater consent on the battlefield, and ultimately into higher levels of military effectiveness through greater morale.[11]

This proposed connection between a state's political system or ideology and its battlefield military effectiveness has received a great deal of empirical scrutiny from military historians and sociologists. The available evidence is mixed. There is an older though substantial body of research that argues that political ideology plays no role in determining the morale or motivations of troops. A famous 1948 study interviewed American-held German prisoners of war (POWs) during World War II, leading the authors to conclude that German military effectiveness emerged from the solid bonds of friendship and allegiance to one's primary group rather than affinity to political ideology. On the American side, the landmark study *The American Soldier* conducted interviews with American soldiers during World War II. There, the authors found that political ideology was not a principal motive for American soldiers aside from a general affinity to the materialism of the United States and the belief that the United States had no choice but to fight following Pearl Harbor. Other studies, drawing on these themes identified in the American and German armies of World War II, applied it to the American Army in the Civil War, Korean War, Vietnam War, and post-Vietnam era with similar results.[12] Others have found support for it in other countries, such as postcolonial democratic India.[13]

Some historians and other scholars have disagreed with this disconnection of political ideology from battlefield performance and motivation. Carl von Clausewitz emphasized the importance of nationalism in the Napoleonic Wars; nationalism remains as a motivating force in modern armies of countries as diverse as North Vietnam and Israel. More broadly, the emergence of the modern nation-state in the decades immediately before World War I saw democracy and nationalism combine to form powerful incentives for citizens to serve and fight for states to which they now felt linked in more powerful ways than previously.[14]

Debates continue to rage over the role of ideology in particular wars. A growing number of scholars now emphasize the role of political ideology in motivating soldiers to fight. An array of modern scholarship now refutes the idea that the German Wehrmacht was a professional military divorced from Nazi ideology. The regular army as well as SS units were devoted to Hitler's rule and his racist ideas about *lebensraum* and Aryan superiority, viewing the war in the East in particular as a racial war of extermination.[15] Political ideology motivated both Union and Confederate soldiers during the American Civil War. Union soldiers wanted to keep the Union whole and abolish slavery, while Confederate soldiers equated states' rights with freedom and saw slavery as an institution worth defending. Interestingly, both sides saw themselves as upholding the spirit of 1776.[16]

More recently, historians have begun to reexamine the motivations of American soldiers in World War II—refuting, in part at least, the earlier studies showing an absence of ideological motivation for American soldiers. In the 1990s the historian Stephen Ambrose published a series of studies of the American Army in the 1944–45 campaigns in Europe. His basic theme was that the American soldier outfought the German soldier. The superiority of the Americans was traceable largely to the influences of democracy, both because Americans fought with better initiative and because they were more strongly motivated to defend and advance freedom. Another study pointed to three victorious democratic marches— the Athenians under Epaminondas into the Peloponnese in the fourth century BCE, the Union Army under Sherman at the close of the Civil War, and the Third Army under Patton in 1944—to argue for the ability of democratic armies to muster superior morale and fighting power to crush oppressive foes.[17]

Our contribution to the rich and diverse historical literature on this point is the application of statistical tests to a broad array of cases. Doing so helps us step back from the trees of individual cases to get a better sense of the forest of the last two centuries of warfare. As such, we apply statistical analysis to test the following proposition:

Proposition 3.1: *Democratic soldiers fight with higher levels of morale than other soldiers.*

Significantly, the morale advantage enjoyed by democratic armies may be only fleeting. One of the central themes in this book is that democracies seek wars that are relatively easy to win, low cost, and short. This last point emerges from a fundamental impatience among democratic citizens, which we discuss in detail in chapter 7. The accumulation of casualties without victory erodes consent for the war within both society and the military, causing all to question how elusive the expected victory truly is. Recognizing that few would wish to fight in a drawn-out, losing effort, we would expect, then, that the morale of democratic soldiers will decline as the war drags on, which leads us to our next proposition.

Proposition 3.1a: *The later in a war a battle takes place, the lower will be the morale for democratic soldiers.*

The Effectiveness of Individuality on the Battlefield

Democratic, liberal culture emphasizes the importance of the individual. Indeed, the very essence of liberal democracy is the guarantee that the individual is minimally fettered, whether in politics, speech, art, religion, or commerce. Armies are microcosms of the societies they come from, and to a large extent, the military mirrors the qualities of the society from which it is drawn. The emphasis on individual initiative in liberal political culture, therefore, spills over into superior initiative on the battlefield. Alexis de Tocqueville made this point, observing that democracies are likely to enjoy the tactical advantage of having soldiers acting on reason rather than on instinct, without threatening military discipline. Superior initiative and inspired leadership demand just this kind of flexibility on the part of individual soldiers. Modern warfare requires the display of individual initiative on the battlefield to exploit best emergent but fleeting opportunities and to cope with unanticipated conditions. During the Middle Eastern Wars, for example, the differences in fighter pilot performance between democratic Israel and its autocratic Arab neighbors emerged from the greater emphasis on individual initiative in liberal Israeli culture. The exercise of individual initiative is especially important for the successful execution of mobile and maneuver-based strategies, as their very premise is allowing lower-ranked officers and troops the freedom to exploit a fluid battlefield.[18]

Israelis themselves see their military prowess as inextricably intertwined with their democratic form of government. The first prime minister of Israel, David Ben-Gurion, explained it as such: "A look at our defence system, the most disciplined organization we have in the country, indicates just how much we predicate our very existence on democracy and on the popular consent that only this form of government can elicit. I think the citizen aspect of the IDF [Israeli Defense Force] makes for both imaginative thinking in military affairs and for exemplary conduct above and beyond the call of duty."[19] Just as democratic societies exhibit personal initiative at home, so do democratic armies on the battlefield; hence our next proposition.

Proposition 3.2: *Democratic soldiers will demonstrate higher levels of initiative on the battlefield.*

Democracy, Loyalty, and a Soldier's Decision to Surrender

Liberal societies' emphasis on the fair and equal treatment of the individual has a second important advantage, beyond increasing the initiative of one's own soldiers. Specifically, it serves to erode the loyalty of opposing soldiers, inducing the surrender of enemy forces. Facing long odds and an autocratic opponent, soldiers from a democratic state will be more likely than their autocratic counterparts to take the personal initiative and continue to resist rather than admitting defeat and passively accepting capture.

The decision to surrender deserves special attention because of its considerable effects on battle and war outcomes. A widespread inclination to surrender can devastate an army's combat effectiveness, making it impossible to rally from early defeats in a war. An army with a higher rate of surrender will find itself drained of manpower on the battlefield. The torrent of German surrender on the Western Front in the fall of 1918, for example, triggered the end of World War I. Indeed, captured POWs sometimes fight alongside the captor's army; at Stalingrad, the Germans used some 50,000 Soviet POWs and citizens alongside Wehrmacht forces. Additionally, belligerents can use captured prisoners as laborers who may make a substantial contribution to the war effort on the home front. German General Erich Ludendorff commented after World War I that "Prisoners of war were of the utmost importance in all fields of war activity. We could not have kept our economic structure together without the aid of enormous numbers of Russians taken in the East." Nazi Germany also made good use of POW labor, putting to work at one time as many as 1.9 million POWs. Even democratic belligerents are not shy about exploiting prisoner labor; in the final three years of World War II, POWs held by the United States contributed more than 90 million person-days of work to the Allied war effort, offsetting local labor shortages.[20]

What causes a soldier to drop his or her weapon and submit to capture by the enemy? The horrifying and chaotic nature of the battlefield has led some to think about this decision from a small-group social psychological perspective. However, even in the most hellish environs, soldiers retain the notion to avoid undesirable outcomes and pursue desirable ones.[21]

When captured, a soldier may be treated well or poorly in the extreme. Being treated well is, of course, a relative term, though in accord with twentieth-century conventions, it means that captured soldiers are kept in a POW camp away from combat zones, are not executed or tortured, and have their basic physical needs (including food and medical care) attended to by their captors. Conversely, being treated poorly can include being shot immediately upon capture, tortured to extract military information, left to die of starvation or disease in a concentration camp, and so forth. Soldiers of course prefer to avoid such harsh treatment and are far more likely to surrender if they are confident their potential captors will treat them well than if they expect to be treated poorly.

Democracies will have an easier time convincing enemy soldiers that, if captured, their captors will treat them well. Autocracies, on the other hand, will be hard pressed to convince enemy soldiers to accept capture and the ill treatment it will likely entail. How is it that soldiers come to believe their potential captors will treat them badly or well? States formalize their commitments to honor the rights of POWs by signing international treaties. There have been a string of treaties since the end of the nineteenth century that have delineated the rights of enemy POWs, and nearly all states have signed these treaties.[22] However, a signature on a piece of paper does not always translate into the action demanded by the treaty. Some states are more likely than others to honor written commitments. Soldiers the world over are aware of these treaties, but when do they believe that a state will honor its commitment to the fair treatment of POWs? The mere signature of the treaties is not sufficiently demonstrative, as there is no global authority to enforce adherence to international treaties. The key question becomes: Will soldiers believe that states will adhere to their international commitments to safeguard the rights of enemy POWs?

First, note that it is in the interest of *all* states to treat POWs well, in order to seduce the enemy to surrender.[23] Treating captured soldiers badly reduces the likelihood that other opposing soldiers will willingly give themselves up for capture. Democratic armies have a comparatively easy time convincing authoritarian soldiers that they will come to no harm if taken prisoner. Respect for the rights of all individuals is central to liberal culture, as discussed. Further, respect for the law is at the core of democratic political institutions, a proposition postulated by enlightenment thinkers such as Alexis de Tocqueville and recently bolstered by modern, formal analysis.[24] Soldiers facing a democratic army will be likely to believe that if they are captured there is a good chance that their democratic captors will abide by international POW treaties and safeguard at least their basic physical safety and welfare.

It is more difficult for the army of an authoritarian state to convince opposing soldiers that it will respect their rights following capture. An autocratic government does not build its political legitimacy on norms of honoring legal commitments, but rather through the repression of dissent and coercion. Autocratic leaders and soldiers alike have a difficult time making a credible commitment to treating opposing soldiers fairly when the state does not even commit to the fair treatment of its own citizens.[25] Further, authoritarian states are more likely to thrive on war cultures that require the brutalization of POWs. Japan's behavior in the early part of the twentieth century is a prime example of this type of national culture. During the 1930s Japan became an extensively militarized society, and during this period its armed forces became increasingly fanatical. Part of this trend was that both civil society in general and the military in particular stressed the glory of dying for the emperor and the total disgrace of surrender. Overall, the changing military culture enhanced Japanese military effectiveness because it ensured high morale on the battlefield, and soldiers that were willing to fight to the death. Stressing the unacceptability of surrender of Japanese forces guided the Japanese military toward policies of brutal treatment of enemy POWs.[26] This treatment showed up in the horrifying mortality rates of Allied soldiers, sailors, and airmen captured by the Japanese, as 27 percent of Anglo-

American POWs died in Japanese captivity. In comparison, the conditions for Japanese POWs held in the United States were quite good, and accordingly they suffered lower mortality rates. The Korean War demonstrated similar dynamics. Some 38 percent of Americans taken prisoner died in captivity. American forces recognized this and resisted surrender: despite three years of fighting with hundreds of thousands of American forces deployed in Korea absorbing tens of thousands of fatalities, only 7,190 Americans were taken prisoner. Similarly, during the Vietnam War, fewer than 600 Americans allowed themselves to be captured by the North Vietnamese; the vast majority of these were aviators shot down over enemy territory. In contrast, over 50,000 Vietnamese soldiers surrendered to the South.[27]

The Nazi German approach to the war with the Soviet Union also led to decisions not to protect the rights of Soviet POWs. In the months before launching the invasion of Russia in 1941, Hitler told his generals that the war against Russia would be a racial war of extermination, in which there would be no restraint and in particular no humane treatment of POWs. Hitler and the Wehrmacht made the war in the East a brutal and racial one, using maltreatment of Soviet POWs to reinforce this barbaric military culture. The results were appalling: nearly two-thirds of the POWs taken by Germany on the Eastern front were dead by 1944.[28]

Numerous examples exist of situations where expectations of postsurrender treatment affected the decisions of enemy soldiers to surrender. If they expect the worst, soldiers will voluntarily accept death in battle rather than surrender willfully. During the Vietnam War, the poor treatment of American POWs led to some startling responses on the part of American soldiers. The North Vietnamese rarely transferred American commandos captured in Cambodia or Laos to POW camps. Instead, they tortured most, ritualistically killed many. Rather than deterring American soldiers from continuing to fight, it had a perverse effect. Knowing they would not survive capture, on several occasions American soldiers deliberately called in tactical air attacks directly on their own positions when they were in danger of being overrun by North Vietnamese forces. The logic in the minds of these American commandos? It was better to take the chance that one might survive an air attack than to choose certain death at the hands of the North Vietnamese. In at least one instance, North Vietnamese troops captured and subsequently killed an entire unit of American special operations soldiers because a horrified American aviator could not bring himself to napalm his comrades' position.[29]

The Wehrmacht's policy of treating Soviet POWs brutally also undercut German military effectiveness on the Eastern front. Hitler had to override the requests of several high-ranking Nazi officials to treat Soviet prisoners of war humanely for the pragmatic purpose of inducing their surrender. Even Alfred Rosenberg, minister for the Occupied Eastern

Territories who was put in charge of the treatment of Soviet POWs, felt that brutalization of Soviet POWs was responsible for bolstering the fighting spirit of the Red Army "and thereby also for the deaths of thousands of German soldiers. . . . An obvious consequence of this politically and militarily unwise treatment has been not only the weakening of the will to desert but a truly deadly fear of falling into German captivity." Hitler, however, ignored these and other pleas to treat soldiers humanely and induce greater Soviet surrender. Instead, Hitler's army continued to treat captured soldiers according to the same sort of racial typology used to classify civilians. Conversely, Hitler actually wanted the Soviets to treat German POWs badly, to discourage German soldiers from surrendering. Hitler even went so far as to destroy an arriving batch of mail from Soviet-held German POWs, to maintain the image of a barbaric enemy.[30]

When facing democratic armies, soldiers of autocracies have been more likely to surrender to democracies, spurred by the hopes of fair treatment. During World War II, Germans were much more willing to surrender to American and British forces in the West than to Soviet forces in the East. As one Panzer corporal put it, "In Russia, I could imagine nothing but fighting to the last man. We knew that going into a prison camp in Russia meant you were dead. In Normandy, one always had in the back of his mind, 'Well, if everything goes to hell, the Americans are human enough that the prospect of becoming their prisoner was attractive to some extent.'"[31] The difference between treatment by the Americans (and British) and treatment by the Soviets was no secret even to the high German command, as evidenced by German Admiral Karl Doenitz's failed attempt in 1945 to engineer a surrender of all German forces to the American and British armies only. More recently, during the 1991 Gulf War between the American-led coalition and the autocratic Iraq, over 86,000 Iraqis surrendered in just a few days of ground combat.[32]

In sum, democracies can more credibly commit to fair treatment of captured soldiers. This means that soldiers are more likely to surrender to democratic foes than to autocratic foes. This provides an important advantage to democratic armies, as it enables them to siphon off enemy strength. Hence, our third proposition of this chapter highlights a tangible, but indirect, source of democratic power on the battlefield.

Proposition 3.3: *Soldiers are more likely to surrender to democratic armies than to authoritarian armies.*

Democracy and Military Leadership

Superior leadership is also an important part of battlefield effectiveness. Good combat leaders can rally demoralized troops, implement doctrine and battle plans competently, and adapt to changing battlefield conditions. Democratic armies are likely to enjoy superior military leadership. This is because civil-military relations within a democracy are likely to engender relatively more meritocratic militaries that promote the competent over the politically connected. Progress away from monarchy and aristocracy and toward democracy engenders social leveling and the general spread of egalitarian norms throughout society. This facilitates egalitarianism and a meritocracy within the government in general and the military in particular. In turn, this means that military organizations will run on relatively more meritocratic rather than class-based principles.

Conversely, authoritarian militaries are likely to be less meritocratic and in turn, on average, will have relatively inferior leadership.[33] Given the weaker or nonexistent institutionalized civilian control of the military in autocratic regimes, a nondemocratic political leader is more likely than a democratic leader to perceive that the armed forces may pose a domestic political threat. The tendency for autocrats to staff their militaries with politically dependable ethnic confreres rather than effective leaders is especially notable in the Middle East. Syrian strongman Hafez al-Assad stocked his military with Alawis; King Hussein of Jordan promoted to senior positions officers from the East Bank region; and Saddam Hussein of Iraq has made sure his officer corps is dominated by minority Bathists. Making matters worse, autocrats rotate officers relatively more frequently to prevent them from developing close ties to their troops, and they squelch rather than listen to constructive criticism from within the officer corps. Sometimes autocrats literally shoot the messenger, as Saddam Hussein did when an Iraqi junior officer (presciently) argued that a planned frontal attack during the war with Iran would end in disaster.[34]

The need for officers in a nondemocratic state to be politically unthreatening will generate lower effectiveness throughout the military. The propensity for Arab authoritarian leaders to install political toadies in high positions undercuts Arab military effectiveness. Some scholars have argued that the disastrous performance of the Red Army in 1941 was due to the purges of the officers' ranks in the years immediately before the German invasion. During 1937 alone, 36,671 Soviet officers were executed, imprisoned, or dismissed. Independent-thinking, high-ranking officers suffered most as Stalin ordered the execution of 403 of 706 brigade commanders or higher. Especially damaging was the arrest and execution of Marshal Mikhail Tukhachvsky, the leading Soviet advocate of maneuver-based warfare. His purge removed one of the most innovative strategic minds in the Red Army, which stifled doctrinal innovation and led to predictably disastrous results in the early stages of the Soviet war with Germany.[35] Leadership, a key component of military effectiveness, although difficult to observe before a war begins, can be critical to military victory. Our last proposition of this chapter links leadership to democratic institutions and their subsidiary attributes.

Proposition 3.4: *Democratic armies enjoy superior levels of leadership.*

The Historical Record

Though the existing literature is dubious of the proposition that democratic armies fight with higher levels of military effectiveness, the empirical methods employed by others thus far have been limited to either analysis of highly suspect survey data of soldiers or case studies. The former method involves soldiers answering questions that essentially ask them whether or not they are motivated by the desire to defend the ideals of their country. This technique suffers from certain biases inherent in ascertaining an individual's motives through direct inquiry after the fact. For example, some armies share a strong cultural norm against deliberate shows of or statements favoring patriotism. None of the surveys of soldiers taps their attitudes the moment when loyalty or courage is most threatened. Instead, researchers ask soldiers to consider retrospectively what motivated them sometime before events the soldiers may not care to revisit in any detail. While we do not question the soldiers' apparent sincerity, empirical research on survey methodology points to the malleability of survey responses over time, and hence leads to our skepticism about many of the standard findings in this area.

The latter method, the case study approach, is likely to produce highly valid results for the wars or battles examined, but the small number of cases necessarily limits how widely we can generalize based on the findings of just a few cases. The empirical tests conducted here offer an important new line of inquiry on questions about the linkages between regime type and battlefield military effectiveness by using quantitative tests on the performance of armies in literally hundreds of battles. This technique allows us simultaneously to analyze a large sample of cases, and it permits us to avoid the pitfalls survey techniques face in this area.

We tested the propositions laid out above (with the exception of the POW Proposition 3.3[36]) using the HERO/CAA data on battles.[37] HERO developed a list of all major battles that took place from 1600 to 1982, with the aim of developing a systematic theory of combat effectiveness.[38] Military historians evaluated and systematically coded dozens of aspects of each battle based on primary and secondary historical sources; members of the U.S. government and civilian consultants then critically evaluated their judgments.

This data set is quite useful for our purposes here, as the authors of the data set made judgments based on historical accounts as to which side of each battle fought better (more on the measures of effectiveness below) for literally hundreds of battles across space and time, enabling us to conduct large statistical tests and draw broader generalizations. Further, the HERO authors and subsequent CAA analysts were not interested in testing the propositions of interest here, so we can be confident that their after-the-fact codings are not rigged to favor one or another of our propositions.[39] Though the data set has some quirks (discussed in greater detail in appendix 3.1), it has been used successfully to predict battle outcomes, and it is the only cross-temporal, large-sample, quantitative data set on individual battles in existence. Focusing on who wins these battles will help us understand who wins wars, for in almost every war covered by the CAA data set the side that won more battles won the war.[40]

Our empirical analyses will test the above hypotheses on battles that have taken place since 1800. There were 572 battles from 1800 to 1982, with 1,094 separate observations. Again, we use three measures of battlefield effectiveness:[41]

Morale: This is the "prevailing mood and spirit conducive to willing and dependable performance, steadiness, self-control, and courageous, determined conduct despite danger and privations."

Leadership: This is the "art of influencing others to cooperate to achieve a common goal, including, for military leaders at all command strata, tactical competence and initiative."

Initiative: This is "an advantage gained by acting first, and thus forcing the opponent to respond to one's own plans and actions, instead of being able to follow one's own plans."

So how do democracies perform on the battlefield? We present here straightforward summaries of the data, encouraging the interested reader to look to appendix 3.1 for a more sophisticated discussion of the statistics. Overall, our findings are striking: democracies win battles. Specifically, the more democratic side won 76 percent of its battles.[42]

This is a first cut at the data; our next step is to look a bit closer. The statistical analysis is complex. One can conduct analysis on the entire data set of more than 500 battles. However, the data set contains an overrepresentation of battles from the American Civil War and the two world wars; fully two-thirds of the battles come from these three wars (49 from the Civil War, 124 from World War I, and 193 from World War II). We reduce this bias in our analysis by constructing a reduced data set that includes essentially one battle per war.[43] Though this reduces the total amount of information we use to analyze the data, this is an acceptable sacrifice to reduce the sampling bias.

After making these adjustments, what results emerge? We found that democratic militaries enjoy significantly higher levels of both initiative and leadership. This offers strong evidence for our hypothesis that the emphasis on the individual in democratic political culture is actually a benefit rather than a hindrance on the modern battlefield. In other words, an army of free-thinkers more likely to exploit opportunities on a fluid battlefield and seize the initiative will do better than an army of subservients who act only on the basis of orders from their higher commanders.

Superior leadership and initiative have helped democratic armies triumph on the battlefield. The D-Day invasion of June 6, 1944, was a victory rather than a catastrophe in large part because of the superior leadership and initiative of American soldiers during truly trying times on the battlefield. As American soldiers lay on the beaches of Normandy, facing apparently insurmountable odds,

> This was the critical moment in the battle. It was an ultimate test: could a democracy produce young men tough enough to take charge, to lead? As Pvt. Carl West put it, "It was simple fear that stopped us at that shingle and we lay there and we got butchered by rocket fire and by mortars for no damn reason other than the fact that there was nobody there to lead us off that goddamn beach. Like I say, hey man, I did my job, but someone had to lead me." They huddled together with some other men, "just trying to stay alive. There was nothing we could do except keep our butts down. Others took cover behind the wall." All across Omaha, the men who had made it to the shingle hid behind it. Then Cota, or Canham or a captain here, a lieutenant there, a sergeant someplace else, began to lead. They would cry out, "Follow me!" and start moving up the bluff. In Sergeant Lewis' case, "Lt. Leo Van de Voort said, 'Let's go, goddamn, there ain't no use staying here, we're all going to get killed!' The first thing he did was to run up to a gun emplacement and throw a grenade in the embrasure. He returned with five or six prisoners. So then we thought, hell, if he can do that, why can't we. That's how we got off the beach." That was how most men got off the beach.[44]

However, our statistical analysis also demonstrates that democratic armies do not fight with statistically significantly higher levels of morale, nor does morale decline significantly faster in democratic than in other armies. Contrary to a common argument made as far back as ancient China and Greece, soldiers drawn from democracies are no more enthusiastic about their task than are soldiers drawn from other kinds of systems. Rather, it is consistent with the view that soldiering is frequently a terrible, dirty business that few people share much enthusiasm for, regardless of the nature of the political institutions in the country. Democratic soldiers carry out their grim tasks with no more enthusiasm, but with greater efficiency, than do their autocratic counterparts. Our lack of support for the morale proposition is perhaps not surprising, as many autocratic governments (such as North Vietnam and Nazi Germany) were able to use calls to nationalism to motivate their troops effectively just as democracies use liberty and freedom in their attempts to motivate their soldiers. Morale as measured in this study is more likely the result of how soldiers believe their unit and general army to be faring in the war. Losing sides display low morale, and winners tend to have higher morale, independent of political system. The null result combines with the positive support for the initiative and leadership propositions to paint a more complex picture of the democratic solider, specifically that democratic soldiers fight better, with superior levels of initiative and leadership, but not with more enthusiasm or spirit—that is, they are no more willing to accept death on the battlefield than their autocratic counterparts.

Democracy and the Art of Battle

Must a democratic society be inferior in the art of war? Though this has been a persistent criticism of liberalism, this chapter presents evidence to the contrary, that along multiple dimensions democratic soldiers actually outperform authoritarian soldiers on the battlefield. Of the D-Day invasion, one historian argued that "The job the Army did in creating and shaping the leadership qualities of its junior officers—just college-age boys, most of them—was also one of the great accomplishments in the history of the Republic." This is not to say that democracies always outperform authoritarian states on the battlefield; some might think of the shocking German conquest of France in 1940, though importantly the German victory was due to French intelligence failure and strategic blunders rather than the French being outfought soldier for soldier.[45]

Note that we did not find support for all of our hypotheses. There is a power of the individual on the battlefield, as democratic armies enjoy superior levels of initiative. Depoliticizing the military also has its payoffs, as the emphasis on competence rather than political loyalty in democratic militaries has meant better leadership as well. However, democratic soldiers do not fight with higher morale than authoritarian soldiers.

In short, this chapter provides some evidence for the superiority of democratic armies. In the following two chapters, we examine two other theories of democratic military prowess. In chapter 4 we see if democracies win because they band together during wartime, and in chapter 5 we determine whether democracies can extract more from their economies for the war effort. This will flesh out our understanding of exactly how democracies differ from other kinds of states in their wartime behavior.

Appendix 3.1 Battlefield Effectiveness

In this appendix, we present more detail on the data set we use and our statistical methodology. In an earlier publication, we used the same data set to explore whether democratic armies enjoy higher levels of logistics, intelligence, or technology. They do not.[46]

We test the hypotheses in this chapter using the 1990 Historical Evaluation and Research Organization (HERO) and U.S. Army Concepts Analysis Agency (CAA) data on battles. HERO and CAA examined all major battles that took place from 1600 to 1982, with the aim of developing a systematic theory of combat effectiveness. Each case is a single side in a battle. Each battle has two sides, providing more than 1,200 cases for some 57 wars. Military historians evaluated and systematically coded dozens of aspects of each battle on the basis of primary and secondary sources; members of the U.S. government then critically evaluated their judgments. Though the data set has some quirks (to be discussed below), it has been used successfully to predict battle outcomes, and it is the only cross-temporal, large-sample, quantitative data set on individual battles in existence.[47] Analyzing the HERO battle data set provides useful purchase for analyzing who wins wars, as for almost every war the state that won the war also won the majority of the battles listed in the HERO data set.

Our empirical analyses test the above hypotheses on battles that took place since 1800, the first year of the Polity III data set, which provides quantitative codings of the regime types of states. There are 572 battles from 1800 to 1982, for 1,094 cases. It is worth noting that the wars covered by the battles within the HERO data set are not coequal with the interstate wars listed in the Correlates of War (COW) project. COW defined interstate wars as military conflicts between recognized members of the international system that produced at least 1,000 battle casualties; see chapter 2 for more discussion. All wars in the HERO data set are listed in appendix 3.2. First, from before 1815 the battles of the War of 1812 and the Napoleonic Wars are included. Second, the battles of a handful of civil and extrasystemic wars are included, namely, the American Civil War, the Latin American Wars of Independence, the War of Texan Independence, the Zulu War, the Transvaal Revolt, colonial conflicts between Britain, Egypt, and the Sudan in the 1880s and 1890s, the Italo-Ethiopian War of 1895, the Boer War, and the Spanish Civil War. Third, a battle between Jordan and Israel in 1968 is included as a new interstate war. Fourth, there are a number of interstate wars listed by the COW project not accounted for by the HERO data.

An additional potential sampling problem concerns the determination of which battles from each war were included. HERO does not appear to have a systematic rule for how wars were included or excluded from the data set, though it does comment that "The purpose of this study was to undertake a comprehensive analysis of the factors which have significantly influenced the outcomes of the major battles of modern history." Unfortunately the authors do not provide a precise definition of "major."[48]

Significantly, availability of historical data probably strongly determined which battles were included. Wars involving the United States tend to have many more battles than other wars. For example, of the 572 battles from 1800 to 1982, 28 are from the 1945 Okinawa campaign near the end of World War II, whereas there are only 4 battles from the Russo-Polish War, Russo-Finnish War, and 1940 Campaign for France combined. Generally, the sample is heavily weighted toward a few wars, as the Civil War, World War I, and World War II account for about three quarters of the battles.

We deal with this source of bias by conducting our analyses on two samples. In the first, we use all cases in the HERO data set. However, one could argue that this sample contains biases because certain wars contain disproportionately more battles than other wars. Our second sample avoids this problem by sampling each country only once per war. If there are, for example, 10 battles from a given war between countries A and B, HERO provides 20 cases. From these 20 cases, we randomly sample 2, perhaps side A in the third battle and side B in the ninth battle. In wars that include battles between more than two participants (the Western Front in World War I, for example, includes armies from France, Britain, the United States, and Germany), each participant is sampled once. This substantially reduces the oversampling bias problem. We did not sample the two sides from one battle per war because of potential autocorrelation problems. Many of our primary variables are coded comparatively, that is, in any given battle, side A is coded as having superior morale to side B, rather than side A getting a morale rating on a scale of 1 to 10, for example. Inclusion of both sides of a battle, therefore, would introduce severe autocorrelation between those two sides, for if one side is coded superior the other is necessarily inferior. These modifications ultimately yield 82 cases.[49]

Empirical Estimates of the Determinants of Battlefield Military Effectiveness

Morale

The HERO project assessed the morale of each army for each battle in the data set. We will use a variable that HERO calls "Morale," defined as "Prevailing mood and spirit conducive to willing and dependable performance, steadiness, self-control, and courageous, determined conduct despite danger and privations." Significantly, HERO codes this variable in a relative manner, that is, it does not assess an army's level of morale on a scale against all other armies of all time, but rather it compares the morale levels of two armies in a particular engagement. The scale is as follows:

$+2$ = Favors the attacker.

$+1$ = Somewhat favors the attacker.

0 = Favors neither side.

-1 = Somewhat favors the defender.

-2 = Favors the defender.[50]

Home Territory

Soldiers are likely to fight harder when defending their own territory. Therefore, when morale is a dependent variable, we include as an independent control variable whether or not the army is fighting on its home territory. This variable is coded as 1 if the battle was fought on the army's prewar home territory and 0 otherwise.[51] Note that for some battles neither side gets a coding of 1, such as clashes between German and American forces in occupied France during 1944. A few special cases are worth noting. Battles during the Civil War that took place in Confederate territory are considered to be on the home territory of the Confederacy and not the Union. In the 1973 October War, the Sinai Peninsula and Golan Heights are considered to be Egyptian and Syrian, respectively, though Alsace-Lorraine is German in 1914. Iwo Jima and Okinawa are not considered part of the Japanese homeland. There were some battles in which the armies of several nations were combined into a multinational army, and the battle was fought on the home territory of one of the allies. In these cases, the home army's fraction of the allied forces is the coding, so that, for example, in the battle of Fuentes de Onoro in the Peninsular Campaigns of the Napoleonic Wars, Spanish forces composed one-third of the combined Anglo-Spanish Army, providing a coding of 0.33.

Democracy

We use two measures of democracy, both based on data from Polity.[52] The first is a state's Democracy score, ranging from 0 to 10.[53] However, the dependent variables are measured in comparative terms, that is, whether an army has a morale advantage in comparison to its battlefield foe. Efficient hypothesis testing of the effects of regime type on factors like morale requires that we convert regime type into a relative score. So, for example, our hypothesis is not that the army of a democratic state is likely to have higher morale, but rather that on the battlefield an army that comes from a more democratic state is likely to have a morale advantage over its opponent. To permit this test, we created a relative regime type score by subtracting each state's Democracy-Autocracy score from that of its battlefield opponent, producing a scale of -20 to 20. A score of -20 indicates that the army in question comes from a country that is substantially less democratic than its battlefield foe, and 20 indicates that the army in question comes from a substantially more democratic state than its battlefield foe. We call this variable Relative Democracy. Note that a country's Relative Democracy score is 0 if it has the same regime type as its opponent, whether that regime type is extremely repressive, a mixed or anocratic regime, or mildly democratic.

Leadership

Leadership is "the art of influencing others to cooperate to achieve a common goal, including, for military leaders at all command strata, tactical competence and initiative."[54] This variable is coded in a similar manner as the morale variable, $+2$ to -2.

Initiative

Initiative is "an advantage gained by acting first, and thus forcing the opponent to respond to one's own plans and actions, instead of being able to follow one's own plans."[55] This variable is coded in a similar manner as the morale variable.

Measures of Battlefield Success

We directly assessed the significance of the above factors in determining battlefield success. HERO codes the outcomes of all of its battles as win, lose, or inconclusive.[56]

Results

We first consider whether our three measures of battlefield effectiveness—Morale, Leadership, and Initiative—correlate with battlefield victory. Table 3.1 provides results of two ordered probit regressions, one on the limited sample of 82 cases, and the other on the full population. In both models, all three measures are statistically significant and positively correlated with victory.

Tables 3.2 and 3.3 present the results of several regression models.[57] Here the indicators of success, which had been our independent variables in table 3.1, become the objects of analysis. As such, they now serve as our dependent variables. Table 3.2 presents results on the limited sample,

TABLE 3.1

Ordered Probit Analysis of Determinants of Battle Outcomes, 1800–1982

Independent Variable	Model 1—Limited Sample	Model 2—Full Population
Initiative	0.818***	0.393***
	(.244)	(.0828)
Leadership	1.83***	0.933***
	(.446)	(.125)
Morale	2.12**	0.790***
	(.901)	(.145)
Cut 1	0.206	−0.139***
	(.225)	(.0213)
Cut 2	0.538	0.139***
	(.208)**	(.0213)
Pseudo r-squared	0.555	0.263
Log likelihood	−31.152114	−683.87768
n	82	1024

Note: Robust standard errors used; in Model 2, standard errors were clustered on the battle. Model 1 replicates table 1 of Reiter and Stam, "Democracy and Battlefield Military Effectiveness," 271.

**Significant at 0.01 level.

***Significant at .001 level.

and table 3.2 provides results on the full sample. In both tables we present analysis of both of our measures of democracy: a state's 0–10 Democracy score and its Relative Democracy score.

In both tables and for both Democracy codings, Democracy is significantly and positively related to Initiation and Leadership. The results on Morale are mixed. In the limited sample (table 3.2), which has less bias but draws from a smaller set of information, Democracy is not significantly related to Morale. In table 3.3, Democracy is significantly and positively related to Morale, but using Absolute Democracy, Morale declines over time for democratic armies (though there is no decline over time using the Relative Democracy measure). While the relatively low r^2 in some of our models (ranging from 0.04 to 0.26) indicates that other factors are likely at play in determining battlefield effectiveness, we can be certain that there is a military advantage associated with democracies at the tactical level, and it is most likely in the form of individual initiative and leadership. With regard to morale, our substantive findings indicate that democracies appear to enjoy an advantage here as well, but the statistical significance is low in the one case per war sample, so we cannot be as confident in these results as we are for the initiative and leadership findings.

TABLE 3.2

Regression Analysis of Effects of Democracy on Battlefield Military Effectiveness, 1800–1982, Limited Sample

Dependent Variable	Model 3 Initiative	Model 4 Initiative	Model 5 Leadership	Model 6 Leadership	Model 7 Morale	Model 8 Morale
Absolute Democracy	0.0862*** (0.0260)	—	0.0931*** (0.0280)	—	0.0120 (0.0189)	—
Relative Democracy	—	0.0437*** (0.00839)	—	0.0522*** (0.00917)	—	-0.000515 (0.00943)
Abs. Dem. * Time	—	—	—	—	-0.000186 0.000355	—
Rel. Dem. * Time	—	—	—	—	—	0.0000321 (0.000229)
Home	—	—	—	—	-0.164 (0.116)	-0.169 (0.117)
Constant	-0.157 (0.136)	0.145 (0.0858)	-0.314* (0.147)	0.0135 (0.0888)	0.0777 (0.0741)	0.109 (0.0640)
n	82	82	82	82	80	80
r-squared	0.11	0.21	0.12	0.26	0.031	0.026

Note: Coefficient estimates reported, robust standard errors in parentheses. Models 3, 5, and 7 replicate components of table 2 in Reiter and Stam, "Democracy and Battlefield Effectiveness," 273.

*Significant at 0.05 level.

***Significant at 0.001 level.

TABLE 3.3
Regression Analysis of Effects of Democracy on Battlefield Military Effectiveness, 1800–1982, Complete Sample

	Model 9	Model 10	Model 11	Model 12	Model 13	Model 14
Dependent Variable	Initiative	Initiative	Leadership	Leadership	Morale	Morale
Absolute Democracy	0.0563*** (0.00708)	—	0.0392*** (0.00563)	—	0.0504*** (0.00825)	—
Relative Democracy	—	0.0225*** (0.00298)	—	0.0155*** (0.00227)	—	0.0112**
Abs. Dem. * Time	—	—	—	—	-0.0008*** (0.000192)	—
Rel. Dem. * Time	—	—	—	—	—	-0.0000050 (0.000085)
Home	—	—	—	—	0.00211 (0.0585)	0.0237 (0.0577)
Constant	-0.276*** (0.0359)	(dropped)	-0.197*** (0.0279)	(dropped)	-0.141*** (0.0281)	-0.00603 (0.0157)
n	1006	988	1006	988	997	985
r-squared	0.068	0.097	0.049	0.070	0.050	0.039

Note: Coefficient estimates reported, robust standard errors (clustered on individual battles) in parentheses.
**Significant at 0.01 level.
***Significant at 0.001 level.

Appendix 3.2   List of "Wars" Covered by the HERO Data, 1800–1982

War	Years of Battles Included	Number of Battles
Second Coalition	1800	3
Third Coalition	1805–1807	5
Peninsular	1808–1813	8
War Against Austria	1809	4
Napoleon's Last Campaigns	1812–1814	9
Hundred Days	1815	3
1812	1813–1815	4
Latin American Independence	1819–1824	6
Texan Independence	1836	1
U.S.-Mexican	1846–1847	8
Crimean	1854	2
Austria, France, and Piedmont	1859	2
American Civil War	1861–1865	49
Seven Weeks	1866	2
Franco-Prussian	1870–1871	10
Zulu	1879	2
Transvaal Revolt	1881	1
Egypt and the Sudan	1882, 1898	2
Italo-Ethiopian, 1895–1896	1896	1
Boer	1899–1900	5
Spanish-American	1898	1
Russo-Japanese	1904–1905	6
Balkan	1912–1913	5
WWI, Western and Middle Eastern Fronts	1914–1918	108
WWI, Eastern Front	1914–1917	16
WWI, Western Front, 1914	1914	16
WWI, Eastern Front, 1914	1914	9
WWI, Serbian Front, 1914	1914	2
WWI, Western Front, 1915	1915	5
WWI, Eastern Front, 1915	1915	2
WWI, Italian Front, 1915	1915	4
WWI, Turkish Fronts, 1915	1915	4
WWI, Western Front, 1916	1916	5
WWI, Turkish Fronts, 1916	1916	1
WWI, Eastern Front, 1916	1916	2
WWI, Turkish Fronts, 1916	1916	1
WWI, Eastern Front, 1916	1916	2
WWI, Italian Front, 1916	1916	4
WWI, Western Front, 1917	1917	6
WWI, Italian Front, 1917	1917	3
WWI, Turkish Fronts, 1917	1917	5

War	Years of Battles Included	Number of Battles
WWI, Western Front, 1918	1918	53
WWI, Italian Front, 1918	1918	1
WWI, Turkish Fronts, 1918	1918	1
Russo-Polish	1920	2
Spanish Civil War	1937	1
Manchurian Incident	1938–1939	5
Russo-Finnish	1939–1940	1
WWII, France	1940	1
WWII, Malay	1941	1
WWII, North Africa, 1942–1943	1942–1943	8
WWII, Italy-Salerno, 1943	1943	9
WWII, Italy-Volturno, 1943	1943	20
WWII, Italy-Anzio, 1944	1944	11
WWII, Italy-Rome, 1944	1944	23
WWII, North Italy Campaign, 1944	1944	1
WWII, Northwest Europe, 1944	1944	24
WWII, Ardennes Campaign, 1944	1944	3
WWII, Eastern Front, 1941–1945	1941–1945	28
WWII, Manchuria	1945	1
WWII, Japan, 1943–1945	1943, 1945	4
WWII, Okinawa Campaign	1945	28
1967 Arab-Israel: West Bank	1967	5
1967 Arab-Israel: Sinai Front	1967	11
1967 Arab-Israel: Golan Front	1967	3
1968 Arab-Israel	1968	1
1973 Arab-Israel: Suez Front	1973	16
1973 Arab-Israel: Golan Front	1973	16
1982 Israel-Lebanon	1982	4

FOUR

BALANCERS OR BYSTANDERS?

THE LACK OF FRATERNAL DEMOCRATIC
ASSISTANCE DURING WAR

About the Russian pact Hitler said that he was in no ways
altering his fundamental anti-bolshevist policies; one had to
use Beelzebub to drive away the devil.
—*German Ambassador Ulrich von Hassell, August 29, 1939*

I can't take Communism nor can you, but to cross this
bridge I would hold hands with the Devil.
—*Franklin Delano Roosevelt*

If Hitler invaded Hell, I should at least make a favourable
reference to the Devil in the House of Commons.
—*Winston Churchill*

THE GREATEST THREATS to Western civilization since the
height of the sixteenth century's Ottoman invasion came in three
sustained blows during the twentieth century. In World War I,
Germany threatened to establish a European hegemony. In World War II,
the Axis powers gambled all in a bid for worldwide dominance. During
the Cold War, the Soviet Union headed a global bloc of Communist
states intent on spreading universal political oppression. In all three cases,
groups of democratic states banded together to confront and eventually
defeat the threat to liberal civilization.

Does the emergence of these democratic coalitions contain the real
explanation for why democracies win wars? Are democracies especially
likely to come to each other's aid and create overwhelming countercoalitions to strike down threats to one of their own? More generally, do
liberal democracies share a sense of international community that pre-
vents conflict between them and draws them together in times of trouble? This mechanism for democratic victory differs substantially from
those identified in chapters 2 and 3. It claims the existence of a sense of
international community or family among democracies. In this view, democracies win because they stand together and treat individual threats as
common threats, which they resist collectively.

We explore this democratic community proposition in this chapter. Specifically, we ask: Do democracies win wars because they band together to rescue democratic targets of aggression? We first present the theoretical arguments made to support this proposition. Next, we investigate the evidence supporting the proposition that democracies come to each other's aid in war. Last, we look at specific cases in which democracies have fought on the same side in war, examining whether democracies pave their path to victory with bricks made by allies of similar political ilk. Our findings are straightforward: democratic fraternity is not responsible for democratic victory. Before we dismiss this democratic community argument, however, let us first review the theory's origins.

Theoretical Foundations of Democratic Fraternity

Immanuel Kant was an eighteenth-century Prussian philosopher well known for discourses on metaphysics and ethics. He also laid out a plan for world peace: the development of a federation of democratic republics, ruled by law and devoid of war. For Kant, democratic republics were especially likely to be peaceful. Since a country's citizens must bear war's burdens, the political system that devolves power most broadly to them will be the least likely to take up weapons against other nations, thereby reducing the risk of death for children and siblings. More recently, some of those who argue that the international system is evolving to a state of universal democracy invoke Hegel's ideas about the evolution of history. These ideas, when combined with Kant's arguments, may ultimately mean the abolition of war and the arrival at a utopian system knowing perpetual peace.[1] Other liberal scholars may shy away from this predicted arrival of global democracy and peace, though they do argue that democracies are especially unlikely to fight each other due to the reduced imperialist pressures within democracies and the resultant reduction in fear among them.[2]

Though democracies may be more peaceful among themselves, as we saw in chapter 2, democracies are willing to fight autocracies. Indeed, democracies even initiate wars against repressive states. This leads to an important question: What motives are sufficient to push a democracy to declare war? One possible answer is that they do so to rescue other democracies under attack. Some versions of liberalism envision the existence of an international community of democracies within which there are not only lower levels of conflict, but also a mutual willingness to defend against aggressors seeking to isolate and attack single democracies. The lack of conflict within the community and the mutual willingness to defend the community against common threats provide a possible mechanism through which democracy will survive and thrive in the international system. Note that in this view, no single democracy must be stronger than any autocracy, as democracies' strength lies in both numbers and the willingness to band together to counter aggression. Democratic military power would more closely resemble that of the Lilliputians, small individuals whose strength lay in their numbers and commitment to the common task, rather than that of Gulliver, the solitary giant.

Liberal scholars have pointed to a number of strong ties that should inspire democracies to assist each other during war. The general argument is that democracies, in theory anyway, share the common goal of defeating authoritarian aggression. Some propose rent-seeking theories of the state, arguing that the greater abilities of authoritarian states to extract rents pose a threat to all democracies. Others maintain that democracies recognize they are jointly pacific but that autocratic states are both fundamentally aggressive and potential enemies of the democratic community. This recognition forces democracies to accept that a threat today against a democratic neighbor may tomorrow be a threat against oneself.[3] Further, liberal states have an economic stake in defending other liberal states and the liberal economic order in general. Democracies, particularly in the postwar period, have high levels of economic interdependence with each other, and some argue that states with strong economic ties are especially likely to intervene militarily on each other's behalf when one is under attack.[4]

Karl Deutsch coined the term "security communities" to characterize groups of states that experience low levels of conflict and high level of cooperation within the group. Liberal theorists often apply this concept to democracies, arguing that democracies are especially likely to form such communities. Others have connected the idea of a security community concept to psychological theories, which focus on the formation of in-groups and out-groups, specifically equating security communities with in-groups.[5] This liberal vision of an international democratic community, whether driven by geopolitical, economic, or social psychological factors, bears the promise of offering a simple answer for the central question of this book, why democracies win wars. Specifically, the central proposition that we investigate in this chapter is as follows.

Proposition 4.1: *Among states under attack, democratic targets are especially likely to attract the assistance of other democracies.*

We deliberately draw this proposition somewhat narrowly. It excludes the potentially related proposition that democracies will assist a democracy on the offensive. The assumptions that form the foundation of liberal theory specifically predict that democracies will help other democracies defend themselves, not that they will assist in wars of aggression or empire. Indeed, the very basis of the liberal prediction of democratic pacifism assumes that democracies are less likely to launch aggressive wars for empire or for any other purpose. Hence, liberalism does not expect democracies to launch such aggressive wars. Moreover, if for some reason a democracy deviated from liberalism's pacific expectations by initiating an aggressive war, we would then expect other democratic nations to be especially unlikely to assist such an illiberal venture.

Observing that, in fact, democracies do occasionally start wars, some liberal theorists develop an aggressive twist on liberalism, proposing that democracies may sometimes launch crusading wars to spread democracy abroad.[6] One could then argue that perhaps other democracies would jump on the revisionist liberal bandwagon. However, such crusading democratic bandwagons are inconsistent with the common notion of liberalism. For instance, one argument as to why democracies might attack other states revolves around security dilemma-type assumptions and maintains that democracies may use force against illiberal states because they fear illiberal states, not because they wish to crusade against them and transform them into democracies.[7]

Authors who make the argument that democracies aid each other in war are explicit on this point. One posed the question and answered it in this way: "Why do expansionary powers always seem to lose major wars? [O]ther powerful republics always join the liberal leader's alliance and are never part of the expansionary power's alliance." Another made a similar claim about the supposed balancing behavior of liberal states: "[D]emocratic states will tend to be less expansionist than autocratic states. . . . [T]o the extent that states balance against threats, rather than power . . . , democratic states should form overwhelming counter coalitions against autocratic states. Not only are autocracies more likely to seek territorial expansion, they are more likely to target democracies."[8]

To sort out these competing claims, some might argue that it is worth examining instances when democracies initiate wars preemptively, that is, when they attack only because they perceive that they are imminently at risk of destruction. Democratic intervention on behalf of the preemptor would then be consistent with liberal theory, as other democracies might see a threatened democracy launch a defensively motivated war and then come to its aid to help safeguard democracy. This argument does not, however, square with the empirical record. As we noted in chapter 2, preemptive wars almost never happen, and there is only one instance of a democracy launching a preemptive war, Israel in 1967. Further, this case provides no support for the democratic community argument at all. Israel attracted no democratic interveners when it launched its preemptive attack against the Arabs. For democratic states, preemption introduces certain dramatic political risks. It is far more difficult to build public consent for striking first (even if defensively motivated) than for defending against another nation's aggression.

The risk of appearing the aggressor and thereby alienating potential supporters in the international community often is sufficient to dissuade states intent on retaining the status quo from launching the first attack in a war. While most states seek to build support before a war—Bismarck used this strategy to good effect in the nineteenth century, for example— democracies have an especially acute need to generate contemporaneous consent before going to war. Fears of alienating tenuous international support for the government dissuaded Israel from launching a preemptive attack against the Arabs in October 1973 and stopped the United States from launching air strikes against missile bases in Cuba in October 1962. Moreover, no democratic great power has ever launched a preventive war, that is, a war to forestall a long-term, unfavorable shift in the balance of power.[9]

A final question is whether the more general security community theory predicts similar behavior within other classes of states, for example, whether fascist regimes should intervene on behalf of other fascist regimes in the same way some expect that democracies should intervene for democracies. The liberal theoretical assumptions would not make this prediction; the liberal emphasis on law and respect for the individual, which brings about peace and cooperation, is of course unlikely to be present among the more repressive regimes. Psychological theory provides a more tenable basis for this proposition. If democracies form an in-group among themselves, then perhaps other kinds of political systems might also form in-groups that could develop into highly cooperative security communities. However, the focus here is specifically on democracy-democracy cooperation, because the ultimate goal is to assess whether or not such cooperation explains the tendency of democracies to win wars. If autocracies are also especially likely to intervene on each other's behalf, then this might provide support for the psychological hypothesis, but it would not explain why democracies win wars because bandwagoning among autocracies would counter any democratic balancing advantage.

The Historical Record

Do democracies protect each other from predation in the international system? A first cut at this question might be to examine whether or not democracies are especially likely to ally with each other in peacetime as well as wartime. Perhaps surprisingly, the answer is that in general they do not. Most rigorous studies have found that before 1945 states of similar regime type were not especially likely to ally with each other, and others have found that democracies may actually be significantly *less* likely than other kinds of states to honor their alliance commitments in wartime.[10]

Sorting this out during the Cold War is a bit more difficult than before World War II. During the Cold War the superpower competition between the United States and the Soviet Union polarized literally the entire world of organized states. Research reveals that after 1945 there was a tendency for similar states to ally with each other. However, this was not an advantage unique to democracy, as most of the world divided into two ideological spheres, each dominated by a common economic ideology that frequently, but not necessarily, equated with political regime type. While it is true that there is some observable tendency for democracies to ally with one another during the Cold War, the tendency was neither lockstep nor driven by liberal community concerns. Instead, democratic tendencies to ally were an artifact of the mutually exclusive economic ideologies underpinning the Cold War competition. For instance, democracy was never a requirement for entering the American system of alliances, as the United States formed alliances with many illiberal states, including notoriously authoritarian regimes in South Korea, Portugal, and Pakistan. Regarding Portugal, not only was it dictatorial when it joined the North Atlantic Treaty Organization (NATO) in 1949, but the Salazar government refused even to pay lip service to the North Atlantic Treaty's rhetorical embrace of democratic principles, instead calling such ideas "unfortunate" and "doctrinaire." Further, when some democratic American allies reverted to authoritarianism, such as Turkey, Greece, and South Korea at various times, they remained in the American alliance structure and received no sanctions from the United States or NATO.[11]

During the Cold War, the general mindset of American leaders focused not on the goal of spreading democracy, but rather on thwarting Soviet expansion and defeating Communism. Most agreed that serving this end might require alliances with nondemocratic states. George Kennan, originator of the containment doctrine, made this Cold-War-ends-over-democratic-means point in 1950:

> Where the concepts and traditions of popular government are too weak to absorb successfully the intensity of the communist attacks, then we must concede that harsh government measures of repression may be the only answer; that these measures may have to proceed from regimes whose origins and methods would not stand the test of American concepts of democratic procedure, and that such regimes and such methods may be preferable alternatives, and indeed the only alternatives, to further communist success.[12]

From the perspective of our empirical investigation, the key observation is that the Cold War democratic alliances did not contribute to a single wartime democratic military victory: the only instances of democratic allies fighting on the same side during the Cold War—the Korean and Vietnam wars—both ended in draws.[13] In other words, in the only period when there may have been a tendency for democracies to ally with each other, this did not help any of them win any wars.

Unlike peacetime alliance behavior, one question that has not received much attention is whether democracies are especially likely to assist each other in times of war, specifically, sending military assistance to aid a democracy under attack. This gets at the heart of our main puzzle, understanding why democracies win wars. If democracies are especially likely to intervene on each other's behalf during war, then this may be important evidence favoring the proposition that democracies win wars because they band together.

We take a number of different tacks to get at whether or not democracies win wars because they ally during wartime. We begin with a simple question: Are democratic targets more likely to attract assistance of any kind than are autocratic targets? Among the 76 states targeted in wars from 1816 to 1992, 11 were democracies.[14] Among these 76 targets, 18 attracted assistance from third parties. Table 4.1 provides a cross-tabulation of whether the target state was a democracy and whether it attracted a defender.

The results indicate that though democratic targets are slightly more likely to attract assistance (27 percent of the time) than are nondemocratic targets (20 percent of the time), this difference is not statistically significant. This small difference (27 percent vs. 20 percent) is about what we would anticipate, given expected variation in two random samples drawn from the same population. Therefore, we must reject the proposition that democratic targets are systematically more likely than autocratic targets to attract allies. This in itself is important: there is little if any evidence to suggest that democratic targets are more likely to attract assistance of any kind during war than are nondemocratic states.[15] Note that here we do not distinguish between democratic and autocratic assistance to targets, examining simply whether democracies are more likely to attract assistance of any sort than are autocracies.

Consider another tack: Are democracies especially likely to intervene in favor of targeted democracies? This gets back to the theoretical discussion above: democracies win wars because other democracies recognize an international liberal community and are willing to rescue targeted democracies from attack. We explore this idea by asking the specific question: What causes bystanders to intervene on behalf of targeted states? If the liberal arguments discussed above are correct, then we would expect that among potential interveners, democracies should be especially likely to take action to defend other democracies that find themselves under

TABLE 4.1

Cross Tabulation of Target's Democracy and Defender Intervention in Wars, 1816–1992

	No Potential Defender Intervened	At Least One Defender Intervened	Total
Nondemocratic Target	52	13	65
	(80%)	(20%)	(100%)
Democratic Target	8	3	11
	(73%)	(27%)	(100%)
Total	60	16	76
	(79%)	(21%)	(100%)

Pearson chi squared (1) = 0.30
$P = 0.58$

attack by autocracies. We conducted statistical analysis to analyze this question and controlled for other factors that are likely to affect a state's decision to intervene. The data we analyzed included all opportunities for states in the international system to intervene on behalf of all targeted states from 1816 to 1992. Although we found that factors like geographical contiguity, trade in goods and services, international alliances, and national power may affect a state's decision to intervene to assist another state, democracies are not more likely to intervene to save targeted democracies (see the appendix 4.1 for discussion of results). In short, the domestic political characteristics of the target state do not have any systematic effect on whether or not a potential intervener acts on the target's behalf. This surprising nonresult deserves closer exploration. Are there instances of democracies winning wars because of the contributions of democratic allies? If so, what were the conditions surrounding the decision to intervene? Do they support the liberal theory predicting democratic balancing, or do they point in different directions? To answer these questions, we now turn to a closer look at the specific instances in which democratic states joined other democracies. In each, we will look at the motives behind one democracy's decision to join another in times of war.

Cases of Democratic Balancing

As we step back from the aggregate data and look at what motivated states to join democracies at war, we want to see if that decision affected the outcome of the war. In other words, we want to assess two things in the few cases where democracies did join other democracies at war: First, did they join because the state at war was a democracy? Second, did the choice to join affect the war's outcome? To work toward a solution for this puzzle, consider the eight wars since 1815 in which at least two democracies fought on a side.[16] These cases are the Boxer Rebellion, the two world wars, the Korean War, the Suez War, the Vietnam War, the 1991 Gulf War, and the 1999 Kosovo War.

Of these eight wars, one (Korea) was clearly a draw, and in another (Vietnam) the democratic coalition either lost or fought to a draw. Hence, democratic balancing cannot count as contributing to victory in these two cases. In the six cases in which the democratic coalition won, the important question to ask is whether democracies entered the war to rescue a fellow democracy from defeat, or if the democracies were fighting on the same side for other reasons. In two of the wars, the Boxer Rebellion and the Suez War, the answer is clearly the latter, as the democratic coalition was the aggressor seeking to alter the status quo.

In another, the 1991 Gulf War, democracies came to the rescue of an autocratic state (Kuwait). However, realist motives alone, such as access to oil and maintaining a regional balance of power, not democratic fraternalism, drove the democrats' intervention. The Korean and Vietnam wars were similar: democracies were assisting autocratic targets out of geopolitical motivations. In the Gulf War, then Secretary of State James Baker explained the American motivation for war on November 13, 1990: "The economic lifeline of the industrial world runs from the Gulf, and we cannot permit a dictator such as this to sit astride that economic lifeline. To bring it down to the level of the average American citizen, let me say that means jobs. If you want to sum it up in one word: it's jobs."[17] Further, the participation of multiple democracies in the Gulf War was unnecessary for victory, as the only two states truly necessary for military victory were the United States and Saudi Arabia, and the latter was not a democracy.[18]

In the more recent Kosovo War, NATO intervened not to protect another democracy but rather to prevent "ethnic cleansing" of a stateless people. The leaders of the Kosovars shortly afterward demonstrated everything but democratic inclinations. In addition, as in the case of the Gulf War, the United States made the principal military contributions to the Kosovo operation and, unlike the Gulf War, the military outcome was only an ambiguous success for the coalition.

This leaves two wars in which democratic coalitions won defensive wars: the two world wars. Are these examples of democracies coming to each other's rescue to protect the liberal democratic community? The answer is at best mixed.

World War I

In World War I, democratic Belgium and France became involved when attacked by Germany. Britain joined the war for principally realist reasons: to protect the balance of power in Europe, to maintain its reputation, and to honor its commitment to Belgian neutrality. Years later, Sir Edward Grey, British foreign secretary in 1914, recalled in his memoirs that "The real reason for going into the war was that, if we did not stand by France and stand up for Belgium against this aggression, we should be isolated, discredited, and hated; and there would be before us nothing but a miserable and ignoble future." Indeed, until the Belgian government triggered the British treaty commitment by making an official request for assistance on August 3, the British cabinet showed little unity in its support for war during the opening stages of the summer 1914 crisis.[19]

A lack of democratic fraternalism was present at the same time on the other side of the Atlantic. Though President Woodrow Wilson has become the leader most closely associated with liberalism and a multilateral view of international relations, a desire to rescue other beleaguered democracies is not the best explanation of the motives behind Wilson's decision to request American intervention into World War I. Indeed, we should not view the American entry into World War I as an instance of liberalism's finest hour; to the contrary, the United States let its democratic confrères fight unassisted for three bloody years, desperately trying to maintain its neutrality. Unable to generate significant domestic consent for war, the American administration sat on the side in the early years of the war as literally millions of soldiers and civilians from European democracies perished.

When American intervention did come in the spring of 1917, Wilson favored it not because he feared an imminent German victory over America's European ideological counterparts, although this was a distinct possibility. Rather, Germany's unrestricted submarine warfare in the Atlantic played a substantial role in spurring American intervention. German submarines threatened American commerce and maritime traffic throughout the Atlantic; this was unacceptable to both Wilson and, eventually, the U.S. public. Further fanning the smoldering enmity between the United States and Germany, the Germans proposed in the now infamous January 1917 Zimmermann telegram that Mexico join Germany in a potential war against the United States. In exchange for assisting the Germans, Mexico was to receive back the territories of New Mexico, Arizona, and Texas.[20]

Wilson's secretary of state, Robert Lansing, thought that this telegram unified public opinion in favor of war with Germany, generating critical contemporaneous consent for joining the war in Europe. In the words of one of Wilson's confidants, "No single more devastating blow was delivered against Wilson's resistance to entering the war."[21] In short, America hesitantly entered World War I because of infringements on its national interests and the growth of public sentiment favoring action. Leading Wilson scholar Arthur Link expressed it as such:

> Wilson did not accept the decision for war because he thought that the Allies were fighting altogether for worthy objectives and the Germans altogether for unworthy ones. . . . It is almost abundantly clear that Wilson simply concluded that there was no alternative to full-fledged belligerency. The United States was a great power. It could not submit to Germany's flagrant—so it seemed to Wilson and his contemporaries—assault on American sovereignty without yielding its honor and destroying its influence for constructive work in the world.[22]

The United States did not enthusiastically leap into World War I, driven by desires to rescue other members of the international democratic community. Far from it. But what about the next Great War, not the War to End All Wars, but the largest global conflagration ever seen, World War II? Should we consider World War II, which appeared to many at the time to be truly the exemplar of the ultimate war of good against evil, to be the case upon which we can build a theory of liberal internationalism?

World War II

Britain and France declared war on Germany in September 1939, coming to the rescue of autocratic Poland. Earlier that year both stood aside, and arguably took an active role, during the spring 1939 demise of the democratic Czechoslovak republic, in spite of (in the French case) formal alliance commitments to the Czechs. Once the war started, the small democratic neutrals in Europe did not voluntarily jump on the democratic bandwagon. Some—Ireland, Switzerland, and Sweden—did not join the democratic coalition at all. Others—Belgium, the Netherlands, Luxembourg, Norway, and Denmark—joined only after the Germans invaded. One—Finland—joined the Axis. The only small European state firmly to ally itself with the Allies from the outset was Portugal, an autocracy. In almost every case, the lessons learned from these small states' World War I experiences, not concerns about the survival of other democracies, drove their decision-making.[23]

The most powerful democracy in the world, the United States, did not enter the war when it broke out in 1939. It did not come quickly to the rescue of either democratic France or Britain, even in the summer of 1940 when France fell and Britain faced mortal danger during the Battle of Britain, the preparatory phase before Operation Sea Lion, the German plan to invade Britain itself. The United States did not enter the war in Asia until Japan, at war principally with autocratic Nationalist China, attacked Pearl Harbor on December 7, 1941. The United States declared war against Japan immediately after the Pearl Harbor attack, but Roosevelt refused to request that Congress declare war immediately on Germany and Italy, due in part to divisions in public opinion. Completely countermanding liberalism's policy expectations, the United States never took proactive steps to declare war against the two countries consuming Europe's democracies at a terrifying pace. America entered the war in Europe only after Hitler and Mussolini first declared war against the United States on December 11, 1941.[24] America's two years of neutrality are doubly vexing for the democratic balancing proposition, as international system structure theories of international relations would predict that the United States should have intervened sooner to protect the balance of power in Europe.[25] Not only did the United States not jump to the aid of the threatened European democracies, it did so while resisting other systemic pressures to join the fray.

In sum, even anecdotal evidence to support the proposition that democracies win wars because they help each other in war is quite scant. In only two of the eight wars in which two democracies fought on the same side and in defense against aggression—World Wars I and II—did the democratic coalitions emerge victorious while protecting the interests of democratic targets. In both the world wars, however, realist motivations spurred the democratic belligerents to action, not liberal fraternalism.[26]

A potential case of democratic intervention in favor of a democratic target was the planned but never executed Allied intervention on behalf of Finland during the 1939–1940 Winter War with the Soviet Union. At this point, the Soviet Union was a non-belligerent in the Anglo-Franco-German conflict and was nominally an ally of Germany because of the August 1939 Molotov-Ribbentrop Pact. Early Finnish military successes surprised the Allies and encouraged the French in particular to consider sending troops in Finland's defense.[27]

However, this case is weak thread on which to hang the case that democratic balancing wins wars. To begin with, Britain and France did not see this as an opportunity to rescue a beleaguered democracy. Rather, viewing the Winter War through a realist lens, they saw the potential rescue of Finland as a means by which they might bring Norway and Sweden into the war, which would have the important benefit of endangering German access to critical Swedish iron ore.[28] The most obvious point, however, is that the commitment was too late; we will never know if it would have been too little as the war ended with a Soviet victory on March 20 before any Allied troops arrived. Further, after the Winter War,

Finland felt that its goals of reclaiming territory trumped any ephemeral desire to make the world safe for democracy. In 1941 it joined Germany in its war against the Soviet Union, making it formally an adversary of Britain and the United States.

Counter to the democratic community theory, especially telling is the story behind the fatal delay of the Allied mission. To be able to reach the fighting in Finland, an Anglo-French expeditionary force would require permission from democratic Norway and Sweden in order to cross their territories. Both Norway and Sweden, from the democratic community perspective, should have been highly motivated to facilitate such a mission: within the liberal framework, they would be helping to defend a fellow democracy and thereby protect the international democratic community. Aside from communitarian concerns, it would also be low cost to them. Britain did not ask Norway or Sweden to contribute any of their own troops; instead, Britain simply requested them to provide the same sort of tacit assistance that Sweden and Switzerland later provided Germany as supposed neutrals. Indeed, both Norway and Sweden might have seen that stopping Soviet adventurism in Finland could serve their own national security interests, given that Norway and Sweden are of course adjacent to Finland, and they might someday face the prospect of fending off a still expansionist Soviet Union themselves. Yet, despite all these motivations, both Norway and Sweden refused to permit Anglo-French troops' access to Finland. Instead, they preferred to safeguard closely their own neutral stances, their historical commitments to neutrality strongly bolstered by their experiences in avoiding entanglement in World War I. Sweden was particularly opposed to this mission. Its refusal to become involved was a continuation of previous illiberal behavior toward Finland that began when Sweden turned down a Finnish request for a mutual defense commitment in the weeks before the Soviet attack in 1939.[29]

Military Assistance Short of a Declaration of War

Some might argue that democracies offer needed assistance to each other short of sending troops; the American dispatch of military aid to Israel during the 1973 Yom Kippur War is one example. The Yom Kippur War, however, serves as a dubious anecdote favoring the liberal community argument, for two reasons. First, it was concern over potentially adverse American reaction that persuaded the Israelis *not* to launch a preemptive attack on October 6, which in turn would have afforded them an important military advantage at the outset of the war that was soon upon them anyway.[30] Hence, close relations with the democratic United States did not provide an unmitigated military advantage for Israel. Second, the eventual American decision to resupply Israel was driven, again, by the United States' broader realist concerns, as American leadership acted to counter Soviet support of Egypt, and to safeguard continued Western access to Persian Gulf oil.[31]

Instances of democratic assistance to democratic targets aside from direct intervention such as the 1973 example are isolated. One might contrast the Yom Kippur War with the American arms embargo toward Israel during its 1948 War of Independence. Similarly, the French decision to *suspend* arms transfers to Israel the day before the 1967 Six-Day War runs counter to liberalism's expectations. Nor do we find support for liberal fraternalism in the American decision to restrict military sales to democratic India during the 1971 Indo-Pakistani War or the U.S. decision to send its aircraft carrier the USS *Enterprise* to the Indian Ocean to show support for its autocratic ally Pakistan. When it does come, this sort of fraternal military aid is often too little or too late to prevent defeat, such as the aid Sweden sent to Finland during the Winter War.[32]

What should we make of American actions in the early years of the world wars, before the United States actually declared war? One might argue that although the Americans delayed their declaration of war in each case, the United States made important economic contributions while it was still neutral. Unfortunately for the liberal thesis, here the record is again mixed at best. In World War I the preferred policy of the United States was to treat all belligerents alike, lumping democratic Britain and France along with autocratic Germany and Austria-Hungary. In practice, this meant trading with all of them. On August 6, 1914, days after the war broke out, the United States officially asked each of the principal belligerents if they would abide by the 1909 Declaration of London, which laid out the rights of neutrals to trade with all belligerents at war, regardless of domestic political institutions. Germany and Austria-Hungary agreed to the proposal with delight. Firm adherence to the 1909 Declaration would largely nullify the tremendous British naval advantage, which could, of course, be used to control maritime trade. The source of the Wilson administration's motivation to seek trade with all belligerents was quite straightforward: domestic political pressure groups from various industrial and trading interests would profit greatly from trade with all of Europe.[33] Wilson's concern with maintaining contemporary public support of America's industrialists pushed him toward a foreign policy that did not back the threatened democracies at the expense of the autocrats in the war that was rapidly spreading throughout Europe. Instead, Wilson's concerns about domestic political consent trumped concerns about protecting the nascent global democratic community.

World War II presents perhaps the better-known case. Britain purchased war materiel from the United States outright up through the end of 1940. It soon became apparent to both the British and the Americans, however, that because of looming currency reserve shortages Britain could not continue this policy in 1941. Roosevelt responded in early 1941 by proposing the Lend Lease Bill, which broadened American aid to Britain, providing for programs like the destroyers-for-bases swap. In later years in the war, after the United States became an explicit participant, Lend Lease did help the British war effort. The critical question for liberal theory is: Did these programs actually prevent a British defeat before the United States became a belligerent in December 1941 because of Pearl Harbor and the German and Italian declarations of war? Probably not. Regardless of Lend Lease, Britain would likely have survived until Germany, Japan, and Italy sowed the seeds of their mutual demise through their declarations of war against the United States.

Our point here is not to discount the importance of America's role in determining the outcome of World War II. Obviously, it was critical to the defeat of Germany, Italy, and Japan. Rather, we want to ascertain the effect of aid resulting from liberal motivations at the earliest stages of the war before the United States became totally committed to the war effort following the Axis attack on American sovereignty, which then provided very clear national security (or realist) motivations for the support of Britain and the other European democracies.

Let us then assess the effects of pre–Pearl Harbor aid, which we might attribute to democratic fraternalism. First, Lend Lease provided relatively little to the British war effort in 1941. In that year, Lend Lease accounted for only 2.4 percent of all munitions supplied to the forces of the British Commonwealth. In naval operations, American contributions were also quite limited in 1941. American shipyards provided relatively little to help maintain the supply convoys to Europe and to replace losses from U-boat attacks. In 1941 American shipbuilding capacity was less than one million tons a year, less than what British shipyards could produce and far short of the eight million tons needed for the war in Europe. The famous destroyers-for-bases deal, executed in September 1941, sent to Britain fifty World War I vintage American destroyers in exchange for leasing rights at a number of Western Hemisphere bases. Though these vessels surely made a contribution to the British naval effort, particularly in convoy service later in the war, their need for refitting meant that at the time of the Japanese attack on Pearl Harbor in December, only a handful were ready for duty.[34] These relatively small efforts were certainly not significant in fending off a possible starvation-induced British surrender before American entry into the war.

Second, and perhaps most important, German conquest of Britain became very unlikely after the Royal Air Force (RAF) won the Battle of Britain with British (that is, not American developed or supplied) fighter aircraft and radar installations. Once the German Luftwaffe failed to destroy the RAF, Hitler abandoned Operation Sea Lion, the plan for the invasion of Britain. The second year of the war, 1940 did not offer much good fortune to other democracies—Norway, Denmark, the Netherlands, Belgium, Luxembourg, and France all fell to Nazi conquest as the United States stood by, largely idle. Again, this is not to say that the United States did not ultimately play a pivotal role in the allied victory over Germany, but rather that American aid was not responsible for keeping Britain in the war during Germany's attempt at conquest. Notably, even following the American declaration of war, the Battle of the Atlantic's outcome was unclear until 1943.[35] By that time, American forces accounted for a substantial proportion of the overall war effort. At the same time, however, the nature of the war had begun to change from one of aiding an isolated democracy attempting to stave off defeat, to the American great power fighting to pursue its nascent superpower interests by defeating rival great powers, Germany and Japan.

Perhaps the most important factor constraining Roosevelt's decisions to aid Britain in the years 1939–1941 was his need to maintain constantly the consent of a majority of the American public. Roosevelt's first decisive shift toward more active support for Britain came after the French defeat in June 1940. A striking shift in American public opinion gave Roosevelt the limited freedom of action he needed to begin Lend Lease and other smaller-scale programs to aid Britain. In May only 47 percent of those polled in a public opinion survey supported selling military aircraft to Britain and France. This number jumped to 80 percent in June following the German invasion of France. Roosevelt's December 1940 "arsenal of democracy" speech in which he called for active American support of Britain met with an enthusiastic response, with public opinion polls indicating a majority supporting aiding Britain even at the risk of war. This strong support encouraged Roosevelt to push for Lend Lease. Notably, he understood the importance of garnering public consent in advance of a policy change as important as Lend Lease. He told Secretary of the Treasury Henry Morgenthau that "We don't want to fool the public, we want to do this thing right, out and out." Even after Lend Lease, Roosevelt understood the importance of remaining within the bounds of what public opinion would allow. In April 1941, following the sentiments found in public opinion surveys, he refused to allow American vessels to escort merchant convoys en route or returning from Britain, remarking that "public opinion was not yet ready for the United States to convoy ships," potentially mortal threats to democratic Britain notwithstanding.[36]

The general picture conveyed here is that the protection of democracy around the world has simply not been a terribly strong motivation in the democratic decision for war. Broader security concerns and potential domestic political costs trump liberal motivations to spread democratic institutions. Consider, for example, that in the twentieth century the United States has had two opportunities to intervene militarily to protect democracy in Hungary. In 1919 it bypassed the opportunity to send troops to turn back the Soviet revolution and save democracy in Hungary, in part because most Americans who were aware of the war viewed it to be costly and unlikely to be successful. Woodrow Wilson recognized the possible folly of such a venture, remarking: "To try and stop a revolutionary movement with field armies is like using a broom to stop a vast flood."[37] Thirty-seven years later, despite public declarations about American commitment to the rollback of Communism in Eastern Europe, President Eisenhower allowed the Soviet Red Army to crush the new democratic regime in Hungary, avoiding what would be at best a dangerous superpower confrontation. More recently, following the collapse of the Soviet Union, Europe and the United States did not move quickly to expand either NATO or the European Union to several of the fledgling democracies of Eastern Europe, instead preferring to pursue narrower economic and security interests by slow and measured expansion of democratic international institutions.[38]

Selection Effects, Again?

Some might argue that a sort of reverse selection effects accounts for the lack of support we find for the liberal community proposition. That is, democracies might be genuinely more likely to join each other in war, but since potential attackers know this, they attack democracies less frequently and attack only those democracies that are for whatever reason particularly unlikely to attract assistance from other democracies.[39] In theory, this argument might be true, since the population we use for several of our empirical tests consists of only those states that actually came under attack. That is, because we do not include those states considered for attack but bypassed by careful aggressors, our tests might miss the emergence of the democratic balancing phenomenon, which might only appear in the peace-to-conflict-initiation phase rather than in the conflict-initiation-to-conflict-joining phase.

Two comments are worth making on this point. First, the proposition we set out to test here—as expressed elsewhere in the literature—is that democracies win wars because of democratic balancing—joining together to face down a common autocratic threat. Hence, the appropriate approach to scarching for evidence supporting this proposition is to look just at the states involved in wars rather than all states. If the selection effects proposition is true in this instance, this means that democracies are not winning wars because of democratic balancing and hence power (though attackers might be *deterred* because they anticipate democratic balancing, but that is an entirely separate question).

Second, there is little empirical evidence in support of this selection effects claim.[40] The principal (and testable) argument drawn from this war avoidance proposition is that autocracies should attack democracies far less frequently than other kinds of states because potential attackers believe that other democracies will join the target in the event of war. However, democracies tend not to have reputations for providing stalwart aid to others in the face of possible aggression; just the opposite. Instead, democracies reputedly lack resolve, which can, in turn, attract rather than repel aggressors.

The events of the July crisis leading to World War I clearly illustrate the problem that democracies commonly face: potential aggressors do not believe that democracies' commitments to come to the aid of one another are credible. Wilhelmine Germany's Schlieffen plan, as executed in 1914, rested on the key assumption that the Germans could avert or delay British intervention on behalf of democratic France and democratic Belgium, particularly if Germany stopped short of utterly crushing France. Key German leaders believed, when push came to shove, that Britain would delay its entry into the war against France despite France's crucial role in balancing German power in Europe. The Germans also heavily discounted Britain's formal agreement to safeguard Belgian sovereignty and a series of British warnings during the summer 1914 crisis.[41] While the outbreak of World War I speaks volumes about the willingness of German oligarchs to take enormous gambles, German actions also shed light on their beliefs about democracies' willingness or ability to honor their international commitments. Specifically, autocrats tend to believe that democracies' requisite needs to generate public consent handcuff their leaders, preventing them from taking swift military action to defend their national interests. Autocrats believe that democracies thereby render their prior commitments to aid one another weak if not worthless.

We can observe this apparent lack of credibility in other important crises, the events that led to World War II providing a notable example. The reluctance of Britain and France to stand by their democratic allies in the 1930s is well known. In 1935 the British government held a plebiscite to gauge whether the Locarno Treaty bound Britain to defend France against a German attack. Some 75 percent of the participants cast their lots against the proposition. This result mirrored the outcome of a famous 1933 Oxford University debate in which a substantial majority of Oxford students passed the resolution that "This House will in no circumstances fight for its King and Country." British leadership took the hint and connived with the French in 1938 to permit the carving up of Czechoslovakia, allowing Nazi Germany first to annex the Sudetenland and then to occupy the entire country. From this, Hitler concluded that he would have a free hand on the continent, observing that "Our enemies are little worms. I saw them at Munich."[42]

Even British and French declarations of war after the invasion of Poland did not improve the international reputation of the Western democracies. A Soviet official warned the Finns in October 1939 during the diplomatic dispute that preceded the Winter War, asking them, "From whom does Finland hope to get help? Poland, it too, had a guarantee." In the Pacific, Japan doubted that the United States would have the stomach to defend itself, due to supposed fundamental character flaws intrinsic to bourgeois, democratic societies. More recently, Saddam Hussein plunged his nation into war with the United States in no small part because he believed the Americans had no stomach for war, finding deterrent claims to the opposite singularly unconvincing. Hussein's remarks about the United States' supposed inability to sustain casualties reflected a global lack of faith in the American's willingness to commit military forces in the wake of the Cold War, encouraging aggressors in the Balkans, Haiti, Somalia, and elsewhere.[43]

Other studies, grounded in statistical analysis, also provide evidence against the supposition that democracies come under attack less frequently because of the deterrent effects of the so-called community of democracy. One study found that crisis participants from 1918 to 1988 were significantly *more* likely to initiate the use of force against democracies than other kinds of targets. This result is completely at odds with the deterrent selection effects story that would render our claims about the lack of solidarity among democratic communities moot. Similarly, two other scholars, using a different data set, found that from 1953 to 1978, democracies were generally *more* likely to be the target of attack and less likely to receive cooperation from other states. Again, counter to the deterrence-from-solidarity selection effects hypothesis, a third group of scholars found that democracies since 1816 were as likely as others, or more so, to find themselves the target of international military aggression, a finding echoed elsewhere.[44] In sum, using a variety of databases, covering different periods, the statistical evidence indicates that democracies are just as likely as other kinds of states to be the targets of international aggression. These findings are strongly inconsistent with the selection effects interpretation summarized above. But perhaps the democratic community advantage lies not in the number of democratic allies that would band together, but in their quality. Might it be that democracies, while no more likely to join together at any one time than other states, when they do choose to fight together, do so more effectively than other groupings of states?

Are Democracies *Better* Allies during Wartime?

A slightly different argument that might explain democratic power, still focusing on allies, is that when democracies fight on the same side, they cooperate more thoroughly and more effectively than their opponents do. Because democracies can safely assume that they pose no threat to each other, when they fight together they may be able to more fully integrate their commands and more easily share military information with one another than more common but less trusting allies can. This then makes the whole greater than the sum of the parts—in theory, anyway. Conventional wisdom holds that the best example of this proposition might be Anglo-American cooperation during World War II.[45]

In general, history reveals that democracies do not always get along well during wartime. They often bicker, jockey for position, and refuse to coordinate their actions or commands, even to the point of hindering other democracies' military operations. British and French coordination was rocky and inefficient during much of World War I. Divergent war aims and strategies led to a number of potentially avoidable blunders on the Western front. In 1914 the Allies' inability to coordinate a single plan of action contributed to the loss of Antwerp and the German occupation of key industrial regions in northern France. This brought the Allies perilously close to defeat and wasted a potential opportunity to win the war in 1914, which would have prevented the horrific costs incurred by both sides in the years to come. The absence of an effective unified command structure barred the Allies from coordinating their military strategy during the middle years of the war. Britain and France did not form their Supreme War Council to coordinate Allied strategy until November 1917, following the disastrous Italian defeat at Caporetto.

American entry into the Great War was not without its problems either. General John J. Pershing, commander of the American Expeditionary Force, clashed frequently with his British and French counterparts. Pershing insisted, for example, on keeping American forces separate from the other Allied armies and under unified American command. Pershing fervently believed that before the American intervention, French and British leaders had negligently wasted the lives of their own citizens in futile frontal attacks on German strongholds. He believed they would happily do the same with American soldiers if given the chance and so refused to permit American soldiers, aside from two all-Black units, to serve under foreign command.[46]

During World War II, the democratic allies did not enjoy unalloyed and universally effective cooperation either. Anglo-French coordination both before and during the German invasion of the West in May–June 1940 was quite poor. British leaders withheld the Royal Air Force from the French campaign in early June for later use in the defense of Britain. The subsequent collapse of the French Army culminated in the eventual panicked evacuation of the British Expeditionary Force from Dunkirk. There, the British soldiers, while fighting a courageous rearguard action to defend their withdrawal, also left behind the majority of their heavy weapons, weakening the British war effort for years to come. Democratic Belgium further hindered British efforts to assist the French, pointlessly clinging to its neutrality to the detriment of Allied military effectiveness. By threatening to shoot down any British aircraft that flew over Belgian territory and refusing to allow British or French forces to use roads through Brussels even after the German invasion had begun, Belgium's democratic elites sealed their nation's fate and provided the nails for France's rapidly closing coffin. Perhaps not surprisingly, the French General Maurice Gamelin remarked that "[t]he two best auxiliaries of Hitler were the Russians and the Belgians."[47]

Though Anglo-American cooperation was better and helped facilitate an Allied victory, it too had its limits. The British kept their own atomic bomb project going because their trust and belief in the Americans only went so far. Lord Cherwell wrote to Winston Churchill, in a memo receiving favorable acceptance, "Whoever possesses such a [nuclear] plant should be able to dictate terms to the rest of the world. However much I may trust my neighbor and depend on him, I am very much averse to putting myself completely at his mercy. I would, therefore, not press the Americans to undertake this work."[48]

During the Cold War, limits to cooperation within the democratic community persisted. Early on, the United States refused to share much information with their NATO allies about nuclear forces or strategies, factors that led, in part, to the French withdrawal from NATO. In the Korean War, America's European allies limited American military effectiveness by refusing to allow U.S. pilots to pursue Communist aircraft into China, and perhaps by discouraging U.S. leadership from considering seriously the use of nuclear weapons.[49] During the Suez War, the United States used the threat of economic coercion to persuade Britain and France to pull back from their successful military operations against Egypt. The French returned the favor when they refused to permit American planes to fly over French territory during the American air strikes against Libya in 1986, which followed Muammer Khadafi's declaration of a "line of death" across the mouth of the Gulf of Sidra in the Mediterranean Sea. Citizens in European democracies expressed their outrage and opposition to the U.S. raids, as anti-American street demonstrations broke out in several cities including West Berlin, Vienna, and Rome.[50]

The Limits of Liberal Community

The weight of history argues strongly against the democratic balancing proposition. When attacked, democracies do not win wars because they attract substantial support from other democracies. Rather, democratic targets are no more likely to attract allies than are other states. Furthermore, democracies are not particularly likely to intervene on behalf of belligerent democracies. Autocratic leaders appear to recognize these facts, as a state gains no significant deterrent effect from being associated with the mythical democratic community. If anything, the opposite appears to be the case. Autocrats, skeptical of democracies' willingness to defend each other, target them as often as they do any other type of state. Examining the handful of cases where democracies did come to the aid of one another reveals that democracies do not intervene to help defend the democratic community of states. Instead, their motivation emerges from realist conceptions of the national interest. Democratic leaders formulate foreign policy while constrained by the bounds of public opinion—the basis of popular consent. While citizens of democracies willingly sanction war to advance their collective notions of the national interest, typically this does not include the spread of democracy.

These results complement other research demonstrating that democracies are not especially likely to cooperate with one another, whether in the form of recognized military alliances or in other contexts.[51] What does this say about the international community of democracies? There is, after all, a veritable mountain of evidence demonstrating that democracies are quite unlikely to fight each other.[52] Significantly, democratic community ties seem to stop at the point of peace among community members. These community bonds are not strong enough to bring members to one another's aid in times of war. While democracies do not shed blood *against* each other, they also seem quite unwilling to shed blood *for* each other.

In summary, the family of democracy appears to have rather loose ties. Concern for the welfare of other democracies has little impact on foreign policy decisions in relation to more general concerns of the national interest. The absence of support for the democratic community proposition contrasts with the evidence we presented in chapters 2 and 3. There we demonstrated strong historical corroboration of the contributions that democratic political structures and culture make in helping democracies win wars. Next, in chapter 5, we consider whether democracies win wars because they can more effectively mobilize their economies in support of their war efforts.

Appendix 4.1: Quantitative Results on Democratic Alliance Behavior

In this appendix, we present the specifics of some statistical analysis, the results of which we discussed in the main body of the chapter. We present a new research design to test Proposition 4.1, that democracies are especially likely to intervene to assist targeted democracies at war.

Previous Research

We first present a brief discussion of previous research to highlight some of the improvements offered by our research design. Some studies looked at whether democracies are especially likely to join another democracy during a militarized interstate dispute (MID). For example, Suzanne Werner and Doug Lemke found that when a state joins a dispute, it is especially likely to join the side with which it has a similar regime type. If true, this finding nevertheless does not render a wartime advantage to democracies, as they find there is autocratic balancing as well as democratic balancing. Robin Moriarty built a slightly different research design. Her population used all MIDs, including those in which no state joined. Each case was a triad of states, which included the challenger, the target, and a potential defender. When a third state did intervene, Moriarty coded it as the potential defender that did, in fact, intervene. When there was no third-state intervention, she used an algorithm to determine who was the most likely intervener and coded that state as the potential intervener that did not intervene. Interestingly, in contrast to Werner and Lemke, Moriarty found that a potential defender was *not* more likely to intervene when its regime type was similar to the regime type of the potential target.[53]

Paul Huth built a different research design to tackle this question. He asked the slightly different question: What causes great powers to intervene in international crises? He used the International Crisis Behavior (ICB) data set, which includes all international crises from 1918 to 1988. His research design was similar to Moriarty's: each case was a triad, with a target, a challenger, and a potential great power defender. When there was no great power intervener (note that neither Moriarty nor Werner/

Lemke limited their studies to great powers), Huth randomly chose a great power as a potential defender, one that necessarily did not intervene. One other significant difference for Huth's data set was that he used a different variable to measure regime similarity between target and potential defender. Whereas Werner/Lemke and Moriarty used Polity III data, Huth created a dichotomous variable coded 1 if both states were democratic (according to Polity II data), or both were fascist or communist.[54] Huth also included a wider array of control variables than the MID-based studies. He found that when there was similar regime type between the great power potential defender and target, the great power was significantly more likely to intervene.

One limitation of the Werner/Lemke, Moriarty, and Huth research designs is the way they treat potential defenders that do not intervene. Werner and Lemke did not examine such states, and both Moriarty and Huth picked one state per MID or crisis as a representative state that did not intervene; Moriarty picked the state systematically, and Huth randomly picked a great power. An alternative approach is to examine all states in the system as potential interveners. This approach has the advantage of not censoring information about which states could have intervened but did not. Michael Mousseau took this approach in his study of states that joined MIDs. He used the triadic approach used by Moriarty and Huth, but for each MID he had triads for all possible joiners in the system. Using this more inclusive approach, he found that democracies are *not* more likely to join MIDs as the target becomes more democratic.[55]

Other studies have also generated mixed findings on whether democracies are especially likely to engage in international cooperation.[56] Arvid Raknerud and Håvard Hegre directly addressed the question, asking, do democracies join each other in war more frequently than would be expected by chance? Their approach was to build a data set composed of dyads for all states for all war initiation years since 1816. They used event history analysis to assess the duration of peace between two states and when it would break down to war. One of their findings is that if one member of the dyad is at war with a third country, then the second member of the dyad is significantly more likely to be at war with the third country if both the first and second countries are democratic.[57]

Though it offered some important methodological advances when published, the Raknerud/Hegre study suffers from some important limitations vis-à-vis testing the hypothesis outlined here. Their study did not distinguish between democracies joining initiators and democracies joining targets. This is important because the liberal bandwagoning theory argues that democracies win wars because other democracies help them win defensive wars. Additionally, their study did not distinguish between states that voluntarily join wars and states that join wars because they are invaded. So, for example, Norway would be coded as freely deciding to join the Allies in 1940, and thereby providing evidence for the hypothesis, when in fact it clung to neutrality until the last possible moment, entering the war only when it was invaded by Nazi Germany. Indeed, if their data is recoded to be put in line with the theory (i.e., to look at democracies that freely join other democracies who were attacked), then the result collapses and democracies are not significantly more likely to join other democracies at war.[58]

Finally, their study does not take full advantage of the opportunities presented by event history analysis. One important advantage of event history analysis in the study of dyads and war is that it enables the analysis of all dyads across all years with a solution to the problem of temporal dependence. However, the Raknerud/Hegre study collects data only on the day on which war breaks out. So, for example, their data set includes data on the Finland–Soviet Union dyad on the day that war breaks out in 1939, but it does not include data during nonwar years, such as a description of the Finland–Soviet Union dyad in 1935. The data set does include information as to how long the dyad has lasted until war broke out, but it has "snapshots" of information on the independent variables only when war does break out. One might argue that the count of the number of days of peace until war breaks out is itself useful, even if information on the independent variable during peacetime is not used. However, this type of peace duration information is of limited use because for each dyad, the data set counts the number of days from January 1, 1816, until the outbreak of war. The more logical alternative would be to count the number of days since both states became members of the international system or the number of days since the last war between the two states ended.

Our Research Design

The specific question we ask is: Are democracies especially likely to intervene to assist democracies that have been attacked? Our sample includes all opportunities for states to join targets for all wars from 1816 to 1992, where a war is a militarized dispute between two recognized members of the nation-state system that generates at least 1,000 battle deaths, and the target is the state that is attacked. More specifically, we use the triad approach: each case includes a state that has been targeted in war, its attacker, and a potential defender. We include all nation-states as potential defenders, so, for example, when the Soviet Union attacks Hungary in 1956, each nation-state in the system is represented as a potential defender in a separate case (the Soviet Union-Hungary-Ecuador triad is one case, the Soviet Union-Hungary-Britain triad is another case, and so forth). The dependent variable is dichotomous, coded as 1 if the potential defender chose to join the target (that is, cases in which a potential defender joined because it was attacked are not coded 1), and 0 otherwise. Joiners are identified on the basis of the Correlates of War and the MID data sets. However, we are only interested in joiners that make at least a minor (as opposed to trivial) contribution to winning the war. Hence, we coded as 0 any country that is coded by COW or MID as joining the war but experiencing less than 1 percent of the casualties of its side. This excludes token joiners who make contributions that have essentially no effect on the war's outcome, like the Greek contribution in the Korean War or the Brazilian contribution in World War II. This separation is important, as the central question is why do democracies win wars, and we need to focus on joiners who make contributions that might actually affect the war's outcome.[59] Triads in which the attacker or target is listed as a potential defender are excluded as cases.

Multilateral wars constitute special cases requiring careful treatment. Some wars are relatively easy: one country attacks another, and then a third country elects to join the defender. When a third country elects to join the attacker, it is included as a case and is of course coded as not joining the target (dependent variable coding of 0). Other cases are more difficult. In some wars, a single attacker simultaneously attacks more than one country. In these cases, one of the initial targets is randomly chosen to be the named target for the data set; the other targets are excluded as potential defenders, because being attacked initially removes their opportunity to choose to join the target. Similarly, in wars with multiple initial attackers, one attacker is randomly chosen.[60]

The most difficult wars to code are large, multilateral wars. In World War I, the initial target is Serbia, but the war quickly becomes about nations other than Serbia and issues larger than the assassination of the Archduke. We treat these wars in a manner to bias the test in favor of supporting the proposition that democracies intervene for each other. We divide World War I into two sets of intervention decisions, the decision(s) to join Serbia in July 1914 and the decision(s) to join France in August 1914.[61] This rigs the test in favor of supporting the hypothesis, as we are assuming that states joining World War I later (like the United States) are doing so to join a democratic coalition, as they are joining democratic France rather than autocratic Serbia. World War II is similarly treated, with one set of decisions being whether or not to join Poland, and the second being whether or not to join Britain.[62] For the Korean War, there are also two sets of decisions, joining South Korea after the June 1950 North Korean invasion, and joining the United States after the Chinese intervention in the war in October. We split the Vietnam War into two wars, before and after the 1973 Peace Agreement, following the method in Stam's book *Win, Lose, or Draw*. The Gulf War is one case, with Iraq the attacker, Kuwait the target, and the rest of the world as potential defenders.

Regime type is measured using Polity data (see chapter 2 for more discussion). A Polity score ranging from − 10 to 10 is generated for each relevant state by subtracting the autocracy score from the democracy score. There is a substantial amount of missing data within the Polity data set, in some instances when an accurate coding is easily obtained. For example, the regime type for Poland 1939 is coded as missing because by the end of the year it was occupied by Nazi Germany. However, after Germany attacked and while the rest of the world had an opportunity to join, Poland had a functioning political system. For many of these cases, particularly regime codings for targets and attackers, the regime codings for the previous year are used (e.g., to acquire data for 1939 Poland the 1938 Poland codings are used). This approach reduces missing data problems while introducing only minimal measurement error. A dichotomous variable measuring Joint Democracy of democracy and target was also built, coded as 1 if both target and potential defender are democratic, where a state is deemed to be democratic if its combined Polity score is 7 or higher (on the − 10 to 10 scale).

A number of control variables are also included, using Correlates of War data.

Defender-Target Alliance

Potential defenders who are allied with the target are more likely to intervene for the target. A dichotomous alliances variable is included, getting coded as 1 if the target and potential defender share a defense pact, and 0 otherwise.[63]

Contiguity

Contiguous potential defenders are more likely to intervene for the target, both because deployment of military forces is easier and because they are more likely to themselves feel threatened by the attacker.[64] A dichotomous variable is used, coded 1 if the distance between the two states is zero, 0 otherwise.

Major Power Status

Major powers have more extensive worldwide interests and are more likely to have an interest in who wins any particular war.[65] This dichotomous variable is coded as 1 if the potential defender is a major power, 0 otherwise.

Balance of Power

Balance of power theory predicts that states are more likely to intervene in favor of a target the more the balance of power between the target and attacker favors the attacker.[66] A balance of power measure was devised using the COW capability scores, with cap(attacker)/cap(target).

Trade

Paul Papayoanou predicted that states are more likely to intervene on behalf of states with which they are economically interdependent, and that states are less likely to intervene on behalf of a target if they are economically interdependent with the attacker. Within our research design, there are two predictions. First, the higher the levels of economic interdependence between target and potential defender, the greater the likelihood that the potential defender will intervene on behalf of the target. Second, the higher the levels of economic interdependence between the potential defender and attacker, the lower the likelihood the defender will intervene on behalf of the target. We have measures of economic interdependence among states for 1950–1992. We coded the level of interdependence between the defender and target and defender and attacker with each triad. For each state within each of these two dyads, the amount of exports plus imports to the other state in the dyad divided by gross national product was determined. The measure of economic interdependence is the lower of the two measures within the dyad.[67]

Since the dependent variable is dichotomous, probit analysis was used.[68] We have strong reason to suspect that there is spatial autocorrelation among the decisions of potential interveners to join a particular target (i.e., the decision of Britain to join the Korean War is probably not independent of the American decision to join that war). This autocorrelation is dealt with in two ways, by using robust standard errors, and by adjusting standard errors within the clusters of various potential defenders deciding whether or not to intervene for specific targets.[69]

Results

There were a total of 5,588 observations (intervention opportunities) for 76 wars; of these, 33 observations were coded 1 and the rest 0.[70] Table 4.2 provides multivariate probit analysis of the factors that determine a potential defender's decision to assist a target.

Model 1 in table 4.2 provides a first cut at our main question of democratic bandwagoning: the Joint Democracy term is not statistically significant at the 0.05 level; Defender's Major Power status, Contiguity, and

TABLE 4.2
Probit Analysis of Decision to Join a Target during Wars, 1816–1992

Variable	Model 1	Model 2: Post-1950 Only	Model 3: Politically Relevant Dyads Only
Joint Democracy: Dichotomy	0.624 (0.401)	—	0.721 (0.449)
Joint Democracy: Lower Pol. Score	—	−0.191 (0.131)	—
Contiguity	0.800*** (0.211)	0.594 (0.388)	—
Defender-Target Alliance	0.923** (0.313)	2.16*** (0.475)	0.669* (.348)
Defender Major Power	0.946*** (0.204)	2.91*** (0.364)	0.704*** (0.231)
Attacker-Target Balance of Power	−0.00841 (0.00677)	−0.102 (0.114)	−0.00517 (0.00688)
Defender-Target Trade	—	−82.7 (65.8)	—
Defender-Attacker Trade	—	−5930* (3268)	—
Constant	−2.97*** (0.146)	−5.21*** (1.26)	−2.71*** (0.189)
Pseudo r-squared	0.238	0.544	0.130
n	5001	3095	1093
Log likelihood	−143.68	−28.07	−106.97

Note: All significance tests are one-tailed. Standard errors in parentheses.
*Significant at 0.05 level.
**Significant at 0.01 level.
***Significant at 0.001 level.

Target-Defender alliance are. The Joint Democracy variable remains insignificant if we use different measures of joint democracy, including making the democracy threshold 5 or higher or 6 or higher, taking the lower of the two Democracy scores, adding the Democracy scores, or taking the difference of the Democracy scores.[71] This provides evidence against Proposition 4.1.

Some have speculated that a true sense of international liberal community emerged only after World War II.[72] In Model 2, we analyzed only cases after 1949. We were able to include the two trade variables, as we have trade data for this period. To generate sufficient variance on the Joint Democracy variable, we used here the lower democracy score instead of the 7 or higher threshold variable. Here too Joint Democracy is statistically insignificant. The Defender-Target trade variable is insignificant, but the Attacker-Target trade variable is statistically significant and in the right direction, indicating that trade ties do not draw a defender to protect a target, but they do repel a defender from becoming embroiled in conflict with a trading partner. This is consistent with evidence elsewhere, which finds that economic interdependence reduces the likelihood of conflict between states. In Model 3, we go back to the 1816–1992 period but use only cases in which the Defender-Target dyad is politically relevant, which is traditionally defined as meaning that the two states are contiguous or at least one state is a major power. Again, Joint Democracy is statistically insignificant (it remains so if Defender Major Power status and Contiguity are dropped from the model).

The quantitative results produce an unmistakable conclusion: when a democracy is attacked, other democracies are not especially likely to rush to its aid. This result is achieved with a variety of control variables. It is robust across a variety of specifications, including varying the coding of the Joint Democracy variable, limiting the sample to politically relevant dyads, and limiting the sample to the postwar period.

FIVE

WINNING WARS ON FACTORY FLOORS?

THE MYTH OF THE DEMOCRATIC
ARSENALS OF VICTORY

We must be the great arsenal of democracy.
—*Franklin D. Roosevelt, December 29, 1940*

THUS FAR, we have looked to complex explanations for democracies' wartime prowess. We have claimed that democratic leaders make better choices, and that soldiers in democracies fight with better leadership and initiative. Both of these themes indicate that the critical difference between democracies and autocracies lies with the people: in democracies they are able to constrain their national leaders at the ballot box, and they make better soldiers in combat. We also examined the proposition that a sense of global democratic community encourages democracies to band together in support of one another during wartime, but we found no evidence to support this claim.

Perhaps there is a simpler explanation of why democracies win wars, one commonly found in the historical literature on war. The solution to the puzzle of why democracies win may be that democracies bring more resources to the battlefield than their opponents. There is no question that the ability to mobilize a country's human and industrial capital is a critical determinant of victory. Perhaps democracies are more effective than their autocratic counterparts at translating the potential energy of society into kinetic energy on the battlefield. For example, the conventional wisdom holds that the key to the Union's victory in the American Civil War was the Union's industrial power, which compensated for the general ineptitude of its leaders in the field. The conventional wisdom suggests again that the principal American contribution to victory in both world wars was its industrial might. During World War I, Edward Grey remarked that the United States was like "a gigantic boiler. Once the fire is lighted under it there is no limit to the power it can generate." During World War II, Franklin Roosevelt called on America to be the "arsenal of democracy" for the Allies. This challenge was indeed met: taking the war as a whole, the United States alone produced as much war materiel as all of the other Allies combined.[1]

What then explains best the democratic tendency to win? Do they bring more equipment and soldiers to the battlefield by more efficiently extracting human and industrial capital? Does democracy's virtue of victory grow from its virtue of prosperity? Liberals such as John Locke expressed the hope that a constrained, republican government would enjoy greater wealth and consequently greater military power. Locke speculated that the "prince, who shall be so wise and godlike, as by established laws of liberty to secure protection and encouragement to the honest industry of mankind, against the oppression of power and narrowness of party, will quickly be too hard for his neighbours."[2] Modern political scientists have also made this point, attributing democracies' tendency to win wars to their ability to produce more tanks, planes, and ships, thereby simply overwhelming their autocratic opponents.[3] The statistical tests presented in chapter 2 certainly show that material industrial and military capabilities significantly affect war outcomes, a finding echoed elsewhere.[4] Is this the key to democracies' apparent power?

In this chapter, we examine the proposition that the key to democratic victory lies in winning the battle on the factory floor. Evaluating this proposition requires first asking the larger question: How do economic factors determine victory in war? Two separate factors link a state's economy to its effort in war.[5] The first is the size of a state's economic base: the more prosperous or wealthy the society, the more resources that can be tapped to fuel the war effort. The second factor is the proportion of the state's economic base that the state can mobilize or extract for the war effort. Regardless of the aggregate level of resources, higher degrees of extraction will provide more resources.[6] We answer the question of whether democracies win wars by investigating each of these factors. First, are democracies in general richer? Second, can democracies extract proportionately more resources from their societies? We answer these questions in turn below using statistical tests to demonstrate the central finding of this chapter: democracies do *not* win wars because of inherent economic advantages.

Base Level of Prosperity:
Building the Economic Foundations for War

Are democracies in general more prosperous? The idea that a liberal political order facilitates prosperity is, of course, at the core of classical liberalism, which argues that commerce is likely to flourish in free societies that exhibit respect for property rights. Immanuel Kant extended this proposition to claim that it meant that democracies would be more powerful than other kinds of states in times of war.[7] During the twentieth century, however, the economic advantages of freedom at times appeared doubtful. While the Western democracies appeared unable to pull themselves out of the Great Depression, Germany's economy boomed under Nazi leadership in the 1930s, leading many conservatives to conclude that fascism would emerge as the more powerful alternative to democracy.[8] In the first decades of the Cold War, many on the Left saw great promise in the Soviet Union's command economy. While Soviet-style Communism drew the respect of the left in both Europe and the United States, it threatened the conservative right in Europe and inspired vitriolic hatred bordering on the pathological in the United States. By the 1960s it appeared to many that the Soviet Union could at least keep up with, if not "bury," the West, as Nikita Khrushchev famously put it in a speech to the United Nations General Assembly in New York.

The end of the Cold War brought about a near universal collapse of faith in socialist economics and dictatorial, one-party political systems, leading some observers to conclude that global society had reached the "end of history." Former Communist nations, particularly those in Eastern Europe, embraced parliamentary democracy and free market economics, hoping to enjoy the fruits of Western freedom and individual prosperity associated with liberal democratic regimes. A number of social scientists revived and expanded liberalisms' core proposition that democracy advances prosperity, an outgrowth of democracies' stress on property rights, their relatively fewer economic distortions, and their respect for the rule of law.[9]

How well placed is this faith in liberal democracy as a guarantor of prosperity? The sources of affluence and growth are, of course, quite complex, and though subjected to a tidal wave of sophisticated research, the relationships between democracy and economic development remain elusive. Some studies have found that democracy and the protection of property rights advance economic development; others have found that democracy does not advance development, but that development may advance democracy; other research has cast doubt on the existence of any significant relationship; while other studies propose that democracies experience inferior economic performance.[10]

In assessing this array of inconclusive findings, we might comfortably say that the democracy-development relationship has varied for different countries. Certainly, for some countries, democratic political institutions have helped to advance prosperity, the United States being a leading example. However, the path to prosperity need not be democratic; in some environments, authoritarian approaches may be more successful. The political system best suited for a country's attempts at industrialization differs along several factors. These include the timing of industrialization, the resources present at the time, and the relative level of industrial development throughout the global economy.[11] More recently, the so-called Asian economic tigers such as Singapore, South Korea, Taiwan, and Thailand achieved remarkable economic growth under relatively repressive social and political conditions. China's per capita GDP skyrocketed during the 1980s and 1990s with little if any political liberalization, to the befuddlement of academics and consternation of politicians. In sum, while democracy has proved advantageous for some, for now, there appears to be no systematic relationship between the process of democratization and increases in states' economic development.

We ask a more straightforward question here, however. Aside from whether or not democracies are in general more prosperous, do democracies win wars because they have larger economies? Recall from chapter 2 that both democracy and military-industrial capabilities make victory more likely, indicating that at the least democracy is contributing in ways beyond economic strength. However, are democracies winning at least in part because they possess greater economic capacity?[12]

To explore this question we conducted extensive statistical analyses on the relationship between a state's level of democracy and its economic capabilities—in particular those capabilities that translate into war materiel on the battlefield (see appendix 5.1). Specifically, we asked the following question: Among states that fought wars, did the democracies have larger economies? Looking at the belligerents in all wars from 1816 to 1990, we found there to be no statistically significant relationship between a state's political institutions and the size of its economy. That is, democratic belligerents did not enjoy larger economies or greater industrial production than did nondemocratic belligerents, whether one uses aggregate measures of military-industrial capability or specific measures such as iron and steel production. There is also no relationship if we restrict our analysis to just those states that won wars, or just those states that initiated wars. This is important evidence against the first proposition in this chapter: democracies that have fought wars over the last two centuries have not won their wars because they had systematically larger economies than their opponents did.

Resource Mobilization for the War Effort

Separate from overall economic prosperity is the question of how much a state can extract from its economy for the war effort. In large part, a nation's real power (as opposed to its theoretical potential) emerges as a product of a state's aggregate material resources and its political capacity for resource extraction during times of need.[13] After World War II, some observers claimed that democratic states make proportionally greater efforts in war than other kinds of states once they become deeply involved in a particular conflict. Critics of American foreign policy, who claimed that it appeared to vacillate in bipolar fashion between detached disinterest and activist furor, included George Kennan and Walter Lippmann. They contrasted democracies' lazy inaction toward the fascist threat during the 1930s with the furious rage of democratic publics during World War II itself. Kennan described the two sides of democratic public opinion, of languor in peacetime but supreme effort during war:

> I sometimes wonder whether in this respect a democracy is not uncomfortably similar to one of those prehistoric monsters with a body as long as this room and a brain the size of a pin: he lies there in his comfortable primeval mud and pays little attention to his environment; he is slow to wrath—in fact, you practically have to whack his tail off to make him aware that his interests are being disturbed; but, once he grasps this, he lays about him with such blind determination that he not only destroys his adversary but largely wrecks his native habitat.

Kennan's colorful metaphor has deep roots: Alexis de Tocqueville made essentially the same point more than a hundred years earlier, contrasting the United States' neglect of military matters during peacetime with a ferocious concentration of effort once war does come.[14]

More recently, political scientists have made roughly similar arguments, that democracies are able to extract more from their societies during wartime than dictators and oligarchs. Some make the simple argument that because democratic governments are more popular, democracies will be able to extract more resources, either human or economic, from society for the war effort, increasing the chances of victory over autocratic states.[15] Others make a more sophisticated claim, arguing that in both peace and war, democracies are better able to provide public goods—those types of goods and services that, if delivered to one, must be delivered to all. National defense or clean air is a classic public good. Private goods, such as cash, land, or patronage positions, can be consumed by a single individual without sharing any of the product with others. Autocrats who are dependent on small groups of individuals to maintain power, according to this line of argument, must devote a disproportionate share of the nations' wealth to the distribution of private goods (to these individuals) in order to maintain power at home.[16] The theoretical implication is that democracies ought to be more able to devote extra public goods to the war effort than should autocratic states, thereby affording an important advantage during wartime. This theory, while elegant and parsimonious, relies on mathematical proof rather than empirical demonstration to establish its veracity. The formal proof relies in turn on the empirical assumption that democracies are able to devote proportionally greater resources to war efforts than are autocracies. What evidence in the historical record is there to support this claim?

Counter to the formal theorists' assumption, history reveals that democracies are *not* more effective at extracting resources during wartime than are other kinds of regimes. Instead, the scholarly literature argues that a state's ability to extract resources from its society correlates with factors other than democracy, such as institutional maturity.[17] In particular, democracies do not extract more from their societies using direct or indirect taxes than do other forms of government. Two scholars found that political capacity is an important determinant of the outcomes of major wars since 1900, but that "differences in the form of government do not determine the degree of political effort." Historical surveys have also revealed, contra Kennan and Lippmann, that democratic war belligerents are not significantly more likely to press for total victory in their war aims than are other kinds of regimes.[18] We conducted further statistical tests that confirm these earlier findings that we present in appendix 5.1.

Another way of thinking about economic extraction for the war effort is to look at the percentage of the population that is serving in the military. This is a useful measure of resource extraction, as putting more people in the armed forces, while obviously advantageous on the battlefield, can strain the national economy and create labor shortages, thereby imposing hardship on the civilian population. We conducted statistical tests to examine whether democracies have put more of their populations under arms since 1816 (see appendix 5.1). We looked at the population of all countries, whether at war or in peace, as well as just that of countries at war. The results indicate that for all states, democracies, in fact, place a significantly *lower* percentage of their populations under arms than do nondemocracies. For states at war, the negative effect remains, though it is not statistically significant.[19]

A slightly different proposition than those above might be that democracies win wars not because they have higher levels of aggregate production, or have more soldiers under arms, but rather because democratic armies have more war materiel available to them on the battlefield than do autocratic armies. This is a potentially important distinction, as higher levels of corruption within autocratic societies may make the translation of industrial production into war goods less efficient. In other words, democracies and autocracies might have equal levels of industrial production, but the democracies may have more weapons available to their troops because of less corruption in their military-industrial complexes.[20]

Analysis of the historical record, however, lends no credence to this argument. To test it, we need a different set of measures, specifically the amounts of war materiel actually available to armies on the battlefield rather than aggregate levels of national production. The HERO data set that we used in chapter 3 contains these measures, specifically providing counts of the number of artillery pieces, tanks, and air sorties flown per side for each major battle since 1800 (see appendix 3.1 for more discussion of the HERO data set). We use these data to test this proposition: The more democratic an army is (or, more literally, the more democratic the state that produced the army), the more tanks and artillery pieces it will field and the more air sorties it will fly per battle. In the statistical analysis, we find that for all three (tanks, artillery, and air sorties), higher levels of democracy mean *lower* levels of tanks, artillery pieces, and air sorties, and in the case of artillery pieces the relationship is statistically significant (for discussion and results, see appendix 5.1; table 5.5 in particular). In short, we can confidently state that democratic armies do not enjoy significantly higher levels of war materiel on the battlefield than do autocratic armies.[21]

An alternative approach to estimating extraction effort, rather than looking at the proportion of society a state puts under arms or the number of weapons it places in the field, is to look directly at what proportion of the economy the state devotes to defense spending. More simply, how much of the total value of goods and services produced in a country is the government spending on guns over butter? One way to measure this is to look at the fraction of the nation's GDP that is devoted to military spending. Analysis of these data supports the proposition that democracies devote proportionally no more or less to their war efforts than other states (see appendix 5.1).

From this additional perspective, again, democracies do not extract more from their populations than do other kinds of states.[22] This result is not surprising; the willingness and ability of autocratic states to invest staggering proportions of their economic and social resources in military and imperial schemes is well known. By one estimate, which we now know to be quite conservative, during the Cold War the Soviet Union invested over one quarter of its gross domestic product in defense and empire, a shocking amount considering that the Soviet Union participated in no major wars during this period. At the same time, the United States extracted only 4–6 percent of its GDP for defense spending, to the consternation of both the political right and left (conservatives felt the United States spent too little in its efforts to contain Communism; liberals, too much). A natural skepticism about the role of the government, or anti-statism, in American political life constrained the American government's ability to mobilize more of the U.S. economy and population for its Cold War containment strategy.[23] Our results indicating no relationship between democracy and extraction rates remain even if we instead look only at war participants, as there is still no significant relationship between democracy and the percentage of revenue devoted to the military (see appendix 5.1).

Thinking about this problem from the domestic political perspective, it is easy to understand the inability or unwillingness of democracies to extract more resources from their populations for war. Democratic states fund marginal increases in military expenditures through either higher taxes or deficit spending, both of which must ultimately lead to reductions in public consumption—the proverbial guns versus butter tradeoff.[24] As Immanuel Kant observed, the public prefers not to spend on military ventures at the expense of individual consumption, and the constraints imposed by democratic political institutions help impose limits on the abilities of democratic elites to raise levels of military spending. More subtle forces may also be at work. Democracies tend to base their economies on trade to a greater degree than autocracies do. Such trade dependence may adversely affect a state's ability to mobilize resources for war, thereby somewhat undercutting a democracy's ability to muster the economic resources necessary for victory.[25]

These results indicate that democracies do not win wars by extracting more from their populations than do autocratic states. This is consistent with the view that the democratic public resists paying high costs for wars, and therefore democratic governments strive to minimize the costs of war so as not to jeopardize public support. During the Vietnam War, for example, President Lyndon Johnson did not call up the reserves as part of the summer 1965 escalation of the war in part because he feared the economic costs of a reserve call-up would threaten his Great Society programs. Three years later, he chose not to escalate the war following the Vietnamese Tet Offensive, in part due to fears that such an action would threaten the U.S. economy, vulnerable because of the concurrent international gold crisis. A change in party in the White House did not free up economic resources for the war. In 1969 budgetary pressures led to scaling back operations in Vietnam, including reducing the number of strategic and tactical air sorties flown, withdrawing two tactical fighter squadrons, and implementing naval reductions.[26] More recently, during the months preceding the 1991 Gulf War, President Bush diffused congressional grumbling over the financial cost of the coming war by securing substantial financial support for the war effort from other countries.[27]

Similarly, in World War II the principal autocratic belligerents, Germany, Japan, Italy, and the Soviet Union, extracted far more from their societies (and imposed far greater suffering on their peoples) than did the principal democratic belligerents, the United States and Britain. For example, the Japanese government imposed grim demands on civilians; particularly biting sacrifices included reduced food supplies for civilians to support increased rations for Japanese soldiers. While British and American per capita caloric consumption did not change much during the war from their relatively high prewar levels, per capita Japanese caloric intake started low and declined by 17 percent from the early 1930s to 1944. By 1945 the average Japanese citizen's caloric intake was 1,680 calories per day, well below the minimum requirement of 2,165 calories. By the end of the war, 20–25 percent of the urban Japanese population suffered from malnutrition, increasing the frequency of diseases such as tuberculosis and beriberi. The Japanese government imposed clothing rationing in 1942, and by 1945 the average Japanese consumer could spend only one-seventh as much on clothing as he or she did before the war. In sharp contrast to the sacrifices made by their fascist counterparts, American consumers saw the real value of their expenditures rise by 5 percent from 1941 to 1944, hardly reflecting large wartime sacrifices brought on by high levels of economic extraction. Over the same period, real Japanese consumer expenditures fell by 28 percent. One historian stated unequivocally, "The Japanese civilian was hit harder by the war than the consumer in Germany, Great Britain, or the United States." The fascist government in Italy also demanded large sacrifices from its people (though not as great as in Japan), as personal consumption of both food and other items declined as the war progressed.[28]

Compared to the effort put forth by their democratic allies, the Soviet citizen living in the totalitarian Stalinist state made almost unimaginable sacrifices for a truly Herculean mobilization effort. By 1943 women made up over half the industrial labor force, and nearly three quarters of the agricultural labor pool. The Soviet administration canceled all holidays and leaves for the entire work force, so workers would not miss a single twelve-to-sixteen-hour day conducted in dangerous and sometimes appalling conditions. To sustain a more rigorous work regimen than other industrial workers maintained during the war, the average Russian was forced to supplement state food rations that were one quarter the food rations of the average German, and one-fifth the rations of the average Briton. Only combat soldiers and manual laborers engaged in especially hazardous work were entitled to an adequate state-provided diet. A twelve-year-old child in Leningrad in the winter of 1941–42 depending only on official rations faced certain death.[29]

We might view Germany as the contrary case to our general claim about the ability of autocrats to make great demands of their societies. The traditional view of economic historians, harking back to the postwar U.S. Strategic Bombing Survey, was that the Nazi government eschewed long-term economic planning and concurrently higher levels of economic extraction from German society at the outset of World War II, hoping that a blitzkrieg strategy would ensure a short, relatively low-cost war.

Part of the motivation behind the German strategy, so the argument goes, was to avoid high levels of resource extraction needed to fuel a sustained war effort that would necessarily reduce civilian consumption, and hence civilian support for the Nazi party's bid for European domination.[30] From this traditional perspective, Germany would be an example of the limits autocracies face in resource extraction, as the Nazi government recognized that the German people would be unwilling to make great economic sacrifices for a repressive government.

However, more recent research has cast serious doubt on the traditional claim that German resource extraction efforts in World War II spared civilian consumption, even in the earliest years of the war. German civilians made substantial sacrifices for the war effort from the outset. Although the output of consumer industries initially rose following the outbreak of the war, the quality of life of the average consumer declined because consumer industries were filling an increasing number of military orders. The German government rationed a variety of consumer goods including some foodstuffs and clothing beginning in September 1939, imposing from the outset the increasingly grim terms of wartime existence upon German civilians: shortages, decline in quality of goods, deteriorating personal health, and so on. Indeed, German civilians made greater economic sacrifices for the war effort in World War II than did British civilians, contra the traditional view. Specifically, in comparison with Britain, German per capita consumer expenditure declined more steeply as the war progressed, a greater percentage of women in society were mobilized to enter the work force, and war expenditure as a percentage of national income was higher. Additionally, Germany devoted a greater percentage of its net national product to military priorities than did Britain virtually throughout the war.[31]

The point we wish to make with the World War II examples is that autocratic leaders were not constrained by fears of waning public support for the war. Leaders in Germany, Italy, Japan, and the Soviet Union alike knew that imposing extremely high levels of extraction on their societies would not dangerously undermine support for either the war effort or their regimes. Only suffering actual conquest would put their political futures at risk. As a result, they were able to impose costs on their societies that would be unthinkable in their democratic counterparts. In Japan, even in the face of total military defeat, the ruling militarists never feared losing control of the government at the hands of the people. The United States government, in contrast, did not need to consider imposing such draconian costs on its consumers, as there was sufficient economic capacity lying idle resulting from the Great Depression that the population did not confront much of a guns versus butter tradeoff. Just as had been the case for the Union side in the Civil War, during World War II in the United States, there was both economic growth *and* mobilization of the economy for the war effort.[32]

World War I also provides an interesting comparison. Did the Allies win because their societies were more willing to make greater sacrifices than the Central Powers were? One study of the military effectiveness of belligerents in World War I reveals that in general, all governments, autocratic and democratic alike, were able to extract the financial, economic, and manpower resources they needed from society for the prosecution of their war efforts. As the war drew to a close in 1918, the German Army collapsed, in part because of material and manpower shortages. Nevertheless, these shortages did not arise because the autocratic German state left some large part of the German society or economy untapped. Indeed, by 1917, with more than a year left in the war, official rations left German civilians in starvation conditions, as official rations provided only 61 percent of the calories needed for a 65–70-kilogram person to perform light physical work.[33] Remarkably, Germany continued to fight for yet another year.

A principal problem for all European combatants during World War I was a continual shortage of manpower and ammunition. The combination of the length of the war, appallingly high casualties on the front, and the never-ending demand for munitions presented by trench warfare strained all of the belligerents' populations and factories, regardless of their political institutions. Some countries, such as Britain, responded by drafting women into the work force and restricting organized labor's activities. However, food availability was less of a problem in the democracies than it was in Germany. In Britain, for example, food rationing did not begin until 1917 despite the ongoing U-boat campaign, and even then, the British consumer easily maintained an adequate diet. Indeed, while German real per capita income fell by 24 percent during World War I, British real per capita income actually rose. The potential of American mobilization remained unknown, as the war ended before the American economy completely switched over to mobilization for war.[34] In short, contrary to the expectation of the extraction argument, the autocratic German government tapped its society far more deeply for the effort in World War I than did its democratic opponents.[35]

From the extraction perspective, a World War I case worth examining a bit more closely is Russia. In 1918 the Bolshevik overthrow of Tsar Nicholas' autocratic regime eventually led to the Russian exit from the war. Is this an example of a society putting sharp limits on what it will sacrifice for an autocratic government's war aims? Probably not. At best, such a claim would be a gross oversimplification of the reality of the time. In contrast to the conditions in Germany during the war years, in Russia, still largely an agrarian society, adequate agricultural production allowed the Nicholas regime to avoid widespread food rationing. By late 1916 there were sporadic food shortages in the cities, but this was due not to declining production, but rather to distribution problems brought on by rural peasants hording food in hopes of higher prices. Mismanagement of grain stocks along with a variety of other conditions conspired to bring starvation conditions to some segments of Russian society by 1917. It is hard to imagine a citizenry under a democratic government being more willing to accept the hardships the Russian peasants bore during the years leading up to and including the war. One prominent historian of the Russian Revolution was blunt in his rejection of the argument that the war caused the revolution: "It is a mistake to attribute the February Revolution to fatigue with the war. The contrary is true. Russians wanted to pursue the war more effectively, and they felt that the existing government was not capable of doing it. Fatigue with the war set in only after the unsuccessful June 1917 offensive launched by the Provisional Government to bolster its prestige and lift national morale. Until then, even the Bolsheviks did not dare to openly call for peace because it was a highly unpopular slogan."[36]

Thus far, our focus has been on the aggregate level of extraction from the economy. Perhaps there is a somewhat more subtle argument linking democracy and economy to victory. Aside from whether democracies devote a higher percentage of their economies to the war effort, perhaps they are more effective at wartime economic management than their autocratic opponents are. Corruption of government officials, for example, tends to be more prevalent in less democratic societies.[37]

How can we assess whether or not democracies win wars because they do more with the economic resources at their disposal during wartime? One approach would be to examine statistically whether democracies extract more military power from each unit of domestic product than autocracies do. However, when we reanalyze the data from chapter 2 on what factors help states win wars, we find that democracies are not more effective at exploiting their military-industrial capability to attain victory than autocrats are.[38]

Wartime economic planning is likely to be most important in long wars. In shorter wars, the conflict may be over before the belligerents have used up their standing stocks of munitions and certainly before moving the economy to a fully mobilized war footing will make a difference in the outcome.[39] For example, during neither the Gulf War in 1991 nor the Kosovo War in 1999 did the United States shift to a wartime footing where we might otherwise expect civilians to make sacrifices for the war effort.

The experience of the world wars illustrates our claim that democracies generally are no better at economic planning during wartime than are nondemocracies. During World War I, autocratic Germany did surprisingly well in holding off a materially superior Allied coalition for several years, pointedly avoiding some of the ammunition shortages, particularly in artillery shells, that Britain and France suffered.[40] In World War II, the United States and Britain did a better job at economic management than did Japan or Germany, though interestingly the Soviet Union under Stalin still managed to get the job done. Specifically, the Soviet state proved up to the task of frantically mobilizing the economy for war in 1941 while simultaneously transporting a substantial portion of industry across hundreds of miles of Soviet territory to the safety of the Urals region. When the immediate crisis brought on by the surprise German invasion passed, the Soviet leadership downshifted the economy, gearing it to fight a longer war that would soon require attention to the general civilian economy (such as the production of rail stock, machinery, and electricity) as well as immediate military needs (the production of tanks, airplanes, bullets, and rifles).[41]

One way to assess wartime economic effectiveness would be to look at wartime economic growth. However, economic growth during wartime is difficult to assess, as a number of idiosyncratic factors contribute to economic growth that are also associated with war-fighting capabilities, such as a state's dependence on raw material imports, or whether the war is fought on its own territory. The United States and Britain did enjoy greater relative growth in their gross national product over the course of World War II than did Germany or the Soviet Union, though all belligerents in World War II experienced a substantial increase in labor productivity. On the other side of the ledger, during wartime, imperial powers are able to extract resources from captured territories, especially those states that use coercive methods—notably, although not exclusively, autocratic regimes.[42]

A more important question is the degree to which regime type affects states' efficacy of wartime resource allocation. That is, what kinds of regimes make the best wartime economic planners? This is a very complicated question, as it gets at regime type issues that do not necessarily match up with the democracy/authoritarian dimension that we have focused on thus far. One key factor determining the effectiveness of wartime economic planning is the fragmentation of the state bureaucracy. Fragmented bureaucracies appear in governments where organizations are largely free to pursue their own agendas, independent of central oversight or without central coordination by a strong executive at the top. These bureaucracies are institutionally similar to a feudal system where each monarch—or agency head—protects his or her own fiefdoms. In the context here, specifically, states with fragmented bureaucracies do worse at wartime economic management and planning. Unified bureaucracies, those controlled and directed by centralized political leadership, will experience higher levels of effectiveness. Importantly, the level of a state's democracy does not correlate in any simple way with bureaucratic fragmentation. Rather, highly democratic states and mature dictatorships tend to experience lower fragmentation, while oligarchs, captured by and dependent on special interests, tend to have higher fragmentation.

Efficient wartime economic planning requires the optimal allocation of resources in the economy toward advancing the total war effort. Inefficiencies arise when critical resources remain untapped for the war effort, and when planners are not able to allocate resources toward optimal provision of the mix of goods necessary to maximizing the chances of winning. Perhaps unexpectedly, wartime production requires that an economy produce a more diverse mix of goods than during peacetime. An economy at peace can narrow the portfolio of goods and services it produces to just those few in which it has a comparative advantage and trade for whatever else it needs. In wartime, the laissez-faire policies that optimize growth in peacetime lead to the underproduction of key goods, which in turn undercuts military effectiveness. States at war need to be more self-sufficient or autarkic than international trade theory would dictate. The state cannot let profit margins determine exclusively what military goods get produced, as it needs a particular balance of aircraft, armored vehicles, fighting ships, merchant ships, transportation, food, and so forth in order to win the war and maintain an adequate standard of living for society under substantially autarkic conditions. Further, the conditions of war may substantially reduce international trade, forcing the national economy to produce a more complete array of consumer items than it otherwise would.

As with all other matters of public policy, states choose from a variety of organizational tools for economic management during wartime. An important variable of wartime economic planning is the degree to which decisions come under centralized control. In a centralized system there is perhaps a war cabinet or even a single policy-making czar that controls all aspects of the economy, including allocation of manpower, wage controls, production priorities, and so on. A more decentralized system exhibits fragmented authority in which there is little central control over an array of ministries, committees, and branches of the military assigned various economic tasks.

Fragmented, decentralized structures are less efficient at producing materials best suited to a particular military strategy. Each authority is responsible for the production of a different product, but they compete for access to the same set of inputs (raw materials, manpower, factory floor space, and so on) located within the same budgetary constraints (the national economy). The fundamental problem is essentially one of collective action: each authority has idiosyncratic and independent preferences about what it wishes to produce, based on its organizational mission or culture. The key point here is that the aggregation of these individual preferences is unlikely to amount to the optimal budget allocation for the war effort. Central coordination of these individual authorities from an executive authority whose single preference is to win the war is an effective method for reducing the collective action problem and maximizing economic effectiveness.

There are two downsides to centralization worth noting. The first is that centralization may reduce innovation, particularly with regard to innovations in military technology. However, this argument is more applicable to peacetime innovation, as countries that have a strong society and a comparatively weak government will experience more weapons innovations emerging from laboratories, best described by a "bottom up" model. The advantage here is that more genuinely novel inventions will emerge than in strong state/weak society countries that will exhibit more "top-down" characteristics, as resources can get mobilized to develop a particular innovation once it has been demonstrated elsewhere or the leadership knows what it is looking for.[43] In wartime, however, some of the most important weapons innovation necessarily occurs in a top-down fashion, as leaders conscript their nation's scientists into the war effort and demand they produce specific weapons.[44] During World War I, for example, First Lord of the British Admiralty Winston Churchill learned that the chemist Chaim Weizmann had discovered a novel laboratory method of producing acetone, a chemical necessary for the manufacture of the explosive materials used in naval shells. In a straightforward and top-down fashion, Churchill allocated the resources that allowed Weizmann to develop his bench-top production of acetone on an industrial scale, which in turn enabled Britain to avoid facing critical ordnance shortages. During World War II, the best example of a centralized effort to develop a specific weapon was the Anglo-American pursuit of the atomic bomb. The Manhattan Project culminated in the sequestration of hundreds of leading scientists at a secret location commanding an industrial base as large as the entire American automobile industry.[45]

A second potential problem with centralization is the rigidity inherent in vertical organizational structures. If all decisions require approval from the highest levels, this may inhibit the ability of the economy to adapt smoothly and dynamically to rapidly changing conditions and, hence, needs. This is a more serious problem than potential constraints on innovation, and the optimal structure of wartime economic planning requires a degree of flexibility, particularly at lower levels.

Regime type has a complex relationship to bureaucratic fragmentation.

Democracies generally are likely to have less bureaucratic fragmentation. A democratic political leadership is more likely to enjoy strong civilian control of the military, and the leadership is more likely to derive its legitimacy for leadership from mass elections than from the support of special interests or branches of the military.[46] Oligarchic or cartelized regimes are, in contrast, more likely to experience bureaucratic fragmentation. Such leaderships draw their support from a small group of special interests, such as branches of the military or particular sectors of industry. Oligarchs are less likely to be able to impose centralized control on their state's bureaucratic organs because politicized sectors, critical to the oligarch's hold on power, may defect from their supporting coalition. Further, civilian control of the military in such regimes tends to be quite weak. Conversely, a dictatorial leader may be able to impose centralized control over the bureaucracy, directly keeping a close watch on those who manage the bureaucracy. In sum, we imagine a curvilinear relationship between regime type and wartime bureaucratic centralization, with democracies and highly repressive regimes being less fragmented and more centralized (and therefore more effective), whereas regimes with mixed characteristics are more fragmented (and less effective).

The experiences of the major belligerents during the two World Wars illustrate the ineffectiveness of fragmented bureaucracies and the complex relationships between regime type and bureaucratic fragmentation. These cases are useful as studies of wartime planning, as the total nature of each state's war aims and the length of the war highlight the importance of effective wartime planning for victory. The cases do not point conclusively in one direction or another. In World War I there appears to be no relationship between regime type and planning efficiency, in World War II both the democracies and the extremely repressive Soviet Union do somewhat better than oligarchic regimes.

Economies at War: World War I

In World War I, the degree of centralized control of the wartime economies varied. Both democratic Britain and autocratic Russia centralized control over their economies once it became apparent that the pre-1914 "short-war" assumption was a pipe dream. In both cases centralization substantially escalated munitions production. Democratic France maintained somewhat higher production, despite the inefficiencies introduced by the uncoordinated morass of boards, committees, and commissions in charge of industrial activities. Germany, exhibiting a mixed political system with both democratic and autocratic elements, had its success limited by political barriers to the centralized control of the economy and inefficiencies in the production of certain key items such as trucks and turbines. American participation in the war was relatively short, though production and efficiency improved in spring 1918 when government control and centralization of national war production decisions increased under the War Industries Board.[47]

One historian has recently dissented from the traditional view that Germany's wartime economic policies and strategies were less competent than those of the Allies. He poses this puzzle: since the Allies possessed a decisive advantage in aggregate material resources (perhaps a 1.5:1 advantage in industrial resources, and a 4.5:1 advantage in manpower), why did the war drag on for so long before Germany finally capitulated? If one believes that aggregate military-industrial capability alone drives war outcomes, Germany should have been defeated in 1915 or 1916, and certainly before the Russian revolutions of 1917. From this empirical puzzle, he argues that Germany's management of its wartime economy was superior to the Allies' management of theirs. Note that this argument is consistent with the theory outlined here, that centralization optimizes wartime economic performance. For example, he argues that the German government was more efficient than the Entente government in allocating manpower to military service and industrial work, and that the German food rationing system was superior to the more market-oriented British approach to food distribution. This argument would point to the economic competence of an autocratic system during war, bolstering the general null hypothesis of this chapter that democracies do not win wars because of superior economic performance.[48]

Economies at War: World War II

World War II demonstrates the relative effectiveness of democratic and totalitarian states in comparison with oligarchic or cartelized regimes. Japan is a good example of a cartelized system. It had a variety of industrial and military groups that vied for power. The government bureaucracy suffered from deep fractures, especially between the army and navy, such that there was very little interservice coordination. The result was inefficient wartime economic planning as both service branches actively competed with each other without central coordination from a higher level. For example, Japanese aircraft production had the potential of reaching 53,000 planes per year but was restricted to 8,000–10,000 planes per year because of army-navy competition that drove each branch to run its own aircraft factories. Indeed, during World War II, the Japanese Army denied naval officers access to army aircraft production facilities, and the Japanese Navy denied army officers access to warships, though German military attachés had open access to both.[49]

Army-navy competition in imperial Japan appeared in other counter-productive ways as well. For example, to support troops stationed on Pacific islands, the Japanese Army built its own submarine from scratch, refusing the navy's offer to share information on submarine design and construction. The government attempted to impose control over this interservice squabbling in November 1943 through the Munitions Company Act, which the Ministry of Munitions, the precursor of the Ministry of International Trade and Industry (MITI), was to enforce. Perhaps not surprisingly, these efforts failed. Munitions Minster Fujihara summarized it neatly after the war: "I was Munitions Minister but my function actually was that of conciliator between Army, Navy, and Air people." The actions of control councils (*toseikai*) created in 1941, intended to consolidate and manage strategic military industries, also undermined the efficient management of the economy itself. These councils were not effectively controlled by the larger industrial cartels (*zaibatsu*), the civilian government, or the military, and they ended up looking more like "ineffective, privately managed cartels" that undermined efficient production in key industries such as automobiles, rolling stock, and machine tools.[50]

Germany in World War II presents a more mixed case of bureaucratic fragmentation. Though German rearmament did proceed and accelerate in the 1930s, short-term time horizons and a lack of central coordination imposed from the top impeded its thoroughness, leaving it somewhat unprepared for the foes it met in 1939–1940. Early on, Hitler used a blitzkrieg strategy, hoping for a short war and forgoing long-term economic planning or mobilization (though he did call on sacrifices from the German consumer from the outset, as described above). Hitler decided to shift the German economy to full mobilization for a long war in early 1942, a decision that coincided with the death of Minister of Armaments and Munitions Fritz Todt and his succession by Albert Speer. Hitler gave Speer greater authority to manage the German economy and improve its efficiency; this in turn enabled Speer to impose greater rationalization on the economy, overcoming the inefficiencies that emerged in the early years of the war in part because industrial and military groups sought to protect their own interests.[51]

However, even after Speer's appointment, bureaucratic fragmentation driven by political pressures undermined efficiency and reduced maximum production. Speer clashed with Hermann Goering, head of the German Luftwaffe, or Air Force, while elsewhere Fritz Sauckel, plenipotentiary-general for labor in Nazi Germany, inhibited Speer's prerogatives and undermined centralized control. Inefficiencies were especially evident in the critical area of aircraft production, where bureaucratic infighting checked Speer's management prerogatives. Further, the SS maintained what amounted to its own economy within an economy, blocking the integration of an important chunk of German resources into the war effort. Another area of inefficiency driven by fragmentation was tank production. Troops in the field, the army's Ordnance Department, and the Ministry of Armaments all took responsibility for developing new tanks. The resulting wide array of types of armored vehicles meant inefficiencies in production, especially in maintenance operations and the supply of spare parts.[52]

The Soviet Union at the outset of World War II had, of course, a highly centralized command economy. We now believe that such centralization is a less preferred means of organizing an advanced industrialized economy. Nevertheless, a highly centralized economy can accomplish certain tasks effectively. Indeed, the disadvantages of a command economy in peacetime can become advantages in wartime. A command economy's rigidity, which is stifling in peacetime, becomes a useful means of rapid mobilization during war. The lack of a real economic market, whose absence undercuts dynamic growth in peacetime, facilitates the state's management of wages and prices in wartime as well as its ability to keep civilian consumption down while simultaneously directing surplus resources to munitions production and critical heavy industries.

During World War II, the Soviet economy exhibited some advantages of a command economy while shedding some of its disadvantages. As mentioned, the Soviet state was quite successful at mobilizing society for the war effort, depressing civilian consumption literally to the point of starvation. Additionally, the command economy facilitated the frantic movement of Soviet industry eastward in the first year of the war, safely behind the Ural Mountains and out of the reach of the initial German advances. On the political side, the bloody transformation of Soviet society under Stalin's purges had, for better or worse, left no significant competing interest groups in the USSR to challenge control of the economy and society from the top. This enabled Stalin to centrally coordinate the production of critical munitions, as he put single individuals in charge of important areas such as airplane and tank production. This helped the Soviets avoid the counterproductive competition between internal groups, such as the army-navy competition in imperial Japan.[53]

Interestingly, the command nature of Soviet economy and society permitted a modicum of much-needed flexibility. The Soviets' immediate need in 1941 was a dramatic increase in military production and the evacuation of Soviet industry to the east. In the first weeks of the war, the command apparatus was adapting too slowly to the crisis imposed by the Nazi invasion. A broad array of emergency measures imposed by individuals granted extensive powers by Moscow replaced the rigid planning then present with more flexible management systems. This new approach was successful, as it served to increase production and industrial evacuation, helped bring in the harvest from frontline regions, and mobilized the population to serve in the military and work for the war effort. The evacuation of industry from western areas of the Soviet Union to eastern regions as distant as Siberia was not completed, but it was successful enough to salvage a substantial portion of Soviet industry and stave off immediate economic collapse and defeat.[54]

Eventually this informal, frantic, and flexible effort led to overmobilization, as the economy focused too much on the production of war goods and not enough on critical civilian items such as food, transportation, steel, and power. The end of the military emergency in 1942 allowed Stalin's autocratic leadership to shift back toward formal, centralized control, which redirected the economy toward a more appropriate balance of priorities. This reimposition of central controls solved the most crucial bottleneck in production, the allocation of labor among industrial needs. In peacetime, the market may be most effective at shifting labor and other factors around toward the most profitable economic activities. In wartime, the needs of the military determine what the economy must produce, making central command of the economy a potentially effective approach. A market economy would be less efficient at producing the optimal mix of goods, as it would require extensive government decisions as to how to price various military goods to assure the right mix. This is not to say, however, that the Soviets imposed a complete command economy in 1942. Factory managers exercised significant discretion to obtain their inputs, and individuals often turned to the black market to obtain goods otherwise unavailable. This odd mix of formal and informal measures worked as an economic model for the Soviet Union. Industrial production recovered from the initial onslaught by late 1942, and Soviet factories began to produce munitions of high quality as well as quantity, such as the La-5-FN fighter aircraft, the Yak-9 dive-bomber, and the T-34 tank, the last of which many armor experts consider to be the best medium tank produced by any belligerent during the war.[55]

Of all the major belligerents in World War II, Britain developed perhaps the most effective economic planning effort. Britain faced critical economic problems, most notably extensive dependence on external economic relations with its trading partners and empire and steep economic demands for the financing of its war effort. To manage these material and financial scarcities, the British state intervened extensively in the management of the economy. As the war progressed, management of the economic side of the war effort became increasingly centralized. At the war's outset, there was an extensive committee system carrying over from the British style of government. When Churchill became prime minster in

May 1940, he streamlined the system down to five committees, reducing them further to three in early 1941. The British planning effort enjoyed success in managing labor relations, distributing resources appropriately within the economy, and exploiting technological advances because of government efforts that minimized bureaucratic infighting through centralization and enjoyed the admirable competence of its leaders at the highest levels.[56]

The American government enjoyed moderate effectiveness at managing the economic portion of the war effort, with management improving as fragmentation decreased throughout the war. The War Production Board (WPB) made its appearance in January 1942 to coordinate war production. Though the board made progress toward managing the various sectors and resources within the economy, it was limited in that its authority did not extend to labor. It also had to contend with independent ordnance departments within the three service branches of the armed forces. Central control improved in late 1942 with the adoption of the British-styled Controlled Material Plan, and in 1943, with the creation of the Office of War Mobilization, designed to act "as supreme umpire over the powerful" and expand executive control. The economy performed smoothest where there was centralized authority, as there was in the energy sector under Secretary of the Interior Harold Ickes.[57]

These observations are not to say that American economic planning during the war was free of inefficiencies. Residual fragmentation of authority led to problems. For example, in 1942 the WPB yielded too much power over production to the military services, which led to tremendous price inflation in military contracts and the misdirection of economic resources away from production of the most needed materials. Excessive fragmentation of authority also contributed to inefficiencies in the allocation of manpower. There was inadequate control and management of interservice clashes over allocation of manpower and resources, due in part to the weakness of the Joint Chiefs of the various service branches. The superior bureaucratic skills of the navy translated into allocation decisions that favored them arguably at the expense of the national interest, sacrificing other priorities such as manpower for the army and the merchant marine.[58]

Democracy, Technology, and Victory

One final point is worth addressing: the role of technology. Some might argue that democracies win wars because they possess and apply superior technology. Open societies that promote free discourse are likely to enjoy more progress in scientific and technological areas, as science thrives on

competition and the free exchange of ideas. These scientific and technological advances may in turn translate into success on the battlefield.[59] We
conducted some statistical tests of this proposition.[60] The HERO data set
described in chapter 3 provides codes of which side enjoyed technological superiority in a particular battle. Our tests using these data were
inconclusive, however. While democracies did enjoy superior levels of
technology, the HERO measures of technology do not correlate with
battlefield success. Hence, these results cannot be interpreted as supporting the proposition that democracies win battles (or wars) because they
have better levels of technology. Other studies that do find a relationship
between measures of technology and war outcomes at the same time find
no relationship between technology and level of democracy.[61]

The examination of individual wars demonstrates the shakiness of the
argument that democracies enjoy better technology and that better technology assures victory. Regarding the first point, consideration of the
wars of the twentieth century shows considerable variance. The United
States enjoyed superior technology over its adversaries in the Gulf War
and the Vietnam War (though it lost the latter), but Israel did not in its
wars with its Arab neighbors and certainly suffered inferiority in the 1973
Yom Kippur War.[62]

The outcomes of both world wars do not clearly reflect decisive military technology. In World War I, the Germans deployed poison gas first
and made use of the submarine, and the British were the first to deploy
the tank, but none of these proved decisive, as the war eventually wound
down when the Central Powers reached the point of exhaustion first.
During World War II, a number of novel technologies proved helpful in
accomplishing individual tasks. However, the development of new technologies was spread around to all the major belligerents. Britain developed radar; the United States developed the atomic bomb; Germany developed the jet aircraft, the missile, and the first submarine that did not
need to resurface to replenish its air; the Soviet Union developed the
T-34 tank; and Japan developed torpedoes designed for use in shallow
depths. In short, it appears that the historical record does not support the
claim that democracies win wars because they enjoy superior technology.

An Absent Democratic Advantage

The conventional wisdom is off the mark: democracies do not win wars
because they have stronger or more efficient economies. Specifically, this
chapter has demonstrated that:

- Democratic war belligerents do not have significantly larger economies
  than other war belligerents.

- Democracies do not extract more from their societies than other states, whether at war or peace.
- Democracies do not mobilize more of their populations into the armed forces than other states, whether at war or peace.
- Democracies do not provide their armies with significantly greater amounts of war materiel.
- Democracies do not provide their armies with significantly better technology.

These conclusions fly in the face of popular understanding of America's greatest strength in warfare: gargantuan economic might. Most think of America's arsenal of democracy sealing an Allied victory in World War II, overcoming fanaticism in the Japanese military and the superior professionalism of the German Wehrmacht and Luftwaffe.[63] This was, of course, an important part of the story, as the American economy had apparently limitless capacity, enabling victory on two fronts (West Europe and the Pacific) while fueling victory on a third (the Russian front). Nevertheless, we should not generalize based on this single case.

Our goal in this book is to move beyond the single case and to be able to generalize about political and social phenomena. Sometimes democratic states are able to win despite being materially overmatched: Israel accomplished a decisive six-day victory over its Arab neighbors in 1967 despite being outnumbered 1.3 to 1 in overall manpower, 2.4 to 1 in aircraft, 2.3 to 1 in tanks, and 4.8 to 1 in artillery pieces. Regarding the United States, we should not lose sight of the fact that its economic power does not always ensure victory. It could not overpower the weaker alliance of China and North Korea in the Korean War, it could not crush the Third World nation of North Vietnam, and it found victory along with its NATO confreres over Serbia in the War for Kosovo surprisingly difficult.[64] Perhaps most notably, the singular economic power of the United States after 1945 is a historical outlier among democratic states, as broad empirical surveys using advanced statistical techniques have cast doubt on the proposition that democracies are more prosperous or that they can allocate more resources toward defense. Lastly, Germany, Japan, and Italy may have lost the battle of the factories in World War II, but this was not, contrary to the theoretical speculation, due to constraints on mobilization driven by fear of the public reaction: these governments squeezed the life out of their populations to support their leaders' imperial dreams.

This null relationship should not be too surprising. An alternative and more accurate picture regarding resource extraction is that democratic leaders fear that fighting wars may endanger their domestic political support. This fear then creates incentives for democratic leaders to minimize the costs of war borne by the population both in terms of economic costs and in terms of lives lost. As we might expect, democracies tend to fight in shorter wars than wars between autocrats (see chapter 7), they suffer fewer casualties when they start wars, and they tend to choose maneuver-based military strategies that promise shorter, less bloody wars.[65]

Thus far, we have found evidence favoring two of our general propositions, and evidence against two other propositions. Democracies do seem to win wars because they are cautious when deciding when to initiate war, and because their soldiers, drawn from the ranks of a participatory society, outfight autocratic armies. Conversely, democracies do not win wars because they band together during war, nor because they enjoy systematic economic advantages. These four findings have moved us a long way toward answering the question posed in chapter 1: Why do democracies win wars? In the next chapter we move to a somewhat different and perhaps more pressing question that flows from the findings in chapter 2, that democracies rarely, if ever, start wars they cannot win: When and why do democracies start wars?

Appendix 5.1: Statistical Analysis of Democracy and the Economic Determinants of Victory

This appendix includes discussion of the statistical analysis used for this chapter. The first analysis concerns whether democracies win wars because they have larger economies. Our data set is the same as that used in chapter 2: participants in all wars from 1816 to 1990. We use an array of dependent variables, each of which measures the economic capabilities of states in different ways. First, we use the same Capabilities measure used in chapter 2. This score is built by first averaging the systemic share each state has of six measures of military-industrial capability, including energy consumption, iron and steel production, military personnel, military expenditures, total population, and urban population. Each state, then, receives a systemic share score ranging from 0 to 1, and then this score is divided by itself plus the systemic share score of the opponent, providing a measure of the state's capability in relation to the capability of its opponent. Our other measures of capability include the state's energy consumption, measured in coal-ton equivalents, and iron and steel production.[66] For both we use the state's share as a fraction of the total of all war participants. Though we would like to use a measure of gross domestic product (GDP), data become scarce for older cases. The composite capabilities index is highly collinear with states' GDP. Additionally, energy consumption, however, is a useful proxy for GDP as it is theoretically appropriate and data are more widely available for older cases.[67] Our principal independent variable is a state's level of democracy, for which we use the -10 to $+10$ scale (where higher scores indicate a more democratic state) described in chapter 2. We also use a variety of control variables, including whether or not the state was the war initiator (as states that initiate are more likely to have greater capabilities, as in general they select themselves into wars they can win).

Our first set of regression results is presented in table 5.1.

These findings indicate that among war participants, democracies do not possess significantly greater economic capabilities; specifically, they do not have significantly higher scores on the aggregate capability index, nor do they have higher levels of energy consumption or iron and steel production. The results do not change if we restrict the analysis to only those states that have won wars.[68]

A second possibility discussed is that democracies are more powerful only among initiators. Table 5.2 explores this possibility, reanalyzing the determinants of capability among war initiators only.

Table 5.2 is evidence against this selection effects speculation. Democratic initiators do not enjoy significantly higher capability levels, whether the dependent variable is Capability Ratio, Energy Consumption, or Iron and Steel production. This increases our confidence that we can reject two hypotheses: that democracies in general win wars because they have higher capabilities, and that democratic initiators win wars because they have significantly higher capabilities than do other kinds of initiators.

A third test discussed in the chapter concerns whether democracies mobilize more of their populations into the military. We test this hypothesis using Correlates of War data for all nation-states from 1816 to 1992.[69] The dependent variable is the number of troops divided by the total population for a particular state in a given year. The principal independent variable is the regime type of a state. This variable is the -10 to $+10$ measure we described in chapter 2, where more democratic nations receive higher scores. Major powers are likely to face more external threats, leading them to put a higher percentage of the population under arms; we include a state's major power status as a dichotomous control variable. We also expect that a state involved in war will have a higher fraction of its population under arms; we include a state's participation in an interstate war in the year in question as an additional dichotomous control variable, coded 1 if the state is a participant and 0 otherwise. Lastly, we expect that states with higher troop quality will need smaller armies; we measure troop quality by dividing total military expenditures by number of troops, affording a dollar per troop measure. We expect the coefficients for Polity, War, and Major Power to be positive, and the coefficient for Troop Quality to be negative.[70]

We use ordinary least squares to analyze these data, assuming AR-1

TABLE 5.1
Regression Analysis of Determinants of Economic Capability among All War
Participants, 1816–1990

Dependent Variable	Model 1 Capability Index	Model 2 Energy Consumption	Model 3 Iron and Steel Production
Democracy	0.00012	0.00062	0.000090
	(0.00096)	(0.0015)	(0.0010)
Initiation	0.21***	0.30***	0.37***
	(0.053)	(0.068)	(0.065)
Constant	0.28***	0.26***	0.20***
	(0.026)	(0.033)	(0.026)
n	234	139	222
r-squared	0.11	0.17	0.22

Note: Coefficient estimates, with robust standard errors (clustering on individual wars) reported in parentheses.
***Significant at 0.001 level, one-tailed test.

temporal autocorrelation and no cross-sectional autocorrelation. We also use panel corrected standard errors.[71] Table 5.3 provides the empirical results.

Model 1 provides analysis of the three independent variables described above. Democracy is significantly related to the fraction of the population mobilized for war, but in the opposite direction predicted by the

TABLE 5.2
Regression Analysis of Determinants of Economic Capability among War
Initiators, 1816–1990

Dependent Variable	Model 1 Capability Ratio	Model 2 Energy Consumption	Model 3 Iron and Steel Production
Democracy	−0.00068	−0.00016	−0.0012
	(0.0015)	(0.0020)	(0.0016)
Constant	0.48***	−0.55***	0.56***
	(0.041)	(0.051)	(0.052)
n	101	61	96
r-squared	0.0021	0.0001	0.0004

Note: Coefficient estimates are reported, with standard errors in parentheses.
***Significant at 0.001 level.
All significance tests one-tailed.

TABLE 5.3
Time Series Analysis of Determinants of Military Mobilization, 1816–1992

Variable	Model 1	Model 2	Model 3
Democracy	− 0.000087	− 0.000077	− 0.000085
	(0.000035) ••	(0.000032) ••	(0.000035) ••
Major Power	0.014	0.010	0.014
	(0.0013)***	(0.0010)***	(0.0013)***
War	0.00085	—	0.00080
	(0.00041)*		(0.00041)*
Troop Quality	− 5.2e-09	− 5.1e-09	− 5.2e-09
	(2.0e-09)***	(2.0e-09)**	(2.0e-09)**
Polity*War	—	—	− 0.000066
			(0.000057)
MID	—	0.00057	—
		(0.00016)***	
Constant	0.0063	0.0065	0.0063
	(0.00054)***	(0.00040)***	(0.00055)***
Pr > Chi2	0.0000	0.0000	0.0000

Note: Cell entries are coefficient estimates, and panel-corrected standard errors are in parentheses. For all three models, there were 152 groups and 177 time periods, yielding 8,140 observations (cases with missing data were dropped).
*Statistically significant at the 0.05 level.
**Statistically significant at the 0.01 level.
•• Statistically significant at the 0.01 level, but not in the predicted direction.
***Statistically significant at the 0.001 level.

extraction power hypothesis. That is, democracies appear to have significantly lower fractions of their population in the armed forces. This is not consistent with the argument that democracies are more effective at extracting resources from their people, but rather with the view that democracies need to maintain popular consent for a war effort, which then sharply limits the levels of sacrifices democracies are able to sustain, during both peace and war. Participation in war, troop quality, and major power status are all significantly related, in the predicted directions.[72] Model 2 is the same as Model 1, though with a state's participation in a militarized interstate dispute exchanged for a state's participation in war, during the year in question.[73] The MID variable is significant, but the results on a state's polity type do not change.

One possible interpretation of these results is that they unjustifiably combine military mobilization during peacetime and wartime. It may be that democracies do not put more people under arms during peacetime, but they definitely do so during wartime. Model 3 gets at this hypothesis, by including an interaction term of war participation in the year in question times the state's −10 to 10 Polity score. If democracies are particularly effective at mobilizing during wartime, then this variable ought to be significant and positive; however, it is neither.

We can provide an even better test of the idea that democracies mobilize an especially large proportion of their populations during wartime, by reducing the scope of analysis to just war belligerents. This reduces any bias that might be introduced by including states at peace, as among these one could argue that democracies would need to spend proportionately less on the military than autocrats who rely, in part, on the military to maintain domestic order and power. Narrowing the scope of the test also permits the inclusion of more control variables. For this test, we use the same dependent variable (total number of military troops divided by total population) and the same Polity variable. We also use a number of variables described in chapters 2 and 3 to test the sources of victory. Specifically, we include troop quality; this may be inversely related to troop mobilization, as higher-quality troops may reduce the need for high numbers of troops. We also include allied assistance, as more allies may reduce the need for mobilizing society. We also code whether the belligerent is the initiator, which may have chosen to fight because it can mobilize more of its population. We include a state's total military industrial capabilities, as it may be inversely related to its need for troops. The regression results are displayed in table 5.4.

Model 1 of table 5.4 indicates that democratic war participants do not mobilize significantly greater fractions of their population into the military than other kinds of states. Model 2 performs the same analysis, confining the sample to initiators of war. Here too, democratic initiators do not mobilize more of their populations into the military than do other kinds of states. We explored the robustness of this result by using a different dependent variable, the percentage of revenue each state spends on its military. Model 3 analyzes all war participants and Model 4 examines all war initiators; in neither sample do democracies devote a significantly higher percentage of government revenue to the military.[74]

An alternative explanation might be that while democracies and autocracies divert roughly the same amount of resources to the military, democracies may be more effective at translating economic investment into actual military resources. Corruption may significantly undercut the ability of autocratic states to convert economic resources into military power. The implication is that in terms of the bottom line of tanks, planes, and guns available to field commanders, democracies may therefore enjoy an advantage over autocracies because they do not suffer from corruption.

One way to test this speculation is to look at actual tallies of equipment available to armies on the battlefield. We use the HERO data set described in chapter 3, which lists all major battles. In addition to provid-

TABLE 5.4
Regression Analysis of Democratic Military Mobilization for War Belligerents,
1816–1990

	Model 1	Model 2	Model 3	Model 4
Dependent Variable	Percent of Pop. in Military	Percent of Pop. in Military	Percent of Rev. to Military	Percent of Rev. to Military
Sample	All Belligerents	Initiators Only	All Belligerents	Initiators Only
Democracy	−0.000093	0.000049	0.00014	−0.00034
	(0.00011)	(0.000040)	(0.00054)	(0.00047)
Troop Quality	−0.00016**	−0.00029**	−0.00086	−0.0018
	(0.000056)	(0.00012)	(0.0014)	(0.0011)
Allies	−0.0071	−0.018	0.0051	0.0055
	(0.0053)	(0.011)	(0.048)	(0.075)
Initiator	0.0042*	—	−0.00027	—
	(0.0025)		(0.021)	
Capabilities	−0.0020	−0.0032	−0.013	−0.054
	(0.0048)	(0.010)	(0.036)	(0.058)
Constant	0.015***	0.022**	0.31***	0.33***
	(0.0030)	(0.0077)	(0.024)	(0.041)
n	233	101	129	61
r-squared	.034	.045	.005	.045

Note: Table entries are coefficient estimates; robust standard errors (clustered on wars) are in parentheses. All significance tests are one tailed.
*Significant at .05 level.
**Significant at .01 level.
***Significant at .001 level.

ing scores on intangible factors such as morale and initiative, the HERO data set also provides measures of available equipment. Each case is one side's army in a battle (such as the German Army in the Battle of the Bulge). We use three different measures for dependent variables: number of tanks, number of artillery pieces, and number of air sorties (missions) flown. Our independent variable is a state's level of democracy; for this we use the −10 to +10 Polity score we have relied on in earlier chapters. Since the dependent variable is a count rather than a normally distributed variable, we use negative binomial regression (chi-squared tests showed that Poisson models were not indicated). We also use robust standard errors as we suspect correlation within battles and wars, clustering on the individual battle.

For the tanks and air sorties variables, we use only post-1914 battles; for artillery pieces, we use all battles from 1800. Note that this substan-

TABLE 5.5

Negative Binomial Regression of Democracy and the Quantity of Tanks,
Artillery Pieces, and Air Sorties in Battles, 1800–1982

Time Period	Tanks 1914–1982	Air Sorties 1914–1982	Artillery Pieces 1800–1982
Polity	−0.018	−0.040	−0.049•
	(0.011)	(0.035)	(0.016)
Constant	5.0***	5.6***	6.2***
	(0.11)	(0.34)	(0.12)
Prob>chi2	0.088	0.24	0.0019
n	602	399	800
Log likelihood	−3096	−1856	−5443

Note: Negative binomial regression used, with robust standard errors clustering on the individual battle.
***Significant at the .001 level, two-tailed test.
•Significant at the .01 level, two-tailed test, but the sign is not in the predicted direction.

tially biases the test toward finding in favor of the democratic extraction advantage hypothesis, because the data set is heavily skewed toward the inclusion of World War II battles, the leading example of a war in which democratic belligerents (U.S./Britain) defeated autocratic belligerents (Japan/Germany/Italy) with superior materiel and firepower. The results are indicated in table 5.5.

Democracy is negatively correlated with all three indicators, contrary to the proposed relationship, but it is statistically significant only for artillery pieces. This is strong evidence supporting the null hypothesis that democracy is not positively correlated with higher amounts of war materiel available to armies in the field. This result is robust, in that the coefficients remain insignificant if we instead use the one-battle-per-war sample also used in chapter 3, or we use the complete data set of 1800 forward for tanks and air sorties.

SIX

DEMOCRACY, CONSENT, AND THE PATH TO WAR

Public opinion in this country is everything.
—Abraham Lincoln

THUS FAR, the focus in this book has been on why democracies win wars. We have found that democracies emerge victorious because they start winnable wars and because their soldiers fight with higher military effectiveness. We have also demonstrated that democracies do not win wars because their economies are stronger or because they join together when one is attacked.

What do these findings tell us about the origins of war? Specifically, what can we say about when democracies start wars and when they do not? Our earlier chapters provide some purchase on this question. From chapter 2 we know that democracies almost always start only those wars they will go on to win. This is an important factor that distinguishes democracies from autocracies: members of the latter group are more prone to engage in risky foreign policy behavior and therefore more likely to stumble into wars that eventually turn out disastrously. From chapter 4 we also know that democracies do not enter wars in order to rescue other democracies, indicating the weakness of the sense of community among democracies.

In this chapter, we explore more deeply why democracies start wars. We do this by building on the selection effects framework presented in chapter 2. There, we made the simple proposition that democracies are different because their institutional structures force leaders to be concerned with maintaining the consent of the governed. From this, we found that democracies win the wars they start because the fear of the domestic political consequences of fighting a losing war pushes elected leaders to start only winnable wars.

Focusing on consent can also explain the connection between democracy and the initiation of war. We argue here that consent holds the key to understanding when and why democracies initiate wars: Democratic decisions for war are determined and constrained by public consent. We further propose that democratic publics are not necessarily pacific. They sometimes consent to the use of force for the advance of empire, for the brutal repression of weaker peoples, and even against other democracies.

This is not an uncontroversial claim. An alternative perspective on democracy and the initiation of war focuses on norms of behavior rather than consent. Holding that democratic political culture emphasizes the peaceful resolution of disputes, it proposes that democracies are generally averse to the use of force in their foreign policies and only resort to force defensively as a means of protection.

Which of these perspectives better characterizes democratic foreign policy-making? Are democratic governments at the mercy of public whims, whether their peoples cower from confrontation or scream for blood and national glory? Or, are democratic governments guided by a set of cultural norms that steer them away from the use of force except as a last resort? Our argument is that the former of these statements is more true: for better or worse, democratic foreign policy is driven by public desires rather than by a fundamental pacifism. Our aim is to demonstrate the broad validity of a focus on consent: that it explains both when democracies initiate wars and why they initiate them. In the next chapter, we show that concern for consent also shapes how democracies fight wars, namely, with the aim of early termination.

Consent and the Initiation of War

The center of the selection effects argument presented in chapter 2 is a focus on the importance of consent. Elected leaders are more dependent on public consent than are autocrats, though the latter are not completely insulated from the public will. As a result, democracies avoid risky military ventures and win those wars that they start.

This specific proposition contains a more general assumption about democratic foreign policy-making, namely, that democratic leaders are sensitive to the demands of citizens. This general assumption has more traditionally been applied toward understanding the connection between democracy and the causes of war. An early interpretation of this assumption was that democracies ought to be, in general, less likely to become involved in wars. Immanuel Kant made this point late in the eighteenth century: "If . . . the consent of the citizens is required to decide whether or not war is to be declared, it is very natural that they will have great hesitation in embarking on so dangerous an enterprise. For this would mean calling down on themselves all the miseries of war. . . . But under a constitution where the subject is not a citizen, and which is therefore not republican, it is the simplest thing in the world to go to war."[1]

Several scholars have used Kant's claim that democratic governments are dependent on public consent to generate explanations of the democratic peace—the observation that democracies rarely fight each other—relying on a variety of methodologies and intermediate assumptions.[2]

Not everyone, however, has reached Kant's conclusion, that the need to generate popular consent forces democracies to be necessarily more pacific. The *Federalist Papers*, for example, stressed the common tendency of both republics and monarchies to wage war. Of parliamentary Britain Alexander Hamilton declared that "Few nations, nevertheless, have been more frequently engaged in war; and the wars in which that kingdom has been engaged have, in numerous instances, proceeded from the people."[3]

An important assumption of this perspective is that consent cannot be easily manufactured by democratic leaders. If democratic leaders could manipulate public opinion into supporting military ventures, then of course public opinion would provide little constraint on democratic foreign policy, as it could be actively molded to support the foreign policy aims of the leadership. The open marketplace of ideas in democracies helps undercut fallacious claims made by leaderships about foreign threats, however, reducing the ability of leaders to shape public opinion. In contrast, authoritarian leaders have an easier time controlling the flow of information to create an unchallenged image of the enemy.[4] Though democratic leaders can sometimes shift public opinion at the margins, in general it is more accurate to think of the public as controlling the actions of its elected leaders rather than dancing on strings pulled by the leadership as puppet master. The findings in chapter 2 are evidence to this effect, indicating that it is very difficult for a democratically elected leadership to hoodwink the public into sanctioning a risky military venture. Relatedly, there appears to be little support for the existence of the infamous "Wag the Dog" phenomenon, that mere participation in war automatically rallies public support for the leadership.[5] Democratic leaders seem to recognize this, as leaders generally do not resort to force when their own popularity levels are low as a means of diverting public attention away from domestic problems.[6]

An orientation on consent pushes us to ask this question: When does the public offer its consent to initiate a war for the protection of national security? Or, more broadly, what is the public conception of what the national security requires? If we can understand the conditions under which publics are likely to give their consent for war, then we will be able to forecast when democracies launch attacks.

There is, of course, a long tradition of skepticism about the public's abilities to make judgments about foreign policy issues. Alexis de Tocqueville, that great observer of the democratic experiment in early America, was frankly concerned that democratic political institutions would constitute a potentially crippling handicap on the conduct of foreign policy. These critiques were renewed in the twentieth century, when observers such as George Kennan and Walter Lippmann looked back in disgust at the inability of the Western democracies to recognize and confront the rising fascist threat in the 1930s in Europe and Asia. With Germany bent literally on global domination, the argument goes, popular opposition to international involvement helped create the image of a myopic public that failed to recognize very real threats to national security.[7]

These criticisms of the alleged shortsightedness of American public opinion and the supposed vulnerability of democratic foreign policy to the vagaries of public opinion are overblown. Most during this period underestimated the nature of the German threat. Even Joseph Stalin, the definitive modern paranoid, underestimated the German threat up until the actual German attack on the Soviet Union in June 1941, having ignored dozens of warnings and intelligence reports about the likelihood of German invasion.[8]

For Americans, the true nature of the threat posed by the Axis to the United States was uncertain until December 1941. In the minds of many, the two oceans still presented substantial moats protecting North America. Before the Japanese attack on Pearl Harbor in 1941, the strategic significance of the aircraft carrier group had not been demonstrated; amphibious warfare had not been vindicated since the disasters at Gallipoli in 1915; and long-range bombers had yet to fly, to say nothing of the coming development of German missile technology. Of course, submarine warfare threatened maritime commerce, but the level of the submarine threat was inversely correlated to one's adherence to neutrality. Most importantly for those advocating isolation, submarines could not carry invasion forces or deliver bombs.

Regarding the intentions of the Axis powers, they too were uncertain at the outset of World War II. While Japan obviously had imperial designs on East Asia and the West Pacific, prior to war's outbreak no one thought it intended to attack North America. President Franklin Roosevelt was personally stunned that the Japanese attack came as far east as Pearl Harbor. In Europe, the situation appeared more complex to the main protagonists than it seems today in retrospect. In September 1939 the American ambassador to Britain, Joseph Kennedy, called on Roosevelt to negotiate a peace following the German conquest of Poland, and that autumn, Hitler called for peace negotiations to stop the war. As late as 1941, it was not clear whether the real threat to the United States was from Germany or the Soviet Union. Then U.S. Senator Harry S. Truman publicly remarked in June 1941 after the German invasion of Russia: "If we see that Germany is winning we ought to help Russia and if Russia is winning we ought to help Germany and that way let them kill as many as possible."[9]

In short, then, the 1930s experience does not necessarily indicate that constraining foreign policy to public opinion is dangerous, both because Western leaders were also unwilling to confront the rising fascist threat and because from the standpoint of the time the actual nature of the threat remained uncertain. More generally, modern political science research has refuted the traditional view of public opinion as being irrational and erratic, portraying it instead as being relatively stable and reacting relatively predictably to changes in the policy environment.[10]

This does not close the discussion, however, as there is great variability among democracies in different eras as to the conditions that are sufficient to generate public consent for the use of force against some other state. Put differently, what is a reasonable cause for war for one public may not be reasonable for another. Public opinion has ranged widely from being supportive of imperialism and colonialism (Britain, France, and the United States at the end of the nineteenth century) to being unwilling to consent to war even at reasonable odds to forestall a very real and imminent threat to national security (Britain and France unwilling to confront Germany in 1936 and 1938). The public has also been occasionally willing to follow what seems in hindsight to be rather specious logic about the needs of national security (for example, the American public accepting domino theory as a justification for intervention in Vietnam).[11]

The central factor determining whether a public will consent to war is its definition of the national interest. A very narrow definition of the national interest will imply a short list of circumstances under which a public will consent to initiating war. A more expansive definition of the national interest will imply a longer list of such circumstances. One important factor determining a public's sense of national interest is national power. Publics of great powers are more likely to consent to war under a larger range of circumstances, recognizing that a great power has more extended security interests than does a minor power. As American economic power grew after the Civil War, the national sense of great power status spread, culminating in the 1890s with public consent for participation in the Spanish-American War, the War in the Philippines, and the Boxer Rebellion.[12]

Power, however, is not a complete determinant of the nature of public consent. Other factors determine the conditions under which a public will consent to war. For example, higher levels of external threat are likely to encourage the public to grant consent under a wide range of conditions. The high degree of threat Israel faces means the government knows there are a wide range of conditions under which the government knows it can initiate war with public consent. Specifically, since independence Israel has initiated three wars, in 1956, 1967, and 1982. In contrast, publics in states facing relatively low levels of threat—such as Switzerland—are unlikely to consent to war frequently.

Another important factor affecting the nature of public consent is a state's past history. An inclination to isolation or international engagement is frequently strongly driven by a state's past experiences. For example, America's seesawing between isolation and engagement in the twentieth century is frequently attributed to differing experiences that speak either to the hollow rewards of internationalism or the dangers of isolation. These dynamics are present among small powers, as well. In the twentieth century, minor powers' proclivities to join alliances—significantly, alliance membership is a literal expression of public consent, as alliance treaties lay out conditions under which the members bind themselves to go to war—have been strongly determined by their experiences during the world wars.[13]

This sketch of public opinion allows for the initiation of war to advance a variety of national interests. Democratic publics do recognize that the initiation of war is sometimes necessary to advance their states' national interests, even under a conception of national interest that reaches beyond direct threats to the security of the homeland. The American interventions in Korea, Vietnam, and Kuwait all enjoyed wide public support, as did the British action in the Falklands. This is not to say that in hindsight the public always makes the wisest choices. The American involvement in South Vietnam is a prominent example of a case where it appears in retrospect that American national interests were not truly at stake. Nevertheless, democratic publics are willing to support military action abroad when they feel that the national interest is involved.

Democracy, Nonviolent Norms, and the Initiation of War

The main theoretical proposition found throughout this book is that we can best understand democratic foreign policy by focusing on the leadership's institutional dependence on public consent. However, this is but one perspective on democratic foreign policy-making. A different outlook focuses on the policy makers' personal norms of behavior rather than institutionally created demand for public consent.[14] Some scholars speculate that the best way to characterize liberal democratic political culture is to focus on policy makers acting on the basis of shared and peaceful norms of conflict resolution. In democracies, so goes the characterization, if some group desires political change, it engages in nonviolent actions such as open debate, participation in the political process, or litigation in the courts as a means of furthering its agenda. In contrast, in authoritarian states political actors must use violent means, such as open repression of dissent, coup d'état, or revolution.

From this initial assumption about the political behavior within states, some speculate that these norms of nonviolent conflict resolution found among the nation's leaders percolate into the country's foreign policy behavior. Specifically, this norms orientation predicts that democracies are reluctant to resolve conflicts violently in international relations. Instead, they rely on nonviolent means of dispute resolution, such as negotiation, the submission of disputes to international tribunals, and the invitation of third-party arbitrators. The boldest proposition emerging from the norms-based argument is that these nonviolent norms account for the fact that democracies apparently do not fight each other. The norms argument accounts for the occurrence of wars between democracies and nondemocracies by explaining that democracies may use force defensively, specifically in reaction to or anticipation of the use of force by a nondemocratic adversary.[15]

We believe, however, that the norms-based explanation of democratic foreign policy is more a caricature than an accurate characterization. It turns out, if we carefully review the historical record, that there is little empirical evidence consistent with the normative explanation of why democracies initiate wars. When liberal democracies initiate the use of force (as described in chapter 2), defensive motivations, as envisioned by the normative explanation, rarely drive the democrats' attacks on autocrats or oligarchs. Indeed, Israel in 1967 is perhaps the *only* example of a democracy launching a defensive preemptive war, and no democratic great power has ever launched a preventive war.[16]

In stark contrast to the normative view's emphasis on peaceful conflict resolution, democratic leaders sometimes recognize that the pursuit of their state's national interests may require them to go to war even when the adversary otherwise might be willing to offer complete political capitulation. For example, after Iraq's 1990 invasion of Kuwait, the Bush administration recognized that the problem they faced was not just the loss of Kuwaiti sovereignty, but also the relative regional dominance of Iraqi military power. In a meeting in August of that year, Bush and his advisers recognized that war would be necessary to destroy Iraqi military assets, in particular their weapons of mass destruction. As a result, a complete and immediate Iraqi withdrawal from Kuwait would be a strategic disaster for the United States, as it would leave the Iraqi threat in the Persian Gulf region intact. At the time, Bush stated it blackly: "We have to have a war." Bush's bellicose attitude did not change even as Iraq's deteriorating strategic position on the ground led Hussein to consider accepting a negotiated solution to end the crisis. Bush felt a deep sense of relief following the failure of the U.S. State Department's final diplomatic effort for peace at a January 9, 1991, meeting between American Secretary of State James Baker and Iraqi Foreign Minister Tariq Aziz. President Bush's emphatic desire for war also pushed the American administration to reject Iraqi peace offers in February. At the time, Bush told General Colin Powell, "If they crack under force, it is better than withdrawal."[17]

To illustrate the mechanisms of our consent model, in the next two sections of this chapter we describe several cases in which democracies initiated the use of organized military force. In each case, a democracy initiated forceful action against a less powerful state or society. Further, in each of the cases, the democracies' target in question is at least quasi-democratic. Each of these cases presents a strong challenge to the pacific norms story of democratic foreign policy. The instances of the use of force between democracies we present are not isolated examples either; another study found that between 1974 and 1991 alone there were 51 instances in which one democracy employed overt military pressure to influence the policies or practices of another democracy.[18] The initiation or threat of force by one democracy against another is particularly puzzling for the normative explanation. Recall that the norms explanation proposes that in the case of conflicts between democracies, nonviolent means of conflict resolution, best characterized by compromise and mutual respect for sovereignty, should prevail. The consent model we propose does not assume that it would be impossible to generate consent for the use of force in one democracy against another and hence can better explain the forceful actions taken by one democracy against other democracies described below.

Imperial Wars

The first class of conflicts we will look at in detail includes wars of empire. These are wars where the belligerent's primary motivation was the expansion of its economic and political spheres of influence for reasons other than immediate national defense. Democracies that initiate such wars offer particularly compelling evidence against the normative explanation. The essential parts of the norms explanation argue that democracies engage in wars out of fear of exploitation by nondemocratic states. However, the initiation of wars of empire against weaker states to expand democracy's interests and influence at the expense of weaker societies is inexplicable from the liberal norms perspective. The contemporaneous consent model, on the other hand, can better account for wars fought over a variety of stakes, including aggressive, imperialist wars. Imperialist wars are likely to be against small, relatively weak, and technologically unsophisticated opponents. As a result, in a democracy initiating such a war, both the political elite and the general public will see victory to be likely, at low cost, and in short order.

What makes imperial wars especially disturbing to the liberal conscience is that they demonstrate also that it is easier to generate public consent if the target is racially or ethnically different from the attacker. While it may sound a bit trite, for most people, killing other people is a fundamentally difficult thing to do, and it requires overcoming a deeply ingrained natural human aversion. People are far more willing to accept and implement the use of deadly force against other peoples if their leaders demonize the potential target, making the target's citizens seem less than human. During the Pacific War, an imperial war that escalated into part of the Axis' global war for world domination, subhuman images of the enemy on both the American and Japanese sides contributed to particularly brutal combat conditions. It was under these conditions, framed by racially tinged images, that surrendering soldiers were shot, corpses mutilated, prisoners of war tortured and executed, captured women sexually enslaved by military officers, and hundreds of thousands of civilians incinerated in bombing raids that culminated in the first and only use of atomic weapons in combat.[19] Clearly, however, Japan in 1941 was not a democracy, nor did the United States initiate the war. Next, we discuss three wars of empire initiated by the United States against foes that were racially different and at least quasi-democratic.

The American Assault on the Cherokee Nation

The willingness of the United States government to use deadly force to carry out a broad program of relocation and extirpation of the Native American nations in the nineteenth century provides a powerful example of democracy demonstrating a complete lack of pacific norms. Many of these Native American nations were organized around democratic principles of governance; indeed, ideas of democracy among some Native American tribes powerfully affected and contributed to the evolution of democracy in the United States of America. However, a sense of white racial superiority, thought by many at the time to be grounded in unavoidable biological differences, permeated the dominant white American view of the Indians. Leaders and mass publics alike believed that the expansion of the American state and economy required the evacuation of Native Americans from areas throughout North America to provide living space for white settlers. The United States government's actions toward Native American nations are a far cry from the patterns of respect for law and negotiations envisioned by the normative model. Instead, U.S. behavior included consistent and routine violation of treaties, military aggression, and the massacre of both warriors and innocents, including women and children.[20]

The United States government's dealings with the Cherokee nation in the early nineteenth century provide a particularly compelling example of publicly debated and accepted national interest motivating policy that completely ignored any norms of nonviolent conflict resolution or respect for legal contracts and negotiations with other democracies. By 1820 the Cherokee nation was a cohesive and established group of Native Americans located within the American state of Georgia with firmly established democratic political procedures and its own constitution based on the American model. As with so many other Native American nations, the existence of the Cherokee nation blocked one avenue of the economic and demographic advance of the United States and white Americans. In the 1820s the state of Georgia demanded that the Cherokee people recognize its sovereignty over them. Individual Georgians took it upon themselves to seize and destroy Cherokee property and to commit atrocities against members of the Cherokee nation. The Cherokees responded by taking their case to court, appealing ultimately to the U.S. Supreme Court, which ruled in their favor in 1832. The majority wrote, "The Cherokee Nation, then, is a distinct community occupying its own territory, with boundaries accurately described, in which the laws of Georgia have no force, and which the citizens of Georgia have no right to enter, but with the assent of the Cherokees themselves, or in conformity with the treaties, and with the acts of Congress. The whole intercourse of the United States and this Nation, is, by our Constitution and laws, vested in the government of the United States."[21]

President Andrew Jackson, a president cut from the populist bolt rather than the Jeffersonian republican cloth, believed that ignoring Indian claims to sovereignty both was in the U.S. national interest and was supported by popular consent. After the Supreme Court handed down its decision, Jackson highlighted the court's absent enforcement capacity with the challenge, "John Marshall has made his decision, now let him enforce it." Georgians needed no more hint from the executive branch: they proceeded to ignore the court and dismantle the Cherokee nation. United States Army soldiers eventually forcibly evicted the remaining Cherokees, condemning them to exile in the Far West via the brutal "Trail of Tears."[22]

The Spanish-American War

A second instance of popularly driven democratic imperialism is the Spanish-American War. The American president William McKinley took office in 1897 without a strong imperialist agenda. McKinley ran for office on a proposed program to improve the domestic economy, with a particular focus on big business. In particular, he did not ride to power on a promise to wrest the colony of Cuba from the tyrannical hands of the Spanish at all costs. McKinley did recognize differences between American and Spanish interests over Cuba and its growing rebellion, and he worked with some success using diplomatic means to push for reforms in Cuba diplomacy in 1897. However, the publication of the insults to President McKinley in the Dupuy de Lôme letter and the sinking of the American battleship *Maine* in February 1898 touched off an unquenchable fever for war among the American public, which grew in no small part from a widespread and popular desire for overseas empire. Scholars have proposed a number of arguments as to what fed the popular hunger for war and empire in the late 1890s: desire for economic expansion into new world markets, new ideas about the importance of seapower, the end of the frontier in North America, and genuine outrage over human rights abuses in Cuba. Regardless of which combination of these factors best explains the popular demand or whether the yellow press reflected opinion or created public bellicosity, the lust for war and empire was unmistakable. Anti-imperial figures tried in vain to counsel for peace. Speaker of the House Thomas Reed bitterly scoffed at the notion of stemming the calls for war, claiming that one might as well "step out in the middle of a Kansas wasteland and dissuade a cyclone!" Young men throughout America ran to enlistment offices in droves. Volunteer numbers exceeded recruitment needs and the army's ability to absorb the rapidly expanding ranks by over 100,000 men. Teddy Roosevelt physically commandeered a vessel in Florida to ensure that his Rough Riders would be present when the American fleet sailed for Cuba.[23]

The Spanish-American War demonstrates how public consent, enacted through the people's demands for immediate action, can trump norms of peaceful consultation and compromise. The Spanish presented no direct threat to American national security (it was all the Spanish could do to fight back a colonial insurgency), and they had made a number of concessions in talks with McKinley over Cuba, including accepting decrees of autonomy in Cuba, granting amnesty to Cuban political prisoners, and releasing Americans held in Cuban jails. Consistent with the predictions of pacific norms theory, on the eve of war, the Spaniards agreed to an armistice with the Cuban rebels, using a third-party negotiator (the Pope) to make the critical concessions.[24] The use of a third-party negotiator is particularly interesting, as a central prediction of the normative model is that democracies are open to the use of third parties to help resolve conflicts and avert war.[25] Also noteworthy is that in 1898 the Spanish political system had democratic elements including universal male suffrage and a bicameral legislature, though it was by no means an advanced, deeply democratic system.[26] However, contrary to the predictions of the normative explanation, neither the democratic trappings of the Spanish political system, nor the absence of any real threat to American national security, nor a series of political concessions on the Cuba issue, nor the use of a third-party mediator to resolve the conflict could dam the tidal wave of American public opinion demanding war against Spain over Cuba. Two months following the explosion of the USS *Maine*'s steam boiler, the United States declared war against Spain.

The American War in the Philippines

The end of the war against Spain brought the opportunity for the annexation of the Philippines. American troops were present on the ground in Manila and elsewhere in the Philippines, and McKinley decided to move for annexation. In the Philippines, a revolutionary force headed by General Aquinaldo had initially cooperated with U.S. efforts to purge the Spanish from the Islands. Indeed, the United States facilitated his return from exile in Hong Kong so that he and his followers could help wage war against the Spanish, which he did to such good effect that the Filipino army numbered over 80,000 when the American Admiral Dewey's fleet arrived in Manila harbor. Quickly, however, Filipinos grew suspicious of U.S. intentions in the Philippines. Aquinaldo had a plan to form a democratic Filipino government for the independent Philippines. To achieve the recognition of Filipino independence, Aquinaldo sent diplomatic agents abroad and attempted to convince the world of the Filipinos' capacity for self-government. In cities liberated from the Spanish, the Filipinos held local elections. During the summer of 1898, however, U.S. plans for expansion in the region escalated from retention of the city of Manila to the annexation of the entire Archipelago. Upon deciding to annex the whole Archipelago, the U.S. government signed with Spain the "Treaty of Paris" in December 1898. The treaty gave the United States the right to exercise sovereignty in the Philippines on behalf of Spain. The effective transfer of power from one imperialist to another was presented to the Filipinos as a fait accompli. Spain and the United States signed the treaty without consulting Aquinaldo or other Filipino leaders. The Filipino-American alliance initially forged under the pressure of necessity soon gave way to mutual hostility. In the meantime, in January 1899, the Filipino leaders promulgated the "Malolos Constitution," which included many of the trappings of institutional democracy and inaugurated the Philippine Republic with Aquinaldo as president.

The war between Philippines and the United States grew out of the Iloilo incident, when American and Filipino patrols exchanged shots on February 4, 1899, with the American soldiers firing first. During the middle of December 1898, American troops attempted to enter the city of Iloilo, ostensibly to rescue soldiers trapped earlier in the city during the fighting between the Spaniards and the Filipinos. Upon their offshore arrival, General Marcus Miller was surprised to find that members of the German Navy had already freed the trapped soldiers and that the Spanish had already surrendered the city to the Filipino Army. The Filipino forces initially denied the newly arrived Americans landing rights. In January the American forces finally landed to find much of the city sacked, and the Filipino Army surrounding the city. Initial small arms fire initiated by American soldiers escalated quickly, and in a matter of hours, several hundred American and Filipino soldiers lay wounded or dead.

With the help of the opportune Iloilo incident, on February 6, 1899, the American Senate ratified the Treaty of Paris by a single vote over the two-thirds majority needed to carry the day.[27] This treaty formally ended the war with Spain and transferred formerly Spanish-held territory to the United States. Following the armistice with Spain, over the next three years, fighting a numerically and technologically outmatched opponent, the United States waged a large-scale war to conquer the entire Philippines archipelago. Ultimately, 126,500 American soldiers served, out of which over 7,000 casualties emerged, with 4,200 paying the ultimate price. As costly as the war was for the Americans, the Filipinos suffered a far worse fate. Some 20,000 Filipino soldiers died during the guerrilla campaign, and an estimated 200,000–500,000 civilians died in massacres, military targeting of civilian areas, and deliberately induced famine.[28]

The Philippines War presents problems for the normative model. It is clearly a war of imperialism; the Filipino people posed no conceivable threat even to global American interests, much less to American national security. President McKinley's motives are complex; in one interview he claimed to believe that American annexation was in the best interest of the Filipinos, as they were "unfit for self-government" and "there was nothing left for us to do but to take them all, and to educate the Filipinos, and uplift and civilize and Christianize them."[29] Annexation of the Philippines also, of course, served other interests, as the provision of a naval base would enable the projection of American naval power and the protection of American trade in the West Pacific and East Asia.

In addition to being an imperial war, the Philippines War was also an antidemocratic war, in that it sought to impose American annexation against the preferences of the Filipino people. Aquinaldo was quite popular; even General Arthur MacArthur conceded: "When I first started in against these rebels, I believed that Aquinaldo's troops represented only a faction. . . . I have been reluctantly compelled to believe that the Filipino masses [were] loyal to Aquinaldo and the government he heads."[30] The government that Aquinaldo headed was a nascent democracy. There existed significant democratic components in the Philippines Republic of 1898; the "Malolos Constitution"—the organic law of the Philippines

Republic—was democratic and progressive. One historian pointed out that "this state was democratic and liberal and was pledged to a careful regard for the protection and development of the masses of its citizens."[31] The Malolos Assembly, elected by popular vote, chose President Aquinaldo. A representative of the Aquinaldo administration conveyed the democratic nature of the new native Filipino government to American President McKinley directly in the fall of 1898.[32] Contrary to claims of American imperialists, Filipinos had substantial potential for self-government, and by the last quarter of the nineteenth century, the Filipinos possessed a certain degree of national consciousness. Claims by imperialists that "savages" and "savages" alone populated the Philippines notwithstanding, Filipinos in urban areas developed a sophisticated society enriched by cultural and commercial contact among themselves and with their neighbors. Filipinos had developed obedience to, and respect for, law and established authority, violent revolts being the exception rather than the rule.[33] Even scholars who claim that the Philippines War does not qualify as a war between democracies concede that the war was "an authentic war of resistance against colonialism" and that "the Philippines in 1899 was, probably, a nascent democratic state."[34]

American elites initially carried on debate along the lines anticipated by the normative explanation of the democratic peace, but it proved an inadequate constraint in the face of popular support for the war. The Treaty of Paris itself passed because the ambitious William Jennings Bryan shocked his supporters by voting in its favor. For Bryan, it was a calculated recognition of where public sentiment lay. He saw that the issue of silver, which served him so well in the 1890s, would not grant him the Democratic nomination for president in the 1900 campaign. Imperialism, however, was sufficiently popular that it could carry him and the Democratic Party to the White House. Among the anti-imperialists, Democratic Senator Bacon supported ending the war by recognizing the new Filipino nation. George Hoar, a staunch Republican anti-imperialist in Congress, praised Aquinaldo as a brave and honest man, proclaimed the political competence of the Filipinos, and accused the McKinley administration of hypocrisy. At the time, academics argued against the war. Professor Lewis Janes argued that "our war in the Philippines was proof that, for the U.S., 'the democratic spirit' had succumbed to 'the commercial and moneymaking power . . . our imperial policy threatened not only the destruction of the Filipinos but the vitality of popular democracy at home." Professor Felix Adler argued that the United States had destroyed the first true republic in the history of Asia. William James reviled privately that "The way the country puked up its ancient principles at the first touch of temptation was sickening," and he publicly declared that

"We are now openly engaged in crushing out the sacredest thing in this great human world—the attempt of a people long enslaved" to achieve its freedom.[35]

Consent for Wars of Empire

In sum, the Wars against Native American nations, the Spanish-American War, and the Philippines War demonstrate the weaknesses of the normative explanation in relation to the consent model. In each case, a democratic nation waged war against nonthreatening, quasi-democratic or democratizing societies, and in some instances, by bypassing negotiations and ignoring third-party arbiters. Significantly, the push to war in each case came from the mass public, illustrating the significance of consent and public opinion in the democratic decision for war.

These cases also indicate that consent for war is complicated: it is produced not only when there is a clear and present danger to the national security, but also at times against nonthreatening societies that are at least quasi-democratic. Notably, there were significant cultural and racial differences between the United States and the Native Americans, Spanish, and Filipinos. Scientific racism against Native Americans clearly played a role in the generation of consent for war against the Cherokee nation. Spaniards suffered from an especially low image in the popular American eye in the 1890s, seen typically as barbaric, cruel, tyrannical, uncivilized, and backward.[36] In the view of most Americans, the Filipinos were a primitive, savage people.

The power of a government invoking racial differences to assist in the generation of consent for war retains its significance at the dawn of the twenty-first century. Even today, racial differences play a powerful role in democracies' attempts to accomplish humanitarian goals, such as stopping genocide. Cultural dissimilarities play an important role in determining whether democratic publics are willing to expend blood and treasure to save the lives of foreigners. Consider that the United States and other predominantly white democracies were willing to intervene in Kosovo in 1999 in a conflict that cost the lives of perhaps a few thousand white Kosovars. Just a few years earlier, however, many of the same politicians were unwilling to intervene in either the concurrent war in Ethiopia, where tens of thousands died, or the 1994 Rwandan conflict, where war cost the lives of over half a million black Hutu and Tutsi civilians. One might claim the 1999 intervention came in part as the result of learning about the 1994 disaster in Africa, but then how might we interpret the lack of action to help end what contemporary journalists refer to as the World War I of Africa—the ongoing multinational war for control of Congo.

Covert Action and the Circumvention of Consent

A second class of conflicts better explained by the consent view than by the normative perspective includes covert military actions. In the wars we have discussed thus far, we showed that public consent and demand for action can facilitate democratic leaders' decisions to advocate the use of force against other actors, at times even against states that share democratic features. But what happens when democratic leaders wish to act against another state but are unable to generate the public consent needed to use force? One option has been the use of force covertly. Regardless of the motivations for keeping operations covert, such actions by their nature take place outside of the public view, and hence without public consent.[37] Through the use of covert means, democratic elites attempt to keep their actions secret from the people in their own country (thereby circumventing the need to generate consent), fellow elites (thereby circumventing norms of consultation and institutional checks and balances), or other member states in the international system (thereby circumventing norms of third-party consultation and nonviolent conflict resolution). Often, if the anticipated scale of an operation is sufficiently small, when democratic leaders perceive weak public consent for a particular option or outright opposition, they will act covertly or deceptively to circumvent public constraints or sidestep public debate on the merits of the anticipated action. Cases of covert action and the deception of the voting public abound. Examples include Lyndon Johnson's manipulation of the 1964 Gulf of Tonkin incident, the 1970 American invasion of Cambodia, the mining of Nicaraguan harbors in 1983, the Iran-Contra affair of the 1980s, and the French bombing of the Greenpeace vessel *Rainbow Warrior* in a New Zealand harbor.[38]

The use of covert action by democracies has two important implications for democratic foreign policy-making. First, it allows an avenue for the use of forceful means against other democracies. The empirical record reveals a number of instances of a democracy using covert action to undermine another democratically elected leadership: Chile in the 1960s and 1970s; Iran, 1953; Guatemala, 1954; Indonesia, 1955; Brazil, 1950s; Italy in the 1960s and 1970s; New Zealand, 1980s; and numerous others.[39] Henry Kissinger, national security adviser and secretary of state for the Nixon administration, has sought to minimize the role played by the United States in destabilizing the Chilean regime of Salvador Allende. However, the documentary record clearly indicates the commitment of the Nixon administration to overthrow Allende, a democratically elected leader, under Project FUBELT. A memo from a meeting on September 16, 1970, reads:

The Director told the group that President Nixon had decided that an Allende regime in Chile was not acceptable to the United States. The President asked the [Central Intelligence] Agency to prevent Allende from coming to power or to unseat him. The President authorized ten million dollars for this purpose, if needed. Further, the Agency is to carry out this mission without coordination with the Departments of State or Defense. . . . The Director said he had been asked by Dr. Henry Kissinger, Assistant to the President for National Security Affairs, to meet with him on Friday, 18 September to give him the Agency's views on how this mission could be accomplished.[40]

The United States' use of covert violence and subterfuge against democratic Chile is an example of the use of force between two democracies that has important implications for our comparison of the normative and consent theories of foreign policy. The two theories make different predictions about the willingness of democratic governments to use covert force against each other. The normative theory in straightforward terms forecasts that democracies would not use any means, overt or covert, to subvert or to overthrow another democratically elected government, as such action would clearly be a violation of democratic norms. The consent model, on the other hand, does not preclude the use of covert force to subvert another democratic government. For the consent model, the absence of war between democracies is driven not by elite-level norms proscribing the use of force between democracies, but rather by leaders' fear of the domestic political consequences of acting without consent. From the perspective of the consent model, if democratically elected leaders believe that they can circumvent the constraints of public consent through covert action, we would then expect them to take action against other democratic governments.[41]

A second, important implication of covert action is that it increases the risks of policy failure. As we discussed in chapter 2, an advantage that democracies enjoy is that the process by which the leadership seeks to gather and to generate consent necessarily involves public debate and engages the marketplace of ideas; this helps dismiss poorly considered ideas and bolster better ones. When a country's informed citizens broadly participate in the debate surrounding the formation and execution of political choices, superior public policy results. When the government circumvents popular consent rather than open the question to broad debate, the chances of foreign policy success drop and the prospects for disaster begin to loom large.[42] While chapter 2 clearly shows that democracies almost never lose overt wars they initiate, their record when using covert force is far murkier. For instance, it would be difficult to characterize the 1953 installation of the Shah's regime in Iran as a success, and ongoing instability in Latin America was in part a result of failed U.S. policies pursuing regional stability through covert means.[43]

The conventional argument favoring secrecy is, of course, that open disclosure would mean the spread of vital information, which in turn could undermine national security. Advocates of secrecy overstate its benefits, however.[44] Even in the area of weapons development, where we find the strongest arguments in favor of secrecy, there are important benefits to maintaining open information flows. Permitting information flows between civilian and military scientists and allowing open discourse between scientists in different fields are both centrally important factors in maintaining, in Karl Polanyi's terms, the Republic of Science as well as stimulating ongoing weapons innovation. During the Cold War, the United States' science and technology complex was far more open than that of the Soviet Union, affording it a decisive edge in weapons innovation. Some argue that the openness of the American system of weapons innovation had a fatal flaw during the Cold War, namely, creating opportunities for Soviet espionage to collect the secrets of the atomic bomb. Recall, however, that the authoritarian great powers of the time did little better in preventing foreign espionage than did the United States: the Allies kept close tabs on the German nuclear program, fatally disrupting it with commando attacks on heavy water facilities in Norway during the war. Conversely, openness did offer its advantages to the Manhattan Project, which enjoyed free-flowing discourse and exchanges among scientists working in different areas. Significantly, this atmosphere contributed to key advances in the production of the first atomic bombs. The experimental physicist Seth Neddermeyer came up with the crucial idea of an implosion design (used in all nuclear weapons after Hiroshima) while attending an open lecture on explosives ordnance at Los Alamos in 1943.[45]

The circumvention of consent and concomitant public debate has helped contribute to the relatively unsuccessful record of accomplishment of American covert action in the Post War period. Indeed, in the words of former national security adviser McGeorge Bundy, "The dismal historical record of covert military and paramilitary operations over the last 25 years is entirely clear." The disaster of the Bay of Pigs invasion of Cuba in 1961 is a good example of the link between secrecy and policy failure. The plan as conceived began in the Eisenhower administration. President Kennedy gave his personal go-ahead despite several deep flaws, which in all likelihood would have led to reconsideration of the venture if they had been exposed to public debate.[46]

The resort to covert action by democratic governments provides events that pose an exception to the consent model that argues that democracies generally should make better policies than autocracies. The common failures of covert actions also are consistent with the predictions of the general consent theory. It is an exception because covert action constitutes foreign policy taken without the consent of the public. The outcomes are consistent with our theory that the need for public consent leads to better policy in that when democracies do engage in covert actions, democratic foreign policy tends to converge with nondemocratic foreign policy. The broad implication of this is that the differences between democracies and their nondemocratic counterparts lie not so much in differing preferences of the political elites, as unconstrained democratic leaders frequently make much the same choices as their autocratic counterparts. Rather, the distinguishing characteristic of democratic and nondemocratic foreign policy is the way that democratic political institutions bring the people into the public policy debate via the necessity of generating public consent for foreign policy ventures in democratic states. The need to generate public consent may often save democratic elites from their worst foreign policy instincts. In the absence of public consent, if democratic leaders believe the issues at stake warrant the use of force and the means can be held to sufficiently small uses of force as to be executed covertly, democratic foreign policy converges with autocratic policy. Democracies will take covert actions to undermine and overthrow other democratic governments. They also engage in policy that ultimately fails at rates that far exceed the rates of policy failure for actions that survive the forge of public debate.

Democracies win the wars they start because such actions are so large they cannot be covert and therefore are subject to the skeptical approval of the population and the bright light of public scrutiny. Since covert actions do not require consent, they need not pass such tests and are less likely to be successful, similar to autocratic states' decisions for war, which also do not require public consent.

The Consent and Normative Models Revisited

We close this chapter by revisiting the question we began with: When do democracies initiate wars? The consent model offers a better answer to this question than does the normative model. The consent model proposes that the decision to wage war is a matter for debate in the court of public opinion. Democratic governments take action to defend a broadly defined notion of the national interest when such an interpretation enjoys the general agreement of the population. This view of the role and power of public consent enjoys broad empirical support: no American president has taken the nation into war without indication that there is broad public support. Conversely, American presidents have constrained themselves from action when they felt there was insufficient public support as was the case, for example, in the Ford Administration's decision not to rescue South Vietnam from military defeat in 1975. Historical research provides support for this speculation, that the more debate needed to reach consensus, the more risk-averse policy will be, as presidents have been significantly less likely to engage in military disputes when control of the Congress and White House is divided between the parties rather than one party controlling both.[47]

The normative model has only at best a vague answer to the question of when do democracies initiate wars. It allows for the initiation of force by a democracy to confront immediate threats to the national security, but there is barely even anecdotal evidence of such preemptive democratic initiations, whereas there are a disturbing number of cases of democracies initiating wars to advance national power, to create or expand empire, and to extinguish inconveniently located peoples. Aside from grave and imminent threats to national security, the normative model might permit the use of force by democracies if sanctioned by an international body such as the League of Nations or United Nations. But while some American military actions have taken place under the purview of U.N. resolutions (such as the Korean and Gulf wars), these wars are the exception rather than the rule. Contrary to the norms model, the United States has routinely taken action when such U.N. approval was not available, including intervention in Vietnam, its 1983 invasion of Grenada, its 1986 strike on Libya, and the 1999 air strikes on Yugoslavia. Further, the United States has ignored U.N. resolutions that were inconsistent with national policy (and public opinion), such as the 1975 resolution equating Zionism with racism.

It would be inaccurate to characterize democracies simply as peace-loving nations. They do not launch war only as a last possible resort following the exhaustion of all other diplomatic means. Nor are democracies constrained by a culture of nonviolent conflict resolution. Rather, in comparison to their autocratic counterparts, democracies are constrained only by the will of the people. For better or for worse, when the people willingly offer consent for war, even wars of empire or genocide, then democratic governments have obliged.

SEVEN

THE DECLINING ADVANTAGES OF DEMOCRACY

WHEN CONSENT ERODES

A democracy cannot fight a Seven Years War.
—*General George Catlett Marshall*

OREIGN POLICY in a democracy lives and dies with the provision and denial of public consent.[1] In chapter 2, we argued that democratic leaders rarely start risky wars, and that democracies only start wars when their estimated chances of victory are very high. Of course, democracies do not fight indiscriminately; they do not fight every war they could win. In chapter 6, we argued that one of the chief constraining factors holding democratic leaders in check is the need to generate public consent for the potential war at hand. Not only must democratic leaders be able to convince the public that the military can win in good speed, but they must also gain the public's consent for the possible war at hand. Further, democratic leaders must work to maintain public consent for the war after it begins. Just as a state's material chances in a war can ebb and flow with the outcomes of individual battles, so too can the public's consent rise and fall. Our previous analyses of war outcomes in chapter 2 treated each war as a snapshot in which each side won or lost; it did not let us look at what can happen over the course of a war. But what happens when public consent for a war begins to dissipate? Though public support must be high when a war starts, it may decline as a war proceeds. When the promised quick victory does not materialize, and when the numbers of dead friends, neighbors, brothers, and sons begin to mount, the people may reconsider their decision to consent to the war at hand and actively withdraw their support.[2]

The dissipation of popular support for war is less of a problem in authoritarian states than in democracies. Authoritarian leaders do not depend on the support of the public for their hold on power, and they can more easily repress dissenting voices that might otherwise increase resistance to the state's policies. For democratic governments, the erosion of popular support has consequences that are far more serious as policies pursued without public support generate serious long-term domestic political dangers for the party in power. Declining support for war may pose a serious disadvantage for democracies as compared to autocratic states because for the latter popular consent is not a necessary condition to initiate and wage a war. What are the effects of this potential handicap that democratic governments face? In this chapter, we take up this question. We begin by thinking carefully about how wars end and the process that determines a war's winners and losers.

Democracy, Consent, and War Outcomes

At its most basic level, war is an exercise in two-sided or mutual coercion: each opponent seeks to inflict costs, be they human or material, on the other side, hoping to persuade the adversary to capitulate first.[3] In chapter 2, we proposed that democracies' institutional dependence on public consent actually served as an advantage, in that it guided democratic leaders to start only those wars they will go on to win—those wars in which the democracy would be able to bear greater costs than its opponents. Additionally, we also know from other studies that this dependence on public consent causes democracies to start wars that promise low casualties and will end more quickly than is typical, and to be more likely to adopt military strategies that promise quick, bloodless victory.[4]

The argument in chapter 2 focused on prewar decision-making. In this chapter, we focus on the events that take place during war. In our general model of warfare, each state tries to coerce its opponent into quitting the fight by inflicting punishment. When a state has absorbed more punishment than it is willing to bear in the pursuit of victory, it will begin to seek an end to the war, accepting either a loss or a draw. If both sides reach this exhaustion point at about the same time, a draw occurs, such as the draws that ended the Korean War in 1953 and the Iran-Iraq War in 1988. In both cases, after inflicting hundreds of thousands of casualties, both sides proved unwilling to continue the war. If one side reaches its breaking point before the other does, this creates conditions for its defeat.

What factors determine when an actor will reach its breaking point and begin to sue for peace? The stakes of the war are of course important. The greater the stakes or the higher the perceived benefits associated with winning, the more willing leaders and citizens will be to bear the ongoing costs associated with war. When either the leaders or the public perceive the stakes to be smaller, lower costs will be necessary to drive the state into quitting the fight. During World War II, Britain's leaders recognized the magnitude of the stakes in its conflict with Germany and steeled their citizens to fight on to victory no matter how long it took. In Britain's darkest hour following the defeat of France and the evacuation of Dunkirk, Prime Minister Winston Churchill called on the British people for a steadfast commitment to victory:

> We shall prove ourselves once again able to defend our Island home, to ride out the storm of war, and to outlive the menace of tyranny, if necessary for years, if necessary alone. . . . That is the will of Parliament and the nation. . . . We shall not flag or fail. We shall go on to the end, we shall fight in France, we shall fight on the seas and oceans, we shall fight with growing confidence and growing strength in the air, we shall defend our Island, whatever the cost may be, we shall fight on the beaches, we shall fight on the landing grounds, we shall fight in the fields and in the streets, we shall fight in the hills; we shall never surrender.[5]

Though Britain did, in fact, continue to fight until the British people prevailed in their war against Germany, even while engaged in high-stakes wars democracies seek to keep the fighting short and casualties few while in the pursuit of victory. In the summer of 1945, the surrender of Germany in Europe allowed the new American president Harry Truman to focus on the endgame in the Pacific with Japan. A central concern was the possibility that an invasion might be required to conquer Japan. Such an operation would put the final defeat of Japan off until 1946 at the earliest, and the estimates were that American casualties in such a campaign might reach the hundreds of thousands. Strategic bombing seemed one way to hasten Japanese defeat: a spokesman for General Curtis LeMay, commander of the bombing campaign against Japan, explained to the *New Yorker* that summer that such raids "are shortening the war." The successful test of the new atomic bomb in New Mexico on July 16 provided an especially effective new tool that American leaders hoped would make the invasion unnecessary. Truman decided to use the atomic bomb against Japan, a decision driven primarily by a desire to shorten the war and reduce American casualties.[6]

On the cost side of the coercion ledger, the faster that costs pile up, the sooner a state will reach its breaking point—the point at which it becomes willing to accept a draw or defeat to stop the fighting. The character, strategy, and scale of fighting usually drive the rate at which costs accrue. Casualties might accrue very slowly in a smoldering border dispute like the Indo-Pakistani clash over the Siachen Glacier, in comparison to a more open conflict with large armies such as the Korean War in which casualties accumulate more quickly. Similarly, time is a central factor. Regardless of the rate at which casualties mount, the longer the war continues, the more costs will necessarily climb and the more likely that at least one side will reach its breaking point.

From the perspective of our consent model, a critical factor that affects when a state will reach its breaking point is its society's willingness to accept casualties. A long-standing assertion has been that the public has a lower tolerance for casualties than do the ruling elites. The logic behind this distinction is quite simple: typically it is the general public that bears the lion's share of the costs of war, while members of the political elite or upper classes are often shielded from suffering directly the costs of war. Casualties tend to affect the public's support for the war effort more directly than the ruling elite's as the elite typically can use their political power to protect their own sons and brothers. For example, during the Vietnam War, children of the political and economic elite such as George W. Bush and Dan Quayle served out their military obligation in the National Guard, spared the dangers of combat service in Vietnam. For several years attending college would defer one's obligation, which in turn created a class-based bias in who served and ultimately bore the costs of war.

In authoritarian settings, the ability to shield members of the elite from the dangers of fighting war leaves leaders quite immune to the costs of war, as neither they nor their families suffer the direct costs of war and they are better insulated from public discontent, which arises when the costs of war escalate. Conversely, democratic leaders, who at times may be able to protect their friends and children from combat service, nevertheless remain politically vulnerable to the discontent of voters, which grows louder as the death toll mounts.[7] Democratic leaders understand that they are dependent on public consent to be able to continue their war efforts, and, as a result, democratic governments are more sensitive to casualties. This greater sensitivity leads democracies to reach their breaking point in war more quickly, other things being equal, than their autocratic counterparts. This greater sensitivity leads democracies to sue for peace at lower levels of casualties. Democratic elites are also more likely than authoritarian elites to be aware of the true costs of war, as democratic political institutions and their relatively open debate decrease the ability of democratic elites to shield themselves from information about the true state of affairs in an ongoing war.[8]

Our central proposition in this chapter is that democracies tend to reach their breaking points of casualty tolerance sooner than authoritarian states because the democratic leadership is structurally dependent on public consent. From this point we raise several related specific propositions:

Proposition 7.1: *The longer a war continues, democracies will be more likely than autocracies to seek an end to the war.*

Proposition 7.1a: *Democracies will be more likely to accept draws than will autocracies, which will seek victory.*

Once a democracy has reached this casualty threshold point, its primary goal shifts from winning outright to ending the war as quickly as possible. While all states would prefer a draw to decisive defeat, democracies will be more likely to accept draws willingly than will authoritarian states, which are more able to continue to risk defeat in order to hold out for the hope of decisive victory. Authoritarian states tend to be more likely than democracies to press for their opponent's outright capitulation even as casualties pile up rather than accepting a negotiated settlement or a draw. Not facing the political danger of waning support for the war, they choose to risk outright defeat in hopes of victory, whereas risk-averse democracies tend to be willing to retire on less decisive terms of settlement. Similarly, the longer the war lasts, the more likely a democracy will be willing to accept any end to the war, even if it means defeat.

Proposition 7.2: *The longer a war continues, the more likely autocracies are to win.*

If neither side faces the dilemma of declining consent, as might be the case involving two autocrats, this level will not change. This leads us to our third proposition:

Proposition 7.3: *Wars involving two autocracies are less likely to end in draws but last longer than wars involving democracies.*

The Historical Record

To test these propositions relating democracy to the duration and outcome of wars, we again examine all wars from 1816 to 1990. One major change compared to the analysis in chapter 2 is that here we also include draws, or wars that ended with less than decisive outcomes. We investigate the duration of wars by collecting data for every year of a war, then estimating how likely it is that a state will choose to continue to fight given how long it has fought already. We propose that autocracies' decisions to accept a draw (be willing to quit fighting) should be independent of the length of the war, whereas for democracies, their willingness to continue fighting should decline the longer a war continues reflecting declining public support for war over time. The statistical analysis detailed in appendix 7.1 focuses on explaining two phenomena: how long a war will last and what the outcome will be (win, lose, or draw). Our central questions are: How do wars fought by democracies differ from wars fought by authoritarian states? Are they shorter? Can we find evidence that democratic leaders start to search for ways out the longer a war continues? In this section, we present our findings with a minimum of statistical detail. We recommend that readers interested in the specifics of the empirical model consult the appendix to this chapter, which covers a variety of methodological matters. Next, we present a summary of our

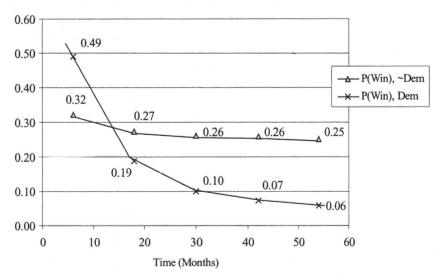

Figure 7.1. Changes in Initiator's Chances of Victory over Time: Democracies and Nondemocracies.

results in three figures that chart the choices that democracies and nondemocracies make as the duration of war increases. The figures provide a first sense of the different kinds of choices and war outcomes we observe between democracies and authoritarian states as the length of wars increase. The results here summarize the average or typical choices that democracies and autocracies made in wars through history. They do not reflect the choices of the states in any single war, but rather, how the two types of states made their choices on average over the past two hundred years.

Figure 7.1 illustrates the relative likelihood that a particular type of state (democracy or not) would win a war having already fought for some period (six months to fifty-four months).

Figure 7.1 demonstrates the democratic advantage we found in chapters 2 and 3. In short wars lasting less than a year, democracies are much more likely to win, 49 percent of the time versus 32 percent. The figure also shows, however, that the probability of a democratic initiator winning a war drops dramatically as a war begins to drag on past the first few months, from 49 percent in the first year to 6 percent if a war continues for five years. Bear in mind, when we note that democracies on average have a 49 percent chance of winning a war they initiated that ended before the first year was out, this does not mean they lost the balance. Rather, in the wars that continued past a year, there are three other possible outcomes: continue to fight (the next most common outcome at this point in a war's progress), draw, or lose. These findings about democracies are even more interesting when contrasted to the choices made by nondemocratic states over time. Note that while the probability of an autocratic initiator winning a war is initially less than that of a democratic initiator winning (32 percent vs. 49 percent), by the second year of a war the nondemocracy is significantly more likely to win, and their probability of winning *does not* decrease significantly as additional time passes. This is quite different from democratic initiators, who become increasingly less likely to win as time goes by. Democracy's prospects decline so precipitously over time that beyond roughly eighteen months, nondemocracies become more likely to win. While these findings might seem inconsistent with those presented in earlier chapters, it is important to note that most wars are quite short: more than half last five months or less—short enough time that declining consent is not a problem for democratic leaders.

Our figures allow for a variety of comparisons, all of which support quite strongly our general arguments about the role of consent and its interaction with democratic political institutions. In figure 7.2, we show how the likelihood of a state choosing to continue fighting changes with the passage of time. Recall our proposition that consent will decline as the costs of war mount, leading democratic leaders to become more hesitant to continue to fight. Generally, the results show that over time democratic initiators become less likely to continue fighting, less likely to win, and much more likely to accept a draw.[9] Democratic initiators have a 32

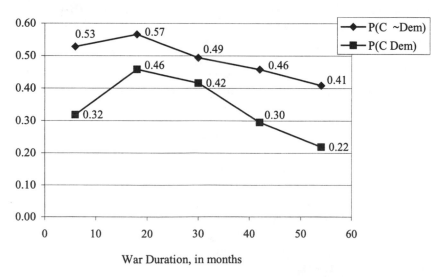

Figure 7.2. Probability War Continues by Time and Initiator Democracy.

percent chance of continuing to fight after the first year of a war. After a second year of war, this probability actually increases somewhat, to 46 percent (this reflects the sharp drop in democracies' chances of victory, which we saw fall precipitously from 49 percent to 19 percent between the first and second year of fighting). Beyond eighteen months of fighting, democratic initiators become less and less willing to continue to fight, the probability dropping significantly, to 29 percent in the fourth year and 22 percent by the fifth year of a war.

Perhaps the most important point shown in figure 7.2 is that nondemocratic war initiators will *always* be more likely to choose to continue fighting than are democratic initiators. Consistent with our consent story, after a war has continued for several years, nondemocracies are twice as likely as a democracy is to continue to fight rather than seeking some sort of negotiated draw or accepting a loss.

In figure 7.3, we show that for a nondemocratic initiator the probability of a draw increases over time but does so much more slowly than it

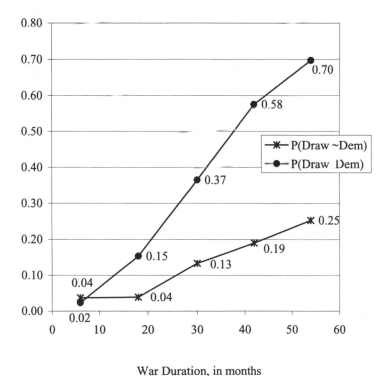

War Duration, in months

Figure 7.3. Probability of Democracies and Nondemocracies Accepting a Draw over Time.

does for democracies. By the time a war has dragged on for more than four years, democracies will accept a draw in almost three out of every four cases. These findings fit with our expectations based on previous research on the public opinion literature and research on victory in war. As costs in war rise over time, the public's consent tends to decline. Since democratic states are more susceptible to declining public support, it follows that democratic war initiators should become more likely to lose or settle for draws as time passes, and they do. It appears that while democracies can maintain enough support and mobilization to avoid losing in long wars, they are much less able to win those long wars than to win short wars.

Overall, nondemocracies do not experience the dramatic fluctuations in outcome probabilities over time that democracies do. Rather, they are able to maintain a substantial probability of victory along with an ability to continue to fight longer than democracies. Nondemocratic initiators sometimes end up fighting wars that end in draws, but much less frequently than do democratic initiators. Both democracies and nondemocracies are, not surprisingly, quite unwilling to settle for a draw at the outset of the war. We also note that wars between autocrats will be less likely to end in draws and more likely to end in decisive outcomes than wars involving a democracy. Autocratic initiators and targets continue to fight longer than democratic leaders and have a lower probability of settling for a draw. Autocratic leaders appear to be willing to hold out for a chance at victory in the future rather then settling for a draw today.

Fighting in the Shadow of Declining Consent

While the figures above demonstrate support for our proposition about the role of consent and democracies' declining prospects over time, they are simply depictions of how states behave on average. To illustrate the way declining consent actually alters leaders' decision-making, we look at two wars in detail, wars in which public opinion researchers are able to show how public opinion in favor and against the war evolved. To understand better the relationship between war termination and public consent, we next examine two important twentieth-century wars, the Vietnam War and the 1991 Gulf War. Here we focus on three issues: How did consent shape each war's duration and its outcome? How did consent affect the way that the United States fought each war? How did the American president's need to maintain public consent for the war affect the military strategy of the opponent? We begin with one of the longest wars of the twentieth century, the Vietnam War.

The Vietnam War

American presidents in the late 1960s and early 1970s knew that they could not continue to fight, much less win, an increasingly unpopular war in Vietnam. Both Johnson and Nixon also suspected that the accumulation of American casualties played a powerful role in determining public support for the war. About the latter point they were quite correct, as U.S. casualties strongly affected American public support for the war. Today, we have a more sophisticated understanding of the relationship between casualties and support for the war. We know that an individual's support for the war was sensitive to escalating casualties of soldiers originally from that individual's hometown or county. We know that this relationship was race-blind, that white Americans' support for the war was just as vulnerable to the deaths of black soldiers as it was to the deaths of whites. We know that casualties that were more recent affected a person's opinion of the war more strongly than the deaths and injuries of soldiers taking place in years before the surveys. We also know that the flow of blood of soldiers drawn from an American's hometown trumped other factors that might have guided public opinion, as local casualty rates were far more important in affecting opinion than newspaper editorials or the antiwar movement.[10]

How did the changing tide of public consent shape the outcome in Vietnam? In 1965, President Johnson faced important decisions about American participation in the Vietnam War. The outlook for the conflict was not promising even at this early stage, though Johnson and his advisers perceived the geopolitical stakes to be substantial enough to warrant a continued American effort. Generally, in 1966 and 1967 Americans supported continuing the war against Vietnam, with some supporting escalation.[11] Johnson's Vietnam policy did not evolve in a vacuum. While he supported the United States' general aims in the region, he was also trying to get a large package of domestic reform legislation passed, known as the Great Society. Johnson believed that if he appeared soft on communism, his political opponents would be able to isolate him from a majority of the American people, dooming his Great Society. Johnson rightly understood that his opponents would judge his attitudes toward communism by his decisions over the war in Vietnam.[12] Knowing that the public supported the continuing support of South Vietnam, Johnson agreed to escalate the war, both with greater commitment of ground troops and with the commencement of Operation Rolling Thunder, a massive bombing campaign. Such a commitment, according to a memo written at the time by Secretary of Defense Robert McNamara, "stands a good chance of achieving an acceptable outcome within a reasonable time."[13]

Though the American leadership did not in 1965 foresee an imminent victory, they did have a strategy. Johnson and his advisors hoped to be able to impose sufficient pain on the North Vietnamese to drive them past their breaking point, to convince the North Vietnamese leaders that the costs of pursing their goals in South Vietnam would vastly exceed whatever they might hope to gain there. The pain would be inflicted largely with airpower and ground-based search and destroy missions. The accounting system would be the body count. According to McNamara, "The body count was a measurement of the adversary's manpower losses; we undertook it because one of Westmoreland's objectives was to reach a so-called crossover point, at which Vietcong and North Vietnamese casualties would be greater than they could sustain. To reach such a point, we needed to have some idea what they could sustain and what their losses were."[14] If all went according to McNamara's plan, this would then end the North Vietnamese support of the Communist insurgency in South Vietnam. Johnson would achieve this goal by deploying tremendous amounts of American firepower. The plan failed—disastrously. Perhaps the central flaw in the American strategy was that the brain trust in the White House significantly underestimated the breaking point of the North Vietnamese. As it was, North Vietnam withstood astonishingly high costs. Between 1954 and 1975 the levels of military casualties were roughly 5 percent of the country's total population, military and civilian casualties combined amounted to almost 10 percent, and more than 30 percent of the civilian population became refugees by the war's end. In comparison, in World War II, the costliest war in history, American casualties were less than one-tenth of those they imposed on the Vietnamese twenty-five years later, only 0.3 percent of the total population. Even Japanese casualties in World War II, 1.4 percent of their population, amounted to one quarter of what the Vietnamese bore.[15]

Importantly, the North Vietnamese government was aware of both the damage it was suffering and the risks of potential future damage. One Hanoi official lamented in 1967, "If we keep fighting five more years, all that will be left of Viet Nam will be a desert." Despite this recognition of the American intention to level the country and slaughter the population, the North Vietnamese government remained in the war, even pursuing an escalatory policy with the 1968 Tet Offensive. The Vietnamese strategy was simple: continue combat operations, even if the ratio of casualties lopsidedly favors the other side, as eventually the United States will flinch first. A North Vietnamese general explained that despite defeats and high casualties, "we never stopped winning the war. Time was on our side. We did not have to defeat you militarily: we had only to avoid losing. A victory by your brave soldiers meant nothing, did nothing to change the balance of forces or to bring you any closer to victory."[16]

As it turned out, this shared conception of the war as a competition in mutual bloodletting turned out to be substantially correct. The American public's support for the war was quite at high at the outset, 78 percent of Americans expressing approval of the administration's handling of the war in October 1965. This figure dwindled slowly but steadily over the next two years. After the January 1968 Tet Offensive, public support collapsed; a March 1968 poll revealed that only 30 percent still approved of the administration's handling of the war. Despite the essential veracity of claims that Tet was a military victory for the American and South Vietnamese forces, the simple fact that it occurred dashed any hopes the American people might have entertained that the North Vietnamese military had been broken and that the end was near. Following Tet, in an astonishing turn of events, Johnson announced that he would not run for reelection. His successor, Richard Nixon, was perhaps more sensitive to the geopolitical costs of withdrawal from South Vietnam than was Johnson, but he was not oblivious to the domestic political constraints imposed by continuing American casualties. President Nixon's new strategy of "Vietnamization" was to facilitate an honorable American exit from the war while reducing American casualties in the process. The strategy did reduce American casualties, which arguably may have bought the administration enough time to negotiate a conclusion to the war, which, at least on paper, looked more like a draw than might have abject American withdrawal.[17]

The American exit from Vietnam brought to a close one of the more divisive events in American history. However, even in wars with more successful outcomes, we can observe how fears about the decline of popular support and the concomitant erosion of consent affect the decisions of elected leaders. In 1991 the United Nations sponsored a U.S.-led war against Iraq that demonstrated the fragile nature of public consent.

The Gulf War

Soon after the August 1990 Iraqi invasion of Kuwait, a consensus formed in the Bush administration that the United States would have to take action. The political context for offensive military operations improved as time passed: diplomatic efforts failed, Saddam Hussein refused to release the so-called hostages, and most of the world lined up in opposition to the Iraqi annexation of Kuwait. In the closing months of 1990, the American leadership began to devise military plans.

What would the war plan look like? As in past wars, American leaders would have to plan to conduct the Gulf War within the constraints of what public consent would allow. This meant pursuing a quick victory with minimal casualties. From the outset, this constrained military options, as "it was well understood within the American military that holding down casualties was a political prerequisite for launching a military offensive." On October 31, for example, American military planners discussed a number of possible plans for action. One called for a Marine invasion via Bubiyan Island of Kuwait, which lay on the Persian Gulf; this option quickly fell from favor because it would incur too many casualties. Military advisors appeared so acutely sensitive to the political costs associated with American casualties that at one point a civilian advisor suspected that the military was intentionally presenting attack plans with especially high casualty estimates in order to move the president away from approving a ground offensive.[18]

More generally, the desire for a short war with few American casualties meant a strategy of immediate and overwhelming force, forgoing the slow escalation strategy previously pursued in Vietnam. As General Colin Powell put it at the time, "I don't believe in doing war on the basis of macroeconomic, marginal-analysis models. I'm more of the mind-set of a New York street bully: 'Here's my bat, here's my gun, here's my knife, I'm wearing armor. I'm going to kick your ass.'" This idea of massive escalation with overwhelming force evolved into what was later called the Powell Doctrine. President Bush's belief that victory could come quickly and cheaply bolstered his commitment to the war. In his memoir he wrote, "Briefing after briefing had convinced me that we could do the job fast and with minimum coalition casualties. . . . I had no fear of making the decision to go."[19]

A central part of Bush's domestic political efforts to rally support for the war was convincing congressional leaders and the public in general that a war against Iraq would be short and victorious with few casualties. Critics predicted a bloody war; the Center for Defense Information predicted that 45,000 American casualties were a possibility. Even political hawks were wary of prewar optimism. William Cohen, then the Republican senator from Maine and later defense secretary in the Clinton administration, commented during the crisis preceding the war that "History is littered with the bones of optimists and generals who thought they were headed for a short war." Cohen may have been thinking of Kaiser Wilhelm's assurance to German soldiers in early August 1914 that "You will be home before the leaves have fallen from the trees." Most importantly, within Bush's inner circle, there was confidence that American casualties would not exceed a few thousand.[20]

The American concern to keep the war brief and casualties few shaped the coalition's military strategy in three major ways. First, it encouraged an extremely intense phase of aerial bombing before the launching of the ground campaign. The air campaign advocates claimed to offer maximum benefits at minimum costs. Specifically, it served to establish total Allied air superiority for the coming ground campaign by eliminating the Iraqi Air Force as a factor, and to degrade Iraqi ground forces. This was accomplished with a minimum of casualties, as downed Allied planes never exceeded a handful despite the fact that more bombing sorties were flown during the Gulf War than by American air forces during World War II.[21]

Second, a prominent awareness among American decision makers was that the war would have to be short with few casualties shaped the planning for the ground campaign. The basic plan of action was for a massive flanking operation to the west of Kuwait itself, encircling Iraqi forces without the need for large-scale set piece battles, which would cause casualty counts to escalate rapidly. The ground operations plan predicted that the Allied forces would meet their military objectives in 144 hours.[22]

Third, motivation to keep the war short drove the termination of the war itself. Shockingly, Allied ground forces defeated Iraqi defensive forces and liberated Kuwait faster and with fewer casualties than the Pentagon had forecast (to say nothing of the predictions of the critics). After four days of combat operations, Kuwait was free. At that point, the American leadership faced a difficult decision. They could continue operations to complete the prewar goal of effectively eliminating Iraq's Republican Guard, they could continue on to Baghdad and attempt to topple Hussein's regime, or they could stop military operations, thereby guaranteeing minimal casualties. Bush and Powell stopped operations and accepted a cease-fire with the Iraqis, in no small part to hold down American casualties. Ground operations stopped after 100 hours, during which time 148 Americans were killed and 467 wounded.[23]

From the outset, Saddam Hussein understood the American need to minimize casualties and to keep the war short. As discussed in chapter 2, he told an American ambassador before the Iraqi invasion of Kuwait that America had no stomach for casualties. In a December 1990 interview with German television, Saddam publicly reemphasized the point, stating that "We are sure that if President Bush pushes things toward war . . . once 5,000 of his troops die, he will not be able to continue the war." Shortly after the invasion, Saddam concentrated all Western civilians in Kuwait and restricted them from leaving. Apparently attempting to prick American fears of bloodshed, he moved some of the civilians to Iraqi defense installations and publicly told Bush that "You are going to receive some American bodies in bags." This tactic failed miserably and only served to demonize Iraq even further in the eyes of the Western publics. The Iraqi belief in American casualty sensitivity persisted, and they based their military strategy around the goal of imposing high casualty counts, hoping that bloodying the nose of the American behemoth would encourage a retreat. This was a primary goal of the unsuccessful January 1991 Iraqi attack on Khafji. Interestingly, the Iraqis could have adopted strategies that would have inflicted higher levels of casualties, such as defending a fortified Kuwait City. Fortunately for the coalition, the Iraqis missed these opportunities, as the tepid public support for military action very likely might have withered in the face of stalled operations and mounting American casualties.[24]

The Hourglass of Public Consent

In this chapter, we have suggested a way of reconciling prior findings about the effects of democracy on states' behavior in war. We started with findings that suggested two things: (1) democracies that initiate wars are more likely to win than nondemocratic states that initiate wars, and (2) public support for war in democracies decreases over time. This raised a puzzle about how democracies can win relatively more wars if the necessary support for war diminishes while wars take place. The answer is quite simple: democracies choose to initiate not just wars that they can win, but wars that they can win quickly. This proposition finds support in the historical record, namely, in our examination of all wars since 1815. Democratic states typically only become involved in wars that can be won quickly. However, democratic states, both initiators and targets, face a substantial risk. If they do not win quickly, they become increasingly likely to end up fighting to a draw. Public consent is like an hourglass: when war starts, the hourglass flips over, and democratic leaders know they must win before the sand runs out. When democratic leaders make accurate forecasts of how the war will unfold, they fight wars that are short, low-casualty, and victorious. When they guess wrong, however, and the war does not end quickly, they eventually must give up on their hopes for victory and seek a draw in order to exit sooner rather than later.

This constitutes an important constraint on the ability of democracies to fight some wars. When the stakes are low to moderate, democratic leaders know that any public consent for action they have amassed at the outset of the war will dwindle eventually below the breaking point as the war drags on and casualties accumulate. Authoritarian states, however, do not face similar constraints and enjoy greater liberty to conduct longer and bloodier wars. Authoritarian leaders recognize this asymmetry and seek to capitalize on it by racking up the casualties of their democratic foes, even if this means accepting higher casualty rates themselves. Democracies cope with this asymmetry by seeking to fight short wars with strategies emphasizing high mobility and few casualties.

Our findings also have implications for a key debate on public opinion, whether public opinion drives elite decisions or elites manipulate public opinion.[25] If the latter is true, then consent washes away as a constraint on national decision-making, as political leaders can spin public opinion in desired directions (for instance, propping up public support even as a war drags on and the casualties accumulate). However, our findings confirm the former viewpoint, that public opinion does not dance on the puppet strings of national leaders but rather emerges autonomously and remains independent enough to be a real constraint on the wartime behavior of democratic states.

Appendix 7.1: Testing a Combined Model of Duration and Outcomes

Testing our proposition that democracies select quick and easy wars requires a different method of analysis than has been used in previous studies of either war outcomes or duration. In chapter 2 we considered only the two outcomes of win or lose, without considering or examining the choice to continue fighting until another day or the possibility of a draw. Previous studies of duration focused solely on whether states choose to continue fighting or end the war.[26] In the analysis below, we focus both on the effects of time and on distinctive outcomes, since in theory, in any given war year, four possible outcomes are possible: the choice to continue to the next year (continuation) and three discrete outcomes (win, lose, or draw). Given that the mutual choice to continue has important implications for understanding domestic institutions, war behavior, and war duration, and given that the odds of achieving one form of war outcome or another may affect the odds of a war enduring, it is important to model all four outcomes rather than just the terminal endpoints we ultimately observe as we did in chapter 2. To do so, we need a dynamic econometric model that is capable of accounting statistically for all four outcomes seen in the theoretical model. This new analysis will also allow us to show that the relationships between the independent variables and outcomes are different in long draws versus short draws and in long victories versus short victories, something not previously possible.

Research Design

Next, we develop a new data set and method appropriate for our analysis. Our theoretical model suggests the appropriate form for both the dependent variable and the unit of analysis. At any point in time, the decisions made by state leaders will lead to either a continuation of a war or one of three decisive outcomes. Although every war will ultimately end with one of the decisive outcomes (win, lose, draw) in this game, until the final iteration of a war, the annual outcome value will be "continue." Because of this change over time, we cannot simply treat the war as the unit of analysis. A cross-sectional design measuring the outcome of each war would not contain the data necessary to judge whether a war was likely to continue or end at a given time, and therefore we would not be able to track the effects of declining consent over time. To model all of the outcomes suggested by our theoretical model, we must specify the unit of analysis as a time period.

We employ a data set in which the unit of analysis is a joint decision iteration, which leads to a data set with multiple observations for each event (war) when the event has several decisions made during its course. Since annual data on the variables included in the model are available, we use the war-year as our unit of analysis, constructing a data set with one observation per war-year. For example, Iran in 1982 during the Iran-Iraq War is an example of a single observation.[27] We capture the passage of time, along with decisive outcomes, by measuring the dependent variable using our four outcome categories per war-year (continue fighting, initiator wins, initiator loses, draw). So, for example, the value on the observation "Vietnam War 1972" is "continue," while the observation on "Vietnam War 1973" is "draw." Wars that last one year or less have one observation in the data set, with the dependent variable coded as either win, lose, or draw.

We do not order the four possible outcomes for each year. We cannot say, for instance, that a war continuation has a "higher" or "lower" value than winning or losing. Rather, it is simply different. Our dependent variable is a categorical coding of whether the initiator won, the initiator lost, the war ended in a draw, or the war continued in the year in question. We use multinomial logit for the statistical analysis.[28]

Because multiple coefficients are produced for each substantive variable, and because coefficients are relative to an excluded category, it is difficult to interpret directly both the statistical significance and substantive effects of the variables in the model. It is quite possible for a variable to appear statistically significant in only some equations but still have an important substantive effect on outcomes. It is also quite possible for a coefficient to have a negative sign in the equation for a particular outcome, but to have a positive effect on the probability of observing that outcome relative to some other outcome. In fact, the direction of marginal effects of a variable on any outcome can be calculated only given knowledge of coefficients across *all* outcomes. We deal with these difficulties by relying on block likelihood-ratio tests,[29] and by using a table of predicted probabilities created by varying values of the variables in X_i and observing the changes in $P(\Upsilon = 0)$, $P(\Upsilon = 1)$, etc. We can then observe which outcome probabilities rise and which probabilities fall as we allow a particular independent variable to increase. Since the predicted probabilities from multinomial logit estimation for any case must sum to 1, whenever the probability of one outcome rises, the probability of at least one of the other outcome(s) necessarily must fall. In addition, given the nonlinearities involved in multinomial logit analysis, it is possible for a probability to rise over some range of variable values and fall over others.

Predictions from the Econometric Model

Ultimately, given a set of values for the independent variables and a particular war-year, our model will predict the probability of an initiator victory, loss, or draw in that year, and the probability that the war will continue into another year. The prediction is thus simultaneously of *duration* (whether the war continues or not) and *outcome* (if the war does end, how it ends). By simultaneously estimating duration and outcome, the combined model we employ can make some exciting predictions. For instance, if we were to examine a hypothetical war and estimate the probability of the initiator winning at 70 percent, while the probabilities of continue, draw, and lose were each 10 percent, we would be predicting a short war likely to be won by the initiator. If on the other hand we were to estimate that the probability of continuation was 70 percent while the probabilities of win, draw, and lose were each 10 percent, we would be predicting a long war whose outcome was quite uncertain.

It is important to note that we are making predictions of both time and outcome with only one set of variables in one equation and thus are answering two questions with one set of independent variables. Because we employ multinomial logit, the models we estimate can appear quite complex. However, one can alternatively see this model as considerably more parsimonious than previous models since we are combining two prior models. One cost to this parsimony, though, is that it increases the difficulty of making accurate outcome predictions in our data set because the distribution of outcomes on our dependent variable is rather skewed. Out of 200 war-years in our final analysis, 111 cases (55 percent) are years in which the war continues into another year. We find only 52 cases (26 percent) of initiator victory, 15 cases of draws, and 22 cases of initiator loss. This skew makes prediction harder than when analyzing either win-lose-draw only, or the continuous variable of war duration. A reduction in the accuracy of our predictions relative to that of previous studies might not be surprising, since we are likely to overpredict war continuation and underpredict decisive outcomes, in the course of simultaneously predicting time and outcome.

Population of Cases and Dependent Variable

Population of Cases. We include in our data set all wars in the Correlates of War list of interstate wars that started after 1816 and ended by 1990. We split a few large wars such as the world wars into multiple wars as we did in chapter 2. As stated previously, wars that span more than one year are split into multiple yearly observations.

Dependent Variable: War Outcomes. War outcomes are coded for each year a war is ongoing as "initiator wins," "initiator loses," "draw," or "continue." "Continue" is coded for a year if the war is ongoing on January 1 of the next year. Initiators are identified, and initiator victory, loss, or draw is coded, following the same procedures we use in chapter 2.[30] Since multinomial logit will produce J sets of coefficient estimates given $J + 1$ possible outcomes, one category of the dependent variable must be used as the omitted category. We use "initiator loses" as this category. Consequently, coefficients will be relative to this category.

Independent Variables

We include in our model many of the variables described in chapter 2. We also include several other variables. These variables have important effects on war durations and war outcomes.[31] Because of this, they should be included in our statistical model as controls although they are not the focus of this chapter. These variables affect either the rate or magnitude of costs (or both) that a state can impose on its opponent. We also expect that several of the variables explored in prior studies will have effects that change over time. Since we are able to model the changing effects of these variables on outcomes and duration for the first time in this study, it is doubly important to include them. In this chapter, remember that our unit of analysis is not the war, or the war participant, but rather the war-year, and we are interested here in whether the initiator wins, the target wins, the two sides negotiate a draw, or the two sides choose to continue to fight. Because the unit is a war-year, we need to set up some of the variables in slightly different fashion than we did in chapter 2.

Initiator and Target Democracy. As demonstrated in chapter 2, democracies win wars more often than repressive states, but now, using a slightly different data set, we will test our expectation that this difference diminishes over time. We again measure democracy using Gurr's ten-point scale of "institutionalized democracy" from the corrected Polity III data set. One important difference in this chapter is that we now include the level of democracy for both the initiator and the target state. Most initiators and targets are quite autocratic. Approximately 60 percent of both initiators and targets have a democracy level of 2 or less, while only about 10 percent of initiators and 20 percent of targets are highly democratic (level 7 or above). There are a number of wars longer than the average war (eleven months) involving either highly democratic initiators or targets. Among these are the U.S.-Mexican War, the two world wars, and the Vietnam War.[32]

Time. In each year, we measure the number of months the war has been ongoing at the end of the fighting in that year.

Democracy/Time Interaction. To capture the diminishing effect of democracy on victory over time, we interact time with the level of democracy as defined above. Following Mueller's argument that popular support for wars in democratic states begins to decline almost as soon as the first soldiers are killed, we expect that democracies will begin to suffer the adverse effects of time almost immediately.

Strategy and Doctrine. As demonstrated in chapter 2, different military strategy combinations are related to the final outcome of a war because they affect both the costs imposed on a target and the rate at which those costs are imposed. Maneuver strategies impose costs quite quickly, and so an initiator employing a maneuver strategy has the highest probability of imposing enough costs on its opponent to cross the opponent's consent threshold or degrading the opponent's capabilities sufficiently to attain victory before the opponent can itself impose similar costs on the initiator.[33] At the other extreme, when an initiator uses a punishment strategy, it is expected that it will take a long time to impose adequate costs to force the target's surrender, and the initiator is itself vulnerable to being defeated if the target can impose costs on the initiator more rapidly. Some states, such as North Vietnam during the Vietnam War, deliberately select strategies that will force the prosecution of a war to slow, allowing for the decline in consent in the opposing state to come into play. Typically, weak opponents choose punishment/guerrilla strategies when they fight against materially stronger opponents.

Here, since some strategy combinations are observed quite rarely, if at all, and to simplify the analysis, we collapse strategy into three dummy variables we designate as "strategic advantage," "strategic disadvantage," and "strategic neutral." We expect the strategy combinations OMDA (offense maneuver—defense attrition), OPDM, ODPA, DPOA, DPOM, and DMOA to give a strategic advantage to the initiator, leading to faster wars, which the initiator is likely to win. We expect the combinations OADM, OMDP, OADP, DAOP, DMOP, and DAOM to give a strategic advantage to the target, leading to longer wars, which the target wins. All other combinations are expected to give a strategic advantage to neither side, leading (all other things being equal) to draws and potentially drawn out wars. Since these dummy strategy variables are mutually exclusive, we must exclude one of them from the analysis. Since it is the most common category, we exclude "strategic neutral" as the base category, including "strategic advantage" and "strategic disadvantage" as variables in the model. It is important to note that compared to our analysis in chapter 2, we now measure strategy annually. Recall that in chapter 2 we measured strategy as the predominant strategy used over the course of the war. Strategy changes as we measure them are relatively rare (important changes occur in the world wars and the Vietnam War), but they do occur. The analysis that follows reflects this.

Terrain. Rough terrain (mountains or jungle) makes finding the enemy difficult and makes it difficult for a state to achieve quick victory. On the other hand, open terrain makes hiding from the enemy more difficult and makes for quick battles and in turn quick wars. Terrain may thus influence victory, loss, and war duration (continuation). We code the terrain on which each war is fought on a scale ranging from 0 for open terrain to 0.75 for very rough terrain. We use the same variable here as was used in the analysis in chapter 2.

Strategy*Terrain. Certain strategies are better suited for particular types of terrain. For example, it is difficult to carry out a strategy requiring rapid movement in very rough terrain, and it is also difficult to carry on a war of punishment involving attacks followed by a retreat to safe hiding places in open terrain. When states choose strategies appropriate for the terrain, we expect initiators to be able to win, and win more quickly, than when their strategy does not fit the terrain. To test this proposition we interact strategy with terrain. We convert the strategy combination variable to a single scale on which we rank strategy combinations based on their estimated speed, and then we interact the resulting scale with our 0 to 0.75 terrain variable. States that make strategy choices that are incompatible with the terrain they face will be more likely to lose.

Balance of Capabilities. We calculate this in the same manner as in chapter 2.

Initiator and Target Repression. Related to the notion of mass-public consent is the problem (from the state's perspective) of active dissent. We expect repressive states to have a higher probability of victory than less repressive states because they are able to suppress mass (or elite) dissent and quickly mobilize forces for use in combat. We measure repression using Gurr's five-point scale of the "Competitiveness of Political Participation" but reverse the scale so that a 1 indicates a nonrepressive (highly competitive) regime while a 5 indicates a repressive (suppressed competition) regime.

Strategy, Capability, Terrain, and Repression Interactions with Time. We expect the effects of the above variables to change over time and so interact each variable with the time measure previously defined. We expect that military strategies will correlate best with outcomes early in the war. Over time, states can adapt to each other's strategy, and so if a strategic advantage does not lead to victory quickly, it is even less likely to do so as time passes. We similarly expect that the effect of capabilities on war outcomes may decrease over time. If a capability advantage does not translate into victory immediately, then there must be some other important factor affecting the war, and so we expect the capability advantage to be relatively neutralized. The muted effect of those capabilities should be reflected by a decrease in their effect over time as other factors continue to gain in importance. Finally, even in repressive states, there is a limit on how long dissent can be suppressed, and so we expect that if sufficient time passes, the advantages of repression will decrease.

Initiator Salience and Target Salience. The more salient (or important) the object in contention, the harder a state should be willing to fight for it, and in democracies, the more likely it will be that the state leaders can maintain consent among the public for the war effort.[34] We code the issues at stake in each war using Kalevi Holsti's categorization of issues.[35] For example, in the 1956 war between Hungary and the Soviet Union, the issues for Hungary include autonomy and government composition, whereas for the Soviet Union the issues include national security, the preservation of alliance unity, and the protection of ideological confreres. We set up a dummy variable for each side marking conflicts involving survival, territory, unification, reputation, and autonomy as salient. Conflicts involving policy, empire, trade, and other issues are coded as nonsalient. We expect that when the issues at stake are salient for a state, it will be more likely to win, less likely to lose, and more likely to continue fighting than to stop.

Distance. Long distances between the initiator and target may make it harder for the initiator to win, both because it is costly and difficult to project power over such distances and because it may be difficult to maintain support for a war effort far from home.[36] We capture some of the effect of distance by discounting national capabilities in the balance of forces variable, but we also include a variable measuring the distance from the initiator to the target in kilometers.

Surprise. Military surprise can help a state win a war (higher probability of victory) and win more quickly (lower probability of a war continuing) by enabling it to impose costs quickly. Based on whether one or both sides achieved strategic military surprise at any point during a war, we calculate the difference in the proportion of military forces surprised between the two sides. The larger the value of our surprise variable, the greater the expected advantage accrues to the initiator.

Total Military Personnel and Population. When states have more personnel or population, they can continue to fight longer than when they have fewer of these resources because they can absorb relatively more costs. In addition, given large forces, two states may be more likely to fight to a draw than if their forces are smaller, since they can both continue to call on military reserves rather than accede to their opponent's policy demands. We thus expect large personnel and population to be associated with higher probabilities of draw outcomes and continuation from year to year.

Duration Dependence, Time, Interactive Time Effects, and the Current Model

One of our goals in this chapter is to simultaneously model war outcomes (win, lose, draw) and the time it takes to reach that outcome, as we earlier hypothesized that democracies should have a stronger preference than autocracies for shorter rather than longer wars, all things being equal. While we do not directly model overall war duration here, by including the "continue" outcome in our annual data set we can predict whether a set of conditions are conducive to a rapid end to conflict or a continuation of fighting. We would expect cases with a high probability of continuation to have a longer overall duration than cases with a low probability of continuing. Modeling duration together with outcome raises interesting questions regarding the role of duration dependence and our expectations about the effects of the independent variables.

Duration dependence is a characteristic of some processes in which the amount of time in a given condition influences expected future time in that same condition. In the case of war, negative duration dependence would occur if a long period of prior fighting led to a conflict becoming entrenched, increasing its chances of continuing longer into the future. Alternatively, positive duration dependence would occur if prior fighting led to war-weariness on the part of the participants, and so an increase in the annual probability of a war ending over time as the war continues. Bennett and Stam found that once strategy, capabilities, and other elements of a model of war duration were properly specified, war did not appear to be duration dependent.[37] What this suggests for this study is that the effect of the variable marking solely the passage of time on the probability of continuation should be near zero. The presence of duration dependence would mean that in each iteration (year) of a war, the duration of the war up to that year is important information. If we have properly accounted for influences on duration, however, the inclusion of a "time" variable should not improve our estimates of whether a conflict will continue or have a decisive outcome in some year. Note, though, that even if war is not duration dependent, time could still have an impact on the relative probabilities of a war ending in a victory, loss, or draw for the initiator. In addition, interactions between other variables and time could still be significant in the absence of duration dependence, because those interactions reflect changes in variable effects over time. These expected interactions have little to do with general duration dependence and our conclusions about it.

Results

Table 7.1 presents the coefficients produced by estimating our multinomial logit model. With four outcomes there are three sets of coefficients that represent estimates of the effects of the variables on the three categories relative to the omitted category, that of the initiator losing. Every variable except for time and strategic advantage interacted with time has an apparent significance level of at least 0.10 in at least one of the outcome equations. However, as discussed previously, it is difficult to rely solely on these individual apparent significance levels in judging whether a variable (or group of variables) has an effect on outcomes. To deal with this problem, we performed a number of likelihood ratio tests using a series of nested models to determine whether variables are having a combined effect on war continuation and war outcomes.

Table 7.2 provides the results of dropping various combinations of variables from the model. For example, for the domestic politics variables, we started by dropping the interactive domestic politics*time terms and progressed to dropping all of the domestic politics variables. The results of the likelihood-ratio tests suggest that whatever block is removed, the variables and interactions we included appear to contribute significantly to the model. We can be quite confident that the interactions between these variables and time are indeed affecting war outcomes systematically.

Table 7.3 shows the success of the model at predicting outcomes across the four outcome categories. Overall, we predict 75 percent of all outcomes correctly. Not surprisingly given the skew in the distribution of outcomes in the data set, we slightly overpredict the modal category of war continuation and underpredict the two rarest outcomes, draws and initiator losses. Thus, our model predicts that 124 war-years should end in a continuation of the war, while there are only 111 actual continuations. We simultaneously predict 12 war-years as draws when there were actually 15, and we predict 10 losses when there were actually 22. Overall, however, the predictions fit actual outcomes rather closely. We can

TABLE 7.1

Coefficient Estimates, Multinomial Logit Model of War Outcomes and Duration

| | Outcomes | | | | | |
| | Continue | | Initiator Victory | | Draw | |
Independent Variable	Coefficient	T-score	Coefficient	T-score	Coefficient	T-score
Strategic Advantage	32.20	.	34.59***	15.81	−65.07	0.00
Strategic Advantage*Time	−0.04	−0.42	−0.03	.	0.50	0.00
Strategic Disadvantage	−6.44**	−2.45	−9.55*	−2.22	−22.96	−1.09
Strategic Disadvantage*Time	−0.06	−0.96	−0.65	−0.89	0.80*	1.97
Terrain	23.40*	1.70	36.07**	2.24	−32.55	−0.40
Terrain*Strategy Scale	−5.25*	−1.82	−6.81**	−2.10	17.23	0.97
Terrain*Time	0.11	1.03	0.12	0.74	−1.76**	−2.67
Balance of Forces	1.71	0.73	4.90*	1.79	36.92**	2.74
Balance of Forces*Time	0.09	0.94	0.34	1.86	−0.97*	−2.19
Sum of Military Personnel	0.00	0.42	0.00	−0.33	0.00*	−2.33
Sum of Population	0.00*	1.91	0.00	1.53	0.00***	3.05

Initiator Democracy	−0.17	−0.74	0.16	0.71	−0.67	−1.37
Target Democracy	−0.07	−0.25	−0.03	−0.11	1.13	1.26
Initiator Democracy*Time	0.00	0.04	−0.02	−1.22	0.09*	2.36
Target Democracy*Time	−0.02	−1.10	−0.02	−1.07	0.13*	2.15
Initiator Repression	−1.31*	−2.29	−0.68	−1.26	−1.28	−0.83
Target Repression	−0.19	−0.31	0.22	0.32	3.04	1.04
Initiator Repression*Time	0.04*	1.78	−0.02	−0.43	0.12*	1.86
Target Repression*Time	−0.05	−1.12	−0.10*	−1.83	0.30*	1.85
Initiator Salience	2.41*	1.73	2.10	1.51	2.47	0.71
Target Salience	0.99	0.94	1.40	1.27	−6.37*	−1.92
Surprise	20.39*	1.77	33.98**	2.39	−69.13	−1.59
Distance	0.00*	2.23	0.00	1.69	0.00*	1.80
Time	−0.03	−0.18	0.26	1.08	−0.69	−1.25
Constant	3.90	1.11	−3.74	−0.95	−56.58*	−2.21

Note: Outcome = Initiator Losses is the comparison group. n = 200 observations (war-years). Log likelihood = −116.4 Log likelihood of model with constant term only = −228.0. P(model) [based on chi-squared test with 72 df] = < 0.001. Significance tests one-tailed.

* p < 0.05.
**p < 0.01.
***p < 0.001.

TABLE 7.2

Block Variable Tests for Variables with Time Interactions

Variables Removed	Degrees of Freedom	Resulting Log Likelihood	Probability (vs. Original Model)
Original model, all variables included)	—	−116.37	—
2 Democracy*Time interactions	6	−126.46	<0.01
4 Democracy variables (raw and interactive)	12	−129.53	0.01
2 Repression*Time interactions	6	−128.32	<0.001
4 Repression variables (raw and interactive)	12	−131.48	<0.01
4 Democracy plus 4 Repression variables	24	−137.49	0.01
1 Capability*Time interaction	3	−125.43	<0.001
2 Capability variables (raw and interactive)	6	−138.76	<0.001
2 Strategy*Time interactions	6	−130.77	<0.001
4 Strategy variables (raw and interactive)	12	−143.92	<0.001
1 Terrain*Time interaction	3	−130.74	<0.001
3 Terrain variables (raw and interactive)	9	−143.23	<0.001

judge how much our model helps us predict outcomes by calculating the proportional reduction in error (PRE) that the model gives us. Without the information provided by the model, we would predict that all war-years would result in the outcome "continue." This would lead to 89 errors. With the predictions of the model, our errors are reduced to 50. The elimination of 39 errors gives us a PRE of 44 percent.

We now turn to the implications of the results for our theoretical arguments, in particular for our arguments about how democracy affects outcomes over time. We begin by creating a table of predicted outcome probability values over various values of the independent variables. In all cases, we present probability values obtained by using the "method of recycled predictions." Generally, the method of recycled predictions uses actual variable values on actual cases but sets variables of interest to particular values for all cases and then assesses the change in outcome probabilities. The probabilities in table 7.4 shows the probability that, given

TABLE 7.3

Predicted vs. Actual Outcomes

		Number of Cases (War-Years) Predicted				
		Continue	Initiator Victory	Draw	Initiator Loss	Total
Actual Number	Continue	96	12	1	2	111
of Cases	Initiator Victory	13	37	1	1	52
(War-Years)	Draw	2	3	10	0	15
	Initiator Loss	13	2	0	7	22
	Total	124	54	12	10	200

Note: 150/200 correct = 75%. Proportional reduction in error (PRE) = 44%.

that a war has lasted for a particular length of time (e.g., six months or eighteen months), the year in consideration will end in each of the four outcomes. The four probabilities P(continue), P(win), P(draw), and P(lose) should sum to 1.0, since in each year, one of the four outcomes must occur.[38]

The table has three main sections, from left to right: The first column lists the duration of the simulated wars, beginning with short wars and continuing down the column to wars that last fifty-four months or more. The second column is where we indicate whether the state in question is a democracy or not. To simplify matters, we only address two types of

TABLE 7.4

Predicted Probabilities of War Outcomes at Different Stages, 1816–1990

War Duration (months)	Initiator	Probability			
		of Continuing	of Win (percent)	of Draw	of Loss
6	Nondemocratic	53	32	4	11
	Democratic	32	49	2	17
18	Nondemocratic	57	27	4	12
	Democratic	46	19	15	20
30	Nondemocratic	49	26	13	11
	Democratic	42	10	37	12
42	Nondemocratic	46	26	19	9
	Democratic	30	7	58	6
54	Nondemocratic	41	25	25	9
	Democratic	22	6	70	3

Note: "Democratic" has Democracy set to 9 (on 1–10 scale). "Nondemocratic" has Democracy set to 2.

states: democracies and nondemocracies. The third group of columns lists the four possible outcomes at each of the different war durations: continue fighting, the war ends and the initiator wins, the war ends in a draw, and the war ends and the initiator loses. We read the table row by row from the top, beginning with the choices that states made, on average after fighting for six months. After fighting for six months, on average, nondemocracies have a 53 percent chance of choosing to continue to fight. Of the nondemocracies that fought in wars of six months or less, 32 percent of them won, 4 percent accepted a draw, and 11 percent lost. For democracies that initiated wars, the chances they would still be fighting after six months are quite a bit less than they are for nondemocracies. By the time six months have passed, only 32 percent of democratic war initiators chose to continue to fight, 49 percent won, 2 percent accepted a draw, and 17 percent lost.

We walk through the application of the method of recycled predictions only in our main results on democracy, but the application would be similar elsewhere. We started with our initial set of data on our 200 cases and the set of coefficients estimated in our main model. We then changed the value on the initiator's democracy variable to the value 2 for all 200 cases, reflecting a low-democracy initiator, set all values of time to six months (reflecting time in the first year of a war), and recomputed interactive variables that involved democracy or time. We then used the coefficients from the model to create predicted probabilities for each of the four outcome categories for each case. At this point, each case in the data has associated probabilities computed *as if* the case were a nondemocratic initiator involved in the early stages of a war, but with all other variables kept at their actual measured values. We then compute and present the average probability across the data set of a war continuation, initiator victory, initiator loss, and draw. We then changed the value of democracy for all cases to a 9, reflecting a highly democratic state, and repeated the process, obtaining new outcome probabilities that we hypothesize would have been observed if all states had been democratic war initiators fighting in the first year of a war. The difference in these predicted probabilities inform us as to whether increasing levels of democracy lead to a higher or lower probability of victory, defeat, and so on.[39]

Although we do not discuss them in detail here, other important elements of the model gain support as well. We find that strategic advantages and disadvantages, terrain, the balance of military forces, the size of military forces and national populations, repression, distance, and surprise all play important roles in determining which of the four outcomes should be expected in any given year. Our nonsignificant results for the variable "time" corroborate Bennett and Stam's earlier arguments that wars are not duration dependent.[40]

EIGHT

WHY DEMOCRACIES WIN WARS

*I must study politics and war that my sons may have liberty
to study mathematics and philosophy.*
—*John Adams*

W E NOW KNOW why democracies win wars. The two key
dimensions of the democratic character that best explain democratic victory are the skeleton of democracy, those political
institutions that hold democratic leaders accountable to the consent of
the people, and the spirit of democracy, with its emphasis on the development of individual rights, responsibility, and initiative. When governments must answer to the will (and anger) of the people, they start only
those wars they are confident they will win. Democracies differ from
other kinds of states in that democratic leaders are, as Tocqueville and
others feared, restrained by the need to generate consent for their actions. Counter to Tocqueville's fears, however, the necessary pause to
generate consent that democratic political institutions build into the
policy-making process leads democratic elites to be far less likely than
other kinds of states to enter into war impulsively, and thereby avoiding
risky and costly military adventures. On the battlefield, democratic political culture imbues democracies' citizens with individual attributes that
serve both the citizens and the state well in war as well as in peace. More
often than not, the sons of democracy outfight the sons of tyranny by
showing better individual initiative and leadership than their counterparts
raised in and fighting for autocratic regimes.

The power of democracy truly does lie with the people and their
unique relationship to the state. Governments of the people and by the
people routinely defeat their autocratic counterparts in battle. Democracies do not win because their political leaders construct powerful coalitions or communities of liberal states, nor do they win because the elites
running their countries are able to extract more of the state's industrial
capacity for war. By retaining a voice in the decision to initiate wars, the
people ensure that foolhardy military gambles are quite rare in democracies, far less common than the risky military adventures all too frequently initiated by dictators. Moreover, on the battlefield itself, citizen
soldiers rise to the challenge and outperform their opposing counterparts.

We have exposed myths—previously accepted explanations of why de-

194   CHAPTER 8

mocracies win wars. The sense of family or community among the leaders
of democracies in the international arena is surprisingly weak. Presidents
and prime ministers are not especially likely to come to each other's aid
during war—they are not especially likely to intervene on each other's
behalf when one comes under attack. Further, democracies do not win
wars by out-producing or out-mobilizing their opponents. Democratic
institutions are not uniquely effective at producing the wealth needed
to build and maintain powerful militaries, nor do they extract proportionately more from their populations than do autocratic systems.

From these findings, we made other important discoveries. Democracies are not as peace-loving as some would hope; they do launch wars
in the pursuit of the national interest and for empire, when the public
provides its consent. When public consent is available, it appears to be
fleeting. Citizens of democracies prefer to cut their losses rather than
continue in the hope that the tide will eventually turn. As a result, leaders
of democracies strive to bring wars to swift conclusion before consent
evaporates entirely. Contrary to explanations of democratic foreign policy
that focus on expectantly benevolent norms of political elites, when public consent is not available, democratically elected leaders sometimes circumvent public opposition by employing covert means, sometimes even
doing so to subvert other democratic governments.

We close this book by reflecting on the broader meaning of our results,
looking beyond the narrower theme of why democracies win wars. We
reflect first on what these findings tell us about the two central concepts
of this book, war and democracy. Then, we look at the normative and
consent perspectives on foreign policy, assessing which one offers a more
accurate outlook on the connections between democracy and war. Finally, we focus on implications of the book for foreign policy. What conclusions can we draw to help guide American foreign policy in the
twenty-first century?

On War

Carl von Clausewitz famously declared, "*war is nothing but the continuation of policy with other means.*"[1] Though written nearly two centuries
ago, these words remain even more true and important today than ever.
Politics and war are inextricably bound. War is not a purely organizational mission, executed by an apolitical military machine. Nor is it un-
derstandable solely by principles of martial strategy and engineering. Its
initiation, prosecution, and termination are all deeply political, all driven
by and infused with political motives and meaning.

Chapter 2 demonstrates that the outbreak of war results from political choice. War does not descend upon nations like locusts or earthquakes. Rather, wars occur because states pick fights to advance political goals. As a result, states that start wars are particularly likely to win them. Further, domestic politics heavily affect the decision to embark on war. Democratic leaders are more politically allergic to foreign policy disasters than are autocratic leaders, and this heightened sensitivity to the costs of war guides them to start only those wars they go on to win. Dependence on consent differentiates democratic war initiation in other ways, as public consent determines which conditions constitute a *casus belli* and which do not.

The German Field Marshal Helmuth von Moltke (the elder) once declared, "The politician should fall silent the moment that mobilization begins."[2] But he had it exactly wrong: the reach of politics is not and cannot be halted with the declaration of war. Combat is not merely a grim reaper's arithmetic of men and munitions, offering victory to the side that tips the scales. It is fundamentally about the skills, motivations, and capabilities of individual soldiers whose behavior reflects the societies from which they come. We have expanded on this traditional belief with an emphasis on the political environment from which soldiers come. Free societies produce freethinking and more effective soldiers. Free societies can also subvert and terminally weaken an opponent's army by seducing its soldiers into laying down their arms in surrender with the promise of fair treatment as prisoners of war.

Lastly, the decision to end war is a deeply political one.[3] Democratic leaders continue to pay attention to the consent and opinion of the public as war proceeds. Democratic governments and their leaders nervously monitor levels of public opinion, knowing they must end their wars quickly. This desire for short wars in turn pushes democratic states to avoid entanglements in long, indecisive wars and to choose military strategies that promise victory quickly and at low cost.

On Democracy

What does it mean for a state to be a democracy? At the outset of this book, we laid out four different possible dimensions or characteristics of democracy: the skeleton, spirit, family, and power of democracy. We found that the skeleton and spirit of democracy explain the tendency of democracies to win wars better than do the family and power of democracy. These sources of democratic military power also say something important about the nature of democratic political institutions. Different types of democracies can exist; a key distinguishing characteristic is the role of mass public consent. In the preceding chapters, we found that forcing leaders to be subject to the consent of the people is an empowering characteristic of certain democratic institutions. Not all democratic theorists would agree with the normative desirability of this proposition, however.

Many, going back to Alexander Hamilton and Thomas Jefferson, felt that the key component of successful democracy is an elite republican aristocracy, in Hamilton's case the landed class. The leaders in Jefferson's republic would not be constrained by a need to generate contemporaneous consent of the masses; instead, they would be free to pursue what they felt was in the best interests of the state, being held accountable after the fact.[4] An early American observer fretted that "The notion that every man that works a day on the road, or serves an idle hour in the militia is entitled as of right to an equal participation in the whole power of government, is most unreasonable, and has no foundation in justice."[5] The *Federalist Papers* are the classic presentation of this conflict, of participatory versus representative democracy.

The early federalists lost the political wars at the founding of the American republic, after which Andrew Jackson and other populists came to realize that the people were not a mob to be constrained by the aristocrats, but rather the source of the state's power. In this way, by creating systems of government where the masses have a say in the decision to go to war through mechanisms of consent, democracies' actions in war show that elite and aristocratic fears of the mob are unfounded. The aristocrats do not bring out the best in the people; rather, it is the so-called mob that brings out the best in the governmental elite. In states where the political leaders are unconstrained by the masses, the aristocrats that the early federalists believed to hold the key to the successful and powerful state all too frequently take risky gambles that place the very future of the state at risk.

The more modern debates over democracy focus on whether democracy is an affordable luxury. Most agree that the democratic process is intrinsically more agreeable to the human condition, as Robert Dahl, one of democracy's most eloquent observers, wrote that democracy is "superior in at least three ways to other feasible ways by which people can be governed. First, it promotes freedom as no feasible alternative can. Second, the democratic process promotes human development, not least in the capacity for exercising self-determination, moral autonomy, and responsibility of one's choices. Finally, it is the surest way (if by no means a perfect one) by which human beings can protect and advance the interests and goods they share with others."[6] Others agree, arguing that democracy provides other important benefits, including offering the best guarantees of distributive justice, acting as a safeguard against genocide, protecting human rights, and reducing the risk of famine.[7]

In contrast, political realists argue that when it comes to international relations, states do not have the luxury of placing considerations such as the distribution of wealth or the individual's moral autonomy at the top of the list of state goals. Rather, in the context of the realist focus on the quest for survival, power and security are the most important imperatives for a state to pursue and to privilege above all other ends. Our findings, however, turn this perspective on its head. Based on the evidence presented here, democracy emerges as the best type of political arrangement, not simply because it is the most just, nor because it is the fairest. In the realm of international politics, there is no need to apologize for advocating the spread of democratic institutions as it is these political institutions that lead to the best, securest, and safest outcomes for the most people. Democracy is the preferred set of political institutions at home. We have now shown that historically, democracy has also been the surest means to power in the arena of battle, allowing states to both serve *and* protect their citizens.

Democracies are able to defend themselves, and they are less likely to initiate foolhardy wars. These two facts result not from aristocratic leaders exercising the exclusive international perquisites of power, but directly because of the people's control over government and their exercise of their rights therein. Political realists have long advocated a separation of normative desires from the analysis of international affairs. They have argued that the future survival and safety of nations is always at stake in the anarchic international system. Because of this, considerations of what type of political system would be "best" for states was seen as a luxury that international relations scholars could not indulge in. By demonstrating that democracies are better able to protect themselves than are other types of states, democracy can now be advocated on realist as well as normative grounds.

Democracy and International Relations

Having reviewed what our findings say about democracies at war and what they may say about the nature of democracy, what does this tell us about how democracies make foreign policy? What does this imply for the foundations of the so-called democratic peace and other observations about the nature of foreign policy in democratic states? In chapters 4 and 6, we laid out two different models of foreign policy incorporating domestic politics: the consent and normative models. The consent model proposes that the foreign policies of democracies differ because democratic governments must answer to the demands of the public. The normative model proposes that the foreign policies of democracies differ because democratic governments forge international liberal communities characterized by norms of peaceful conflict resolution.

Which of these perspectives on the connection between domestic regime type and international relations is favored by the way that states actually behave? Consider two sets of facts that constitute much of the body of empirical knowledge we possess about the behavior of democracies in the international system. The first consists of characteristic types of foreign policy choices that are particular to democracies; the second set of observations particularly regards democracies at war:

Foreign policy choices that democracies make:

1. Democracies rarely, if ever, choose war against one another.[8]
2. Democracies are not especially likely to choose to ally with each other or to assist each other in war (chapter 4).
3. Democracies choose to initiate wars against nondemocracies (chapters 2, 7).
4. Democracies choose to use covert force against other democracies (chapter 6).
5. Democracies sometimes choose to execute genocidal policies in wars of empire (chapter 6).
6. Democracies at war are more likely to choose to settle for draws (chapter 7).
7. Democracies choose not to devote greater material efforts in war than other states (chapter 5).
8. Democracies make better choices of military strategy.[9]

Empirical facts about democracies at war:

1. Democracies are more likely to win interstate wars (chapter 2).
2. Democratic initiators are particularly likely to win wars (chapter 2).
3. Democracies' chances of victory diminish as public support for war drops (chapter 7).
4. Democracies initiate wars of shorter duration (chapter 7).
5. Democracies suffer fewer casualties in wars they initiate.[10]
6. Democraties' use of force declines as casualties mount.[11]
7. Democratic soldiers fight with better leadership and greater initiative (chapter 3).

What specific conclusions can we draw about these fifteen observations? First, they point clearly and unavoidably toward a powerful refutation of the normative theory linking democracy and international relations. A norm of pacifism does not drive democracies to be more peaceful than other states in the international system. Democracies do initiate wars, and they do so when it is seen to be in the national interest, and not as only a last ditch effort to preserve the national defense when diplomacy has failed. Further, they initiate wars against weaker foes, they initiate imperialist wars, and they sometimes use genocidal means in warfare. In addition, there is no international community of democracy emerging from shared liberal norms. Democracies are not especially likely to ally with each other, and they do not intervene on one another's behalf when one comes under attack. Further, democracies are sometimes willing to take forceful action against nascent democracies, resorting to covert action or, sometimes, overt action against primitive peoples.

Conversely, these empirical results quite strongly support the consent perspective. All the empirical evidence points strongly to democratic governments calculating very carefully whether their foreign policy actions are consistent with public opinion. Democratic leaders avoid starting wars that they will lose or that will be bloody, they choose military strategies that help them win cheap and successful wars, they fight short wars, and they start wars only for popular causes. In short, consent matters.

The fifteen observations above are consistent with the following deductions about democracies:

- Democratic leaders make their choices more carefully than leaders in autocracies and dictatorships.
- Democratic elites are not "nicer" than elites in other kinds of states.
- Soldiers from democracies fight better than their counterparts in other kinds of states do.
- Initiating war against a democracy is risky.
- Public consent is a critical, although often overlooked, factor in the study of international relations.
- The ties that bind international democracies together are relatively weak.

One of our central goals in this book has been to demonstrate the importance of public consent in thinking about democracy and international relations. We conclude our discussion of consent by drawing out two slightly different conceptualizations of how consent matters for the determination of a state's foreign policy; our intent is to map out an agenda for future scholarship. These two conceptualizations are the *contemporary consent model* and the *electoral punishment model*.[12]

The key difference between the two models is how democratic leaders are constrained by the nature of public opinion. In our story, they are subject to the constraint of the public at the time of their decision. Alternatively, voters constrain their leaders by evaluating their policies ex post or after they are completed. The contemporary consent model employs the former assumption, proposing that democratic leaders think about the current nature of public opinion when they make their decision. This views democratic leaders as constantly monitoring and campaigning for public support, even when there is no election immediately impending.[13]

The electoral punishment model assumes the latter, that democratic leaders think about what the nature of public opinion will be only after events play themselves out in the international system, and most specifically when elections occur. Even if a foreign policy action is currently unpopular, leaders are willing to take that action if they feel that the action will eventually come to be seen as a wise choice by the electorate, such as if it turns out to be much more successful than the public thinks beforehand.

The central similarity between the contemporary consent and electoral punishment variants is that both focus on public consent for government policies. Both also retain similar assumptions about what kinds of things the public is likely to approve or disapprove of: the public hates to lose wars, dislikes high casualty levels, and so forth. The key difference is the timing of the leadership's concern about public opinion. The contemporary consent model argues that leaders ask the question, "What is the nature of public support right now?" This is consistent with a participatory notion of democracy—contemporaneous consent is necessary for governmental action, and the citizens have a right to have a say in the choices their governments make. The electoral punishment model argues that leaders ask the question, "What will the public's level of support be when I come up for reelection, and how will events today affect their evaluation of my future performance at election time?" This is a more Aristotelian or Jeffersonian notion of republican democracy.[14] Leaders are selected by their citizens, who keep an eye on the future; indirectly then, they hold their leaders accountable for the actions they may take while in office. Significantly, these two theories get at fundamentally different ways of thinking about the nature of government and the constraining effects of public consent. The contemporary consent model sees democratic leaders as aiming to represent the will of the people constantly, whether for self-serving or idealistic reasons. The electoral punishment model sees democratic leaders as disinterested in public opinion except in the quite narrow and instrumental manner in which it directly determines reelection. Regarding war outcomes, the contemporary consent model predicts that democratic leaders virtually never initiate war that is unpopular at the time, preferring instead to wait until consent emerges or they can generate it. As we have shown, there is a great deal of evidence to support this view.

Woodrow Wilson called for American entry into World War I in 1917 when there was sufficient popular American support at the time, due to threats to American shipping and the Zimmermann telegram. Franklin Roosevelt's tentative steps toward American involvement in World War II in the two years preceding illustrate this point: he only pushed American belligerency as far as he felt American public opinion would support it, though he did of course actively work to enlighten American opinion toward favoring involvement by arguing publicly that engagement was in the national interest. As we discussed in chapter 6, the existence of public consent at the time a democracy initiates war is essential. Alternatively, the electoral punishment model envisions the possibility that a democratic leader could initiate a quite unpopular war, if the leadership were confident that the war would turn out better than expected by the population, or if the war would be forgotten by the population by the time the next set of elections occurred.

Our view is that the true nature of the relationship between public consent and democratic foreign policy-making contains elements of both models and likely evolves over time. Democratic leaders are clearly concerned about elections and what their public support will be when elections occur. Sometimes this encourages foreign policy behavior oriented around the timing of elections, such as Lyndon Johnson's October 1968 peace initiative intended to boost the Democrat Hubert Humphrey's chances in the November presidential election, followed by candidate Richard Nixon's countermove of scotching the peace ploy just days before the election. Others have claimed that the 1980 Reagan-Bush presidential campaign endeavored to delay the release of Iranian hostages to prevent the incumbent Jimmy Carter from securing a last-minute foreign policy coup. Or, that John F. Kennedy's decision for action against Cuban missiles in October 1962 was motivated at least in part by concern over the upcoming midterm Senate elections.[15] More generally, however, most of the historical evidence indicates that the timing of elections does not affect profoundly the decision to use force, especially in the post–World War II period.[16] In the fall of 1990, for example, George Bush was motivated to choose war over sanctions as a policy against Iraq because of his falling public support at the time, though ironically the massive wave of public approval (as high as 89 percent) he experienced in the winter of 1991 did not sweep him to reelection in the following year.[17]

The degree to which either of these two models will best explain democratic foreign policy behavior is likely to vary across political systems. Longer spans between elections afford executives less contemporary concern with consent. Executives with more powerful legislatures who themselves face frequent elections may be more constantly concerned with public opinion. The contemporary consent model is more likely to have explanatory power in recent decades with the advent of electronic media and the improvement of the public opinion poll. It is now quite possible for presidents and prime ministers to have very precise estimates of their popularity on a month-to-month or even week-to-week basis as politicians seek to alter their behavior not just in synch with the election cycle, but in rhythm to the daily news cycle.

American Foreign Policy in the Twenty-First Century

What advice do we have for policy-makers? Our first and happiest conclusion is that the democratic experiment can and will continue to survive. Contrary to the fears of some naysayers, democracies have consistently been able to fight off attacks from autocratic predators and will continue to endure. They wisely avoid foolish wars, and when they are forced to fight, their soldiers typically perform better than do their autocratic counterparts. This gives us confidence in the sustainability of the international trend to democracy. Several factors are pushing an increasing number of nations to democratize. Among these, rising global levels of material prosperity, the appearance of other democracies themselves, and the decreased ability of autocrats to manage and manipulate news information make the further spread of democracy more likely.[18] In addition to these factors, we can say confidently that democracies can safely defend themselves from the threat of outside predators. But what sort of policies or doctrine should the United States pursue as the acknowledged international system leader at the dawn of the twenty-first century?

During the Cold War, the doctrine of containment served as the basic foreign policy strategy for both parties. Following the collapse of the Soviet Union, the future of U.S. foreign policy is once again open to far-ranging debate. The 2000 American presidential campaign highlighted one of the major cleavages in foreign policy in the post-Cold War period. On one side are advocates of an interventionist doctrine, known to its critics during the Clinton years as the Albright "do-ability" doctrine: Use force in ways that were doable to improve the lot in life of various peoples around the world. While ambassador to the United Nations, Madeleine Albright expressed this extreme willingness to use force when she told Colin Powell in 1993, "What's the use of having this superb military you're always talking about if we can't use it?"[19] This might better be called an interventionist doctrine—force, while obviously to be used to wage wars against other states, might also be used in more limited ways to intervene in the domestic affairs of other nations, notably to spread democratic institutions.

An alternative view is that American military forces ought to be used only to fight more traditional wars, and only to defend American geopolitical interests. This view emerges from two central assumptions, that the spread of democracy and protection of human rights are not central to the American national interest, and that the armed forces are ill-equipped at fighting unconventional conflicts or nation-building. At this writing, it appears that the new George W. Bush administration holds beliefs close to but not coequal with this view. During the 2000 campaign, Bush proposed that "There may be some moments when we use our troops as peacekeepers, but not often." Colin Powell, the secretary of state under the George W. Bush administration, has also expressed skepticism about the use of military force for such nation-building and peacekeeping operations, growing from similar views expressed as part of the "Powell Doctrine," formulated when he was chairman of the Joint Chiefs during the George Bush (Senior) administration.[20] The main ideological divide today between these two views is over the conditions that would justify an intervention in the internal affairs of a foreign country. While the Albright do-ability interventionist doctrine allows for a wider range of conditions that include the protection of human rights and advance of democracy, the alternative view is more narrow and would be unlikely ever to accept intervention to spread democracy or protect human rights.

Based on the research presented here, we believe there is a middle ground, a more enlightened interventionist policy. What sorts of rules of thumb can we provide for the use of force in the twenty-first century? In the context of our arguments about the role of democracy in international relations, we need to ask two questions: How valuable to the national interests of the United States is the international spread of democracy? What does it take to transform a previously autocratic regime into a democracy? Regarding the former, the spread of democracy is good both for individual states and the international system. American interests are served by a more peaceful world order, and democracies (even new ones) are unlikely to fight each other.[21] The bottom line of our argument is that democracies provide security for themselves by empowering their citizens and crafting more prudent foreign policies. An international system populated with prudent and nonwarring states would be a more stable and safer system than one populated with risk-acceptant dictatorships, both from a military security perspective and from an economic one, as domestic and international stability in a region is a necessary condition for economic growth and investment. In other words, the spread of democracy serves the goals of both viewpoints on intervention, as it advances the human condition by protecting freedom and directly serves the American national interest by helping sustain a peaceful, more prosperous world.

Now, regarding the second point, what does it take to transform the political institutions of state, to make a state into a democracy? We know that building democracy is not an easy task, far from it. To ensure that a transition to democracy will "take," or persist into the future, there are important antecedent conditions. For a state to successfully make the transition to democracy, there first must be a basic respect for the rule of law and a collective sense that reform of the nation's governing political institutions will lead them to serve the interests of the country and its citizens. Democracy can only work if its citizens are confident that the rule of law will ensure real and fair political competition and protect their rights to participate in the political process. Second, there also needs to be an economic middle class sufficiently large to provide a political counterweight to other social and economic classes. Relatedly, democracy becomes more likely to succeed as per capita gross domestic product grows.[22]

If the conditions are right, then sustained democratization is possible. The transformation of an autocratic state into a liberal democratic one is in the interest of both the people of that society and their neighbors and the international system leader, the United States. So when or under what conditions should American leaders consider intervening to advance democracy abroad? First, the United States should only dispatch troops when there is public consent. Fortunately, post–Cold War surveys of public opinion indicate that the public is open to sending American troops abroad to intervene in nontraditional conflicts such as peace-keeping, even if such operations do not serve a narrow conception of the national interest.[23] Second, the general emphasis on caution in the Powell Doctrine, that military force should only be used when the objective is clear and there is high probability of attaining it, is well worth remembering. A central finding of our book is the virtue of caution in the use of force. Democracies win wars in large part because they attack only when they are very confident they can win. This emphasis on caution is especially important regarding the use of force to establish democracy or long-term political stability, given past difficulties in accomplishing this mission in Somalia and elsewhere. Importantly, though, complete pessimism is unwarranted; military force can promote social stability and the advance of democracy. We urge policy-makers to be willing to use force for this end if the conditions for success, especially a society that enjoys the proper institutional, cultural, and economic conditions, seem to be present.

Our findings offer a reassuring if counterintuitive conclusion: consent breeds success and democracy builds security. Foreign policy is not necessarily best left to political and military leaders; obeying the whims of the public tends to steer a state away from military disasters, rather than leading it to them. As John Jay pointed out in the *Federalist Papers*, "absolute monarchs will often make war when their nations are to get nothing by it, but for purposes and objects merely personal, such as a thirst for military glory, revenge for personal affronts, ambition, or private compacts to aggrandize or support their particular families or partisans. These and a variety of other motives, which affect only the mind of the sovereign, often lead him to engage in wars not sanctified by justice or the voice and interests of his people."[24] By acting only when the interests and the voice of the people are at stake and with their consultation, state leaders reduce tremendously their chances for folly in the international arena. Further, the temptations of circumventing consent through covert action are best left to pass by the wayside. Bypassing public approval means bypassing public dialogue and debate. Ill-founded plans that might otherwise have had their fatal flaws exposed live on, their subsequent implementation then leading to probable failure.

Liberal democratic governments need not undermine their very democratic natures to survive and thrive in the international arena. The institutions that define a state as democratic—the vote, separation of powers, a free press—are also those that make its foreign policy effective and help it win wars. Contrary to long-standing belief, the freedom and rewards that democratic institutions provide individual citizens are not something that we should view as a luxury that incurs unavoidable risks in international politics. Rather, democratic political institutions hold the key to prudent and successful foreign policy. The installation of democracy presents no Faustian bargain, no dangerous tradeoff in the face of global anarchy. Counter to the fears of many scholars and politicians, national leaders need not subvert liberty in order to preserve it.

NOTES

CHAPTER 1

1. The text of the address is available at http://www.pub.whitehouse.gov/uri-res/I2R?urn:pdi://oma.eop.gov.us/1994/1/26/1.text.1.

2. A discussion of the twentieth century's most prescient critic of liberalism, Carl Schmitt, can be found in John McCormick, *Carl Schmitt's Critique of Liberalism*. On Marx and the democratic petty bourgeois, see David McLellan, *Karl Marx*, 279.

3. Immanuel Kant, "Perpetual Peace: A Philosophical Sketch," in *Kant's Political Writings*; Zeev Maoz and Bruce M. Russett, "Normative and Structural Causes of Democratic Peace, 1946–1986."

4. Francis Fukuyama, *The End of History and the Last Man*.

5. *The Federalist Papers*, ed. Garry Wills, no. 8; Alexis de Tocqueville, *Democracy in America*, 228; Sherman quoted in Gerald F. Linderman, *Embattled Courage*, 36–37. Secretary of State Dean Acheson agreed: "In the conduct of their foreign relations democracies appear to me decidedly inferior to other governments." Quoted in Michael D. Pearlman, *Warmaking and American Democracy*, 10. See also Zbigniew Brzezinski, "War and Foreign Policy"; Hans J. Morgenthau, *Politics among Nations*, 153; Jean-François Revel, *How Democracies Perish*.

6. See Scott Sigmund Gartner, "Opening Up the Black Box of War," and the June 1998 special issue of the *Journal of Conflict Resolution*.

7. Robert A. Dahl, *Democracy and Its Critics*.

8. Kant, "Perpetual Peace." See also Bruce Russett and John Oneal, *Triangulating Peace*, Karl Deutsch, *Political Community and the North Atlantic Area*, and Thomas Risse-Kappen, *Cooperation among Democracies*.

9. For a discussion of how this view played out in the context of World War II, see Alan S. Milward, *War, Economy and Society 1939–1945*.

10. Note that we might expect autocrats and command economies to be able to extract proportionately more from their societies, organized around the state and the collective, as opposed to democracies, organized around the individual's pursuit of his or her own self-interest.

CHAPTER 2

1. Geoffrey Blainey provides a standard argument as to why wars are chosen and not accidental in *The Causes of War*, 3d ed. (New York: Free Press, 1988). Some scholars have stressed that wars can be accidental, whether because of mechanical accident, cognitive misperception, or stress-induced decision-making pathologies. See Scott Sagan, *The Limits of Safety*; Robert Jervis, *Perception and Misperception in International Politics*; Richard Ned Lebow, *Between Peace and War*.

2. The model we present here is conceptually similar to that of Scott Sigmund Gartner and Randolph M. Siverson, "War Expansion and War Outcome."

3. Here we do not attempt to specify the necessary and sufficient conditions under which states would consider going to war. Our point here is not to contest other scholars' theories about why wars begin, but rather to point out that a complete theory of war must include the initiating side's expectations about victory. In appendix 2.1, we conduct a simple test of war initiation that confirms our speculation that democracies are more risk-averse when starting wars than are more repressive states.

4. Joffre quoted in David G. Herrmann, *The Arming of Europe and the Making of the First World War*, 152–153; Larry Berman, *Planning a Tragedy*, 140; McGeorge Bundy, *Danger and Survival*, 453.

5. On Clausewitz and unpredictability, see Alan Beyerchen, "Clausewitz, Non-linearity, and the Unpredictability of War." See also Erik Gartzke, "War Is in the Error Term." For the 90 percent prediction, see Allan C. Stam III, *Win, Lose or Draw*, 199.

6. Bruce Bueno de Mesquita, *The War Trap*; Kevin Wang and James Lee Ray, "Beginners and Winners"; Gartner and Siverson, "War Expansion and War Outcome."

7. James D. Fearon, "Rationalist Explanations for War." See also Blainey, *Causes of War*; Steven Rosen, "War Power and the Willingness to Suffer"; Suzanne Werner, "The Precarious Nature of Peace"; R. Harrison Wagner, "Bargaining and War."

8. Fearon discusses this and some other possible reasons in "Rationalist Explanations." See also Wagner, "Bargaining and War"; Werner, "Precarious Nature of Peace"; Blainey, *Causes of War*; and Rosen, "War Power."

9. Fearon makes this point in "Rationalist Explanations," 393–395.

10. Janice Gross Stein, "Deterrence and Compellence in the Gulf, 1990–91."

11. Richard Ned Lebow, "Miscalculation in the South Atlantic." In this case, Argentina was the aggressor, an autocratic initiator that was a likely loser.

12. Richard Andres, "The Relative Selection Effect and Winning Disputes." See also, Stephen Van Evera, *The Causes of War*, 57–58. Similarly, Germany lulled the Soviets into complacency in 1941, prior to the initiation of Operation Barbarosa.

13. Max Jakobson, *The Diplomacy of the Winter War*, esp. 131.

14. Jonathan Mercer argues that this view, while widely held by scholars and policymakers alike, is likely empirically incorrect. *Reputation and International Politics*.

15. Donald Kagan, *On the Origins of War and the Preservation of Peace*, 8–9; Anthony F. Upton, *Finland: 1939–1940*, 32. On salami tactics, see Thomas C. Schelling, *Arms and Influence*.

16. Barbara W. Tuchman, *The Guns of August*, 102. Belgium's military forces were quite weak despite the fortress system around Liège. John Keegan, *The First World War*, 80.

17. In recent years several important papers have used selection effects models in one way or another to improve our understanding of international conflict. See, for example, Alastair Smith, "Alliance Formation and War"; James D.

Fearon, "Signaling versus the Balance of Power and Interests"; David L. Rousseau et al., "Assessing the Dyadic Nature of the Democratic Peace, 1918–1988"; William Reed, "A Unified Statistical Model of Conflict Onset and Escalation."

18. Significantly, even Henry Kissinger, one of the century's central realist figures, recognized that democratic publics punish leaders who incur foreign policy disasters. *Years of Renewal*, 1068.

19. Pearlman, *Warmaking and American Democracy*, 13.

20. Quoted in Colin L. Powell, *My American Journey*, 499.

21. Bruce Bueno de Mesquita and Randolph M. Siverson, "War and the Survival of Political Leaders."

22. Darrell Bates, *The Fashoda Incident of 1898*, 151–159.

23. David Holloway, *Stalin and the Bomb*, 265.

24. Gad Barzilai, "War, Democracy, and Internal Conflict," 318.

25. On democratic initiators and casualties, see Randolph M. Siverson, "Democratic and War Participation"; and Karl R. DeRouen, Jr., "Presidents and the Diversionary Use of Force." On the sensitivity of democratic publics to casualties, see John E. Mueller, *War, Presidents and Public Opinion*; John Mueller, Scott Sigmund Gartner and Gary Segura, "War, Casualties, and Public Opinion"; Scott Sigmund Gartner and Gary Segura, "Race, Casualties, and Opinion in the Vietnam War"; and Edward N. Luttwak, "A Post-Heroic Military Policy." For a skeptical view, see James Burk, "Public Support for Peacekeeping in Lebanon and Somalia."

26. Benjamin I. Page and Robert Y. Shapiro, *The Rational Public*; Bruce W. Jentleson, "The Pretty Prudent Public," Bruce W. Jentleson and Rebecca L. Britton, "Still Pretty Prudent."

27. John J. Mearsheimer, *Conventional Deterrence*, 157–158; Kissinger, *Years of Renewal*, 412; Ernest R. May, *Strange Victory*, 23.

28. Stein, "Deterrence and Compellence in the Gulf," 175; U.S. News and World Report, *Triumph Without Victory*, 205; Barry M. Blechman and Tamara Cofman Wittes, "Defining Moment," esp. 5; Mark Bowden, *Black Hawk Down*, esp. 110.

29. H. E. Goemans, *War and Punishment*. An example of this type of strategic shift is Germany's massive offensive in the spring of 1918.

30. Jack Snyder, *Myths of Empire*; Stephen Van Evera, "Hypotheses on Nationalism and War," 32–33; Dan Reiter, "Political Structure and Foreign Policy Learning," 47–49; Cheney quoted in Powell, *My American Journey*, 479.

31. Kenneth M. Pollack, "The Influence of Arab Culture on Arab Military Effectiveness," chap. 3; Blechman and Wittes, "Defining Moment," 14.

32. Snyder, *Myths of Empire*.

33. See also Goemans, *War and Punishment*.

34. See Stam, *Win, Lose, or Draw*, for a lengthy discussion of this approach. See also Robert A. Pape, *Bombing to Win*, and Schelling, *Arms and Influence*.

35. See David A. Lake, "Powerful Pacifists: Democratic States and War," and Stam, *Win, Lose, or Draw*. An alternative view is that war is about the revelation of private information. See Fearon, "Rationalist Explanations," and Wagner, "Bargaining and War." The important distinction between these models and our institutional cost benefit argument has to do with the results on our initiation

variables. Information revelation or bargaining approaches imply there should be no particular bias in outcomes tilted toward initiators. See Gartzke, "War Is in the Error Term," for an extensive discussion of this point. Our model strongly points to a selection process bias that is observable in systematically different outcomes for targets and initiators.

36. There are some other, more minor arguments as to why democracies might fight wars more effectively. One could argue that democracies enjoy more advanced military technology because the open nature of democratic societies is more nurturing of innovations. We take up this question briefly in chapter 5 and control for technology, using admittedly crude measures in the tests in appendix 2.1. Alternatively, one could argue that autocratic regimes are more likely to use the military to repress internal dissent, which in turn trades off with battlefield military effectiveness. Stanislav Andreski, "On the Peaceful Disposition of Military Dictatorships." Notably, empirical analysis has revealed that democracies are not more likely to submit to coercion via aerial bombardment. Michael Horowitz and Dan Reiter, "When Does Aerial Bombing Work?"

37. John J. Mearsheimer, "Back to the Future"; Christopher Layne, "Kant or Cant"; Joanne Gowa, *Ballots and Bullets*; Kenneth N. Waltz, "Structural Realism after the Cold War."

38. On democracies having no advantage, see Quincy Wright, *A Study of War*, 163. See also Morgenthau, *Politics among Nations*, 143–146.

39. Even in these three cases of preemption, other goals supplanted preemptive concerns. Germany attacked Russia in 1914 to preempt the Russian mobilization and to address domestic political problems. Israel attacked in 1967 to preempt what was perceived to be an imminent Arab attack and to restore deterrent credibility. China intervened in the Korean War in November 1950 because it feared that the United Nations forces were about to cross the Yalu River and attack the Chinese mainland, and because the Chinese leadership saw an opportunity to sweep non-Communist forces off the Korean peninsula entirely. On the rarity and costs of preemption, see Dan Reiter, "Exploding the Powder Keg Myth." On the nonadvantage of surprise, see Stam, *Win, Lose, or Draw*, 111–132.

40. The focus on conflicts between states (interstate wars) to the exclusion of conflicts between states and nonstate entities such as rebel movements in colonies (termed extrasystemic wars) is standard in the study of conflict. We do not include extrasystemic wars because we want to keep the focus on interstate wars, which are qualitatively different from extrasystemic wars in their causes. Interstate wars usually emerge relatively quickly from an international crisis following high-level diplomacy, whereas extrasystemic wars usually escalate very slowly, with the imperial/colonial power being drawn in piecemeal with key decisions frequently being made by agents and officers abroad rather from the national government. These wars also differ in their prosecution, as interstate wars mean the clash of regular armies, but extrasystemic wars involve a minimum of conventional warfare and greater occurrence of clashes with unarmed or very lightly armed natives, guerrilla and sniper warfare against imperial/colonial troops, and nonmilitary actions by the imperial/colonial side in the way of economic development, political propagandizing, and incarceration of suspected rebels. We cannot analyze interstate and extrasystemic wars together, as there are not data for extrasystemic wars

for several crucial interstate war variables. However, we analyzed all extrasystemic wars since 1816 using the Correlates of War data set, including as cases each metropole power, and we found that democratic metropoles are significantly more likely to win extrasystemic wars than are other types of metropoles, including as control variables initiation, population size, and size of armed forces (n = 137). See J. David Singer and Melvin Small, "Correlates of War Project."

41. Some wars end in what is essentially the prewar status quo (for example, the Korean War). Wars such as this can best be thought of as draws. At this point we drop these cases, as our theory does not bear on what happens in democracies as time passes after wars begin, though inclusion of draws does not change our core results. In chapter 7 we return to this question and present a more elaborate theory and empirical data about the nature of draws in war. Again, the bargaining perspective views all war outcomes as draws, or wars with a negotiated settlement, and as such, coding winning and losing does not make much sense.

42. Including control variables is an important part of robustly testing for relationships between variables. We include variables other than regime type here, just as one would also include, if one were testing the effect of race on income, factors such as gender, age, education, and so on. For a statistical discussion of this point, see Eric A. Hanushek and John E. Jackson, *Statistical Methods for Social Scientists*, esp. 80.

43. We are confident that the statistical models of war outcomes are reasonably good representatives of reality. First, if we split the data and use the estimates from half of the sample to predict the results of the other half, we are successful in predicting the outcomes 90 percent of the time. Second, if we set all the variables to their mean and predict the outcome of the average war, the outcome becomes 50/50, win/lose.

44. On the movement for East Pakistani autonomy, see Sumit Ganguly, *The Origins of War in South Asia*, esp. 104–105. The West Pakistani president was a military general and ruled all of Pakistan with martial law. His calling of national elections in 1970 was the first step of his plan to return the government to civilian leadership.

45. Ibid., 118–119.

46. Ibid., 120.

47. Ibid., 129. It is speculated that by increasing the activities of the guerrilla forces after achieving their diplomatic goals, the Indians provoked West Pakistan into attacking. Waiting for an opponent to begin the attack is a time-honored way states try to deflect responsibility for blame. For example, Bismarck and Prussia waited until France initiated the Franco-Prussian War, and Germany attempted to create similar cover in its war against Poland in World War II, using German soldiers in Polish uniforms to attack a German-run radio station in Poland near the German frontier.

48. Mearsheimer, *Conventional Deterrence*.

49. Compare the Indian behavior in 1971 with the Pakistanis' hasty response to India's 1998 nuclear weapons tests. Following Pakistan's quick tests of its own in response (a decision driven by pressure from the military), the United States was forced to cut off aid to Pakistan, doing substantial damage to the Pakistani economy. Being able to count on an impetuous response, India was able to

weaken Pakistan without firing a single shot. See Samina Ahmen, "Pakistan's Nuclear Weapons Program."

50. Richard Sisson and Leo E. Rose, *War and Secession*, esp. 198, 208–210.

51. In chapter 7 we investigate democracies' preferences for short wars in detail. On the preference of democracies for maneuver strategies, see Dan Reiter and Curtis Meek, "Determinants of Military Strategy, 1903–1994."

52. See Ahmad Faruqui, "The Enigma of Military Rule in Pakistan."

53. Robert Jackson, *South Asian Crisis*, 108.

54. Scott D. Sagan, "The Origins of the Pacific War"; Michael A. Barnhart, *Japan Prepares for Total War.*

55. Quoted in Hiroyuki Agawa, *The Reluctant Admiral*, 243–244. Earlier that year, Yamamoto had argued that a limited war against the United States was unlikely, but his pessimism was in the minority and ignored by other factions. Eventually, Yamamoto reluctantly accepted the plan. See Michael A. Barnhart, "Japanese Intelligence Before the Second World War," and Agawa, *Reluctant admiral*, 291.

56. John W. Dower, *War Without Mercy*, and Barnhart, "Japanese Intelligence," 452.

57. Saburo Ienaga, *The Pacific War, 1931–1945*, 97.

58. Reiter and Meek, "Determinants of Military Strategy." On strategy and war duration, see chapter 7.

59. On Israel, see Mearsheimer, *Conventional Deterrence*. We do not observe that democratic initiators enjoy advantages in any one category (allies, strategy, or troop quality, for example) in our sample of war participants probably because the sample is too small. If our sample were much larger, in the tens of thousands, then statistically significant effects for each of these factors would probably appear.

60. Some might argue that it would be better to focus just on the core dyad of belligerents in each war rather than include all belligerents. See Karen Rasler and William R. Thompson, "Predatory Initiators and Changing Landscapes for Warfare." There are two reasons why including all belligerents is preferable. First, there is no theoretical justification for excluding all but the core dyad if the dependent variable is war outcomes. For war initiation, it may be more important to think about the primary disputants. However, if the focus is on performance during war, it is not as relevant whether or not a belligerent was a member of the initial, core dyad. Second, exclusion of belligerents who were not members of the core dyad would leave out relevant information. We enhance our confidence in the veracity of the results if we can broaden the scope of the empirical sample. Note that Model 6 in table 2.2 includes only core dyads, and the results are largely the same. The Singer and Small data include cases to 1982. Our analysis goes up to 1990. We code the 1985–1987 Sino-Vietnam War as a draw, and it is dropped. We also code the Iran-Iraq War as a draw. We could have included the 1991 Azeri-Armenian conflict, the Iraqi invasion of Kuwait, and the Allied liberation of Kuwait as three new wars. The number of deaths in the Iraq-Kuwait War does not exceed the correlates of war (COW) one thousand battle death threshold. Nevertheless, these wars generally confirm our results: no democracies lose.

61. The COW data set is described in Melvin Small and J. David Singer, *Resort*

to Arms. We also used R. Ernest Dupuy and Trevor N. Dupuy, *The Encyclopedia of Military History from 3500 BC to the Present*.

62. Analyzing the data with draws included does not substantially change the results. One variable that we drop from the analysis, geographic distance, becomes statistically significant if we include draws. States fighting in far-off wars are more likely to settle for draws than states fighting in close proximity to their own borders. In addition, we note that our data set differs from that of Lake, "Powerful Pacifists." From the COW list of wars, Lake (31, 33, 35n) used only wars in which at least one democracy participated, minus the Spanish-American War and wars in which there was no clear victor. Lake also restricted the size of his data set by using a version of the COW data set whose temporal domain extended only to 1965, leaving him with only 20 wars. We believe our data set is richer and likely to contain fewer sources of bias: it includes wars up to 1990 (77 total), includes the Spanish-American War, and does not exclude wars in which no democracy participated. The results do not change significantly if we only use cases up to 1965, though standard errors do increase somewhat. Lastly, Lake did not disaggregate World Wars I and II and the Vietnam War, as we did.

63. James E. Edmonds, *A Short History of World War I*.

64. See, for example, Dupuy and Dupuy, *Encyclopedia of Military History*. The results are quite similar even if we drop the changed wars; because this procedure involves dropping 14 wars (12 in World War II), *all* of the standard errors increase slightly. The coefficient estimates were stable, though the strategy and terrain variables cannot be estimated because of insufficient variance among the independent variables.

65. The COW codings are based in part on an attempt to generate a data set useful for testing propositions about systemic wars and the mechanism through which bilateral wars spread into multilateral ones. The COW outcome codings do not attempt necessarily to reflect the outcome of waging war. For example, while the Germans clearly defeated Poland in World War II, the Polish government in exile remained allied to the United States and British war effort. Consequently, COW codes Poland as being on the winning side, although it was defeated in battle. We are interested in the process of waging war, so we treat each war separately and do not aggregate them into multilateral wars unless that is the way the battles were actually waged. The 1973 Arab-Israeli War is an example of a multilateral war we not disaggregate.

66. Paul F. Diehl, "Arms Races and Escalation."

67. Dupuy and Dupuy, *Encyclopedia of Military History*; Michael Clodfelter, *Warfare and Armed Conflicts*.

68. On the Crimean and First Balkan Wars, see A.J.P. Taylor, *The Struggle for Mastery in Europe, 1848–1918*, and Rene Albrecht-Carrie, *A Diplomatic History of Europe since the Congress of Vienna*. On the treatment of joiners versus initiators, see D. Scott Bennett and Allan C. Stam, "Research Design and Estimator Choices in the Analysis of Interstate Dyads."

69. William Reed and David H. Clark, "War Initiators and War Winners"; Reed, "A Unified Model of Conflict Onset and Outcome."

70. Keith Jaggers and Ted Robert Gurr, "Tracking Democracy's Third Wave with the Polity III Data." Some countries that were invaded and conquered in

the same year (such as Norway in 1940) are coded by Polity III as having missing democracy and autocracy scores. For these cases, we used the democracy and autocracy scores in the previous year, as the "missing" scores reflect the lack of a normal political system during occupation; these countries had functioning polities prior to the invasion and during the war, meaning that our hypotheses can make predictions about how their political systems affected war outcomes.

71. P. Royston and D. G. Altman, "Regression Using Fractional Polynomials of Continuous Covariates."

72. We do not discount nations' material contributions based on when they joined the war. The inevitable imprecision and inaccuracies of any discount formula would outweigh any reduction in bias it might achieve.

73. Paul K. Huth, D. Scott Bennett, and Christopher Gelpi, "System Uncertainty, Risk Propensity, and International Conflict among the Great Powers"; Stam, *Win, Lose, or Draw*.

74. Mearsheimer, *Conventional Deterrence*; Stam, *Win, Lose, or Draw*; Reiter and Meek, "Determinants of Military Strategy."

75. Dupuy and Dupuy, *Encyclopedia of Military History*; Clodfelter, *Warfare and Armed Conflicts*; Kalevi J. Holsti, *Peace and War: Armed Conflicts and International Order 1648–1989*; Trevor Nevitt Dupuy, *Analysis of Factors That Have Influenced Outcomes of Battles and Wars*. In the three cases where there was no clear distinction between maneuver and attrition, we coded the modal strategy of attrition. See D. Scott Bennett and Allan C. Stam III, "The Duration of Interstate Wars," 247n.

76. For more discussion, see Stam, *Win, Lose, or Draw*.

77. Ibid.; Bennett and Stam, "The Duration of Interstate Wars"; Mearsheimer, *Conventional Deterrence*; Dan Reiter, "Military Strategy and the Outbreak of International Conflict." Our model also simplifies reality by ignoring strategy changes made within wars. See Scott Sigmund Gartner, *Strategic Assessment in War*. We code each belligerent as having a single strategy throughout the war. Fortunately, there are very few cases in which belligerents make strategy changes from one of our categories to another. We reduce the potential problem of intra-war strategy change by breaking up three long wars, World Wars I and II and the Vietnam War, into shorter components.

78. *New York Times Atlas of the World*; Dupuy, *Analysis of Factors*; Dupuy and Dupuy, *Encyclopedia of Military History*; Trevor Nevitt Dupuy, *Numbers, Predictions and War*.

79. Including the scale or individually multiplied dummy variables makes little difference in the overall results of the model, as the model fit remains nearly identical.

80. We use the *New York Times Atlas of the World* and Gary L. Fitzpatrick and Marilyn J. Modlin, *Direct-Line Distances*.

81. Karen Rasler and William Thompson ("Predatory Initiators") produced different results, most notably that democratic initiators are not more likely to win but democratic targets are. Their results diverge from ours probably because of differences in research design, which include: each of their cases is a war rather than a belligerent; they do not include military strategy or terrain as control variables; they do not divide up multilateral wars as we do; they have a measure for

"development" rather than our measure of troop quality; they include duration as an independent variable (our analysis of duration, democracy, and war outcomes is presented in a different research design in chapter 7); and they include more initiation interaction terms, which probably increases multicollinearity and raises standard errors. Unfortunately, the authors are unable to provide us with the data that would enable us to replicate the precise results they present in their *Journal of Conflict Resolution* article, so we cannot deduce the exact source of the divergence in results. However, one claim that Rasler and Thompson make is that initiators are not more likely to win after 1945. When we reanalyze our own data such that we only include post-1945 participants, the central results remain, that democratic initiators and democratic targets are more likely to win. Interestingly, however, autocratic initiators are not significantly more or less likely to win in this constricted ($n = 41$) data set.

82. We also fit the same models to the logit distribution. In these models, the parameter estimates are essentially the same; the standard errors increase somewhat. In the baseline model with the logit estimates, the democratic target term does not meet standard levels of significance (p = .052).

83. Models 1 and 2 do not include an estimate for a constant. If included, the absolute value of the standard errors exceeds the estimate of the constant itself. In runs with a constant estimated, the coefficients for all variables remain stable with the p-value for all remaining below 0.05 (one tailed tests).

84. To compare the fit of two (or more) fractional polynomial models, we compared the deviance (D) of the two models. The deviance is defined as -2 times its minimized log likelihood using the formula: $D = n(1 + \log \frac{2\pi RSS}{n})$ where n is the sample size and RSS is the residual sum of squares estimated fitting a linear model. The gain (G) is defined as the deviance estimated for a straight line model minus the deviance estimated for the fractional polynomial model. The test statistic to calculate the p-value for the gain for the polynomial probit model is obtained using the formula $T = D_{k-1} - D_k$. We then compared T to the χ^2 distribution with 2 df. These p-values are approximate and conservative (for an extensive discussion of fractional polynomial models, see Royston and Altman, "Regression Using Fractional Polynomials").

85. We also checked for the possibility that the distance term would have an effect only as an interactive variable with military and industrial capabilities. This hypothesis was not supported. We also estimated a model using capability scores adjusted for distance according to the procedures in Bueno de Mesquita, *The War Trap*. Again, the hypothesis was not supported.

86. To estimate our core dyad model, we reran our basic model but excluded the following cases: in Austro-Sardinian War, excluded Tuscany and Modena; in Roman Republic, excluded France; in Crimean, excluded Britain, Italy, and France; in Italian Unification, excluded France; in Lopez, excluded Argentina; in Seven Weeks, excluded Hanover; in Franco-Prussian, excluded Wurtemberg, Bavaria, and Baden; in Pacific, excluded Bolivia; in second Balkan, excluded Turkey and Romania; in World War II West Europe, excluded United States and Italy; in Yom Kippur II, excluded Jordan and Saudi Arabia; in Ethiopia-Somalia, excluded Cuba; in World War Ib, excluded Turkey; in World War Ic, excluded Britain, United States Italy, Rumania, Bulgaria, Austria, Greece, and Turkey. We

also estimated a model, not in the table, where we drop all cases but initiators. In this case, the politics variable is still associated with greater chances of victory (coefficient 0.044, SE 0.022, p < 0.05).

87. We also analyzed a data set of just initiators and found that among initiators, democracies are significantly more likely to win.

88. Dan Reiter, "Military Strategy and the Outbreak of International Conflict." Reiter and Meek, "Determinants of Military Strategy"; Bennett and Stam, "Duration of Interstate Wars."

89. Bennett and Stam, "Duration of Interstate Wars," Stam, *Win, Lose, or Draw*; Bruce Bueno de Mesquita and David Lalman, *War and Reason*.

90. On the MID data set, see Daniel M. Jones, Stuart A. Bremer, and J. David Singer, "Militarized Interstate Disputes, 1816–1992." We generated the dependent variable and much of the other data using the EUGene computer program, available at eugenesoftware.org.

91. J. David Singer, Stuart Bremer, and John Stuckey, "Capability Distribution, Uncertainty, and Major Power War, 1820–1965," 27–28.

CHAPTER 3

1. Note that if the latter two arguments were the only sources of democratic victory, then when we controlled for size of military and alliance contributions in the statistical analysis in appendix 2.1, the parameter estimate for Democracy should have become indistinguishable from 0, which was not the case.

2. The importance of winning battles is an integral component of Stam's earlier model of victory in war, which focuses on the importance of inflicting costs on the adversary by winning land battles. Stam, *Win, Lose, or Draw*. John H. Cushman pointed out that though battlefield effectiveness is a desirable and perhaps necessary virtue, it is not a sufficient condition for victory, as evidenced by the eventual defeat of the tactically effective German and Japanese militaries in World War II. "Challenge and Response at the Operational and Tactical Levels, 1914–1945," 3:322. Broader empirical surveys point to the importance of battlefield military effectiveness: examining all wars from 1816 to 1980, John Arquilla found that armies with higher skill ratings were significantly more likely to win land wars. *Dubious Battles*.

3. Quoted in A. M. Gray, *Warfighting*, 103n, and in F. M. Richardson, *Fighting Spirit*, 1.

4. Carl Schmitt, *The Concept of the Political*, 71; McCormick, *Carl Schmitt's Critique of Liberalism*, 257. On Lindbergh, see Peter Grose, *Gentleman Spy*, 130; Aleksandr I. Solzhenitsyn, *A World Split Apart*, 13–15.

5. Sun Tzu, *The Art of War*, 64. Chang Yü, a Song dynasty scholar, interpreted Sun Tzu's point as follows: "When one treats people with benevolence, justice, and righteousness, and reposes confidence in them, the army will be united in mind and all will be happy to serve their leaders." Quoted in *The Art of War*, 23. Of course, neither Sun Tzu nor Chang Yü was thinking of democratic governance, but their general point about popular versus unpopular government is still relevant.

6. Herodotus, *The History*, book 5, para. 78.

7. Thucydides, *History of the Peloponnesian War*, book 2, para. 39. The source of the eventual Athenian defeat in the Peloponnesian War is usually attributed to squabbling following Pericles' death, the discrediting of the military leaders Theramenes and Thrasybulus following Alcibiades' disgrace, and other factors. See ibid., para. 65, and Donald Kagan, *The Fall of the Athenian Empire*, 413–426.

8. John Locke, *Second Treatise of Government*, 26; Stephen Holmes, *Passions and Constraint*, 19; Thomas Paine, *Prospects on the War, and Paper Currency*, 17; Thomas C. Walker, "The Forgotten Prophet."

9. Michael Walzer, *Obligations*, 77–98.

10. Jefferson letter to John Adams (August 1, 1816), *Bartlett's Familiar Quotations*, 368; Ronald W. Reagan, "Ronald Reagan's First Inaugural Address," http://grid.let.rug.llnl/~welling/usa/presidents/inaug/reagan1.html, January 20, 1981.

11. On contingent consent, see Margaret Levi, *Consent, Dissent, and Patriotism*. On the importance of trust within military organizations and how it influences battlefield efficiency or lack thereof, see Stam, *Win, Lose, or Draw*. Stam also hypothesized that ethnic and class cleavages, along with political institutions will influence trust within military organizations. Stephen Biddle and Robert Zirkle demonstrate that high levels of trust are a necessary condition for high levels of military and tactical efficiency and effectiveness. "Technology, Civil-Military Relations, and Warfare in the Developing World." Kenneth Pollack investigated the effects of Arab culture and political institutions on the relative efficacy of Arab troops as compared to Israeli troops in the wars of the Middle East from 1948 to 1991. "The Influence of Arab Culture on Arab Military Effectiveness."

12. Edward Shils and Morris Janowitz, "Cohesion and Disintegration in the Wehrmacht in World War II"; Samuel A. Stouffer et al., *The American Soldier*, 430–485; Martin Van Creveld, *Fighting Power: German and U.S. Army Performance, 1939–1945*, 83–89; Gay Hammerman and Richard G. Sheridan, *The 88th Infantry Division in World War II*; Paddy Griffith, *Battle Tactics of the Civil War*; Roger W. Little, "Buddy Relations and Combat Performance"; Charles C. Moskos, Jr., *The American Enlisted Man*; Wm. Daryl Henderson, *Cohesion*, 99–100.

13. Stephen Peter Rosen, *Societies and Military Power*, esp. 214, 248–249. However, Rosen along with others emphasizes the importance of culture and social structure in determining battlefield military effectiveness. See Deborah Yarsike Ball, "Ethnic Conflict, Unit Performance, and the Soviet Armed Forces," and Pollack, "Arab Culture." For a view that democracies do not field armies with higher battlefield military effectiveness, see Cushman, "Challenge and Response."

14. On the Napoleonic Wars, see Michael Howard, *Clausewitz*, as well as Barry Posen, "Nationalism, the Mass Army, and Military Power." For dissent, see Charles J. Esdaile, *The Wars of Napoleon*, 37–70. On North Vietnam and Israel, see Henderson, *Cohesion*. On the emergence of the nation state, see Michael Howard, *War in European History*.

15. Jürgen E. Förster, "The Dynamics of *Volksgemeinschaft*"; Omer Bartov, *Hitler's Army*; Stephen G. Fritz, "'We Are Trying . . . to Change the Face of the World'" Daniel Jonah Goldhagen, *Hitler's Willing Executioners*. These authors have made pointed methodological criticisms of the Shils and Janowitz study, which relied on interviews of an unrepresentative population of German soldiers

who were of course motivated to downplay their allegiance to Nazism in interviews with their captors.

16. James M. McPherson, *For Cause and Comrades*.

17. Stephen E. Ambrose, *D-Day, June 6, 1944*; Stephen E. Ambrose, *Citizen Soldiers*; Victor Davis Hanson, *The Soul of Battle*. Martin Van Creveld (*Fighting Power*, 3–9) argued that the German Army in World War II man for man outfought the American Army. Significantly, however, he reached this conclusion using the same data that we use to demonstrate that in general democratic armies enjoy higher effectiveness, the HERO data generated in Dupuy, *Numbers, Predictions and War*. Dupuy's calculation of German superiority in World War II has not been uncontested; John Sloan Brown reanalyzed the HERO data using slightly different parameters (though the same data) for Dupuy's effectiveness equations and reversed Dupuy's result, finding American superiority in some areas, and in general finding that "American divisions were clearly more efficient overall." "Colonel Trevor N. Dupuy and the Mythos of Wehrmacht Superiority." Interestingly, Dupuy (63) attributes German superiority to an array of factors, as "overall German superiority probably resulted from better utilization of manpower. The remainder could possibly be the result of such factors as more experience, greater mobility, better doctrine, more effective battle drill, superior leadership, or inherent national characteristics." This demonstrates the importance of complementing case studies with quantitative analysis: even if one concludes that the German Army had superior battlefield military effectiveness, this appears to be an isolated case within the context of a more significant pattern of democratic armies fighting better. For another view that German military effectiveness in the 1944–1945 campaign has been overrated, see Robert S. Rush, "A Different Perspective." Lastly, S.L.A. Marshall's older claim that only 15 percent or so of American soldiers actually fired their weapons during World War II has been discredited. See Fredric Smoler, "The Secret of the Soldiers Who Didn't Shoot."

18. John Stuart Mill, *On Liberty*; Rosen, *Societies and Military Power*; de Tocqueville, *Democracy in America*, 658–659; Eliot A. Cohen and John Gooch, *Military Misfortunes*; Pollack, "Arab Culture"; Mearsheimer, *Conventional Deterrence*.

19. David Ben-Gurion, *Recollections*, 95–100.

20. Niall Ferguson, *The Pity of War*, 367–394; Antony Beevor, *Stalingrad*; Ludendorff quoted in Gerald H. Davis, "Prisoners of War in Twentieth-Century War Economies," 630; Milward, *War, Economy, and Society*, 224; George G. Lewis and John Mewha, *History of Prisoner of War Utilization by the United States Army, 1776–1945*, 263.

21. Others models of soldiers' actions that see them as fundamentally rational include Geoffrey Brennan and Gordon Tullock, "An Economic Theory of Military Tactics"; Robert Axelrod, *The Evolution of Cooperation*; William H. Riker, "The Political Psychology of Rational Choice Theory"; Levi, *Consent, Dissent, and Patriotism*.

22. For descriptions and lists of signatories, see Dietrich Schindler and Jiri Toman, eds., *The Laws of Armed Conflicts*.

23. This is a rare instance where behavior advocated by idealists is consistent with the realist position. All too frequently, behavior that might increase a state's

power at the expense of others is inconsistent with the tenets of just war theory. However, in the case of committing to humane norms of conduct toward POWs, one need not choose between might and right.

24. Barry R. Weingast, "The Political Foundations of Democracy and the Rule of Law."

25. James D. Morrow argues that an expectation of reciprocity is the best guarantee that the rights of enemy POWs will be honored. Expectations of reciprocity can help start and sustain cooperation regarding POWs. "The Institutional Features of the Prisoner of War Treaties." However, domestic political concerns can trump reciprocity effects. For example, the Soviet Union sent a number of diplomatic notes just after the German invasion in 1941 proposing that both sides adhere to the Hague Convention. Germany refused the offer. Alfred Streim, "International Law and Soviet Prisoners of War," 296. Further, despite Japan's inhumane treatment of American POWs, the United States treated Japanese POWs humanely and by the letter of the Hague Convention throughout World War II. S. P. MacKenzie, "The Treatment of Prisoners of War in World War II," 516; Martin Tollefson, "Enemy Prisoners of War."

26. Ruth Benedict, *The Chrysanthemum and the Sword*, 30–42; MacKenzie, "The Treatment of Prisoners of War," 513; Olive Checkland, *Humanitarianism and the Emperor's Japan, 1877–1977*, 89–91; Ikuhiko Hata, "From Consideration to Contempt," in *Prisoners of War and Their Captors*.

27. Dower, *War Without Mercy*, 48; Joan Beaumont, "Protecting Prisoners of War, 1939–95," 279; Max Hastings, *The Korean War*, 304; Clodfelter, *Warfare and Armed Conflicts*.

28. Bartov, *Hitler's Army*, esp. 72; Omer Bartov, *The Eastern Front, 1941–45*; Fritz, "'We Are Trying,'"; Dower, *War Without Mercy*, 48.

29. John L. Plaster, *SOG*, 152.

30. Forster, "The Dynamics of *Volksgemeinschaft*," 21–23; Albert Speer, *Inside the Third Reich*, 250n; Leonidas E. Hill, ed., *Die Weizsacker-Papiere 1933–1950*, 327–328. Thanks to Christian Tuschhoff for assistance with translation.

31. Quoted in Ambrose, *Citizen Soldiers*, 33; see also Rush, "A Different Perspective," 500.

32. Karl Doenitz, *Memoirs*, 445–464; Adam Roberts, "The Laws of War in the 1990–91 Gulf Conflict," 160.

33. Note that we do not mean to imply that every general in a democratic army will be a Patton, nor do we fail to recognize the often brilliant military leadership in some dictatorships, notably Germany during the World War II.

34. Risa Brooks, *Political-Military Relations and the Stability of Arab Regimes*, 32–33; Gordon Tullock, *Autocracy*; Khidhir Hamza with Jeff Stein, *Saddam's Bombmaker*, 174–175.

35. Pollack, "Arab Culture"; Risa Brooks, "Institutions at the Domestic/International Nexus; John E. Jessup, "The Soviet Armed Forces in the Great Patriotic War, 1941–5"; Beevor, *Stalingrad*, 23. For dissent on the effects of the Soviet purges, see Roger R. Reese, *Stalin's Reluctant Soldiers*.

36. HERO does not provide data on POWs. Quantitative data on POWs from other sources have severe problems, regarding both missing data and measurement error. Further, statistical efforts to test hypotheses on POW counts suffer

from worrisome sources of bias that are difficult to correct. Hence, we refrain from providing statistical tests here and instead note that examination of a handful of prominent cases (as outlined above) boosts our confidence in Proposition 3.4. One paper using quantitative tests that did find that democracies attract higher levels of enemy surrender is Dan Reiter and Allan C. Stam III, "The Soldier's Decision to Surrender."

37. See Dupuy, *Numbers, Prediction, and War*; Dupuy, "Analysis of Factors That Have Influenced Outcomes of Battles and Wars." Since HERO authored the project, its name has changed to the Dupuy Institute. See also Dupuy, *Understanding War*; Thomas Bauer and Ralph Rotte, "Prospect Theory Goes to War.

38. We use the 1990 CAA version of the data set that includes battles up to 1982. There is an earlier version of the data set that includes battles up to only 1973. The 1990 version adds some battles to pre-1973 wars and incorporates reviews and corrections of the earlier version. For more information, contact the Dupuy Institute in Virginia or Dr. Robert Helmbold of the U.S. Army Concept Analysis Agency.

39. Since codings of the qualities of militaries postdate the outcomes of the battles, one might argue that there is the bias of hindsight; coders are more likely to infer that one side had superior morale because it won the battle. However, the mission of the HERO project was not to assess the simple hypotheses we have presented here; they were more interested in building a complex model of battle outcomes accounting for an array of material and intangible factors. Further, one of the central conclusions of the HERO project was the superiority of German armies (serving autocratic regimes such as Hitler's Third Reich), so we might if anything expect the data set to be skewed against our hypotheses that democracies fight better.

40. One study that used the data set to predict outcomes is Dupuy, *Numbers, Prediction, and War*. The sole case in which the side that won more battles did not also win the war is the 1939–1940 Winter War between the Soviet Union and Finland.

41. See Dupuy, "Analysis of Factors," 2: 13–14.

42. Of 505 battles (some were dropped because of missing data), there were 444 in which one side was more democratic (that is, had a higher Polity score). Within this group, the more democratic side won 338 battles. As described in the appendix, the data set overrepresents some wars. However, if one randomly samples to adjust for the skew, democracies are still significantly more likely to win battles (see appendix 3.1).

43. See appendix 3.1 for full discussion. We also present analysis of the full data set for comparison.

44. Ambrose, *D-Day*, 344.

45. Ibid., 352. An older explanation of French defeat focused on the failure of the French national spirit. Marc Bloch, *Strange Defeat*. More recent scholarship has dismissed this explanation, offering powerful evidence that the French defeat was due primarily to strategic blunders and intelligence failures, most notably leaving the Ardennes region substantially underprotected, which allowed German panzers to crash through and achieve the breakthrough upon which the blitzkrieg vitally depends. See Don W. Alexander, "Repercussions of the Breda Variant";

Len Deighton, *Blitzkrieg*; Robert J. Young, *In Command of France*; Alistair Horne, *To Lose a Battle*; Ernest R. May, *Strange Victory*. Interestingly, some have argued that, soldier-for-soldier, the Wehrmacht did not outperform the French Army during this campaign. Allied troops held their own when they came up against German infantry (which comprised the vast majority of the Wehrmacht) and in general, when they came up against German forces of equal numbers and firepower. See Horne, *To Lose a Battle*, 516; Alexander, "Repercussions," 462–465.

46. Dan Reiter and Allan C. Stam III, "Democracy and Battlefield Effectiveness."

47. Dupuy, *Numbers, Prediction, and War*.

48. Dupuy, "Analysis of Factors," 2:1.

49. In the event that the random number generator drew two sides from the same battle, a new random number was selected, and if there was only one battle in the war then only one case was used.

50. Dupuy, "Analysis of Factors," 2:13. In the original HERO data set, there was a category called "comparable" and another called "no factor." We coded "comparable" as 0, and "no factor" as missing, as the latter probably reflects the prejudgment on the part of the original code that morale did not affect the outcome of the battle, though the existence of the separate "comparable" category implies that "no factor" does not necessarily imply similar levels of morale.

51. Reiter and Stam coded these variables.

52. In a number of cases Polity III provided codings of "missing" because the country in question suffered occupation or internal chaos at some point during the year in question. However, it was often the case that the country did have a functioning political system when the battle occurred, though it lost the war after the battle. For these cases, we used the Polity III codings for the latest available year prior to the year of the battle when occupation or internal chaos missing codings are provided. A handful of cases still had missing data as they are for countries that are not internationally recognized nation-states. They include the rebels during the Latin American Wars of Independence, Texas during the War of Texan Independence, the Zulus during the Zulu Wars, the Boers during the Transvaal Revolt and the Boer War, Egypt and Sudan at the battles of Tel el-Kebir (1882) and Omaurman (1898), and Palestine at the battle of Gaza Strip in the Six-Day War (an independent Palestinian military force fought Israeli forces). The Confederacy during the Civil War was given the same democracy score as the Union, and an autocracy score of 3 to the Union's autocracy score of 0. On the slightly less democratic nature of the Confederacy as compared to the Union, see James Lee Ray, *Democracy and International Conflict*, 111.

53. This replicates the measure we used in Reiter and Stam, "Democracy and Battlefield Military Effectiveness."

54. Dupuy, "Analysis of Factors," 2:14.

55. Ibid.

56. Dupuy, *Numbers, Prediction, and War*, 48–49, 204–205.

57. Some might argue that the army that initiates the battle might exhibit higher levels of battlefield effectiveness, as a field commander would choose to strike when he feels especially confident in his army. The HERO data set does not

provide a battle initiation variable similar to the war initiation variable that we use in chapter 2. We tried including war initiation as a control variable on the limited sample, but it was not significant and did not alter the other results.

CHAPTER 4

1. See, in particular, Alexander Wendt, *Constructing International Politics*. For an empirical take on the subject, see Russett and Oneal, *Triangulating Peace*.

2. Kant, *Kant's Political Writings*; Fukuyama, *The End of History and the Last Man*; John M. Owen, *Liberal Peace, Liberal War*; Bruce M. Russett, *Grasping the Democratic Peace*.

3. David A. Lake, "Powerful Pacifists," 31; Owen, *Liberal Peace, Liberal War*.

4. On defending the liberal order, Mark R. Brawley, *Liberal Leadership*, 21–22; Kurt Taylor Gaubatz, "Democratic States and Commitment in International Relations." On democracies trading with each other, see James D. Morrow, Randolph M. Siverson, and Tressa E. Tabares, "The Political Determinants of International Trade"; Harry Bliss and Bruce Russett, "Democratic Trading Partners." On economic ties motivating democratic intervention, see Paul A. Papayoanou, *Power Ties*.

5. Deutsch, *Political Community and the North Atlantic Area*; Emanuel Adler and Michael Barnett, eds., *Security Communities*; Risse-Kappen, *Cooperation among Democracies*; Spencer R. Weart, *Never at War*; Colin H. Kahl, "Constructing a Separate Peace"; Margaret G. Hermann and Charles W. Kegley, Jr., "Rethinking Democracy and International Peace."

6. John M. Owen, "How Liberalism Produces Democratic Peace"; Michael W. Doyle, "Kant, Liberal Legacies, and Foreign Affairs, Part 2"; Weart, *Never at War*.

7. Owen, *Liberal Peace*. See also the normative explanation in Russett, *Grasping the Democratic Peace*, as well as the formal model in Bueno de Mesquita and Lalman, *War and Reason*.

8. Brawley, *Liberal Leadership*, 21–22; Lake, "Powerful Pacifists," 28–31. Karen Rasler and William R. Thompson found that democratic targets (but not initiators) are more likely to win, and they speculated that this may be because democracies assist democratic targets. "Predatory Initiators and Changing Landscapes for Warfare," 423–425.

9. Reiter, "Exploding the Powder Keg Myth"; Randall L. Schweller, "Domestic Structure and Preventive War."

10. On democracies not allying with each other, see Brian Lai and Dan Reiter, "Democracy, Political Similarity, and International Alliances, 1816–1992." On democracies not honoring their alliance commitments, see Alastair Smith, "To Intervene or Not to Intervene."

11. Lai and Reiter, "Democracy, Political Similarity, and Alliances"; Dan Reiter, "NATO Enlargement and the Spread of Democracy."

12. Quoted in Leslie Bethell, "From the Second World War to the Cold War," 64–65.

13. The Suez War is another possibility, though Britain and France shared no alliance with Israel, and the outcome is best characterized as victory for Israel and a draw for Britain and France.

14. That is, states with Polity scores of 7 or above on a -10 to $+10$ scale. Setting the democracy threshold at 7 follows the recommendation of the managers of the Polity data set, Keith Jaggers and Ted Robert Gurr, "Tracking Democracy's Third Wave with the Polity III Data," 479. The 7 threshold is also used in other empirical work, such as Kenneth A. Schultz, "Do Democratic Institutions Constrain or Inform?"; Rousseau et al., "Assessing the Dyadic Nature of the Democratic Peace, 1918–1988"; and Dan Reiter, "Does Peace Nurture Democracy?" Setting the threshold at 5 or 6 does not change the results.

15. We also ran probit regression of these 76 cases with the dependent variable being whether or not the target attracted a defender, and independent variables of the target's Polity score and the Balance of Power between the Attacker and Target. Neither variable was statistically significant.

16. A ninth case might arguably be the dispatch of British troops to Norway in 1940 after the German invasion. This case really belongs in a different category, as Britain was already at war with Germany, and so sending troops to Norway was a tactical move as part of their overall war with Germany. Even if the British intervention to aid Norway was counted as a case, it did not prevent the German defeat of Norway, so the case cannot be used as an example offering support for the claim that democracies win wars because they form an alliance.

17. U.S. News and World Report, *Triumph Without Victory*, 179; see also George Bush and Brent Scowcroft, *A World Transformed*, 399–400. Andrew Bennett, Joseph Lepgold, and Danny Unger found that the contributions by the coalition partners were made because of a variety of external and internal factors, none of which includes the desire to safeguard democracy. "Sharing in the Persian Gulf War."

18. David A. Lake dissents somewhat from this point, pointing to a number of contributions made by democratic members of the coalition. However, his bottom line is that absent these contributions, the prewar military buildup would have been "slowed considerably"; that is, he does not go so far as to argue that victory depended on the contributions of countries like Britain and France, noting, for instance, that U.S. strike aircraft delivered over 90 percent of the ordinance dropped on Iraq. *Entangling Relations*, 224–225.

19. Michael Howard, *The Continental Commitment*; Kagan, *On the Origins of War*, 204–205; Luigi Albertini, *The Origins of the War in 1914*, esp. 3:409. Grey quote in Edward Grey, *Twenty-Five Years 1892–1916*, 2:15–16. On uniting the British cabinet, see Winston S. Churchill, *The World Crisis*, 1:211.

20. Ernest R. May, *The World War and American Isolation 1914–1917*, 427; Arthur S. Link, *Wilson*, 342–345.

21. Robert Lansing, *War Memoirs of Robert Lansing, Secretary of State*, 232; quote from Fritz Fischer, *Germany's Aims in the First World War*, 306.

22. Link, *Wilson*, 411–412.

23. Dan Reiter, *Crucible of Beliefs*.

24. Robert Dallek, *Franklin D. Roosevelt and American Foreign Policy*, 312.

25. Randall L. Schweller, *Deadly Imbalances*, 173.

26. Last, we also note that these two cases should not carry any more or less evidentiary weight simply because they were world wars. Bruce Bueno de Mesquita, "Big Wars, Little Wars," 159–160.

27. John H. Wuorinen, ed., *Finland and World War II*, 69–73; May, *Strange Victory*, 332–335.

28. Wuorinen, *Finland and World War II*, 70–71; Winston S. Churchill, *The Second World War, Volume 1: The Gathering Storm*, 489.

29. Reiter, *Crucible of Beliefs*; Jakobson, *The Diplomacy of the Winter War*; Upton, *Finland: 1939–1940*.

30. Moshe Dayan, *Moshe Dayan*; Golda Meir, *My Life*, 420–427.

31. Kissinger, *Years of Upheaval*, 510–515.

32. David Schoenbaum, *The United States and the State of Israel*, 59–92; Abba Eban, *Personal Witness*, 407; Sisson and Rose, *War and Secession*, 261–264; Upton, *Finland: 1939–1940*.

33. Arthur S. Link, *Wilson*, esp. 105–110.

34. On Lend Lease munitions, see Richard J. Overy, "Co-operation, Trade, Aid, and Technology," in *Allies at War*, ed. David Reynolds, Warren F. Kimball, and A. O. Chubarian, 209; on shipbuilding, see Peter Calvocoressi, Guy Wint, and John Pritchard, *Total War*, 1:462; on destroyers for bases, see Nathan Miller, *War at Sea*, 106.

35. Gartner, *Strategic Assessment in War*.

36. Dallek, *Roosevelt*, esp. 257, 261.

37. Quoted in Grose, *Gentleman Spy*, 55.

38. Bruce Russett and Allan C. Stam, "Courting Disaster"; James M. Goldgeier, *Not Whether but When*.

39. See Gartner and Siverson, "War Expansion and War Outcome"; Smith, "To Intervene or Not to Intervene."

40. Kenneth A. Schultz found that when a democracy is a challenger, the target is more likely to back down if the challenger is an autocrat. "Do Democratic Institutions Constrain or Inform?" Note that this argument is driven by the assumption that democracies can signal their intentions with more information, not that democracies are feared to be stronger adversaries in war (because their allies are more reliable, or for whatever other reason). For one to use Schultz's empirical results to claim that states back down from democratic challenges because democratic challengers are more likely to have better allies, one would also have to assume that democracies are willing to help each other accomplish revisionist goals (as challengers usually have revisionist goals, especially given the rarity of preemptive wars [Reiter, "Exploding the Powder Keg Myth"] and, we argued earlier in this chapter, that liberal theory does not predict revisionist democratic bandwagoning).

41. Jack S. Levy, "Preferences, Constraints, and Choices in July 1914"; Fischer, *Germany's Aims*; Lebow, *Between Peace and War*.

42. On the plebiscite, see J. Kenneth Brody, *The Avoidable War*, 178; for Hitler's quote and appeasement in 1930s in general, see Kagan, *Origins of War*, chap. 4.

43. For the Finland quote, see Jakobson, *Diplomacy of the Winter War*, 134; on Japan, see chapters 2 and 7 as well as Dower, *War Without Mercy*, 259–261, and Sagan, "The Origins of the Pacific War," 344; for the Saddam quote, see Stein, "Deterrence and Compellence in the Gulf, 1990–91," 175; on post–Cold War, see Blechman and Wittes, "Defining Moment." Ted Hopf has argued in *Peripheral Visions* that the Soviet Union did not infer from American defeat in Vietnam that it was weak.

44. David L. Rousseau et al., "Assessing the Dyadic Nature of the Democratic Peace"; Brett Ashley Leeds and David R. Davis, "Beneath the Surface"; Kurt Dassel and Eric Reinhardt, "Domestic Strife and the Initiation of Violence at Home and Abroad"; and personal communication with Eric Reinhardt, Emory University, November 3, 1998. These three papers use the Interstate Crisis Behavior, Conflict and Peace Data Bank, and Militarized Interstate Dispute data sets. See also Bennett and Stam, "Research Design and Estimator Choices," 677.

45. Ajin Choi, "Democracy, International Partnerships, and State War Performance."

46. William James Philpott, *Anglo-French Relations and Strategy on the Western Front*, 50; John Keegan, *The First World War*, 350; David F. Trask, *The AEF and Coalition Warmaking*. Anglo-Franco-American cooperation during the 1991 Gulf War also had its bumps, as both Britain and France refused to accept their initial combat assignments in the ground campaign. James F. Dunnigan and Austin Bay, *From Shield to Storm*, 60–61.

47. Brian Bond, *France and Belgium 1939–1940*, 96, 100; Calvocoressi et al., *Total War*, 138; May, *Strange Victory*, 304, 394, 295.

48. Cherwell quoted in Richard Rhodes, *The Making of the Atomic Bomb*, 372.

49. Of course, this European recalcitrance may have also prevented World War III.

50. On Korea, see Risse-Kappen, *Cooperation among Democracies*; on Suez, see Louise Richardson, *When Allies Differ*; on NATO, see Jane E. Stromseth, *The Origins of Flexible Response*.

51. Lai and Reiter, "Democracy, Political Similarity"; Edward D. Mansfield and Rachel Bronson, "The Political Economy of Major-Power Trade Flows." Additionally, Karen Remmer found in "Does Democracy Promote Interstate Cooperation?" that democracies are not particularly likely to sign economic cooperation agreements with each other.

52. Bruce Russett, *Grasping the Democratic Peace*; Rousseau et al., "Assessing the Dyadic Nature"; John R. Oneal and Bruce Russett, "The Kantian Peace."

53. Suzanne Werner and Douglas Lemke, "Opposites Do Not Attract"; Robin Moriarty, "Understanding the Formation and Reliability of International Agreements."

54. Paul K. Huth, "Major Power Intervention in International Crises." The latter two categories were based on Huth's own codings.

55. Michael Mousseau, "Peace in Anarchy," chap. 6. Earlier, Mousseau found that democracies are especially likely to be on the same side at the outset of a dispute, but that design lumps challengers and targets together. Michael Mousseau, "Democracy and Militarized Interstate Collaboration."

56. Ashley Leeds, using the COPDAB data set, found in "Domestic Political Institutions, Credible Commitments, and International Cooperation," that jointly democratic dyads were more likely to cooperate in the 1953–1978 period than jointly autocratic dyads, and mixed dyads are less likely to cooperate than are jointly democratic or jointly autocratic dyads. Neta Crawford proposed that the Iroquois League provides an example of security cooperation among democratic nations, though David Rousseau and Karl Mueller disputed the claim, arguing that the Iroquois nations were not democratic. Crawford, "A Security Regime among Democracies"; Rousseau and Mueller, "Peaceful Democrats or Pragmatic Realists?" Relatedly, some have argued that alliances between democracies should last longer, but the most sophisticated research design addressing this question (D. Scott Bennett, "Testing Alternative Models of Alliance Duration") found that this hypothesis is supported only when democracy is defined using Michael Doyle's codings ("Liberalism and World Politics") not when the more conventional Polity data are used. John Lewis Gaddis proposed that the democratic institutions of Western states helped NATO outlast the Warsaw Pact. *We Now Know*, 288–289.

57. Arvid Raknerud and Håvard Hegre, "The Hazard of War." See also Nils Petter Gleditsch and Håvard Hegre, "Peace and Democracy."

58. Thanks to Håvard Hegre for provided data and assistance. The recoded data and results are available from the authors.

59. Casualty data from Small and Singer, *Resort to Arms*. For the Gulf War, we instead used the percentage of troops contributed by each nation, due to the strange nature of coalition casualties in that war.

60. In the 1907 Central American War, Honduras is randomly picked over El Salvador as the target; in the Second Balkan War, Greece is randomly picked as the target over Serbia; in the Nomohan War, the Soviet Union is randomly picked as the target over Mongolia; in the Six-Day War, Syria is randomly picked as the target; in the Papal States War, Austria is the attacker; in the First Balkan War, Bulgaria is randomly picked as the attacker; in the Hungary-Allies War, Romania is picked as the attacker.

61. We alternatively could have made the second decision about whether or not to join Belgium (rather than France). Choosing one or the other is unlikely to affect results, as both are democratic.

62. This means that Britain and France are coded as intervening on behalf of Poland. Note that we code the decision to declare war, not the decision to send troops. So, when Norway is invaded by Germany in 1940, Britain is not included as a potential defender case because it is already at war with Germany.

63. Smith, "To Intervene." COW alliance data are available up through 1984. We updated this data set to 1992. We also ran a model with a variable for an alliance between the potential defender and attacker; the defender-attacker alliance variable was not significant.

64. Randolph M. Siverson and Harvey Starr, *The Diffusion of War*.

65. Kenneth N. Waltz, *Theory of International Politics*.

66. Stephen M. Walt, *The Origins of Alliances*.

67. Papayoanou, *Power Ties*. We used data from John R. Oneal and Bruce Russett, "Assessing the Liberal Peace with Alternative Specifications."

68. Some might argue that a better approach would be to use hazard analysis, examining how long it takes states to join wars once war breaks out. Probit analysis is probably more likely to find in favor of the democratic bandwagoning hypothesis, as it does not account for some delays in democratic bandwagoning, such as American entry into both world wars.

69. Specifically, the cluster command was used (in STATA 6.0).

70. Due to missing data, 587 observations were dropped from the 5,588. We also have little fear the results are significantly affected by multicollinearity. Among the four independent variables, Target-Defender Mutual Democracy, Defense Pact, Contiguity, and Defender Major Power, partial correlations are always below 0.25.

71. Another possibility is that democracies only defend each other when there is an alliance between them. However, if we include a variable of Mutual Democracy*Defense Pact it is not significantly related, as there are no cases of an intervention by a democratic defender on behalf of a democratic target in which there is an alliance between them. Additionally, if we change the dependent variable such that it measures either intervention on behalf of only attackers rather than defenders, or intervention on behalf of both attackers and defenders, Mutual Democracy remains insignificant.

72. Henry S. Farber and Joanne Gowa, "Common Interests or Common Polities?"

CHAPTER 5

1. Grey quoted in Winston S. Churchill, *The Second World War, Volume 3: The Grand Alliance*, 540, on U.S. war production, see Harold J. Clem, *Mobilization Preparedness*, esp. 47.

2. Locke, *Second Treatise of Government*, 26; see also Holmes, *Passions and Constraint*, 18–20.

3. Lake, "Powerful Pacifists." In appendix 5.1 we address Lake's claim and find no systematic relationship between a state's level of democracy and the number of artillery, tanks, and aircraft. See in particular table 5.5.

4. Stam, *Win, Lose, or Draw*; Paul Kennedy, *The Rise and Fall of the Great Powers*, Rosen, "War Power and the Willingness to Suffer."

5. See Milward, *War, Economy, and Society*, 19–21. A.F.K. Organski and Jacek Kugler also emphasized aggregate resources and the extractive capacity of the state in their study of war outcomes, *The War Ledger*.

6. For a detailed formal presentation of the tradeoffs between mobilization of national resources for consumption and security, see Robert Powell, *Bargaining in the Shadow of Power*.

7. See Baron de Montesquieu, *The Spirit of the Laws*, 340–341; Kant, *Political Writings*, 50. For discussion of the links among democracy, property rights, and economic growth, see David A. Leblang, "Property Rights, Democracy and Economic Growth," and "Political Democracy and Economic Growth."

8. Schmitt, *Concept of the Political*.

9. On the end of history, see Fukuyama, *The End of History and the Last Man*. Martin C. McGuire and Mancur Olson, Jr., provided a more recent, formal state-

ment of the proposition that democracy facilitates development. They argued that a society in which the government is responsible to a rational, wealth-seeking majority will be more prosperous than an autocratic society; that is, it will produce more private goods. "The Economics of Autocracy and Majority Rule." See also Mancur Olson, "Autocracy, Democracy, and Prosperity." This argument is similar to the rent-seeking argument made by Lake, "Powerful Pacifists." In a later article, "Dictatorship, Democracy, and Development," Olson also stressed that only democracies are likely to safeguard property rights over the long run, an important prerequisite of democracy. Similarly, Kenneth A. Schultz and Barry R. Weingast argued in "Limited Governments, Powerful States" that democracies have better long-run economic stamina in rivalries because they have better access to credit. In contrast, Ronald Wintrobe proposed in *The Political Economy of Dictatorship* that democracies do not necessarily experience greater prosperity than dictatorships, as the performance of dictatorships is likely to vary greatly.

10. Larry Diamond, "Economic Development and Democracy Reconsidered"; Leblang, "Property Rights"; Philip Keefer and Stephen Knack, "Why Don't Poor Countries Catch Up?;" Ross E. Burkhart and Michael S. Lewis-Beck, "Comparative Democracy"; John F. Helliwell, "Empirical Linkages Between Democracy and Economic Growth"; Robert J. Barro, *Determinants of Economic Growth*; Yi Feng, "Democracy, Political Stability and Economic Growth"; Adam Przeworski et al., *Democracy and Development*; John B. Londregan and Keith T. Poole, "Does High Income Promote Democracy?"; Yi Feng and Paul Zak, "The Determinants of Democratic Transitions"; William Easterly, "Life during Growth"; Mark J. Gasiorowski, "Democracy and Macroeconomic Performance in Underdeveloped Countries"; Matthew A. Baum and David A. Lake, "The *Political Economy* of Growth."

11. Alexander Gershenkron, *Economic Backwardness in Historical Perspective*.

12. In chapter 2, in our statistical analysis, we controlled for a state's relative share of the system's military-industrial resources. There, we found that even when controlling for the proportion of resources a state controls, the state's level of democracy is still significantly related to its propensity to win. In this chapter we conduct much more fine-grained analysis focusing on each possible component of victory.

13. Organski and Kugler, *The War Ledger*.

14. George F. Kennan, *American Diplomacy*, esp. 66; Walter Lippmann, *Essays in the Public Philosophy*; de Tocqueville, *Democracy in America*, 654–658.

15. See Lake, "Powerful Pacifists," 30; Alan C. Lamborn, *The Price of Power*, 84; Levi, *Consent, Dissent, and Patriotism*. The Schultz and Weingast ("Limited Governments," 17) argument could be applied here, as it might imply that democracies can access greater resources in wartime by having more credit availability, enabling them to "finance larger and longer wars." It is an interesting point, which they demonstrate nicely in the Dutch Revolt against Spain and the seventeenth-century Anglo-French rivalry. Its applicability to modern circumstances may be more limited, however; modern democracies might be less likely to exploit these financial advantages in a long war, as since 1815 they have tended to fight short wars to maintain support at home (see chapter 7).

16. Bruce Bueno de Mesquita et al., "Institutional Explanation of the Democratic Peace." They explain their argument as follows: "If war occurs, then leaders

must decide how much effort to make to achieve military victory. By this we mean what proportion of available resources a leader is prepared to allocate to the war effort rather than to other purposes. . . . This means that [democracies] are willing to spend more resources on war effort and only engage in fights they anticipate winning. . . . Democrats are more likely to win wars then autocrats . . . if they need to, democrats try hard, spending resources on the war to advance their public policy goals. . . . Democrats, by their superior level of effort, often defeat autocratic foes and achieve successful policy outcomes" (794). They conclude: "We demonstrated [formally] that democratic leaders, when faced with a war, are more inclined to shift extra resources into the war effort than are autocratic leaders" (804).

17. See, for example, Samuel P. Huntington, *Political Order in Changing Societies*. Robert Jackman also discussed legitimacy as a determinant of political capacity, though he argued that nondemocratic regimes can accrue legitimacy through, for example, fast economic growth. Regardless, the notion of legitimacy is a slippery one to define or to measure. *Power Without Force*, 96–97.

18. On taxation, see José Antonio Cheibub, "Political Regimes and the Extractive Capacity of Governments," for the capacity quote, see Jacek Kugler and William Domke, "Comparing the Strength of Nations," 66, as well as Jacek Kugler and Marina Arbetman, "Relative Political Capacity"; on democracy and total victory, see Suzanne Werner, "Negotiating the Terms of Settlement."

19. This finding is indirect evidence against Levi's (*Consent, Dissent, and Patriotism*) model that predicts that democratic governments enjoy higher levels of popular consent toward conscription policies.

20. We discuss a similar argument about effectiveness of wartime economic management later in the chapter. The argument we are summarizing here has to our knowledge not been made in print, and specifically it is not explicitly made in Bueno de Mesquita et al., "Institutional Explanation." We thank Bruce Bueno de Mesquita for discussions on this point.

21. This result parallels the finding that there was not consistent evidence that among great powers since 1860, democracies built more capital ships than did nondemocracies. Sean Bolks and Richard J. Stoll, "The Arms Acquisition Process."

22. Though this dependent variable might offer some theoretical advantages over looking at demographic mobilization, there are substantially more missing data. We use military spending as a percentage of GDP, as measured in the state's local currency, for 1970–1992; data are provided by the *World Development Indicators on CD-ROM*. Out of 3,838 observations of nation-years for this time-span, there are 1,748 missing observations (45.5 percent) for the dependent variable alone. Further, data are not randomly missing, as we might expect that data are more likely to be missing for Third World and repressive countries. Conducting panel data analysis indicates that none of the independent variables of Model 1 in table 5.1 is statistically significant. Such panel analysis, however, may be distorted due to the considerable gaps in the data. Interestingly, ordinary least squares (OLS) regression on these data provides a similar result as indicated in Model 1 of table 5.1, namely, that democracy is significantly and negatively correlated with defense spending as a fraction of GDP. Even given the problems with using OLS on panel data, this bolsters our confidence that there is not a positive relationship,

for while OLS may bias standard error estimates, it is unlikely to cause coefficients to change their signs.

23. On the Soviet Union, see David F. Epstein, "The Economic Cost of Soviet Security and Empire." For a liberal critique of American Cold War policy, see Richard Ned Lebow and Janice Gross Stein, *We All Lost the Cold War*; for a conservative critique, see Colin S. Gray and Keith Payne, "Victory Is Possible." On constraints in the United States, see Aaron Friedberg, *In the Shadow of the Garrison State*. Friedberg argues, however, that antistatism provides advantages to democracies by boosting technological progress and by generating greater economic growth and development. For more discussion, see below.

24. The exception would be wars of empire, where, literally, to the victor go the spoils.

25. On democracies' dependence on trade, see Daniel Verdier, *Democracy and International Trade*; on trade dependence, resource mobilization, and war, see David M. Rowe, "World Economic Expansion and National Security in Pre–World War I Europe."

26. Berman, *Planning a Tragedy*, 122–127; Robert S. McNamara, *In Retrospect*, 198; George C. Herring, *America's Longest War*, 222–223; Lyndon Baines Johnson, *The Vantage Point*, 406–407; Lewis Sorley, *A Better War*, 124–125.

27. George Bush and Brent Scowcroft, *A World Transformed*, 359–360.

28. Jerome B. Cohen, *Japan's Economy in War and Reconstruction*, 353; Richard B. Frank, *Downfall*, 351; see also Akira Hara, "Japan: Guns Before Rice," 256. On Italy, see Vera Zamagni, "Italy," 190–191.

29. Richard Overy, *Why the Allies Won*, John Barber and Mark Harrison, *The Soviet Home Front, 1941–1945*.

30. Alan S. Milward, *The German Economy at War*, 10–11; Lothar Burchardt, "The Impact of the War Economy on the Civilian Population of Germany," 62–64.

31. Werner Abelshauser, "Germany," Harrison, 152–153; Richard J. Overy, *War and Economy in the Third Reich*, 283–285, 312; Mark Harrison, "Resource Mobilization for World War II," 184.

32. On Japan, see Ienaga, *The Pacific War, 1931–1945*, 223; Pape, *Bombing to Win*. There was some rationing in the United States during World War II, but it was much more limited and was frequently temporary. On the United States during World War II, see Harold G. Vatter, "The Material Status of the U.S. Civilian Consumer in World War II," and Robert Higgs, "Wartime Prosperity? A Reassessment of the U.S. Economy in the 1940s"; on the Civil War, see Bruce Catton, *Glory Road*, 235–251.

33. Millett and Murray, eds., *Military Effectiveness*, vol. 1; Burchardt, "The Impact of the War Economy," 43.

34. On Britain, see Sir Llewellyn Woodward, *Great Britain and the War of 1914–1918*, 498–513; Sidney Pollard, *The Development of the British Economy, 1914–1990*, 19; Ferguson, *The Pity of War*, 276. On the United States, see James A. Huston, *The Sinews of War*, 328.

35. The shortages in Germany or the relative abundance of consumer goods in Britain cannot be attributed to differences in the two states' degree of democratization. More important was the fact that Germany had far fewer outlets by

which it could import food, whereas Britain could import from its colonies and trade with overseas states such as the United States. France suffered tremendously in large part because much of the war was fought on French soil, principally in the industrial areas in the north of France.

36. The quote is from Richard Pipes, *Three "Whys" of the Russian Revolution*, 27. See also Norman Stone, *The Eastern Front 1914–1917*, and Richard Pipes, *The Russian Revolution*, 205–206, 245.

37. See Wayne Sandholtz and William Koetzle, "Accounting for Corruption." Interestingly, those two authors argue (48) that the military spending effects of corruption are likely to be that corruption outside the military sector reduces the flow of resources into the military sector. We find evidence against that claim in this chapter, in that democracies do not devote a greater percentage of their economies to military spending. Nor do we find support for Bueno de Mesquita et al.'s ("Institutional Explanation") argument that corruption in autocratic regimes reduces the numbers of weapons they are able to acquire with similar levels of resources as their democratic counterparts. See table 5.4 for details.

38. Specifically, we estimated a statistical model using Model 5 in appendix 2.1, including an interaction variable of its -10 to $+10$ Politics score multiplied by its Industrial Capability score. The interaction term was not statistically significant.

39. Note also that the median duration of interstate wars is just over four months. Wars such as the world wars that require long-term mobilization of civil society are quite rare. On war duration, see Bennett and Stam, "The Duration of Interstate Wars."

40. This is particularly telling as both sides in the war recognized the importance of artillery on the battlefield.

41. On World War I, see Ferguson, *Pity of War*, 260–263; on World War II, see Barber and Harrison, *The Soviet Home Front*, 198; Overy, *Why the Allies Won*. Our point is not that centrally planned economies like the Soviet system are in general superior, but rather that such centralization can accomplish some tasks well, such as rapid military mobilization of the economy.

42. On growth, see Harrison, "Resource Mobilization," 185; on productivity, see Milward, *War, Economy, and Society*, 230; on imperial extraction, see Peter Liberman, *Does Conquest Pay?*

43. Matthew Evangelista, *Innovation and the Arms Race*.

44. For a discussion of the effects of wartime innovation as it may affect war duration and outcomes, see Stam, *Win, Lose, or Draw*, 186–196.

45. Rhodes, *The Making of the Atomic Bomb*, esp. 88–89.

46. Snyder, *Myths of Empire*.

47. Millett and Murray, *Military Effectiveness*; Pollard, *Development of the British Economy*; John H. Morrow, Jr., "Industrial Mobilization in World War I," 51; Daniel R. Beaver, "The Problem of American Military Supply, 1890–1920"; Clem, *Mobilization Preparedness*. For an argument that German agricultural problems during World War I were driven by outmoded ideas more than inferior bureaucratic structures, see Joe Lee, "Administrators and Agriculture."

48. Ferguson, *Pity of War*.

49. Cohen, *Japan's Economy in War and Reconstruction*, 74–75; Gerhard Krebs, "The Japanese Air Forces," 233n.

50. Quote from Cohen, *Japan's Economy*, 79; see also 73; Richard J. Samuels, *"Rich Nation, Strong Army,"* 105; Chalmers Johnson, *MITI and the Japanese Miracle*, 167–168; David Friedman, *The Misunderstood Miracle*, 60–70.

51. Wilhelm Deist, *The Wehrmacht and German Rearmament*; Overy, "War and Economy in the Third Reich," 343–375.

52. Milward, *The German Economy at War*; R. L. DiNardo, *Germany's Panzer Arm*, 12–13.

53. Barber and Harrison, *The Soviet Home Front*.

54. Ibid., 198; Alexander Werth, *Russia at War*, 213–224.

55. Barber and Harrison, *The Soviet Home Front*; Werth, *Russia at War*, 619–628.

56. Williamson Murray, "British Military Effectiveness in the Second World War," 3:92; Richard Overy, "Great Britain: Cyclops," 113–144.

57. Milward, *War, Economy, and Society*, 112–113; Huston, *Sinews of War*, 457–461; Theodore A. Wilson, "The United States," 184–185.

58. Harold G. Vatter, *The U.S. Economy in World War II*, 72–73; Wilson, "The United States"; Joel R. Davidson, *The Unsinkable Fleet*.

59. Vannevar Bush, *Modern Arms and Free Men*; Evangelista, *Innovation and the Arms Race*; Friedberg, *In the Shadow*.

60. Reported in Reiter and Stam, "Democracy and Battlefield Military Effectiveness."

61. Stam, *Win, Lose or Draw*; Dan Reiter and Allan C. Stam III, "Democracy, War Initiation, and Victory."

62. Pollack, "The Influence of Arab Culture on Arab Military Effectiveness."

63. On American perceptions of the Japanese in World War II, see Dower, *War Without Mercy*. As we discussed in chapter 3, there is a substantial debate among historians about whether soldier for soldier the German Army outfought the American Army. Our empirical results in chapter 3 indicate that democracies enjoy important advantages in superior initiative and leadership, however.

64. On Israel, see Ian J. Bickerton and Carla L. Klausner, *A Concise History of the Arab-Israeli Conflict*, 152. For an argument that North Vietnam won the Vietnam War because of superior political capacity, see Organski and Kugler, *The War Ledger*.

65. Hein Goemans in *War and Punishment* extends this argument to oligarchs and also finds a strong relationship between war duration and regime type. In his model and data, democracies initiate the shortest wars, oligarchs the longest, and dictators' wars fall in between the two extremes. On casualties, see Siverson, "Democratic and War Participation; DeRouen, "Presidents and the Diversionary Use of Force"; and R. J. Rummel, "Democracies ARE Less Warlike than Other Regimes." On strategy, see Reiter and Meek, "Determinants of Military Strategy."

66. J. David Singer, "Reconstructing the Correlates of War Data Set on Material Capabilities of States."

67. See Kenneth A. Bollen, "Political Democracy and the Timing of Development."

68. In some wars, no state produces any iron or steel. For these wars, we assumed that each state had equal iron and steel production to avoid the problem

of dividing by zero. If we instead drop all cases in which no war participant produced any iron or steel, the results do not change.

69. We use the Correlates of War data set on membership in the international system. It includes all states that are recognized as members of the international system whose membership exceeds 500,000.

70. The partial correlations for all four of these variables are in all cases below 0.10.

71. Nathaniel Beck and Jonathan N. Katz, "What to Do (and Not to Do) with Time-Series Cross-Section Data."

72. If the COW aggregate capabilities score is substituted for major power status, the results do not change.

73. On the MID data, see Jones, Bremer, and Singer, "Militarized Interstate Disputes."

74. For defense expenditure as a percentage of government revenue, we used Arthur S. Banks, "Cross-National Time Series, 1815–1997." We used annual data; the null result holds whether one uses the highest percentage of revenue spent on defense for any one year during the war, or if one averages the percentage spent on defense across all years of the war. Unfortunately, revenue data are missing for 45 percent of the cases.

CHAPTER 6

1. Kant, *Kant's Political Writings*, 100.

2. See, for example, Bueno de Mesquita and Lalman, *War and Reason*; Russett, *Grasping the Democratic Peace*; Lake, "Powerful Pacifists"; James D. Fearon, "Domestic Political Audiences and the Escalation of International Disputes"; Bueno de Mesquita et al., "Institutional Explanation of the Democratic Peace."

3. Alexander Hamilton, James Madison, and John Jay, *The Federalist Papers*, 25 (Federalist No. 6).

4. Snyder, *Myths of Empire*.

5. Bradley Lian and John Oneal, "Presidents, the Use of Military Force, and Public Opinion"; Mueller, *Policy and Opinion in the Gulf War*, 96–112.

6. For scholarship skeptical of the diversionary effect, see, for example, James Meernik, "Modeling International Crises and the Political Use of Military Force by the USA"; Jack S. Levy, "The Diversionary Theory of War: A Critique." For examples of scholarship that claim to find the presence of diversionary effects, see T. Clifton Morgan and Kenneth N. Bickers, "Domestic Discontent and the External Use of Force," and T. Clifton Morgan and Christopher J. Anderson, "Domestic Support and Diversionary External Conflict in Great Britain."

7. Tocqueville, *Democracy in America*; Walter Lippmann, *Essays in The Public Philosophy*; and Kennan, *American Diplomacy*.

8. Barton Whaley, *Codeword BARBAROSSA*.

9. On 1939, see Robert Dallek, *Franklin D. Roosevelt and American Foreign Policy*, 207. The quote is from Richard Rhodes, *Dark Sun*, 57.

10. Page and Shapiro, *The Rational Public*. See also Jentleson, "The Pretty Prudent Public"; Jentleson and Britton, "Still Pretty Prudent."

11. Mueller, *War, Presidents and Public Opinion.*

12. On the requirements of great power status, see Waltz, *Theory of International Politics.* On the United States, see, for example, Ernest R. May, *Imperial Democracy.*

13. Reiter, *Crucible of Beliefs.* On the United States, see also Ernest R. May, *"Lessons" of the Past.*

14. Norms have been defined as "standards of behavior defined in terms of rights and obligations." Stephen D. Krasner, "Structural Cases and Regime Consequences," 2.

15. Russett, *Grasping the Democratic Peace.* See also William J. Dixon, "Democracy and the Peaceful Settlement of International Conflict"; William J. Dixon, "Democracy and the Management of International Conflict"; William J. Dixon, "Dyads, Disputes, and the Democratic Peace"; Risse-Kappen, *Cooperation among Democracies.* The empirical evidence regarding the claim that democracies are more likely to arbitrate their conflicts peacefully is mixed. Though Dixon has generally found evidence supporting this claim, Beth Simmons found in "See You in 'Court'?" that among dyads with territorial disputes, democratic dyads are not significantly more likely to agree on a bilateral arbitration agreement regarding their conflicting claims. Interestingly, Eric Reinhardt found in "Aggressive Multilateralism" that among GATT members, democracies are significantly more likely to file trade disputes against each other.

16. Reiter, "Exploding the Powder Keg Myth"; Schweller, "Domestic Structure and Preventive War."

17. Bob Woodward, *Shadow,* 184–185; Bush and Scowcroft, *A World Transformed,* 477; Colin L. Powell, *My American Journey,* 400.

18. Charles W. Kegley and Margaret G. Hermann, "Putting Military Intervention into the Democratic Peace." There are debates about whether or not there has ever been an actual war between democracies, where war is defined as being a militarized conflict between two nation-states that incurs at least 1,000 casualties. Close calls include the Spanish-American War, the American Civil War, the Boer War, Finnish participation in World War II as a member of the Axis, and others. See Russett, *Grasping the Democratic Peace,* and Ray, *Democracy and International Conflict.* The 1999 India-Pakistani War may have been the most incontrovertible case yet of a war between democracies, as there were probably at least a thousand casualties, and both India and Pakistan are rated as democracies in 1998 by the latest version of the Polity data set (that is, both have 7 or higher on the -10 to $+10$ scale).

19. On aversion to killing, see Dave Grossman, *On Killing: The Psychological Cost of Learning to Kill in War and Society.* On World War II, see Dower, *War Without Mercy.* More generally on clashes across lines of ethnicity or civilization, see Samuel P. Huntington, *The Clash of Civilizations and the Remaking of World Order.* The quantitative evidence on whether ethnic differences make international conflict more likely or international cooperation less likely is preliminary, with some initially suggestive results. See Errol Anthony Henderson, "The Democratic Peace Through the Lens of Culture"; Lai and Reiter, "Democracy, Political Similarity, and International Alliances."

20. Donald A. Grinde Jr. and Bruce E. Johansen, *Exemplar of Liberty;*

Reginald Horsman, "Scientific Racism and the American Indian in the Mid-Nineteenth Century," *American Quarterly* 27 (May 1975): 152–168; Dee Brown, *Bury My Heart at Wounded Knee* (New York: Bantam Books, 1970). In many instances, including public remarks by the president of the United States, the rhetoric in nineteenth-century America justifying white immigrants' need for living space to be provided at the expense of the native Americans, disconcertingly parallels that heard in Germany in the 1930s regarding the Nazi German *lebensraum* justification of their invasion of Eastern Europe and subsequent murder and enslavement of millions.

21. Grinde and Johansen, *Exemplar of Liberty*, 33–35; John Tebbel and Keith Jennison, *The American Indian Wars*, 224–225.

22. Russel Lawrence Barsh and James Youngblood Henderson, *The Road*; Tebbel and Jennison, *The American Indian Wars*, 229; Robert M. Utley and Wilcomb M. Washburn, *Indian Wars*. Andrew Jackson's personal history is filled with impertinent actions. Jackson participated in several duels, even after such behavior had been banned. At the Battle of New Orleans his forces initiated battle and routed the British Forces *after* the peace treaty between the United States and Britain had already been signed. His veto of the renewal of the Second National bank legislation in 1832 outraged elites throughout the United States. For a detailed discussion of Jackson's role in U.S. constitutional development, and in particular his role in shaping the power of public consent, see Arthur M. Schlesinger, Jr., *The Age of Jackson*.

23. Ray, *Democracy and Conflict*; Gerald F. Linderman, *The Mirror of War*; Reed quoted in Barbara W. Tuchman, *The Proud Tower*, 174.

24. Lewis L. Gould, *The Spanish-American War and President McKinley*, 30, 45.

25. Gould, *The Spanish-American War*, 10; Dixon, "Democracy and the Management of International Conflict."

26. The question of whether or not Spain is a democracy has been discussed in the context of the democratic peace. See Russett, *Grasping the Democratic Peace*, 19; Ray, *Democracy and International Conflict*, 111–115; Owen, *Liberal Peace, Liberal War*, 170–181.

27. Opportune from the perspective of those desiring war.

28. Teodoro Agoncillo and Oscar Alfonso, *History of the Filipino People*.

29. Quoted in Gould, *The Spanish-American War*, 109. See also Ernest R. May, *Imperial Democracy*, 252–253.

30. Quoted in Stuart Miller, *Benevolent Assimilation*, 94.

31. Joseph Hayden, *The Philippines*, 32.

32. Teodoro Agoncillo, *Malolos*, 322–325.

33. Elidoro Robles, *The Philippines in the Nineteenth Century*, 290.

34. Russett, *Grasping the Democratic Peace*, 17; Ray, *Democracy and International Conflict*, 115.

35. Richard Welch, *Response to Imperialism*, 69, 63, 121; Tuchman, *Proud Tower*, 185–186.

36. Linderman, *The Mirror of War*; Michael H. Hunt, *Ideology and U.S. Foreign Policy*.

37. David N. Gibbs, "Secrecy and International Relations"; Miroslav Nincic, *Democracy and Foreign Policy*, 148–149.

38. Herring, *America's Longest War*; William Shawcross, *Sideshow*; John Prados, *Presidents' Secret Wars*.

39. David P. Forsythe, "Democracy, War, and Covert Action." On Iran, see also James Risen, "Secrets of History."

40. Memo available from the Gerald Ford Library and at www.seas.gwu.edu/ nsarchive/NSAEBB/NSEBB8/ch03-01.htm. See also Henry Kissinger, *Years of Upheaval*.

41. On covert action and the democratic peace, see Forsythe, "Democracy, War, and Covert Action"; Russett, *Grasping the Democratic Peace*, 120–124; Michael W. Doyle, "Kant, Liberal Legacies, and Foreign Affairs," 215n; and Patrick James and Glenn E. Mitchell II, "Targets of Covert Pressure." The norms argument makes strong claims about the power of normative constraints in the context of the democratic peace. The restraints are so powerful, some authors claim, that they account for the virtual lack of war between democracies for close to two hundred years. Our position is that if these norms are so strong, they should show up elsewhere in the democratic nonuse of force. Our discussion of the covert use of force simply calls into question the normative finding and leads us to pursue other logical lines of argument. In the end, we feel the normative claim fails, not because of any single case, but because we develop an alternative explanation (consent) that explains more than does the norms argument.

42. On participation, see Michael X. Delli Carpini and Scott Keeter, *What Americans Know about Politics and Why It Matters*. On secrecy, see Daniel Patrick Moynihan, *Secrecy*.

43. On Iran, see Michael S. Sherry, *In the Shadow of War*. On the failure of U.S. policy in Latin America, see Walter LaFeber, *Inevitable Revolutions*.

44. Moynihan, *Secrecy*.

45. On military innovations during the Cold War, see Evangelista, *Innovation and the Arms Race*. On the Manhattan Project, see Rhodes, *The Making of the Atomic Bomb*, and Rhodes, *Dark Sun*.

46. McGeorge Bundy, *New York Times*, June 10, 1985; Prados, *Presidents' Secret Wars*.

47. David H. Clark, "Agreeing to Disagree."

CHAPTER 7

1. Many of the ideas in this chapter were originally published as D. Scott Bennett and Allan C. Stam III, "The Declining Advantages of Democracy." Our thanks to Scott Bennett for permitting us to build on that earlier paper here.

2. See Bruce M. Russett, *Controlling the Sword*; Mueller, *War, Presidents and Public Opinion*; Gartner and Segura, "War, Casualties and Public Opinion"; Scott Sigmund Gartner, Gary Segura, and Michael Wilkening, "All Politics Are Local." This is related to the political choice of whom to mobilize for the war effort, a question we do not address here. In some instances politicians have based their choice of who shall serve (and therefore who shall suffer the immediate costs of war) on their desire to maintain political support for war in key constituencies. This means that the costs of war tend not to be borne equally across location,

social class, or racial group. This politicization of mobilization is not restricted to the United States or even to democracies in general. Nondemocracies are especially likely to have uneven mobilization, as the ability of nondemocratic governments to stay in power frequently rests on the ability to maintain the support of a small number of critical groups. These distorted mobilization strategies may in turn affect the choice of military strategy. See Stam, *Win, Lose or Draw*, and Reiter and Meek, "Determinants of Military Strategy."

3. Beyond this very simple notion, there are several different ways that modern scholars characterize war. Sophisticated theoretical analysis began with Clausewitz's *On War*. Recently, some have come to view war as a means by which two sides use force to reveal information about their relative capabilities, which then determines the division of goods in a bargaining game. See, for example, Wagner, "Bargaining and War." Others view war from an attrition perspective, with both sides seeking to reduce the other side's military resources, wars ending in this variant when one side realizes that it faces likely elimination if it continues to fight, and hence will sue for peace. On this type of theory, see Alastair Smith, "Fighting Battles, Winning Wars." Most of the applied research that military organizations rely on when they forecast war outcomes focuses on exchange rate variants of the attrition approach. For a highly developed exchange rate attrition model, see Joshua M. Epstein, *Strategy and Force Planning*.

4. Siverson, "Democratic and War Participation"; Bennett and Stam, "The Duration of Interstate Wars"; Reiter and Meek, "Determinants of Military Strategy." For example, in the late 1990s, democratic Russia in its war in Chechnya relied on air strikes and artillery rather than close-quarters combat in order to minimize their own casualties. *The Military Balance*, 108.

5. June 4, 1940, to House of Commons. Full text available at www.winstonchurchill.org/beaches.htm.

6. LeMay quoted in Bundy, *Danger and Survival*, 67. On Truman's decision, see also Douglas J. MacEachin, *The Final Months of the War with Japan*, 31. Some have claimed that the actual estimates of American casualties from an American raid would be more on the order of 46,000. See Gar Alperovitz, "Hiroshima." For effective critiques, see MacEachin and D. M. Giangreco, "Casualty Projections for the U.S. Invasions of Japan."

7. On the links between casualties and public support for war, see Mueller, *War, Presidents and Public Opinion*, and Gartner and Segura, "War, Casualties and Public Opinion."

8. See Levi, *Consent, Dissent, and Patriotism*, esp. 208–211.

9. The results when a target is democratic are similar to our results when the initiator is democratic. In particular, the probability of a war ending in a draw is higher when the target is democratic rather than nondemocratic and rises dramatically over time when the target is a democracy. In addition, the probability of an initiator losing to a democratic target starts higher than the probability of losing to a nondemocratic target, but by the third year, the initiator is more likely to lose to a nondemocratic target. Interestingly, initiators are always more likely to win against nondemocratic targets than democratic ones, but those probabilities remain relatively stable over time.

10. See citations in note 2, as well as Gartner and Segura, "Race, Casualties, and Opinion in the Vietnam War"; Melvin Small, *Johnson, Nixon, and the Doves*; Joseph Furia, "Mass Public Opinion and the Tet Offensive."

11. Mueller, *War, Presidents, and Public Opinion*.

12. Berman, *Planning a Tragedy*; Robert Dallek, *Flawed Giant*, 244–246.

13. Quoted in McNamara, *In Retrospect*, 204.

14. Ibid., 236.

15. Gartner, *Strategic Assessment in War*; Andrew F. Krepinevich, *The Army and Vietnam*; John E. Mueller, "The Search for the 'Breaking Point' in Vietnam"; Organski and Kugler, *The War Ledger*.

16. Quotes in Cecil B. Currey, *Victory at Any Cost*, 263, 258. A well-known anecdote conveys the same point. In April 1975 Colonel Harry Summers told a North Vietnamese counterpart, "You know you never defeated us on the battlefield," who replied, "That may be so, but it is also irrelevant." Col. Harry G. Summers, *On Strategy*, 1. During the 1993 Somalia operation, General William Garrison had similar fears about the effects of taking casualties even in the context of a tactical success, remarking: "If we go into the vicinity of the Bakara Market, there's no question we'll win the gunfight, but we might lose the war." Quoted in Bowden, *Black Hawk Down*, 21.

17. Gartner, Segura, and Wilkening, "All Politics Are Local," 678; Dallek, *Flawed Giant*, 502–513; Scott Sigmund Gartner, "Differing Evaluations of Vietnamization."

18. Michael R. Gordon and Bernard E. Trainor, *The Generals' War*, 133; *U.S. News and World Report, Triumph Without Victory*, 171; H. Norman Schwartzkopf, *It Doesn't Take a Hero*, 362.

19. Powell quoted in *U.S. News and World Report, Triumph Without Victory*, 172; Bush quote from Bush and Scowcroft, *A World Transformed*, 462.

20. On CDI casualty estimates, see Mueller, *Policy and Opinion in the Gulf War*, 124. Cohen quoted in *U.S. News and World Report, Triumph Without Victory*, 185–186. Kaiser Wilhelm quoted in Tuchman, *The Guns of August*, 119. Administration casualty estimates from Powell, *My American Journey*, 498–499.

21. The contributions and effectiveness of the aerial bombardment are somewhat controversial. See, for instance, Stephen Biddle, "The Gulf War Debate Redux."

22. Powell, *My American Journey*, 485; *U.S. News and World Report, Triumph Without Victory*, 275–276.

23. Gordon and Trainor, *Generals' War*, 476; Mueller, *Policy and Opinion in the Gulf War*, 69.

24. Saddam quotes in *Gulf War Air Power Survey* 1:92, and *U.S. News and World Report, Triumph Without Victory*, 129. On Khafji, see Gordon and Trainor, *Generals' War*, 269–271. On American public opinion, see Mueller, *Policy and Opinion in the Gulf War*, 125–129.

25. See Russett, *Controlling the Sword*.

26. Bennett and Stam, "The Duration of Interstate Wars."

27. Given that most wars are relatively short, monthly data would be preferred to annual data. Unfortunately, these data are not available for the vast majority of the cases we analyze. However, it is also important to note that decisions about

wars may also be made on a roughly annual basis, since nearly all military theaters have a seasonal weather cycle that leads to an annual lull in fighting that allows reassessment. Blainey, *The Causes of War*, 98.

28. Detailed discussions of multinomial logit appear in many texts, including William H. Greene, *Econometric Analysis*. Multinomial logit produces estimates of the probability that each outcome will occur given a set of data while making no assumptions about the order of the possible outcomes. Specifically, multinomial logit estimates the probability that the dependent variable Y will take on each of a set of discrete outcomes, given a set of independent variables X. Given $J + 1$ outcomes, J equations (sets of coefficients β) are estimated that show the effects of the independent variables on producing a particular outcome. In our analysis, we have four outcomes (continue, victory, draw, loss) and thus estimate three equations. Estimates for the three equations are made relative to a base category, the selection of which is arbitrary. Then, given $J + 1$ outcomes numbered 0, 1, 2,..., J, the predicted probability that any given case (set of data x_i) will have a particular outcome Y is as follows:

$$\text{Probability } (Y = j) = \frac{e^{x_i\beta_j}}{1 + \sum_{k=1}^{J} e^{x_i\beta_k}} \text{ for } j = 1, 2, \ldots, J.$$

$$\text{For the base case, Probability } (Y = 0) = \frac{1}{1 + \sum_{k=1}^{J} e^{x_i\beta_k}}.$$

29. We use likelihood ratio tests to assess whether a variable has any statistically significant effect on differentiating between outcomes as a whole. See Gary King, *Unifying Political Methodology*.

30. In most cases, the state that initiates war is also the aggressor or offensive state, that is, the state that desires to change the status quo. In a few wars (about 10 percent), this is not the case. For instance, in 1967 Israel initiated a defensive war in a preventive action against Arab states, and in 1939, Britain and France declared war against Germany, initiating the major theater of World War II. Because some analysts may dispute whether the technical initiator of such wars is really the most important state (another state is really the instigator of the conflict), we also analyzed the data when it was coded as "offensive state wins." The results were unremarkable.

31. See discussion in chapter 2. For a detailed discussion of war durations, see Bennett and Stam, "Duration of Wars."

32. Note that our argument does not require us to focus solely on long wars initiated by states with the highest level of democracy. Our argument is that states that are relatively more democratic will be relatively more susceptible to declining support even over short periods.

33. Our assumption that democracies prefer shorter wars implies that maneuver strategies should be particularly attractive to democracies. For a discussion and empirical test whose results support this proposition, see Reiter and Meek, "Determinants of Military Strategy."

34. William Zimmerman, "Issue Area and Foreign-Policy Process"; Stam, *Win, Lose, or Draw*.

35. Holsti, *Peace and War*.

36. Bueno de Mesquita, *The War Trap*.

37. Bennett and Stam, "Duration of Interstate Wars."

38. It is important to note that these probabilities assume that a war has reached the year in question. That is, these probabilities are not the joint probability *both* that a conflict will reach a particular point *and* that it will have a particular outcome. If we wanted to calculate the probability at the start of a war that the war would continue for *n* years and then end in a particular outcome, we could do so by multiplying the P(continue) as given in tables 7.4 for the number of years in question, and then by the probability of the particular outcome in question.

39. Without modifying any variables, the observed probability of continue was 55 percent, the probability of initiator victory 26 percent, the probability of draw 7 percent, and the probability of initiator loss 12 percent.

40. Bennett and Stam, "Duration of Interstate Wars."

CHAPTER 8

1. Carl von Clausewitz, *On War*, 69. Emphasis in original.

2. Quoted in Jack Snyder, *The Ideology of the Offensive*, 25.

3. On the political aspects of war termination, see Werner, "Negotiating the Terms of Settlement"; Goemans, *War and Punishment*.

4. This notion of ex post accountability is more consistent with the model of prospective voting laid out best in Bueno de Mesquita et al., "Institutional Explanation of the Democratic Peace."

5. Quoted in Schlesinger, *The Age of Jackson*, 13.

6. *Democracy and Its Critics*, 311.

7. Ian Shapiro, *Democratic Justice*; R. J. Rummel, *Power Kills*; Steven C. Poe and C. Neal Tate, "Repression of Human Rights to Personal Integrity in the 1980s"; Amartya Kumar Sen, *Development as Freedom*.

8. Russett, *Grasping the Democratic Peace*.

9. Reiter and Meek, "Determinants of Military Strategy."

10. Siverson, "Democratic and War Participation."

11. DeRouen, "Presidents and the Diversionary Use of Force."

12. An advanced version of the electoral punishment model is formulated in Bueno de Mesquita et al., "Institutional Explanation." See also Kurt Taylor Gaubatz, *Elections and War*.

13. For instance, lame ducks are subject to and abide by the same constraints.

14. Dahl, *Democracy and Its Critics*, 26–30.

15. Stephen E. Ambrose and Douglas G. Brinkley, *Rise to Globalism*, 225; Gary Sick, *October Surprise*; Lebow and Stein, *We All Lost the Cold War*, 95–98; Graham Allison and Philip Zelikow, *Essence of Decision*, 330–347.

16. See, for example, Joanne Gowa, "Politics at the Water's Edge"; Brett Ashley Leeds and David R. Davis, "Domestic Political Vulnerability and International Disputes"; Karl R. DeRouen Jr., "The Indirect Link"; James Meernik and Peter

Waterman, "The Myth of the Diversionary Use of Force by American Presidents"; Patrick James and Athanasios Hristoulas, "Domestic Politics and Foreign Policy."

17. Mueller, *Policy and Opinion in the Gulf War*, 116.

18. Adam Przeworski et al., *Democracy and Development*; John O'Loughlin et al., "The Diffusion of Democracy, 1946–1994."

19. Lawrence Korb, "The Use of Force," 24.

20. Holger Jensen, "Vote Cliffhanger Highlights Foreign Policy Differences."; Korb, "The Use of Force," esp. 24. Powell and George W. Bush have expressed support for some humanitarian interventions, including the 1989 Panama intervention and the 1994 Haiti intervention.

21. On the point that new democracies are less war-prone, see Michael D. Ward and Kristian S. Gleditsch, "Democratizing for Peace"; John R. Oneal and Bruce M. Russett, "The Classical Liberals Were Right."

22. On the requirements of democracy, see Przeworski et al., *Democracy and Development*, and Samuel P. Huntington, *The Third Wave*.

23. Steven Kull and I. M. Destler, *Misreading the Public*. For example, 68 percent of those surveyed in April 1995 agreed with the following statement: "When innocent civilians are suffering or are being killed, and a UN peacekeeping operation is being organized to try to address the problem, in most cases the U.S. should be willing to contribute some troops, whether or not it serves the national interest" (104).

24. *The Federalist Papers*, no. 4, 46.

BIBLIOGRAPHY

Achen, Christopher H. *The Statistical Analysis of Quasi-Experiments*. Berkeley: University of California Press, 1986.

Adler, Emanuel, and Michael Barnett, eds. *Security Communities*. New York: Cambridge University Press, 1998.

Agawa, Hiroyuki. *The Reluctant Admiral: Yamamoto and the Imperial Navy*. Translated by John Bester. New York: Harper and Row, 1979.

Agoncillo, Teodoro. *Malolos: The Crisis of the Republic*. Quezon City, Philippines: University of the Philippines, 1960.

Agoncillo, Teodoro, and Oscar Alfonso. *History of the Filipino People*. Quezon City, Philippines: Malaya Books, 1967.

Ahmed, Samina. "Pakistan's Nuclear Weapons Program: Turning Points and Nuclear Choices." *International Security* 23 (Spring 1999): 178–204.

Albertini, Luigi. *The Origins of the War in 1914*. Volume 3. Translated and edited by Isabella M. Massey. London: Oxford University Press, 1957.

Albrecht-Carrie, Rene. *A Diplomatic History of Europe since the Congress of Vienna*. New York: Harper & Row, 1958.

Alexander, Don W. "Repercussions of the Breda Variant." *French Historical Studies* 8 (Spring 1974): 458–488.

Allison, Graham, and Philip Zelikow. *Essence of Decision: Explaining the Cuban Missile Crisis*. Second edition. New York: Longman, 1999.

Alperovitz, Gar. "Hiroshima: Historians Reassess." *Foreign Policy*, no. 99 (Summer 1995): 15–34.

Ambrose, Stephen E. *Citizen Soldiers: The U.S. Army from the Normandy Beaches to the Bulge to the Surrender of Germany, June 7, 1944–May 7, 1945*. New York: Simon and Schuster, 1997.

——. *D-Day, June 6, 1944: The Climactic Battle of World War II*. New York: Simon and Schuster, 1994.

Ambrose, Stephen E., and Douglas G. Brinkley. *Rise to Globalism: American Foreign Policy since 1938*. Eighth revised edition. New York: Penguin, 1997.

Andres, Richard. "The Relative Selection Effect and Winning Disputes." Presented at the Annual Meeting of the American Political Science Association, August 31–September 3, 2000, Washington, DC.

Andreski, Stanislav. "On the Peaceful Disposition of Military Dictatorships." *Journal of Strategic Studies* 3 (December 1980): 3–10.

Arquilla, John. *Dubious Battles: Aggression, Defeat and the International System*. Washington, DC: Taylor and Francis, 1992.

Auerswald, David P. "Inward Bound: Domestic Institutions and Military Conflicts." *International Organization* 53 (Summer 1999): 469–504.

Avant, Deborah D. "The Institutional Sources of Military Doctrine: Hegemons in Peripheral Wars." *International Studies Quarterly* 37 (December 1993): 409–430.

Axelrod, Robert. *The Evolution of Cooperation*. New York: Basic Books, 1984.

Ball, Deborah Yarsike. "Ethnic Conflict, Unit Performance, and the Soviet Armed Forces." *Armed Forces and Society* 20 (Winter 1994): 239–258.

Banks, Arthur S. "Cross-National Time Series, 1815–1997" [Computer File]. Binghamton: Computer Solutions Unlimited, 1998.

Barber, John and Mark Harrison. *The Soviet Home Front, 1941–1945: A Social and Economic History of the USSR in World War II.* London: Longman, 1991.

Barnhart, Michael A. *Japan Prepares for Total War: The Search for Economic Security, 1919–1941.* Ithaca: Cornell University Press, 1987.

———. "Japanese Intelligence before the Second World War: 'Best Case' Analysis." In *Knowing One's Enemies: Intelligence Assessment before the Two World Wars.* Edited by Ernest R. May, 424–455. Princeton: Princeton University Press, 1984.

Barro, Robert J. *Determinants of Economic Growth: A Cross-Country Empirical Study.* Cambridge: MIT Press, 1997.

Barsh, Russel Lawrence, and James Youngblood Henderson. *The Road: Indian Tribes and Political Liberty.* Berkeley: University of California Press, 1980.

Bartlett's Familiar Quotations. Sixteenth edition. New York: Little, Brown, 1992.

Bartov, Omer. *The Eastern Front, 1941–45, German Troops and the Barbarization of Warfare.* Houndsmill, UK: Macmillan, 1985.

———. *Hitler's Army: Soldiers, Nazis, and War in the Third Reich.* New York: Oxford University Press, 1991.

Barzilai, Gad. "War, Democracy, and Internal Conflict: Israel in a Comparative Perspective." *Comparative Politics* 31 (April 1999): 317–336.

Bates, Darrell. *The Fashoda Incident of 1898: Encounter on the Nile.* London: Oxford University Press, 1984.

Bauer, Thomas, and Ralph Rotte. "Prospect Theory Goes to War: Loss-Aversion and the Duration of Military Combat." Ms. Department of Economics, Rutgers University, 1997.

Baum, Matthew A., and David A. Lake. "The *Political* Economy of Growth: Democracy and Human Capital." Presented at the Annual Meeting of the American Political Science Association, Washington, DC, September 2000.

Beaver, Daniel R. "The Problem of American Military Supply, 1890–1920." In *War, Business, and American Society: Historical Perspectives on the Military-Industrial Complex.* Edited by Benjamin Franklin Cooling, 73–92. Port Washington, NY: Kennikat Press, 1977.

Beck, Nathaniel. "Reporting Heteroskedasticity Consistent Standard Errors." *The Political Methodologist* 7 (Spring 1996): 4–6.

Beck, Nathaniel, and Jonathan N. Katz. "What to Do (and Not to Do) with Time-Series Cross-Section Data." *American Political Science Review* 89 (September 1995): 634–647.

Beevor, Antony. *Stalingrad*, New York: Viking, 1998.

Benedict, Ruth. *The Chrysanthemum and the Sword: Patterns of Japanese Culture.* Boston: Houghton Mifflin, 1946.

Ben-Gurion, David. 1970. *Recollections.* Edited by Thomas R. Bransten. London: Macdonald Unit Seventy–Five, 1970.

Bennett, Andrew, Joseph Lepgold, and Danny Unger. "Burden-Sharing in the Persian Gulf War." *International Organization* 48 (Winter 1994): 39–75.

Bennett, D. Scott. "Testing Alternative Models of Alliance Duration, 1816–1984." *American Journal of Political Science* 41 (July 1997): 846–878.

Bennett, D. Scott, and Allan C. Stam III. "The Declining Advantages of Democracy: A Combined Model of War Outcomes and Duration." *Journal of Conflict Resolution* 42 (June 1998): 344–366.

———. "The Duration of Interstate Wars, 1816–1985." *American Political Science Review* 90 (June 1996): 239–257.

———. "Research Design and Estimator Choices in the Analysis of Interstate Dyad: When Decisions Matter." *Journal of Conflict Resolution* 44 (October 2000): 653–685.

Berman, Larry. *Planning a Tragedy: The Americanization of the War in Vietnam.* New York: W. W. Norton, 1982.

Bethell, Leslie. "From the Second World War to the Cold War: 1944–1954." In *Exporting Democracy: The United States and Latin America.* Edited by Abraham F. Lowenthal, 41–70. Baltimore: Johns Hopkin University Press, 1991.

Betts, Richard K. *Soldiers, Statesmen, and Cold War Crises.* Cambridge: Harvard University Press, 1997.

Beyerchen, Alan. "Clausewitz, Nonlinearity, and the Unpredictability of War." *International Security* 17 (Winter 1992/93): 59–90.

Bickerton, Ian J., and Carla L. Klausner. *A Concise History of the Arab-Israeli Conflict.* Englewood Cliffs, NJ: Prentice Hall, 1991.

Biddle, Stephen. "The Gulf War Debate *Redux*: Why Skill *and* Technology Are the Right Answer." *International Security* 22 (Fall 1998): 163–174.

———. "Victory Misunderstood." *International Security* 21 (Fall 1996): 139–180.

Biddle, Stephen, and Robert Zirkle. "Technology, Civil-Military Relations, and Warfare in the Developing World." *Journal of Strategic Studies* 19 (June 1996): 171–212.

Blainey, Geoffrey. *The Causes of War.* Third edition. Basingstoke: Macmillan, 1988.

Blechman, Barry M., and Tamara Cofman Wittes. "Defining Moment: The Threat and Use of Force in American Foreign Policy." *Political Science Quarterly* 114 (Spring 1999): 1–30.

Bliss, Harry, and Bruce Russett. "Democratic Trading Partners: The Liberal Connection, 1962–1989." *Journal of Politics* 60 (November 1998): 1126–1147.

Bloch, Marc. *Strange Defeat: A Statement of Evidence Written in 1940.* Translated by Gerard Hopkins. New York: Oxford University Press, 1949.

Bolks, Sean, and Richard J. Stoll. "The Arms Acquisition Process: The Effect of Internal and External Constraints on Arms Race Dynamics. " *Journal of Conflict Resolution* 44 (October 2000): 580–603.

Bollen, Kenneth A. "Political Democracy and the Timing of Development." *American Sociological Review* 44 (August 1979): 572–587.

Bond, Brian. *France and Belgium 1939–1940.* London: Davis-Poynter, 1975.

Bowden, Mark. *Black Hawk Down: A Story of Modern War.* New York: Penguin, 1999.

Brawley, Mark R. *Liberal Leadership: Great Powers and Their Challengers in Peace and War.* Ithaca: Cornell University Press, 1993.

Brennan, Geoffrey, and Gordon Tullock. "An Economic Theory of Military Tactics: Methodological Individualism at War." *Journal of Economic Behavior and Organization* 3 (1982): 225–242.

Brody, J. Kenneth. *The Avoidable War: Lord Cecil and the Policy of Principle 1932–1935.* New Brunswick, NJ: Transaction Publishers, 1999.

Brooks, Risa. "Institutions at the Domestic/International Nexus: The Political-Military Origins of Strategic Integration, Military Effectiveness and War." Ph.D. diss., University of California, San Diego, 2000.

———. *Political-Military Relations and the Stability of Arab Regimes.* Oxford: Oxford University Press, 1998.

Brown, Dee. *Bury My Heart at Wounded Knee: An Indian History of the American West.* New York: Bantam Books, 1970.

Brown, John Sloan. "Colonel Trevor N. Dupuy and the Mythos of Wehrmacht Superiority: A Reconsideration." *Military Affairs* 50 (January 1986): 16–20.

Brzezinski, Zbigniew. "War and Foreign Policy: American-Style." *Journal of Democracy* 11 (January 2000): 172–178.

Bueno de Mesquita, Bruce. "Big Wars, Little Wars: Avoiding Selection Bias." *International Interactions* 16, no. 3 (1990): 159–160.

———. *The War Trap.* New Haven: Yale University Press, 1981.

Bueno de Mesquita, Bruce, and David Lalman. *War and Reason: Domestic and International Imperatives.* New Haven: Yale University Press, 1992.

Bueno de Mesquita, Bruce, and Randolph M. Siverson. "War and the Survival of Political Leaders: A Comparative Study of Regime Types and Political Accountability." *American Political Science Review* 89 (December 1995): 841–855.

Bueno de Mesquita, Bruce, James D. Morrow, Randolph Siverson, and Alastair Smith. "An Institutional Explanation of the Democratic Peace." *American Political Science Review* 93 (December 1999): 791–807.

Bundy, McGeorge. *Danger and Survival: Choices about the Bomb in the First Fifty Years.* New York: Vintage, 1988.

———. *New York Times*, June 10, 1985.

Burchardt, Lothar. "The Impact of the War Economy on the Civilian Population of Germany during the First and Second World Wars." In *The German Military in the Age of Total War.* Edited by Wilhelm Deist, 40–70. Warwickshire, UK: Berg, 1985.

Burk, James. "Public Support for Peacekeeping in Lebanon and Somalia: Assessing the Casualties Hypothesis." *Political Science Quarterly* 114 (Spring 1999): 53–78.

Burkhart, Ross E., and Michael S. Lewis-Beck. "Comparative Democracy: The Economic Development Thesis." *American Political Science Review* 88 (December 1994): 903–910.

Bush, George, and Brent Scowcroft. *A World Transformed.* New York: Alfred A. Knopf, 1998.

Bush, Vannevar. *Modern Arms and Free Men: A Discussion of the Role of Science in Preserving Democracy.* New York: Simon and Schuster, 1949.

Calvocoressi, Peter, Guy Wint, and John Pritchard. *Total War: The Causes and Courses of the Second World War.* Volume 1. Revised second edition. New York: Pantheon, 1989.

Carlson, Lisa J. "A Theory of Escalation and International Conflict." *Journal of Conflict Resolution* 39 (September 1995): 511–534.

Caron, François. *An Economic History of Modern France*. Translated by Barbara Bray. New York: Columbia University Press, 1979.

Catton, Bruce. *Glory Road*. New York: Anchor Books, 1952.

Checkland, Olive. *Humanitarianism and the Emperor's Japan, 1877–1977*. New York: St. Martin's Press, 1994.

Cheibub, José Antonio. "Political Regimes and the Extractive Capacity of Governments: Taxation in Democracies and Dictatorships." *World Politics* 50 (April 1998): 349–376.

Choi, Ajin. "Democracy, International Partnerships, and State War Performance, 1816–1992." Ph.D. diss., Duke University, forthcoming.

Chopra, Pran. *India's Second Liberation*. Cambridge: MIT Press, 1974.

Churchill, Winston S. *The Second World War, Volume 1: The Gathering Storm*. Boston: Houghton Mifflin, 1948.

———. *The Second World War, Volume III: The Grand Alliance*. Boston: Houghton Mifflin, 1950.

———. *The World Crisis*. Volume 1. New York: Charles Scribner's Sons, 1923.

Clark, David H. "Agreeing to Disagree: Domestic Institutional Congruence and U.S. Dispute Behavior." *Political Research Quarterly* 53 (June 2000): 375–400.

Clark, David H., and William Reed. "A Unified Model of War Onset and Outcome." Ms., Binghamton, NY, 2000.

Clausewitz, Carl Von. *On War*. Edited by Michael Howard and Peter Paret. Princeton: Princeton University Press, 1976.

Clem, Harold J. *Mobilization Preparedness*. Washington, DC: National Defense University, 1983.

Clodfelter, Micheal. *Warfare and Armed Conflicts: A Statistical Reference to Casualty and Other Figures, 1618–1991*. 2 vols. Jefferson, NC: McFarland, 1992.

Clogg, Richard. *A Short History of Modern Greece*. Cambridge: Cambridge University Press, 1986.

Cohen, Eliot A., and John Gooch. *Military Misfortunes: The Anatomy of Failure in War*. New York: The Free Press, 1990.

Cohen, Jerome B. *Japan's Economy in War and Reconstruction*. Minneapolis: University of Minnesota Press, 1949.

Crawford, Neta C. "A Security Regime among Democracies: Cooperation among Iroquois Nations." *International Organization* 48 (Summer 1994): 345–385.

Cumings, Bruce. *Korea's Place in the Sun: A Modern History*. New York: Norton, 1997.

Currey, Cecil B. *Victory at Any Cost: The Genius of Viet Nam's Gen. Vo Nguyen Giap*. Washington: Brassey's, 1997.

Dahl, Robert A. *A Preface to Democratic Theory*. Chicago: University of Chicago Press, 1956.

———. *Democracy and Its Critics*. New Haven: Yale University Press, 1989.

Dallek, Robert. *Flawed Giant: Lyndon Johnson and His Times, 1961–1973*. New York: Oxford University Press, 1998.

———. *Franklin D. Roosevelt and American Foreign Policy, 1932–1945*. Oxford: Oxford University Press, 1979.

Dassel, Kurt, and Eric Reinhardt. "Domestic Strife and the Initiation of Violence at Home and Abroad." *American Journal of Political Science* 43 (January 1999): 56–85.

Davidson, Joel R. *The Unsinkable Fleet: The Politics of U.S. Navy Expansion in World War II.* Annapolis: Naval Institute Press, 1996.

Davis, Gerald H. "Prisoners of War in Twentieth-Century War Economies." *Journal of Contemporary History* 12 (October 1977): 623–634.

Dayan, Moshe. *Moshe Dayan: Story of My Life.* New York: William Morrow, 1976.

Deighton, Len. *Blitzkrieg: From the Rise of Hitler to the Fall of Dunkirk.* New York: Alfred A. Knopf, 1980.

Deist, Wilhelm. *The* Wehrmacht *and German Rearmament.* Toronto: University of Toronto Press, 1981.

Delli Carpini, Michael X., and Scott Keeter. *What Americans Know about Politics and Why It Matters.* New Haven: Yale University Press, 1996.

DeRouen, Karl R., Jr. "The Indirect Link: Politics, Economics, and the Use of Force." *Journal of Conflict Resolution* 39 (December 1995): 671–695.

———. "Presidents and the Diversionary Use of Force: A Research Note." *International Studies Quarterly* 44 (June 2000): 317–328.

Deutsch, Karl. *Political Community and the North Atlantic Area: International Organization in the Light of Historical Experience.* Princeton: Princeton University Press, 1957.

Diamond, Larry. "Economic Development and Democracy Reconsidered." *American Behavioral Scientist* 35 (March/June 1992): 450–499.

Diehl, Paul F. "Arms Races and Escalation: A Closer Look." *Journal of Peace Research* 20, no. 3 (1983): 205–212.

DiNardo, R. L. *Germany's Panzer Arm.* Westport, CT: Greenwood Press, 1997.

Dixon, William J. "Democracy and the Management of International Conflict." *Journal of Conflict Resolution* 37 (March 1993): 42–68.

———. "Democracy and the Peaceful Settlement of International Conflict." *American Political Science Review* 88 (March 1994): 14–32.

———. "Dyads, Disputes, and the Democratic Peace." In *The Political Economy of War and Peace.* Edited by Murray Wolfson, 103–126. Boston: Kluwer, 1998.

Doenitz, Karl. *Memoirs: Ten Years and Twenty Days.* Translated by R. H. Stevens. Cleveland: World Publishing Company, 1959.

Dower, John W. *War Without Mercy.* New York: Pantheon, 1986.

Downs, George W., and David M. Rocke. "Conflict, Agency, and Gambling for Resurrection: The Principal-Agent Problem Goes to War." *American Journal of Political Science* 38 (May 1994): 362–380.

Doyle, Michael W. "Kant, Liberal Legacies, and Foreign Affairs." *Philosophy and Public Affairs* 12 (Summer 1983): 205–235.

———. "Kant, Liberal Legacies, and Foreign Affairs, Part 2." *Philosophy and Public Affairs* 12 (Fall 1983): 323–353.

———. "Liberalism and World Politics." *American Political Science Review* 80 (December 1986): 1151–1169.

Dunnigan, James F. and Austin Bay. *From Shield to Storm: High-Tech Weapons, Military Strategy, and Coalition Warfare in the Persian Gulf.* New York: William Morrow, 1992.

Dupuy, R. Ernest, and Trevor N. Dupuy. *The Encyclopedia of Military History from 3500 BC to the Present.* Second revised edition. New York: Harper and Row, 1986.

Dupuy, Trevor Nevitt. *Analysis of Factors That Have Influenced Outcomes of Battles and Wars: A Database of Battles and Engagements, Final Report.* 6 vols. Dunn Loring, VA: Historical Evaluation and Research Organization, 1983.

———. *Numbers, Predictions and War: Using History to Evaluate Combat Factors and Predict the Outcome of Battles.* Indianapolis: Bobbs-Merrill, 1979.

———. *Understanding War: History and Theory of Combat.* New York: Paragon House, 1987.

Easterly, William. "Life during Growth." *Journal of Economic Growth* 4 (September 1999): 239–275.

Eban, Abba. *Personal Witness: Israel Through My Eyes.* New York: G. P. Putnam's Sons, 1992.

Economic History of the USSR in World War II. London: Longman, 1991.

Edmonds, James E. *A Short History of World War I.* London: Oxford University Press, 1951.

Epstein, David F. "The Economic Cost of Soviet Security and Empire." In *The Impoverished Superpower: Perestroika and the Soviet Military Burden.* Edited by Henry S. Rowen and Charles Wolf, Jr., 127–154. San Francisco: Institute for Comparative Studies, 1990.

Epstein, Joshua M. *Strategy and Force Planning: The Case of the Persian Gulf.* Washington, DC: Brookings Institution, 1987.

Esdaile, Charles J. *The Wars of Napoleon.* London: Longman, 1995.

Evangelista, Matthew. *Innovation and the Arms Race: How the United States and the Soviet Union Develop New Military Technologies.* Ithaca: Cornell University Press, 1988.

Farber, Henry S., and Joanne Gowa. "Common Interests or Common Polities? Reinterpreting the Democratic Peace." *Journal of Politics* 59 (May 1997): 393–417.

Faruqui, Ahmad. "The Enigma of Military Rule in Pakistan." Ms. Palo Alto, CA, 2000.

Fearon, James D. "Domestic Political Audiences and the Escalation of International Disputes." *American Political Science Review* 88 (September 1994): 577–592.

———. "Rationalist Explanations for War." *International Organization* 49 (Summer 1995): 379–414.

———. "Signaling versus the Balance of Power and Interests: An Empirical Test of a Crisis Bargaining Model." *Journal of Conflict Resolution* 38 (June 1994): 236–269.

The Federalist Papers. Edited by Garry Wills. New York: Bantam, 1982.

Feng, Yi. "Democracy, Political Stability and Economic Growth." *British Journal of Political Science* 27 (July 1997): 391–418.

Feng, Yi, and Paul Zak. "The Determinants of Democratic Transitions." *Journal of Conflict Resolution* 43 (April 1999): 162–177.

Ferguson, Niall. *The Pity of War.* New York: Basic Books, 1999.

Finnemore, Martha. *National Interests in International Society.* Ithaca: Cornell University Press, 1996.

Fischer, Fritz. *Germany's Aims in the First World War*. New York: W. W. Norton, 1967.

Fitzpatrick, Gary L., and Marilyn J. Modlin. *Direct-Line Distances*. Metuchen, NJ: Scarecrow Press, 1986.

Forster, Jürgen. "The German Army and the Ideological War against the Soviet Union." In *The Policies of Genocide: Jews and Soviet Prisoners of War in Nazi Germany*. Edited by Gerhard Hirschfeld, 15–29. London: German Historical Institute, 1986.

Forsythe, David P. "Democracy, War, and Covert Action." *Journal of Peace Research* 29, no. 4 (1992): 385–395.

Frank, Richard B. *Downfall: The End of the Imperial Japanese Empire*. New York: Random House, 1999.

Friedberg, Aaron. *In the Shadow of the Garrison State: America's Anti-Statism and Its Cold War Grand Strategy*. Princeton: Princeton University Press, 2000.

Friedman, David. *The Misunderstood Miracle: Industrial Development and Political Change in Japan*. Ithaca: Cornell University Press, 1988.

Fritz, Stephen G. "'We are Trying . . . To Change the Face of the World'—Ideology and Motivation in the Wehrmacht on the Eastern Front: The View from Below." *Journal of Military History* 60 (October 1996): 683–710.

Fukuyama, Francis. *The End of History and the Last Man*. New York: Avon, 1992.

Furia, Joseph. "Mass Public Opinion and the Tet Offensive." Ms., Yale University, 2000.

Gaddis, John Lewis. *We Now Know: Rethinking Cold War History*. Oxford: Clarendon Press, 1997.

Ganguly, Sumit. *The Origins of War in South Asia: Indo-Pakistani Conflicts since 1947*. Boulder: Westview Press, 1986.

Gartner, Scott Sigmund. "Differing Evaluations of Vietnamization." *Journal of Interdisciplinary History* 29 (Autumn 1998): 243–262.

———. "Opening Up the Black Box of War." *Journal of Conflict Resolution* 42 (June 1998): 252–258.

———. *Strategic Assessment in War*. New Haven: Yale University Press, 1997.

Gartner, Scott Sigmund, and Gary Segura. "Race, Casualties, and Opinion in the Vietnam War." *Journal of Politics* 62 (February 2000): 115–146.

———. "War, Casualties, and Public Opinion." *Journal of Conflict Resolution* 42 (June 1998): 278–300.

Gartner, Scott Sigmund, Gary Segura, and Michael Wilkening. "All Politics Are Local: Local Losses and Individual Attitudes toward the Vietnam War." *Journal of Conflict Resolution* 41 (October 1997): 669–694.

Gartner, Scott Sigmund, and Randolph M. Siverson. "War Expansion and War Outcome." *Journal of Conflict Resolution* 40 (March 1996): 4–15.

Gartzke, Eric. "War Is in the Error Term." *International Organization* 53 (Summer 1999): 567–587.

Gasiorowski, Mark J. "Democracy and Macroeconomic Performance in Underdeveloped Countries: An Empirical Analysis." *Comparative Political Studies* 33 (April 2000): 319–349.

Gaubatz, Kurt Taylor. "Democratic States and Commitment in International Relations." *International Organization* 50 (Winter 1996): 109–139.

————. *Elections and War: The Electoral Incentive in the Democratic Politics of War and Peace*. Stanford: Stanford University Press, 1999.

Gerschenkron, Alexander. *Economic Backwardness in Historical Perspective: A Book of Essays*. Cambridge, MA: Belknap Press, 1962.

Giangreco, D. M. "Casualty Projections for the U.S. Invasions of Japan, 1945–1946: Planning and Policy Implications." *Journal of Military History* 61 (July 1997): 521–582.

Gibbs, David N. 1995. "Secrecy and International Relations." *Journal of Peace Research* 32 (May 1995): 213–228.

Gleditsch, Nils Petter, and Håvard Hegre. "Peace and Democracy: Three Levels of Analysis." *Journal of Conflict Resolution* 41 (April 1997): 283–310.

Goda, Norman J. W. *Tomorrow the World: Hitler, Northwest Africa, and the Path toward America*. College Station: Texas A&M Press, 1998.

Goemans, H. E. *War and Punishment: The Causes of War Termination and the First World War*. Princeton: Princeton University Press, 2000.

Goldgeier, James M. *Not Whether but When: The U.S. Decision to Enlarge NATO*. Washington: Brookings, 1999.

Goldhagen, Daniel Jonah. *Hitler's Willing Executioners: Ordinary Germans and the Holocaust*. New York: Alfred A. Knopf, 1996.

Gordon, Michael R. and Bernard E. Trainor. *The Generals' War: The Inside Story of the Conflict in the Gulf*. Boston: Little, Brown, 1995.

Gould, Lewis L. *The Spanish-American War and President McKinley*. Lawrence: University of Kansas Press, 1982.

Gowa, Joanne. *Ballots and Bullets: The Elusive Democratic Peace*. Princeton: Princeton University Press, 1999.

————. "Politics at the Water's Edge: Parties, Voters, and the Use of Force Abroad." *International Organization* 52 (Spring 1998): 307–324.

Gray, A.M. *Warfighting*. New York: Doubleday, 1994.

Gray, Colin S., and Keith Payne. "Victory Is Possible." *Foreign Policy*, no. 39 (Summer 1980): 56–91.

Greene, William H. *Econometric Analysis*. Third edition. New York: Macmillan, 1993.

Grey, Edward. *Twenty-Five Years 1892–1916*. Volume 2. New York: Frederick A. Stokes, 1925.

Griffith, Paddy. *Battle Tactics of the Civil War*. New Haven: Yale University Press, 1987.

Grinde, Donald A. Jr., and Bruce E. Johansen. *Exemplar of Liberty: Native America and the Evolution of Democracy*. Los Angeles: American Indian Studies Center, 1991.

Grose, Peter. *Gentleman Spy: The Life of Allen Dulles*. Boston: Houghton Mifflin, 1994.

Grossman, Dave. *On Killing: The Psychological Cost of Learning to Kill in War and Society*. Boston: Little, Brown, 1995.

Gulf War Air Power Survey. Volume 1. Washington, DC: United States Government Printing Office, 1993.

Hammerman, Gay, and Richard G. Sheridan. *The 88th Infantry Division in World War II: Factors Responsible for its Excellence*. Dunn Loring, VA: Historical Evaluation and Research Organization, 1982.

Hamza, Khidhir, with Jeff Stein. 2000. *Saddam's Bombmaker: The Terrifying Story of the Iraqi Nuclear and Biological Weapons Agenda.* New York: Scribner, 2000.

Hanson, Victor Davis. *The Soul of Battle: From Ancient Times to the Present Day, How Three Great Liberators Vanquished Tyranny.* New York: Free Press, 1999.

Hanushek, Eric A., and John E. Jackson. *Statistical Methods for Social Scientists.* San Diego: Academic Press, 1977

Harris, George S. *Troubled Alliance: Turkish-American Problems in Historical Perspective, 1945–1971.* Washington, DC: American Enterprise Institute, 1972.

Harrison, Mark, ed. *The Economics of World War II: Six Great Powers in International Comparison.* Cambridge: Cambridge University Press, 1999.

———. "Resource Mobilization for World War II: The U.S.A., U.K., U.S.S.R., and Germany, 1938–1945." *Economic History Review* 61 (May 1988): 171–192.

Hastings, Max. *The Korean War.* New York: Touchstone, 1987.

Hayden, Joseph. *The Philippines: A Study in National Development.* New York: Macmillan, 1942.

Helliwell, John F. "Empirical Linkages Between Democracy and Economic Growth." *British Journal of Political Science* 24 (April 1994): 225–248.

Henderson, Errol Anthony. "The Democratic Peace Through the Lens of Culture, 1820–1989." *International Studies Quarterly* 42 (September 1998): 461–484.

Henderson, Wm. Darryl. *Cohesion: The Human Element in Combat.* Washington, DC: National Defense University Press, 1985.

Hermann, Margaret G., and Charles W. Kegley, Jr. "Rethinking Democracy and International Peace: Perspectives from Political Psychology." *International Studies Quarterly* 39 (December 1995): 511–533.

Herodotus. *The History.* Translated by David Grene. Chicago: University of Chicago Press, 1987.

Herring, George C. *America's Longest War: The United States and Vietnam, 1950–1975.* Third edition. New York: McGraw-Hill, 1996.

Herrmann, David G. *The Arming of Europe and the Making of the First World War.* Princeton: Princeton University Press, 1996.

Higgs, Robert. "Wartime Prosperity? A Reassessment of the U.S. Economy in the 1940s." *Journal of Economic History* 52 (March 1992): 41–60.

Hill, Leonidas E., ed. 1974. *Die Weizsacker-Papiere 1933–1950.* Frankfurt: Propylaen Verlag.

Holloway, David. "Military Power and Political Purpose in Soviet Policy." *Daedalus* 109 (Fall 1980): 13–30.

———. *Stalin and the Bomb: The Soviet Union and Atomic Energy, 1939–1956.* New Haven: Yale University Press, 1994.

Holmes, Stephen. *Passions and Constrain: On the Theory of Liberal Democracy.* Chicago: University of Chicago Press, 1985.

Holsti, Kalevi J. *Peace and War: Armed Conflicts and International Order 1648–1989.* Cambridge: Cambridge University Press, 1991.

Hopf, Ted. *Peripheral Visions: Deterrence Theory and America Foreign Policy in the Third World, 1965–1990.* Ann Arbor: University of Michigan Press, 1994.

Horne, Alistair. *To Lose a Battle: France 1940.* London: Macmillan, 1969.

Horowitz, Michael, and Dan Reiter. "When Does Aerial Bombing Work? Quantitative Empirical Tests, 1917–1999." *Journal of Conflict Resolution* 45 (April 2001): 147–173.

Horsman, Reginald. "Scientific Racism and the American Indian in the Mid-Nineteenth Century." *American Quarterly* 27 (May 1975): 152–168.

Howard, Michael. *Clausewitz*. Oxford: Oxford University Press, 1983.

———. *The Continental Commitment: The Dilemma of British Defence Policy in the Era of the Two World Wars*. London: Ashfield Press, 1972.

———. *War in European History*. London: Oxford University Press, 1976.

Hunt, Michael H. *Ideology and U.S. Foreign Policy*. New Haven: Yale University Press, 1987.

Huntington, Samuel P. *The Clash of Civilizations and the Remaking of World Order*. New York: Touchstone, 1996.

———. *Political Order in Changing Societies*. New Haven: Yale University Press, 1968.

———. *The Third Wave: Democratization in the Late Twentieth Century*. Norman: University of Oklahoma Press, 1991.

Huston, James A. *The Sinews of War: Army Logistics 1775–1953*. Washington, DC: United States Army, 1966.

Huth, Paul K. *Extended Deterrence and the Prevention of War*. New Haven: Yale University Press, 1988.

———. "Major Power Intervention in International Crises, 1918–1988." *Journal of Conflict Resolution* 42 (December 1998): 744–770.

Huth, Paul K., D. Scott Bennett, and Christopher Gelpi. "System Uncertainty, Risk Propensity, and International Conflict among the Great Powers." *Journal of Conflict Resolution* 36 (September 1992): 478–517.

Ienaga, Saburo. *The Pacific War, 1931 1945: A Critical Perspective on Japan's Role in World War II*. New York: Pantheon Books, 1978.

Jackman, Robert W. *Power Without Force: The Political Capacity of Nation-States*. Ann Arbor: University of Michigan Press, 1993.

———. *South Asian Crisis*. London: Chatto & Windus, 1975.

Jaggers, Keith, and Ted Robert Gurr. "Tracking Democracy's Third Wave with the Polity III Data." *Journal of Peace Research* 32 (November 1995): 469–482.

Jakobson, Max. *The Diplomacy of the Winter War: An Account of the Russo-Finnish War, 1939–1940*. Cambridge: Harvard University Press, 1961.

James, Patrick, and Athanasios Hristoulas. "Domestic Politics and Foreign Policy: Evaluating a Model of Crisis Activity for the United States." *Journal of Politics* 56 (May 1994): 327–348.

James, Patrick, and Glenn E. Mitchell II. "Targets of Covert Pressure: The Hidden Victims of the Democratic Peace." *International Interactions* 21, no. 1 (1995): 85–107.

Jensen, Holger. "Vote Cliffhanger Highlights Foreign Policy Differences." *Denver Rocky Mountain News*, November 9, 2000, 38A.

Jentleson, Bruce W. "The Pretty Prudent Public: Post Post-Vietnam American Opinion on the Use of Military Force." *International Studies Quarterly* 36 (March 1992): 49–74.

Jentleson, Bruce W., and Rebecca L. Britton. "Still Pretty Prudent: Post–Cold War American Public Opinion on the Use of Military Force." *Journal of Conflict Resolution* 42 (August 1998): 395–417.

Jervis, Robert. *Perception and Misperception in International Politics*. Princeton: Princeton University Press, 1976.

Johnson, Chalmers. *MITI and the Japanese Miracle: The Growth of Industrial Policy*. Stanford: Stanford University Press, 1982.

Johnson, Lyndon Baines. *The Vantage Point: Perspectives of the Presidency, 1963–1969*. New York: Holt, Rinehart, and Winston, 1971.

Jones, Daniel M., Stuart A. Bremer, and J. David Singer. 1996. "Militarized Interstate Disputes, 1816–1992: Rationale, Coding Rules, and Empirical Patterns." *Conflict Management and Peace Science* 15 (Fall 1996): 163–213.

Kagan, Donald. *The Fall of the Athenian Empire*. Ithaca: Cornell University Press, 1987.

———. *On the Origins of War and the Preservation of Peace*. New York: Anchor Books, 1995.

Kahl, Colin H. "Constructing a Separate Peace: Constructivism, Collective Liberal Identity, and Democratic Peace." *Security Studies* 8 (Winter 1998/1999–Spring 1999): 94–144.

Kant, Immanuel. *Kant's Political Writings*. Edited by Hans Reiss. Second edition. Cambridge: Cambridge University Press, 1991.

Katzenstein, Peter J. *Cultural Norms and National Security: Police and Military in Postwar Japan*. Ithaca: Cornell University Press, 1996.

Keefer, Philip, and Stephen Knack. "Why Don't Poor Countries Catch Up? A Cross-National Test of an Institutional Explanation." *Economic Inquiry* 35 (July 1997): 590–602.

Keegan, John. *The First World War*. New York: Alfred A. Knopf, 1998.

Kegley, Charles W., and Margaret G. Hermann. "Putting Military Intervention into the Democratic Peace: A Research Note." *Comparative Political Studies* 30 (February 1997): 78–107.

Kennan, George F. *American Diplomacy*. Expanded edition. Chicago: University of Chicago Press, 1984.

Kennedy, Paul. *The Rise and Fall of the Great Powers: Economic Change and Military Conflict from 1500–2000*. New York: Random House, 1987.

Kier, Elizabeth. *Imagining War: French and British Military Doctrine Between the Wars*. Princeton: Princeton University Press, 1997.

King, Gary. *Unifying Political Methodology: The Likelihood Theory of Statistical Inference*. Cambridge: Cambridge University Press, 1989.

Kissinger, Henry. *Years of Renewal*. New York: Simon and Schuster, 1999.

———. *Years of Upheaval*. Boston: Little, Brown, 1982.

Korb, Lawrence. "The Use of Force." *Brookings Review* 15 (Spring 1997): 24–25.

Krasner, Stephen D. "Structural Cases and Regime Consequences: Regimes as Intervening Variables." In *International Regimes*. Edited by Stephen D. Krasner, 1–21. Ithaca: Cornell University Press, 1983.

Krebs, Gerhard. "The Japanese Air Forces." In *The Conduct of the Air War in the Second World War: An International Comparison*. Edited by Horst Boog, 228–234. Berg: New York, 1992.

Krepinevich, Andrew F. *The Army and Vietnam.* Baltimore: Johns Hopkin University Press, 1986.

Kugler, Jacek, and Marina Arbetman. "Relative Political Capacity: Political Extraction and Political Reach." In *Political Capacity and Economic Behavior.* Edited by Marina Arbetman and Jacek Kugler, 11–45. Boulder: Westview Press, 1997.

Kugler, Jacek, and William Domke. "Comparing the Strength of Nations." *Comparative Political Studies* 19 (April 1986): 39–69.

Kull, Steven, and I.M. Destler. *Misreading the Public: The Myth of a New Isolationism.* Washington, DC: Brookings, 1999.

LaFeber, Walter. *Inevitable Revolutions: The United States in Central America.* New York: Norton Press, 1984.

Lai, Brian, and Dan Reiter. "Democracy, Political Similarity, and International Alliances, 1816–1992." *Journal of Conflict Resolution* 44 (April 2000): 203–227.

Lake, David A. "Powerful Pacifists: Democratic States and War." *American Political Science Review* 86 (March 1992): 24–37.

———. *Entangling Relations: American Foreign Policy in Its Century.* Princeton: Princeton University Press, 1999.

Lamborn, Alan C. *The Price of Power: Risk and Foreign Policy in Britain, France, and Germany.* Boston: Unwin Hyman, 1991.

Lansing, Robert. *War Memoirs of Robert Lansing, Secretary of State.* New York: Bobbs-Merrill, 1935.

Layne, Christopher. "Kant or Cant: The Myth of the Democratic Peace." *International Security* 19 (Fall 1994): 5–49.

Leblang, David A. "Political Democracy and Economic Growth: Pooled Cross-Sectional and Time Series Evidence." *British Journal of Political Science* 27 (July 1997): 453–472.

———. "Property Rights, Democracy and Economic Growth." *Political Research Quarterly* 49 (March 1996): 5–26.

Lebow, Richard Ned. *Between Peace and War: The Nature of International Crisis.* Baltimore: Johns Hopkins University Press, 1981.

———. "Miscalculation in the South Atlantic: The Origins of the Falklands War." In *Psychology and Deterrence.* Edited by Robert Jervis, Richard Ned Lebow, and Janice Gross Stein, 89–124. Baltimore: Johns Hopkins University Press, 1985.

Lebow, Richard Ned, and Janice Gross Stein. *We All Lost the Cold War.* Princeton: Princeton University Press, 1994.

Lee, Joe. "Administrators and Agriculture: Aspects of German Agricultural Policy in the First World War." In *War and Economic Development: Essays in Memory of David Joslin.* Edited by J. M. Winter, 229–238. Cambridge: Cambridge University Press, 1975.

Leeds, Brett Ashley. "Domestic Political Institutions, Credible Commitments, and International Cooperation." *American Journal of Political Science* 43 (October 1999): 979–1002.

Leeds, Brett Ashley, and David R. Davis. "Beneath the Surface: Regime Type and International Interaction, 1953–1978." *Journal of Peace Research* 36, no. 1 (1999): 5–21.

———. "Domestic Political Vulnerability and International Disputes." *Journal of Conflict Resolution* 41 (December 1997): 814–834.

Levi, Margaret. *Consent, Dissent, and Patriotism*. Cambridge: Cambridge University Press, 1997.

Levy, Jack S. "The Diversionary Theory of War: A Critique." In *Handbook of War Studies*. Edited by Manus I. Midlarsky, 259–288. Boston: Unwin Hyman, 1989.

———. "The Offensive/Defensive Balance of Military Technology: A Theoretical and Historical Analysis." *International Studies Quarterly* 28 (June 1984): 219–238.

———. "Preferences, Constraints, and Choices in July 1914." *International Security* 15 (Winter 1990/91): 151–186.

Lewis, George G., and John Mewha. *History of Prisoner of War Utilization by the United States Army, 1776–1945*. Washington, DC: Center of Military History, U.S. Army, 1988.

Lian, Bradley, and John Oneal. "Presidents, the Use of Military Force, and Public Opinion." *Journal of Conflict Resolution* 37 (June 1993): 277–300.

Liberman, Peter. *Does Conquest Pay? The Exploitation of Occupied Industrial Societies*. Princeton: Princeton University Press, 1996.

Linderman, Gerald F. *The Mirror of War: American Society and the Spanish-American War*. Ann Arbor: University of Michigan Press, 1974.

Link, Arthur S. *Wilson: Campaigns for Progressivism and Peace*. Princeton: Princeton University Press, 1965.

———. *Wilson: The Struggle for Neutrality, 1914–1915*. Princeton: Princeton University Press, 1960.

Lippmann, Walter. *Essays in the Public Philosophy*. Boston: Little, Brown, 1955.

Lipset, Seymour Martin, Kyoung-Ryung Seong, and John Charles Torres. "A Comparative Analysis of the Social Requisites of Democracy." *International Social Science Journal*, no. 136 (May 1993): 155–175.

Little, Roger W. "Buddy Relations and Combat Performance." In *The New Military: Changing Patterns of Organization*. Edited by Morris Janowitz, 195–223. New York: Russell Sage Foundation, 1964.

Locke, John. *Second Treatise of Government*. Edited by C. B. Macpherson. Indianapolis: Hackett, 1980.

Londregan, John B. and Keith T. Poole. "Does High Income Promote Democracy?" *World Politics* 49 (October 1996): 1–30.

Luttwak, Edward N. "A Post-Heroic Military Policy." *Foreign Affairs* 75 (July–August 1996): 33–44.

MacEachin, Douglas J. *The Final Months of the War with Japan: Signals Intelligence, U.S. Invasion Planning, and the A-Bomb Decision*. Langley, VA: Center for the Study of Intelligence, 1998.

MacEachin, Douglas J., and D.M. Giangreco, "Casualty Projections for the U.S. Invasions of Japan, 1945–1946: Planning and Policy Implications," *Journal of Military History* 61 (July 1997): 521–582.

MacKenzie, S. P. "The Treatment of Prisoners of War in World War II." *Journal of Modern History* 66 (September 1994): 487–520.

McCormick, John P. *Carl Schmitt's Critique of Liberalism: Against Politics as Technology*. Cambridge: Cambridge University Press, 1997.

McGuire, Martin C., and Mancur Olson, Jr. "The Economics of Autocracy and Majority Rule: The Invisible Hand and the Use of Force." *Journal of Economic Literature* 36 (March 1996): 72–96.

McLellan, David. *Karl Marx: Selected Writings*. Oxford: Oxford University Press, 1977.

McNamara, Robert S. *In Retrospect: The Tragedy and Lessons of Vietnam*. New York: Times Books, 1995.

McPherson, James M. *Embattled Courage: The Experience of Combat in the American Civil War*. New York: Free Press, 1987.

———. *For Cause and Comrades: Why Men Fought in the Civil War*. New York: Oxford University Press, 1997.

Mansfield, Edward D. and Rachel Bronson. "The Political Economy of Major-Power Trade Flows." In *The Political Economy of Regionalism*. Edited by Edward D. Mansfield and Helen V. Milner, 189–208. New York: Columbia University Press, 1997.

Maoz, Zeev, and Bruce M. Russett. "Normative and Structural Causes of Democratic Peace, 1946–1986." *American Political Science Review* 87 (September 1993): 624–638.

May, Ernest R. *The World War and American Isolation 1914–1917*. Cambridge: Harvard University Press, 1959.

———. *Imperial Democracy: The Emergence of America as a Great Power*. New York: Harcourt, Brace, and World, 1961.

———. *"Lessons" of the Past: The Use and Misuse of History in American Foreign Policy*. Oxford: Oxford University Press, 1973.

———. *Strange Victory: Hitler's Conquest of France*. New York: Hill and Wang, 2000.

Mearsheimer, John J. "Back to the Future: Instability in Europe after the Cold War." *International Security* 15 (Summer 1990): 5–56.

———. *Conventional Deterrence*. Ithaca: Cornell University Press, 1983.

Meernik, James. "Modeling International Crises and the Political Use of Military Force by the USA." *Journal of Peace Research* 37 (September 2000): 547–562.

Meernik, James, and Peter Waterman. "The Myth of the Diversionary Use of Force by American Presidents." *Political Research Quarterly* 49 (September 1996): 573–590.

Meir, Golda. *My Life*. New York: G. P. Putnam's Sons, 1975.

Mercer, Jonathan. *Reputation and International Politics*. Ithaca: Cornell University Press, 1996.

The Military Balance, 1999–2000. London: Oxford University Press, 1999.

Mill, John Stuart. *On Liberty*. Edited by Alburey Castell. New York: Appleton Century Crofts, 1947.

Miller, Nathan. *War At Sea: A Naval History of World War II*. New York: Scribner, 1995.

Miller, Stuart. *"Benevolent Assimilation": The American Conquest of the Philippines, 1899–1903*. New Haven: Yale University Press, 1982.

Millett, Allan R. "Patterns of Military Innovation in the Interwar Period." In *Military Innovation in the Interwar Period*. Edited by Williamson Murray and Allan R. Millett, 329–368. Cambridge: Cambridge University Press, 1996.

Millett, Allan R., and Williamson Murray, eds. *Military Effectiveness*. 3 vols. Boston: Allen and Unwin, 1988.

Milward, Alan S. *The German Economy at War*. London: Athlone Press, 1965.

———. *War, Economy, and Society: 1939–1945*. Berkeley: University of California Press, 1977.

Montesquieu. *The Spirit of the Laws*. Translated and edited by Anne M. Cohler, Basia Carolyn Miller, and Harold Samual Stone. Cambridge: Cambridge University Press, 1989.

Moore, Bob, and Kent Federowich, eds. *Prisoners of War and Their Captors in World War II*. Oxford: Berg, 1996.

Morgan, T. Clifton, and Christopher J. Anderson. "Domestic Support and Diversionary External Conflict in Great Britain, 1950–1992." *British Journal of Political Science* 61 (August 1999): 799–814.

Morgan, T. Clifton, and Kenneth N. Bickers. "Domestic Discontent and the External Use of Force," *Journal of Conflict Resolution* 36 (March 1992): 25–52.

Morgenthau, Hans J. *Politics among Nations: The Struggle for Power and Peace*. Fifth edition, revised. New York: Alfred A. Knopf, 1978.

Moriarty, Robin. "Understanding the Formation and Reliability of International Agreements: The Case of Alliances." Ph.D. diss., Emory University, 1998.

Morrow, James D. "The Institutional Features of the Prisoner of War Treaties." *International Organization* 55 (2001).

Morrow, James D., Randolph M. Siverson, and Tressa E. Tabares. "The Political Determinants of International Trade: The Major Powers, 1907–1990." *American Political Science Review* 92 (September 1998): 649–661.

Morrow, John H. "Industrial Mobilization in World War I: The Prussian Army and the Aircraft Industry." *Journal of Economic History* 37 (March 1977): 36–51.

Moskos, Charles C., Jr. *The American Enlisted Man: The Rank and File in Today's Military*. New York: Russell Sage Foundation, 1970.

Mousseau, Michael. "Democracy and Militarized Interstate Collaboration." *Journal of Peace Research* 34 (February 1997): 73–87.

———. "Peace in Anarchy: Democratic Governance and International Conflict." Ph.D. diss., SUNY Binghamton, 1998.

Moynihan, Daniel Patrick. *Secrecy: The American Experience*. New Haven: Yale University Press, 1998.

Mueller, John E. "The Search for the 'Breaking Point' in Vietnam: The Statistics of a Deadly Quarrel." *International Studies Quarterly* 24 (December 1980): 497–519.

———. "Pearl Harbor: Military Inconvenience, Political Disaster." *International Security* 16 (Winter 1991/1992): 172–203.

———. *Policy and Opinion in the Gulf War*. Chicago: University of Chicago Press, 1994.

———. *War, Presidents and Public Opinion*. Lanham: University Press of America, 1985.

Murray, Williamson. "The German Response to Victory in Poland: A Case Study in Professionalism." *Armed Forces and Society* 7 (Winter 1981): 285–298.

New York Times Atlas of the World: In Collaboration with the Times of London. New York: Times Books, 1983.

Nincic, Miroslav. *Democracy and Foreign Policy: The Fallacy of Political Realism.* New York: Columbia University Press, 1992.

O'Loughlin, John, et al. "The Diffusion of Democracy, 1946–1994." *Annals of the Association of American Geographers* 88 (December 1998): 545–574.

Olson, Mancur. "Autocracy, Democracy, and Prosperity." In *Strategy and Choice.* Edited by Richard J. Zeckhauser, 132–157. Cambridge: MIT Press, 1991.

———. "Dictatorship, Democracy, and Development." *American Political Science Review* 87 (September 1993): 567–576.

Oneal, John R., and Bruce Russett. "Assessing the Liberal Peace with Alternative Specifications: Trade Still Reduces Conflict." *Journal of Peace Research* 36 (July 1999): 423–442.

———. "The Classical Liberals Were Right: Democracy, Interdependence, and Conflict, 1950–1985." *International Studies Quarterly* 41 (June 1997): 267–294.

———. "The Kantian Peace: The Pacific Benefits of Democracy, Interdependence, and International Organizations, 1885–1992." *World Politics* 52 (October 1999): 1–37.

Oren, Ido, and Jude Hays. "Democracies May Rarely Fight One Another, but Developed Socialist States Rarely Fight at All." Presented at the Annual Meeting of the International Studies Association, San Diego, April 1996.

Organski, A.F.K., and Jacek Kugler. *The War Ledger.* Chicago: University of Chicago Press, 1980.

Overy, Richard J. *War and Economy in the Third Reich.* Oxford: Clarendon Press, 1994.

———. *Why the Allies Won.* London: Jonathan Cape, 1995.

Owen, John M. "How Liberalism Produces Democratic Peace." *International Security* 19 (Fall 1994): 87–125.

———. *Liberal Peace, Liberal War: American Politics and International Security.* Ithaca: Cornell University Press, 1997.

Page, Benjamin I., and Robert Y. Shapiro. *The Rational Public: Fifty Years of Trends in Americans' Policy Preferences.* Chicago: University of Chicago Press, 1992.

Paine, Thomas. *Prospects on the War, and Paper Currency.* First American edition. Baltimore: S. and J. Adams, 1794.

Papayoanou, Paul A. *Power Ties: Economic Interdependence, Balancing, and War.* Ann Arbor: University of Michigan Press, 1999.

Pape, Robert A. *Bombing to Win: Air Power and Coercion in War.* Ithaca: Cornell University Press, 1996.

Pearlman, Michael D. *Warmaking and American Democracy: The Struggle over Military Strategy, 1700 to the Present.* Lawrence: University Press of Kansas, 1999.

Petraeus, David H. "Military Influence and the Post-Vietnam Use of Force." *Armed Forces and Society* 15 (Summer 1989): 489–505.

Pevehouse, Jon C. "International Influences and Democratic Consolidation." Presented at the Annual Meeting of the American Political Science Association, Atlanta, September 2–5, 1999.

Philpott, William James. *Anglo-French Relations and Strategy on the Western Front, 1914–18.* New York: St. Martin's, 1996.

Pipes, Richard. *The Russian Revolution.* New York: Alfred A. Knopf, 1990.

———. *Three "Whys" of the Russian Revolution.* New York: Vintage Books, 1995.

Plaster, John L. *SOG: The Secret Wars of America's Commandos in Vietnam.* New York: Onyx Books, 1998.

Poe, Steven C., and C. Neal Tate. "Repression of Human Rights to Personal Integrity in the 1980s: A Global Analysis." *American Political Science Review* 88 (December 1994): 853–872.

Pollack, Kenneth M. "The Influence of Arab Culture on Arab Military Effectiveness." Ph.D. diss., Massachusetts Institute of Technology, 1996.

Pollard, Sidney. *The Development of the British Economy, 1914–1990.* Fourth edition. London: Edward Arnold, 1992.

Posen, Barry. "Nationalism, the Mass Army, and Military Power." *International Security* 18 (Fall 1993): 80–124.

———. *The Sources of Military Doctrine: France, Britain and Germany between the World Wars.* Ithaca: Cornell University Press, 1984.

Powell, Colin L., with Joseph E. Persico. *My American Journey.* New York: Random House, 1995.

Powell, Robert. *In the Shadow of Power: States and Strategies in International Politics.* Princeton: Princeton University Press, 1999.

Prados, John. *Presidents' Secret Wars: CIA and Pentagon Covert Operations since World War II.* New York: Morrow, 1986.

Przeworski, Adam, Michael Alvarez, Jose Antonio Cheibub, and Fernando Limongi. *Democracy and Development: Political Institutions and Well-Being in the World, 1950–1990.* Cambridge: Cambridge University Press, 2000.

Przeworski, Adam, and Fernando Limongi. "Modernization: Theories and Facts." *World Politics* 49 (January 1997): 155–183.

Raknerud, Arvid, and Håvard Hegre. "The Hazard of War: Reassessing the Evidence for the Democratic Peace." *Journal of Peace Research* 34, no. 4 (1997): 385–404.

Rasler, Karen, and William R. Thompson. "Predatory Initiators and Changing Landscapes for Warfare." *Journal of Conflict Resolution* 43 (August 1999): 411–433.

Ray, James Lee. *Democracy and International Conflict: An Evaluation of the Democratic Peace Proposition.* Columbia: University of South Carolina Press, 1995.

Reed, William. "Alliance Duration and Democracy: An Extension and Cross-Validation of 'Democratic States and Commitment in International Relations.'" *American Journal of Political Science* 41 (July 1997): 1072–1078.

———. "The Relevance of Politically Relevant Dyads." Presented at the Annual Meeting of the Peace Science Society, East Brunswick, October 13, 1998.

———. "A Unified Statistical Model of Conflict Onset and Escalation." *American Journal of Political Science* 44 (January 2000): 84–93.

Reed, William, and David H. Clark. "War Initiators and War Winners: The Consequences of Linking Theories of Democratic War Success." *Journal of Conflict Resolution* 44 (June 2000): 378–395.

Reese, Roger R. *Stalin's Reluctant Soldiers: A Social History of the Red Army 1925–1941.* Lawrence: University Press of Kansas, 1996.

Reinhardt, Eric. "Aggressive Multilateralism: The Determinants of GATT/WTO Dispute Initiation, 1948–1998." Unpublished manuscript, Emory University, February 16, 2000.

Reiter, Dan. *Crucible of Beliefs: Learning, Alliances, and World Wars.* Ithaca: Cornell University Press, 1996.

———. "Does Peace Nurture Democracy?" *Journal of Politics* (August 2001).

———. "Exploding the Powder Keg Myth: Preemptive Wars Almost Never Happen." *International Security* 20 (Fall 1995): 5–34.

———. "Military Strategy and the Outbreak of International Conflict, 1903–1992." *Journal of Conflict Resolution* 43 (June 1999): 366–387.

———. "NATO Enlargement and the Spread of Democracy." *International Security* 25 (Spring 2001): 41–67.

———. "Political Structure and Foreign Policy Learning: Are Democracies More Likely to Act on the Lessons of History?" *International Interactions* 21 (March 1995): 39–62.

Reiter, Dan, and Allan C. Stam III. "Democracy and Battlefield Effectiveness." *Journal of Conflict Resolution* 42 (June 1998): 259–277.

———. "Democracy, War Initiation, and Victory." *American Political Science Review* 92 (June 1998): 377–389.

———. "The Soldier's Decision to Surrender: Prisoners of War and World Politics." Presented at the Annual Meeting of the American Political Science Association, Washington, DC, August, 1997.

Reiter, Dan, and Curtis Meek. "Determinants of Military Strategy, 1903–1994: A Quantitative Empirical Test." *International Studies Quarterly* 43 (June 1999): 363–387.

Remmer, Karen L. "Does Democracy Promote Interstate Cooperation? Lessons from the Mercosur Region." *International Studies Quarterly* 42 (March 1998): 25–52.

Revel, Jean-François. *How Democracies Perish.* Translated by William Byron. Garden City, NY: Doubleday. 1984.

Reynolds, David, Warren F. Kimball, and A. O. Chubarian, eds. *Allies at War: The Soviet, American, and British Experience, 1939–1945.* New York: St. Martin's Press, 1994.

Rhodes, Richard. *Dark Sun: The Making of the Hydrogen Bomb.* New York: Simon and Schuster, 1995.

———. *The Making of the Atomic Bomb.* New York: Simon and Schuster, 1986.

Richardson, F. M. *Fighting Spirit: A Study of Psychological Factors in War.* New York: Crane, Russak, 1978.

Richardson, Louise. *When Allies Differ: Anglo-American Relations during the Suez and Falklands Crises.* New York: St. Martin's Press, 1996.

Riker, William H. "The Political Psychology of Rational Choice Theory." *Political Psychology* 16 (March 1995): 23–44.

Risen, James. "Secrets of History: The C.I.A. in Iran—A Special Report." *New York Times*, April 16, 2000, A1.

Risse-Kappen, Thomas. *Cooperation among Democracies: The European Influence on U.S. Foreign Policy*. Princeton: Princeton University Press, 1995.

Roberts, Adam. "The Laws of War in the 1990–91 Gulf Conflict." *International Security* 18 (Winter 1993/94): 134–181.

Robles, Elidoro. *The Philippines in the Nineteenth Century*. Quezon City, Philippines: Malaya Books, 1969.

Roeder, Philip G. *Red Sunset: The Failure of Soviet Politics*. Princeton: Princeton University Press, 1993.

Rosen, Stephen Peter. *Societies and Military Power: India and Its Armies*. Ithaca: Cornell University Press, 1996.

———. *Winning the Next War: Innovation and the Modern Military*. Ithaca: Cornell University Press, 1991.

Rosen, Steven. "War Power and the Willingness to Suffer." In *Peace, War, and Numbers*. Edited by Bruce Russett, 167–183. Beverly Hills: Sage, 1972.

Rousseau, David L., and Karl Mueller. "Peaceful Democrats or Pragmatic Realists?: Revisiting the Iroquois League." Presented at the Annual Meeting of the American Political Science Association, Chicago, September 3, 1995.

Rousseau, David L., Christopher Gelpi, Dan Reiter, and Paul K. Huth. "Assessing the Dyadic Nature of the Democratic Peace, 1918–1988." *American Political Science Review* 90 (September 1996): 512–533.

Rowe, David M. "World Economic Expansion and National Security in Pre–World War I Europe." *International Organization* 53 (Spring 1999): 195–231.

Royston, P., and D. G. Altman. "Regression Using Fractional Polynomials of Continuous Covariates: Parsimonious Parametric Modeling." *Applied Statistics* 43, no. 3 (1994): 429–467.

Rummel, R. J. "Democracies ARE Less Warlike than Other Regimes." *European Journal of International Relations* 1 (December 1995): 457–479.

———. *Power Kills: Democracy as a Method of Nonviolence*. New Brunswick, NJ: Transaction Publishers, 1997.

Rush, Robert S. "A Different Perspective: Cohesion, Morale, and Operational Effectiveness in the German Army, Fall 1944." *Armed Forces and Society* 25 (Spring 1999): 477–508.

Russett, Bruce M. *Controlling the Sword: The Democratic Governance of National Security*. Cambridge: Harvard University Press, 1990.

———. *Grasping the Democratic Peace: Principles for a Post–Cold War World*. Princeton: Princeton University Press, 1993.

———. *No Clear and Present Danger: A Skeptical View of the United States Entry into World War II*. New York: Harper Torchbooks, 1972.

Russett, Bruce M., and Allan C. Stam. "Courting Disaster: An Expanded NATO vs. Russia and China." *Political Science Quarterly* 113 (Fall 1998): 361–382.

Russett, Bruce M., and John Oneal. *Triangulating Peace: Democracy, Interdependence, and International Organizations*. New York: Norton, 2001.

Sagan, Scott D. *The Limits of Safety: Organizations, Accidents, and Nuclear Weapons*. Princeton: Princeton University Press, 1993.

————. "The Origins of the Pacific War." In *The Origin and Prevention of Major Wars*. Edited by Robert I. Rotberg and Theodore K. Rabb, 323–352. Cambridge: Cambridge University Press, 1988.

Sagan, Scott D., and Kenneth N. Waltz. *The Spread of Nuclear Weapons: A Debate*. New York: W. W. Norton, 1995.

Samuels, Richard J. *"Rich Nation, Strong Army": National Security and the Technological Transformation of Japan*. Ithaca: Cornell University Press, 1994.

Sandholtz, Wayne, and William Koetzle. "Accounting for Corruption: Economic Structure, Democracy, and Trade." *International Studies Quarterly* 44 (March 2000): 31–50.

Schelling, Thomas C. *Arms and Influence*. New Haven: Yale University Press, 1966.

Schindler, Dietrich, and Jiri Toman, eds. *The Laws of Armed Conflicts: A Collection of Conventions, Resolutions and Other Documents*. Geneva: Henry Dumont Institute, 1988.

Schlesinger, Arthur M., Jr. *The Age of Jackson*. Boston: Little, Brown, 1945.

Schmitt, Carl. *The Concept of the Political*. Translated by George Schwab. New Brunswick: Rutgers University Press, 1976.

Schoenbaum, David. *The United States and the State of Israel*. New York: Oxford University Press, 1993.

Schultz, Kenneth A. "Do Democratic Institutions Constrain or Inform? Contrasting Two Institutional Perspectives on Democracy and War." *International Organization* 53 (Spring 1999): 233–266.

Schultz, Kenneth A., and Barry R. Weingast. "Limited Governments, Powerful States." In *Strategic Politicians, Institutions, and Foreign Policy*. Edited by Randolph M. Siverson. Ann Arbor: University of Michigan Press, 1998.

Schwartzkopf, General H. Norman. *It Doesn't Take a Hero*. New York: Bantam, 1992.

Schweller, Randall L. "Domestic Structure and Preventive War: Are Democracies More Pacific?" *World Politics* 44 (January 1992): 235–269.

————. *Deadly Imbalances: Tripolarity and Hitler's Strategy of World Conquest*. New York: Columbia University Press, 1998.

Sen, Amartya Kumar. *Development as Freedom*. New York: Knopf, 1999.

Shapiro, Ian. *Democratic Justice*. New Haven: Yale University Press, 1999.

Shawcross, William. *Sideshow: Kissinger, Nixon and the Destruction of Cambodia*. New York: Simon and Schuster, 1979.

Sherry, Michael S. *In the Shadow of War: The United States since the 1930's*. New Haven: Yale University Press, 1995.

Shils, Edward, and Morris Janowitz. "Cohesion and Disintegration in the Wehrmacht in World War II." In *Center and Periphery: Essays in Macrosociology*. Edited by Edward Shils, 345–383. Chicago: University of Chicago Press, 1975.

Sick, Gary. *October Surprise: America's Hostages in Iran and the Election of Ronald Reagan*. New York: Times Books, 1991.

Simmons, Beth. "See You in "Court"? The Appeal to Quasi-Judicial Legal Processes in the Settlement of Territorial Disputes." In *A Road Map to War: Territorial Dimensions of International Conflict*. Edited by Paul F. Diehl, 205–237. Nashville: Vanderbilt University Press, 1999.

Simon, Michael W., and Erik Gartzke. "Political System Similarity and the Choice of Allies: Do Democracies Flock Together, or Do Opposites Attract?" *Journal of Conflict Resolution* 40 (December 1996): 617–635.

Singer, J. David. "Reconstructing the Correlates of War Data Set on Material Capabilities of States, 1816–1985." In *Measuring the Correlates of War*. Edited by J. David Singer and Paul F. Diehl, 53–71. Ann Arbor: University of Michigan Press, 1990.

Singer, J. David, and Melvin Small. "Correlates of War Project: International and Civil War Data, 1816–1992" [Computer file]. Ann Arbor: Inter-University Consortium for Political and Social Research, 1994.

Singer, J. David, Stuart Bremer, and John Stuckey. "Capability Distribution, Uncertainty, and Major Power War, 1820–1965." In *Peace, War and Numbers* Edited by Bruce Russett, 19–48. Beverly Hills: Sage, 1972.

Sisson, Richard, and Leo E. Rose. *War and Secession: Pakistan, India, and the Creation of Bangladesh*. Berkeley: University of California Press, 1990.

Siverson, Randolph M. "Democracies and War Participation: In Defense of the Institutional Constraints Argument." *European Journal of International Relations* 1 (December 1995): 481–489.

Siverson, Randolph M., and Harvey Starr. *The Diffusion of War: A Study of Opportunity and Willingness*. Ann Arbor: University of Michigan Press, 1991.

Siverson, Randolph M., and Juliann Emmons. "Birds of a Feather: Democratic Political Systems and Alliance Choices in the Twentieth Century." *Journal of Conflict Resolution* 35 (June 1991): 285–306.

Small, Melvin, and J. David Singer. *Resort to Arms: International and Civil Wars, 1816–1980*. Beverly Hills: Sage, 1982.

Small, Melvin. *Johnson, Nixon, and the Doves*. New Brunswick: Rutgers University Press, 1988.

Smith, Alastair. "Alliance Formation and War." *International Studies Quarterly* 39 (December 1995): 405–425.

———. "Fighting Battles, Winning Wars." *Journal of Conflict Resolution* 42 (June 1998): 301–320.

———. "International Crises and Domestic Politics." *American Political Science Review* 92 (September 1998): 623–638.

———. "To Intervene or Not to Intervene: A Biased Decision." *Journal of Conflict Resolution* 40, no. 1 (1996): 16–40.

Smoler, Frederic. "The Secret of the Soldiers Who Didn't Shoot." *American Heritage* 40 (March 1989): 37–45.

Snyder, Jack. *The Ideology of the Offensive: Military Decision Making and the Disasters of 1914*. Ithaca: Cornell University Press, 1984.

———. *Myths of Empire: Domestic Politics and International Ambition*. Ithaca: Cornell University Press, 1991.

Solzhenitsyn, Aleksandr I. *A World Split Apart*. New York: Harper and Row, 1978.

Sorley, Lewis. *A Better War: The Unexamined Victories and Final Tragedy of America's Last Years in Vietnam*. New York: Harcourt Brace, 1999.

Speer, Albert. *Inside the Third Reich: Memoirs by Albert Speer*. Translated by Richard and Clara Winston. New York: Macmillan, 1970.

Spiro, David E. "The Insignificance of the Liberal Peace." *International Security* (Fall 1994): 50–86.

Stam, Allan C., III. *Win, Lose, or Draw: Domestic Politics and the Crucible of War.* Ann Arbor: University of Michigan Press, 1996.

Starr, Harvey. "Democracy and Integration: Why Democracies Don't Fight Each Other." *Journal of Peace Research* 34 (May 1997): 153–162.

Stein, Janice Gross. "Deterrence and Compellence in the Gulf, 1990–91: A Failed or Impossible Task?" *International Security* 17 (Fall 1992): 147–179.

Stone, Norman. *The Eastern Front 1914–1917.* London: Hodder and Stoughton, 1975.

Stouffer, Samuel A., Edward A. Suchman, Leland C. DeVinney, Shirley A. Star, and Robin Williams, Jr. *The American Soldier: Adjustment during Army Life.* Princeton: Princeton University Press, 1949.

Streim, Alfred. "International Law and Soviet Prisoners of War." In *From Peace to War: Germany, Soviet Russia and the World, 1939–1941.* Edited by Bernd Wegner, 293–308. Providence, RI: Berghahn Books, 1997.

Stromseth, Jane E. *The Origins of Flexible Response: NATO's Debate over Strategy in the 1960s.* New York: Macmillan, 1988.

Summers, Col. Harry G. *On Strategy: The Vietnam War in Context.* Carlisle Barracks, PA: Strategic Studies Institute, 1981.

Sun Tzu. *The Art of War.* Translated by Samuel B. Griffith. London: Oxford University Press, 1963.

Taylor, A. J. P. *The Struggle for Mastery in Europe, 1848–1918.* Oxford: Clarendon Press, 1954.

Tebbel, John, and Keith Jennison *The American Indian Wars.* New York: Harper, 1960.

Thompson, William R , and Richard Tucker. "A Tale of Two Democratic Peace Critiques." *Journal of Conflict Resolution* 41 (June 1997): 428–454.

Thucydides. *History of the Peloponnesian War.* Translated by Rex Warner. Harmondsworth, UK: Penguin, 1954.

Tocqueville, Alexis, de. *Democracy in America.* Edited by J. P. Mayer. Translated by George Lawrence. Garden City, NY: Anchor Books, 1969.

Tollefson, Martin. "Enemy Prisoners of War." *Iowa Law Review* 22 (November 1946): 50–68.

Trask, David F. *The AEF and Coalition Warmaking, 1917–1918.* Lawrence: University Press of Kansas, 1993.

Tuchman, Barbara W. *The Guns of August.* New York: Bantam Books, 1962.

———. *The Proud Tower: A Portrait of the World before the War 1890–1914.* New York: Bantam Books, 1966.

Tullock, Gordon. *Autocracy.* Boston: Kluwer Academic Publishers, 1987.

U.S. News and World Report. *Triumph Without Victory: The Unreported History of the Persian Gulf War.* New York: Random House, 1992.

Upton, Anthony F. *Finland: 1939–1940.* London: Davis-Poynter, 1974.

Utley, Robert M., and Wilcomb M. Washburn. *Indian Wars.* New York: American Heritage, 1985.

Van Creveld, Martin. *Fighting Power: German and U.S. Army Performance, 1939–1945.* Westport, CT: Greenwood Press, 1982.

―――. *Technology and War: From 2000 B.C. to the Present.* Revised and expanded edition. New York: Free Press, 1991.

Van Evera, Stephen. *The Causes of War: Power and the Roots of Conflict.* Ithaca: Cornell University Press, 1999.

―――. "Hypotheses on Nationalism and War." *International Security* 18 (Spring 1994): 5–39.

Vatter, Harold G. "The Material Status of the U.S. Civilian Consumer in World War II: The Question of Guns or Butter." In *The Sinews of War: Essays on the Economic History of World War II.* Edited by Geoffrey T. Mills and Hugh Rockoff, 219–242. Ames: Iowa State University Press, 1993.

―――. *The U.S. Economy in World War II.* New York: Columbia University Press, 1985.

Verdier, Daniel. *Democracy and International Trade: Britain, France, and the United States, 1860–1990.* Princeton: Princeton University Press, 1994.

Wagner, R. Harrison. "Bargaining and War." *American Journal of Political Science* 44 (July 2000): 469–484.

Walker, Thomas C. "The Forgotten Prophet: Tom Paine's Cosmopolitanism and International Relations." *International Studies Quarterly* 44 (March 2000): 51–72.

Walt, Stephen M. *The Origins of Alliances.* Ithaca: Cornell University Press, 1987.

Waltz, Kenneth N. "Structural Realism after the Cold War." *International Security* 25 (Summer 2000): 5–41.

―――. *Theory of International Politics.* New York: McGraw-Hill, 1979.

Walzer, Michael. *Obligations: Essays on Disobedience, War, and Citizenship.* Cambridge: Harvard University Press, 1970.

Wang, Kevin, and James Lee Ray. "Beginners and Winners: The Fate of Initiators of Interstate Wars Involving Great Powers since 1495." *International Studies Quarterly* 38 (March 1994): 139–154.

Ward, Michael D., and Kristian S. Gleditsch. "Democratizing for Peace." *American Political Science Review* 92 (March 1998): 51–61.

Weart, Spencer R. *Never at War: Why Democracies Will Not Fight One Another.* New Haven: Yale University Press, 1998.

Weingast, Barry R. "The Political Foundations of Democracy and the Rule of Law." *American Political Science Review* 91 (June 1997): 245–263.

Welch, Richard. *Response to Imperialism: The United States and the Philippine-American War, 1899–1902.* Chapel Hill: The University of North Carolina Press, 1979.

Wendt, Alexander. *Social Theory of International Politics.* New York: Cambridge University Press, 1999.

Werner, Suzanne. "The Effects of Political Similarity on the Onset of Militarized Disputes, 1816–1985." *Political Research Quarterly* 53 (June 2000): 343–374.

―――. "Negotiating the Terms of Settlement: War Aims and Bargaining Leverage." *Journal of Conflict Resolution* 42 (June 1998): 321–343.

―――. "The Precarious Nature of Peace: Resolving the Issues, Enforcing the Settlement, and Renegotiating the Terms." *American Journal of Political Science* 43 (July 1999): 912–934.

Werner, Suzanne, and Douglas Lemke. "Opposites Do Not Attract: The Impact of Domestic Institutions, Power, and Prior Commitments on Alignment Choices." *International Studies Quarterly* 41 (September 1997): 529–546.

Werth, Alexander. *Russia at War 1941–1945*. New York: E.P. Dutton, 1964.

Whaley, Barton. *Codeword BARBAROSSA*. Cambridge: MIT Press, 1973.

Wintrobe, Ronald. *The Political Economy of Dictatorship*. Cambridge: Cambridge University Press, 1998.

Woodward, Bob. *Shadow: Five Presidents and the Legacy of Watergate*. New York: Simon and Schuster, 1999.

Woodward, Sir Llewellyn. *Great Britain and the War of 1914–1918*. London: Methuen, 1967.

World Development Indicators on CD-ROM. Washington, DC: World Bank, 1997.

Wright, Quincy. *A Study of War*. Abridged edition. Abridged by Louise Leonard Wright. Chicago: University of Chicago Press, 1964.

Wuorinen, John H., ed. *Finland and World War II, 1939–1944*. New York: Ronald Press, 1948.

Young, Robert J. *In Command of France: French Foreign Policy and Military Planning, 1933–1940.* Cambridge: Harvard University Press, 1978.

Zimmerman, William. "Issue Area and Foreign-Policy Process: A Research Note in Search of a General Theory." *American Political Science Review* 67 (December 1973): 1204–1212.

INDEX

Beck, Nathaniel, 233n.71
Beevor, Anthony, 218n.20, 219n.35
Belgium, 17, 93, 94, 99, 101, 104, 208n.16
Belligerents. *See* War
Benedict, Ruth, 219n.26
Ben-Gurion, David, 65, 218n.19
Bennett, Andrew, 223n.17
Bennett, D. Scott, 48, 192, 213n.68, 214nn. 73, 75, 77, 216nn. 88, 89, 225n.44, 226n.56, 231n.39, 236n.1, 237n.4, 238n.26, 239n.31, 240nn. 37, 40
Berman, Larry, 208n.4, 230n.26, 238n.12
Bethell, Leslie, 222n.12
Beyerchen, Allan, 208n.5
Bickers, Kenneth N., 233n.6
Bickerton, Ian J., 232n.64
Biddle, Stephen, 217n.11, 238n.21
Bismarck, Otto von, 88
Blainey, Geoffrey, 207n.1, 208nn. 7, 8, 238n.27
Blechman, Barry M., 209nn. 28, 31, 225n.43
Bliss, Harry, 222n.4
Bloch, Marc, 220n.45
Bolks, Sean, 229n.21
Bollen, Kenneth A., 232n.67
Bolsheviks, 124, 125
Bond, Brian, 225n.47
Bowden, Mark, 209n.28, 238n.16
Boxer Rebellion (1900), 92, 148
Brawley, Mark R., 222n.8
Brazil, 109, 159
Bremer, Stuart A., 216nn. 90, 91, 233n.73
Brennan, Geoffrey, 218n.21
Brinkley, Douglas G., 240n.15
Britton, Rebecca L., 209n.26, 233n.10
Brody, J. Kenneth, 224n.42
Bronson, Rachel, 225n.51
Brooks, Risa, 219nn. 34, 35
Brown, Dee, 234n.20
Brown, John Sloan, 218n.17
Bryan, William Jennings, 157
Brzezinski, Zbigniew, 207n.5
Bueno de Mesquita, Bruce, 49, 50, 208n.6, 209n.21, 215n.85, 216n.89, 222n.7, 224n.26, 228n.16, 229n.20, 231n.37, 233n.2, 240nn. 36, 4, 12
Bundy, McGeorge, 161, 208n.4, 236n.46, 237n.6

Burchardt, Lothar, 230nn. 30, 33
Bureaucracy: centralized systems, 127, 128, 130, 132; in democracies, 129; development of information and, 23; fragmented, 126–28, 130, 134; regime type and, 128–29; unified, 127
Burk, James, 209n.25
Burkhart, Ross E., 228n.10
Bush, George H. W., 20, 121, 150–51, 201, 223n.17, 230n.27, 234n.17, 238n.19; administration of, 150. *See also* Persian Gulf War
Bush, George W., 167, 202–3, 241n.20; administration of, 202–3
Bush, Vannevar, 232n.59

CAA. *See* Concepts Analysis Agency (U.S. Army; CAA) dataset
Caillaux, Joseph, 12–13
Calvocoressi, Peter, 224n.34, 225n.47
Cambodia, 159
Carter, Jimmy, 201
Casualties. *See* Democracy and war; War
Catton, Bruce, 230n.32
Center for Defense Information, 176
Checkland, Olive, 219n.26
Cheibub, José Antonio, 229n.18
Cheney, Dick, 24, 209n.30
Cherokee Nation, 152–53, 158
Cherwell, Lord, 104, 225n.48
Chile, 159–60
China, People's Republic of: economic factors, 117; Japan and, 35–36, 37, 95; Korean War and, 16; military strategies and, 42; Taiwan and Taiwan Straits and, 16, 20
Choi, Ajin, 225n.45
Chubarian, A. O., 224n.34
Churchill, Winston: references to, 223n.19, 224n.28, 227n.1; World War II and, 84, 104, 128, 133–34, 165–66
Civil War (U.S.), 63–64, 77, 114, 123–24
Clark, David H., 213n.69, 236n.47
Clausewitz, Carl von, 13, 58, 63, 194, 237n.3, 240n.1
Clem, Harold J., 227n.1, 231n.47
Clinton, William Jefferson, 1; administration of, 2
Clodfelter, Michael, 40, 42, 213n.67, 214n.75, 219n.27
Cohen, Eliot A., 218n.18